The Wonder-Working Lawyers of Talmudic Babylonia

The Theory and Practice of Judaism in its Formative Age

Studies in Judaism

The Wonder-Working Lawyers of Talmudic Babylonia

The Theory and Practice of Judaism in its Formative Age

Jacob Neusner

NIVERSITY
PRESS OF
AMERICA

LANHAM • NEW YORK • LONDON

4720 Boston Way
Lanham, MD 20706

3 Henrietta Street
London WC2E 8LU England

Printed in the United States of America

British Cataloging in Publication Information Available

Library of Congress Cataloging-in-Publication Data

Neusner, Jacob, 1932-
The wonder-working lawyers of Talmudic Babylonia.

(Studies in Judaism)
"The major portion of this text originally appeared in the series A history of the Jews in Babylonia, II-V."—T.p. verso.
Includes bibliographical references and index.
1. Judaism—Iraq—Babylonia—History. 2. Rabbis—Iraq—Babylonia—Office. 3. Talmudic academies. 4. Courts, Jewish. I. Title. II. Series.
BM386.5.B33N48 1987 296.6'1'0935 87-6161
ISBN 0-8191-6287-6 (alk. paper)
ISBN 0-8191-6288-4 (pbk. : alk. paper)

All University Press of America books are produced on acid-free paper which exceeds the minimum standards set by the National Historical Publication and Records Commission.

For my indexer and loyal friend

ARTHUR WOODMAN

Canaan, New Hampshire

In gratitude
and
in celebration of twenty years of reliable and accurate indexing
for upwards of a hundred books.

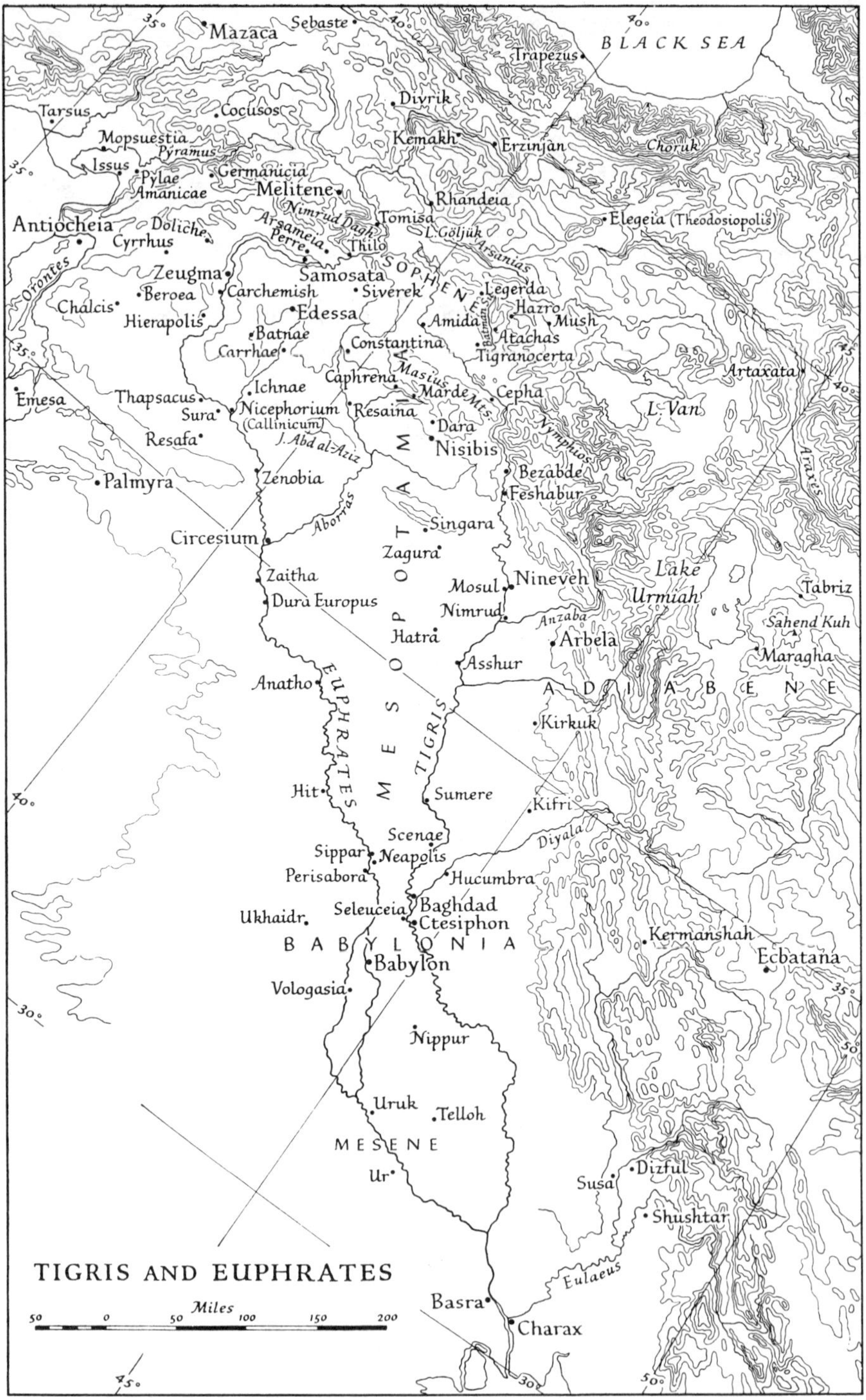

Source: Freya Stark, *Rome on the Euphrates* (John Murray, London, and Harcourt, Brace, and World Inc., New York, © 1966, reproduced by permission.)

CONTENTS

PREFACE

My *History of the Jews in Babylonia* (Leiden, 1965-1970: E. J. Brill) Volumes II-V, presents a systematic picture of the Jews' religious life portrayed by talmudic and other sources. In that work I addressed to the classic documents of the canon of Judaism the agenda of the history of religions. I wanted to know what sort of religious life characterized the Jews as seen by the rabbis of the Talmud, what kind of religious and political institutions gave concrete form to that life, what sort of influence the rabbis (as they portrayed themselves) exercised, what sort of concrete power they were able to bring to bear – in all, to investigate the relationship between the beliefs of the Judaic system and the everyday life of the Jews subjected to the governance of the rabbis who shaped and executed those beliefs in everyday life. In the present work I present four statements, deriving, in succession, from volumes II, III, IV, and V, corresponding to Chapters One through Four of this book, respectively, covering the program at hand.

First I lay out the problem of the relationship between the people and the law of the Torah as sages taught and applied it. We cannot take for granted that everybody did as rabbis thought they should, and the evidence of Talmudic literature one-sidedly maintains that they did not. That chapter adduces in evidence stories that refer to third century figures, from the beginning of Sasanian times, ca. 226, through the end of the reign of Shapur I in 272.

Chapter Two turns to the definition of the rabbi as a holy man, with much attention to the interplay between Torah-study and wonder-working or magic. Here I review materials bearing attributions to sages who flourished between the end of Shapur I's reign and the beginning of Shapur II's, that is, 272-309.

In Chapter Three I pursue the same topic, now with attention to the much broader range of problems of the rabbi as a holy man and the rabbinical institution and estate as a center of supernatural power in Israel, the Jewish people, in Sasanian Babylonia. Here I cover a broad range of institutional and religious-historical issues.

Finally I turn, in Chapter Four, to the rabbis as political figures who actually exercised not merely influence but coercive authority in enforcing Israel's public policy. I cover the courts – corresponding, in our own time, to local administrative agencies with a broad range of practical power and authority – and how rabbis ran them. The stories and sayings reviewed in this chapter refer to figures who flourished from the end of the reign of Shapur II in 372 to the Muslim conquest of Sasanian Iran and the end of the Mazdean, or Zoroastrian, state church, in ca. 640.

Throughout the book I review stories that indicate how rabbis applied the practical law, in addition to urging or influencing people to keep more spiritual rules. The distinction between the practical and the spiritual, of course, is ours, not theirs, but it does correspond to the distinction between stories about influence and coercion through persuasion, on the one side, and those that record concrete and practical decision making, effected through coercion through state power and, if necessary, force, on the other. An understanding of the later history of the Judaism of the dual Torah, which appeals to the Talmud of Babylonia as the definitive statement of the Oral part of the Torah God revealed to Moses, our rabbi, at Mount Sinai, requires a clear picture of the political and social theology of Judaism that that Talmud laid forth. For the Judaism that would flourish from then to nearly our own day not only rested on the law and theology of the Talmud of Babylonia but also appealed to the models of authority and leadership originally defined there.

Now that twenty years have passed since the publication of the first of the four volumes that have contributed chapters to this book, it seems reasonable to think that the work has stood the test of time. No book in any language has presented another picture of the whole of the formative history of Judaism as portrayed in the Talmud and related sources, let alone a systematic and complete account of the problems I dealt with in my *History of the Jews in Babylonia*. A new generation is ready to consider the matter, and in presenting sample chapters containing some of the more representative conclusions, I hope to draw to the *History* as a whole, where complete and systematic discussions of matters, as well as bibliographies, indices, and the like, are to be found, yet another readership. I thank E. J. Brill for permission to copy the original.

JACOB NEUSNER

Rosh Hodesh Heshvan 5747
November 3, 1986

Program in Judaic Studies
Brown University
Providence, Rhode Island 02912-1826 U.S.A.

CHAPTER ONE

THE PEOPLE AND THE LAW

I. The Problem

Our knowledge of Babylonian Jewish history in this period comes to us from essentially legal sources. The data cited in the preceding chapters constitute a very small segment of these sources, and is itself mostly preserved in the context of legal discussions. These discussions focus upon the Mishnah, its interpretation and application. In general, we have three kinds of legal material: explications of the Mishnah itself, statements on theoretical problems elicited by Mishnaic law, but not directly connected to the Mishnah, and citations of cases in which the law was actually applied. For historical purposes, the first two bodies of legal data are of limited value. The historian wants to know *how things were*, not how some people wished they might be.

We have no way whatever of determining how much of Mishnaic law, and the legal doctrines arising from it, actually influenced the life of the people. The language of legal discourse does not vary, whether it is discussing matters which were obviously theoretical, or day-to-day issues of practical law. A few examples of the former will suffice:

> R. Huna, R. Judah, and all the disciples of Rav maintained, A heathen is executed for violation of the seven laws applying to the sons of Noaḥ . . . . .
>
> (b. Sanh. 57a)

The Jewish courts did not, as we have seen, possess the right to inflict capital punishment except under strict Sasanian supervision, if then. It is not likely that they would have had sufficient jurisdiction over non-Jews to enforce the Noaḥide laws among them. Similarly, we have numerous legal dicta regarding the sacrificial cult, which had ceased to exist more than a century and a half earlier:

> R. Zera in the name of Rav stated, If a non-priest slaughtered the Red Heifer, it is invalid because . . .
>
> (b. Men. 6b)

> Samuel to R. Hana of Baghdad said, Bring me ten people and I will teach you in their presence, If drink offerings are defiled, one makes a separate fire for them and burns them.
>
> (b. Zev. 92a)

> R. Judah in the name of Samuel said, If a peace-offering is slaughtered before the doors of the *Heikhal* are opened, it is invalid, as it is said, 'And he shall kill it at the entrance of the tent of meeting' (Lev. 3.2)—when it is open, but not when it is closed.
>
> (b. Zev. 55b)

> Samuel asked R. Huna, How do we know that when one who is unaware engaged in sacrifices, it is invalid . . .
>
> (b. Zev. 46b)

Whether the Red Heifer was actually slaughtered before 70 is not entirely clear, since the Tannaitic traditions on the matter are notoriously inexact,[1] but it is certain that neither the red-heifer, nor peace-offerings had been prepared, and that the defilement of drink offerings had not in fact posed a practical legal problem, for over a century and a half. It is striking that Samuel wished to make a public announcement of his legal view, so that it would be regarded as an official statement. The sacrificial cult is not the only area of law which elicited legal inquiries, but it is the obvious example of how the dedication to study of the Torah, including its legal sections, brought about consideration of matters which could not have practical consequences except when the Messiah came; and of how the appropriate language and procedures differed *not at all* from those relevant to very immediate, commonplace legal problems.

Furthermore, we have legal dicta on matters of normally private concern, for example:

> Rav said, A man who wilfully causes erection is to be placed under ban.
>
> (b. Nid. 13a)

> Samuel said, The domestic and wild goose are forbidden copulation.
>
> (b. Bekh. 8a)

> Rav said, It is forbidden to sleep by day more than a horse's sleep.
>
> (b. Suk. 20b)

Even though the values of the rabbis played a very substantial part in the formation of social mores, a very elaborate police force would have had to have been employed to enforce dicta such as these. For their part, the rabbis tried to encourage obedience to the law by both promises and threats; for example:

> Rav observed, A *mamzer* [illegitimate child] never lives longer than thirty days.
>
> (Lev. R. 33.6)

[1] See my *Life* 51-3, 60-1, 70.

This saying is explained to mean that if a *mamzer* is known as such, he will not survive. Similarly:

> R. Huna said, Once in seventy years, the Holy One blessed be He brings a great pestilence upon the world, and consumes the *mamzerim*, taking the legitimate ones with them . . .
>
> (Lev. R. 33.6)

The rabbis could not invariably enforce their views of what were, and were not, acceptable marriages, but they could, and did, encourage the people to share their view that these marriages could not produce healthy children. They did not find that everyone acted accordingly. In the following case, we see that some of the rabbis possessed greater prestige than others, and the people obeyed whomever they saw fit:

> Rabbah b. Bar Ḥana gave money to Rav, and instructed him, Buy this field for me, but he went and bought it for himself. Did we not learn, What he did is done, yet he has behaved toward him as a cheat? For Rav, they showed respect, but not for Rabbah b. Bar Ḥanah.
>
> (b. Qid. 59a)

Finally, the rabbis themselves acted at variance with the prevailing view of the law:

> Rav once had his harvest gathered for him in the intervening days of the festival. Samuel heard and was annoyed.
>
> (b. M.Q. 12b)

Similarly, the rabbis sought to discourage the people from swearing oaths, because of the possibility of profaning the Divine Name, but all they could do about it was point to the dire consequences, as in the following case:

> R. Judah in the name of Rav, or R. Kahana, said: In a year of scarcity a certain man deposited a dinar of gold with a widow who put it a jar of flour. She baked the flour and gave the loaf to a poor man. The owner came and said, Give me back my dinar, and she said, May death seize upon one of my sons if I have derived any benefit for myself from your dinar, and not many days passed before one of her sons died. When the sages heard, they remarked, if such is the fate of one who swears truly what must be the fate of one who swears falsely.
>
> (b. Git. 35a)

The legal sources cannot, therefore, be used indiscriminately to provide testimony about the conditions of daily life. As we have seen, Mishnaic law treated legal issues which were quite remote, because of historical or other circumstance, from reality. Other kinds of sayings, in a legal formula, concerned actions and attitudes which easily eluded legal enforcement under the best of circumstances. The rabbis themselves differed not only in theory, but in practice, and the famous saying that Nehardea and its environs followed the view of Samuel, and Sura, of Rav, indicates that conformity to a single legal criterion was most difficult to attain.

Even if the rabbis had been unanimous about the great issues of the law, and even if their unanimity concerned specifically those legal problems which most affected day-to-day affairs, however, it would have been very difficult to render the law invariably, or even mostly, effective in the common life. First, even the exilarch did not possess means of physical coercion such as he formerly possessed (and later recovered). Second, even if he had, he was not the sole legal authority in Babylonia. He ruled—at best—only the affairs of his Jewish subjects, while other groups and territories, including those with substantial Jewish populations, were not under his control. One recalls[1] that some Jews, when confronted with rabbinic authority for Sabbath-breaking and having been excommunicated, simply abandoned Judaism and thus placed themselves quite beyond the pale of Jewish law. It does not prove that the rabbis possessed *no* authority whatever; but it does suggest that circumstances limited its effectiveness. Without armies or police, supported only by the *willingness* of Jews to obey the law, because it had been revealed by God to Moses on Sinai, and transmitted faithfully to their own generation, the rabbis had to rely in some measure upon persuasion, in some, upon the inertial force of accepted authority, in some, upon the willingness of the Persian government to accept their decrees, but mostly upon the acquiescence of the people themselves. Because of the precariousness of any kind of government, in an age in which the execution of law was slow and inefficient, and might be impeded by factors out of the control of any Jewish authority the mere proclama-

[1] b. Qid. 72a:

When Rabbi [Judah the Prince] lay dying, he said, There is Humania in Babylonia, which consists entirely of Ammonites. There is Misgaria in Babylonia, consisting entirely of *mamzerim*. There is Birka in Babylonia, which contains two brothers who trade wives. There is Birta diSatya in Babylonia. Today they have turned away from the Almighty. A fishpond overflowed on the Sabbath, and they went and caught fish on the Sabbath, whereupon R. Aḥai son of R. Josiah declared the ban against them, and they renounced Judaism.

See vol. I 147-8.

tion of law meant little practically. The issue of rabbinic authority over the people's life is considerably more complex than has been recognized, and the usefulness of rabbinic laws in recovering a clear notion of how affairs were conducted is somewhat less substantial than is widely assumed.

The rabbinic sources do not, moreover, convey a true and complete picture of how the laws shaped daily affairs, because they mostly suppress, or report only by indirection, actions and conduct contrary to rabbinic dicta. The two great bodies of archaeological evidence provide the most striking examples. No rabbinic source would have permitted us to predict the existence of a synagogue wall such as was unearthed at Dura-Europos; nor is there very adequate assistance in rabbinic literature as presently understood in interpreting the art of that synagogue. The incantation texts from Nippur tell us considerably more about the attitudes of the common people than does the Talmud, and what they tell us is that the people had no hesitation whatever about making use of the best magical science of their day in achieving their life's purposes. We have considered above (p. 35) some of the rabbis' sermons. Even discounting the homiletician's natural hyperbole, one would have to suppose that there were people who did not obey the dietary laws, attend ritual baths, and otherwise comport themselves properly, and that the rabbis had to call down upon their heads the most severe calamities by way of exhortation. The following sayings suggest that the rabbis took a very realistic view of their contemporaries, preaching sermons to encourage the people to behave in a moral manner:

> Rav said, On account of four things is the property of householders confiscated by the state [fiscus]: On account of those who defer payment of laborer's wages, on account of those who withhold the hired laborer's wages, on account of those who remove the yoke from off their necks and place it on the necks of their follows, and on account of arrogance. And the sin of arrogance is equivalent to all the others, whereas of the humble it is written (Ps. 37.11), 'But the humble shall inherit the land and delight themselves in the abundance of peace.'
>
> (b. Suk. 29b)
>
> R. Amram in the name of Rav said: Three transgressions which no man escapes for a single day are sinful thought, calculation on prayer and slander.
>
> R. Judah in the name of Rav said: Most people are guilty of robbery, a minority of lewdness, and all of slander.
>
> (b. B.B. 164b)

> The Master said, Bet Hillel say, he that abounds in grace inclines (the scales) towards grace. How can this be, seeing that it is written, 'And I shall bring the third part through fire' (Zech. 13.9). That refers to wrongdoers of Israel who sin with their body. What are 'wrongdoers of Israel who sin with their body?' Rav said, This refers to the cranium which does not put on the phylactery. Who are the wrongdoers of the Gentiles who sin with their body? Rav said, This refers to [sexual] sin.
>
> (b. R.H. 17a)

Jews lived in Babylonia, therefore, who did not put on phylacteries, and who did not meet the rabbis' standards for ethical economic and social behavior[1]; who did not even respect the rabbis, for Rav defined an 'Apikoros,' who is destined to be denied the blessings of the world to come, as one who insults a scholar (b. Sanh. 99b). However ominous such a lapse may have been under ordinary circumstances, one must suppose that in this period, disrespect was sufficiently serious for the rabbis to set aside a particularly unhappy fate for such a person. If, furthermore, we took the following source as probative, we should have to conclude that the Jews did not fight on the Sabbath:

> R. Judah in the name of Rav said, If foreigners besieged Israelite towns, it is not permitted to sally forth against them, or to desecrate the Sabbath in any other way on their account, and so a Tanna taught as well.
>
> (b. ʿEruv. 45a)

In fact, the narrative about the Jewish state of Anileus and Asineus makes it quite clear that the Jews not only fought on the Sabbath, but did so not merely to overcome a siege, but to mount aggressive attacks on the enemy.

Similarly, the rabbis themselves preserved comments on the mores of their contemporaries which present a picture quite at variance from the one we should derive from strictly legal sources. For example:

> R. Giddal in the name of Rav said, If an inhabitant of Naresh kisses you then count your teeth. If a man of Nehar Pekod accompanies you, then it is because of the fine garments he sees on you. If a Pumeditan accompanies you, change your lodging.
>
> (b. Ḥul. 127a)

> Some thieves came up to Pumbedita and opened many casks. Rava said, The wine is permitted. What was his reason? The majority of

[1] Even the rabbis had lax servants, see b. Beẓah 14b.

thieves [there] are Jews. The same thing happened in Nehardea, and Samuel said, The wine is permitted.

(b. A.Z. 70a)

While the rabbis laid great stress upon proper genealogies, holding the descendants of illegitimate unions might not marry Jews, as we have seen, the people in whole provinces paid no attention whatever to their views, and were declared heretics. On the one hand, the Babylonian rabbis insisted that Babylonia was, from the genealogical viewpoint, the acme of purity:

R. Judah in the name of Samuel said, All countries are as dough in comparison with Palestine, and Palestine is as dough in comparison to Babylonia.

(b. Qid. 69b)

They moreover regarded ethical and social conduct as a suitable measure of genealogical purity:

Rav said, Peace in Babylonia is the mark of pure birth . . . . R. Judah in the name of Rav said, If you see two people continually quarreling there is a blemish of unfitness in one of them and they are [providentially] not allowed to cleave to each other.

(b. Qid. 71b)

Samuel said, He who claims, 'I am descended from the royal house of the Hasmoneans' is a slave, because there remained of them only one maiden who ascended a roof, lifted up her voice, and cried out, 'Whoever says I am descended from the Hasmoneans is a slave.' On that day, many *ketuvot* were torn up in Nehardea. When he went out, they came to stone him [R. Judah, who reported the saying], but he threatened them, If you will be silent, well and good, but if not, I will tell what Samuel said, There are two families in Nehardea, one the House of Jonah, the other, the House of Urbati, and the sign thereof is 'Unclean to unclean', 'Clean to clean'. Thereupon they threw away the stones and created a stoppage in the royal canal.

(b. Qid. 70a)

It was believed that Ezra had taken up with him all of the unsuitable families, leaving Babylonia genealogically uncontaminated. On the other hand, we may reconsider the geographical sayings cited above:

R. Papa in the name of Rav said, Babylonia is healthy, Mesene is dead, and Elam is dying. What is the difference between the sick and the dying? The sick are destined for life, the dying for death. How far does Babylonia extend . . . .

(b. Qid. 71b)

These definitions were provided for genealogical purposes. For instance, Samuel held that Moxoene is genealogically as pure as 'the Exile,' meaning Babylonia; Rav held that Halwan and Nehawand are similarly pure. They clearly reveal, first of all, that the sickness or health of a region was determined by its genealogies; secondly, that large territories were placed beyond the pale; and third, that, even in Babylonia itself were substantial numbers of people whose ancestry concealed a dubious alliance. The rabbis' knowledge of genealogy was regarded as thorough and sound. Rav's visitation and examination of a family was interpreted to mean that he had studied their genealogy. Given the importance ascribed to inherited, as well as acquired, merits, moreover, one can easily understand how the theological importance of proper breeding played such a significant part in the people's choice of marriage-partners. And yet: Mesene is dead and Elam is dying. And in Nehardea itself were many families who had reason to fear rabbinic examination.

One recalls, moreover, that Elam was held to produce students, but not teachers of the law. While a very few rabbis came from Mesene, Adiabene, Armenia, and elsewhere, the bulk of the students in the academies came from, and went back to influence, Babylonia itself. Whatever conditions prevailed in the 'Exile', the outlying districts were probably quite remote from rabbinic law, simply because the institutions and instruments for the propagation and application of the law were unavailable. However useful we may find legal dicta for describing life in the central Babylonian communities, we cannot, therefore, claim to know anything about that in the outlying districts. That is not to say that Jews in Dura, Arbela, Tigranocerta, or Charax Spasinu were not observant. They doubtless kept the bulk of the law, as they understood it; in Dura, provision was made for an *'eruv*, which suggests that the Sabbath laws were observed with considerable care. We have no grounds, however, to believe that they kept the law exactly as the *rabbis* taught it.

The problem of using legal sources in order to describe social life cannot therefore find a simple solution. Here I shall attempt only a very limited step toward a full sociological appreciation of the legal literature. Since the scope of this study is narrowly defined by the first four decades of Sasanian rule, the only material available for study is that in the names of Rav, Samuel, their adult contemporaries, or clearly identified with their times. On such a narrow basis, one cannot even attempt a full description of the life of the people, for no one could reasonably hold that only those laws which Rav and Samuel discussed were actually known in their day, or that only those dicta the observance of which we can demonstrate were actually enforced. Yet a study within narrow chronological limitations will reveal useful information. It can provide evidence on the *minimal* areas of law which were enforced in the daily life of the people, and provide the basis for sound conjecture on those laws, in addition to the obvious ones cited above, which were not enforced, or which were discussed for theoretical purposes only, or which applied to the life of the academy alone. Of the three kinds of legal data, moreover, only the third, the numerous reports about the application and enforcement of the law in popular affairs, is useful here. As we shall see, these reports are by no means scattered evenly through each tractate. This is not to suggest that all legal theory, interpretation of the Mishnah and speculation about hypothetical cases, instruction in the academy, and the like, represented merely exercises of legal fancy. I do not argue that they did. The only exact and concrete evidence we have however, that the law *was* enforced, which therefore helps to provide a picture of the life of the people, is the report of a case that such-and-such a litigation came before one of the rabbis, who decided in such-and-such a manner. This evidence is decisive, and ought to be isolated and examined by itself. I do not know to what extent other kinds of law were carried out by the people. I do know from the kinds of evidence to be studied here that *some* of the law yielded court cases, inquiries to the rabbis from ordinary people, and other kinds of circumstantial evidence that parts of the law in fact influenced the conduct of life.

As I emphasized in the preface, the following pages will by no means exhaust the vast legacy of legal dicta left by Rav, Samuel, and their contemporaries. I do not believe that we shall have touched, in all, more than one-half of all the sayings in the names of early third-century rabbis. Several tractates containing numbers of their Mishnaic interpretations yielded not a single shred of evidence of actual law-enforcement, and will not, therefore, be considered here, even though it is quite reasonable to suppose that parts of such Mishnaic law were actually under practical as well as theoretical consideration. I hope eventually to be able to offer a valid description of Babylonian Jewish social life in Talmudic times, but only after the evidence pertaining to each period has been isolated and examined, and the possibilities of social changes have been taken into account.

II. Agricultural Offerings

The rabbis believed that Babylonia was subject to the agricultural taxes decreed in Scripture or by ordinance of the prophets.[1] Samuel held, moreover, that hybridization is forbidden, not only to Jews but also to gentiles,[2] and that stipulations on land use supposed to have been laid down by Joshua applied in Babylonia as well.[3] We have, in addition, several sayings of Rav, which indicate that he believed the rules on tithing should be enforced, including one which must be theoretical:

> R. Judah in the name of Rav said, If a heathen separated heave-offering from his pile, then we examine him. If he said, I have separated it with the same intention as an Israelite, it is to be handed to the priest . . .
>
> (b. ʿArakhin 6a)

I doubt that many gentiles would have done so. We cannot, nonetheless, conclude that the great number of the people actually observed these laws, since there is only one example of rabbinical enforcement.[4] On the contrary, one recalls the saying of R. Yoḥanan that "Our *rabbis* in the Exile used to separate heave offerings and tithes until the archers came,"[5] which we suggested, following Halevi, referred to the time of the Palmyrene invasion. The language of R. Yoḥanan is significant, for he holds that it was the *rabbis* who were meticulous on the offerings. It is difficult not to suppose that the laymen were not so conscientious. The rabbis, holding both a tradition and an exegesis based upon Lev. 19.19, acted according to their lights, and their discussions on the laws may be based in part upon their own practice. That the average farmer accepted the burden of offerings, which he may well have regarded as required only in Palestine, above the taxes he paid to the Sasanian government, is not likely. I think the people observed the tabu against sowing with mixed seeds, because we have both a case in which Samuel fined a man for breaking it,[6] and an inquiry from an outlying town about whether

---

[1] Mishnah Yadayim 4.3, "The rule touching Babylonia is the work of the prophets". Compare b. Bekh. 27a, giving *terumah* was a 'rabbinical' enactment.

[2] b. Sanh. 60a, Qid. 39a, based on an exegesis of Lev. 19.19.

[3] b. B.Q. 81b.

[4] The case involving Rav in b. Ḥul. 131a, about a Levite who used to snatch the priestly dues, could well have taken place in Palestine. We have no clear evidence on Babylonia whatever, except for y. ʿOrlah 3.7, cited below.

[5] Above, p. 51-2.

[6] Note, however, the discussions of Rav and Samuel on whether the agricul-

certain plants constituted 'mixed seeds' in a vineyard. I do not know about the rest. Where the biblical law was explicit and well-known, the people obeyed it, and consulted the rabbis about how to do so.

On the other hand, the Palestinian rabbis forbade the breeding of 'small cattle' in Palestine, but permitted it in Syria and in unsettled areas, where if the depredations of goats, for example, damaged the basic agricultural economy by ruining the forests, Jewish Palestine would not be affected. When Rav came to Babylonia, he decreed the same rule:

> R. Judah in the name of Rav said, We put ourselves in Babylonia with reference to the law of breeding small cattle on the same footing as if we were in Palestine. (b. B.Q. 80a)

(We have a similar ruling with regard to bills of divorce). In this matter, however, we have no clear evidence that Rav's legal dictum was in fact widely accepted, and I do not think it likely that the rabbis' authority was sufficient to enforce it. It would have required a very extensive reform of agricultural practices, and evidences of such a reform, in the form of court cases, stories of law enforcement, and the like, are not available. What is more likely is that the rabbis and those who were influenced by them, through sermons, study in the academies, and personal contact, may have followed the decree in this matter, but the greater number of Jewish farmers would not, in this period, have accepted it.

On the other hand, several of the rabbis were very rich men. Samuel, for example, was able to influence the price of produce by his marketing practices, in order to keep it down, as did his father.[1] He owned many slaves.[2] Whatever moral influence he may have exerted was certainly strengthened by his economic power, and in the area around Nehardea, he may thereby have been able to convince others to follow his practice.

Though superficially, this is an argument from silence, actually the absence of cases reporting the enforcement of the various agricultural taxes and most of the tabus is practically probative, for we

---

tural offerings and tabus had to be observed, in y. ʿOrlah 3.7. Here we have a case in which Samuel fined a man for disobeying the laws on mixed seeds, "The matter came before Samuel and he fined him". The rabbis were therefore prepared to *enforce* the laws if they could, but this is the only instance we have in which they actually did. See also y. Ḥal. 4.4 on Ḥallah and heave-offerings outside of Palestine, and b. Hul. 134b re R. Sheshet.

[1] b. B.B. 90b.

[2] b. Nid. 47a.

have extensive evidences showing that other kinds of law *were* either enforced or voluntarily carried out by the people, who therefore consulted the rabbis about the proper manner of fulfilling them. It stands to reason that where we have no similar evidence, the law in fact was mainly theoretical.

III. Transfers of Property, Torts, and Damages

There can be no doubt whatever that the rabbis did effectively enforce the law as they saw it in *all* matters of transfer of property, including litigations. The evidence is abundant that they did so. It is, moreover, quite natural to suppose that they did. What the farmers did on their farms would not normally come under the supervision of the rabbis. Disapproved practices would have been easily concealed; the rabbis could not inspect every farm in Babylonia to ensure that their interpretation of the law was followed; nor did they have the right to come to the farmer and extract from him the agricultural offerings due to the priests and others. To do so systematically would have entailed the use of a considerable police force, which the rabbis did not have at their disposal. Transfers of property were quite another matter. They had to be regulated by public authorities; documents had to be written properly; and the rabbis and their scribes *were* the official registrars of such documents. Orderly and permanent transfer of property required public authorization, recognition, and confirmation. It was the rabbis, acting for the exilarchate, and empowered, or at least recognized, by the Sasanian government, who supervised such matters. When the people came to them, the rabbis had a splendid opportunity to act as they thought proper. As judges, therefore they had no difficulty in enforcing the law by their own lights.

It should not, however, be concluded that the rabbis had an entirely free hand. Practices which the people accepted could not easily be changed. For example, the people widely practiced the writing of a *prosbul*, which would annul the affect of the Sabbatical year upon the remission of debts. Samuel said:

> We do not make out a *prosbul* save either in the Court of Sura or in the Court of Nehardea . . . This *prosbul* is an assumption on the part of the judges. If I am ever able, I shall abolish it.
>
> (b. Git. 36b)

The practice, however, continued into the next generation.[1]

[1] b. Git. 37b. See Weiss, *Dor*, III 153.

Samuel tried to limit the need, by decreeing that orphans do not require a *prosbul*,[1] but his most effective limitation was the requirement to obtain the document in only two courts, which would have necessitated considerable travel from other parts of Babylonia if it was to be met. There is no evidence on the progress of Samuel's policy. Since cases would most certainly have arisen, and come for litigation, under Samuel's decree, and since we have no cases of suit to obtain funds claimed to have been remitted because a document was, from Samuel's viewpoint, invalid, we may suppose that his decree was not widely observed, and that people continued to accept documents written elsewhere, without too much rabbinical opposition.

The rabbis did, however, exert considerable authority on the proper form of deeds and documents of all kinds. Deeds of transfer were brought to court, verified, and confirmed for action, and the rabbis laid down rules which were observed widely, for example:

> Samuel said, If one finds a deed of transfer in the street he should return it to the owners .... R. Naḥman said, My father was among the scribes of Mar Samuel's court when I was about six or seven years old, and I remember that they used to proclaim, Deeds of transfer which are found in the street should be returned to their owners . . .
>
> (b. B.M. 16b)[2]

The rabbis adjudicated conflicting claims based upon legal documents; they laid down many rules on how to do so. I have no doubt whatever that these rules were put into effect.[3]

Transfers of inheritance and the execution of wills posed numerous knotty problems to the rabbinical courts. Samuel warned his student, R. Judah, to avoid transferring inheritances, on moral grounds, from a bad to a good son,

> . . . because one never knows what issue will come forth from him, and much more so from a son to a daughter. (b. Ket. 53a)[4]

Questions were addressed to the rabbis from outlying parts:

> The people of ʿAkra diʿAgma asked Samuel, Will our master teach us? What is the law in the case where one was generally held to be the first-born son, but the father declared another to be first born?
>
> (b. B.B. 127b)

---

[1] b. Git. 37a.
[2] Another case is in b. Ket 21a.
[3] For example, b. B.B. 34b-35a, b. Sanh. 28b, B.B. 51b.
[4] Also b. B.B. 133b.

> R. Jeremiah b. Abba reported, The following inquiry was sent from the academy to Samuel: Will our master instruct us? What about a dying man who gave all his estate to strangers in writing, and an act of acquisition took place . . .
>
> (b. B.B. 152b)

Cases were brought to them for adjudication:

> A case in Nehardea arose [in which a man said to his wife, My estate will belong to you and your children] and Samuel allowed her to receive one-half of the estate.
>
> (b. B.B. 143a)

There is no reason to doubt that the rabbis possessed sufficient authority to carry out the law. Since they were judging cases which *had* to be brought to their courts, they quite naturally enforced the law of the Mishnah as they understood it, and the significant number of such cases prevents any doubt whatever about the practical effectiveness of their decisions and opinions.

The principles of adjudication were widely proclaimed, moreover, so that people would not need to be constantly repairing to the courts, but would act, in the first place, according to the law. For instance,

> Samuel said to R. Ḥanan of Bagdad, Go and bring me a group of ten men so that I may tell you in their presence that if title is conferred upon an embryo, [through the agency of a third party] it does acquire ownership.
>
> (b. Yev. 67a)[1]

It was particularly important for people to know the proper way of effecting acquisition of property. In Jewish law, money payment does not constitute acquisition, but a formal action is required. Rav lectured in Kimḥania, near Sura, on how to acquire large cattle,[2] and Samuel issued many dicta on the subject of acquiring fields, trees, and so forth.[3] Cases came to court in which ownership of a property was in dispute:

> A certain lady had the usufruct of a date-tree to the extent of lopping off its branches [for cattle-fodder] for thirteen years. A man came and hoed under it a little, and claimed ownership. He asked Levi [or, Mar ʿUkba] who confirmed title to the land. The woman complained

---

[1] See b. Ket. 7b, Qid. 42a, where Rav provides a Scriptural basis through exegesis of Num. 34.18, B.B. 142b, y. Yev. 4.1.

[2] b. Qid. 25b.

[3] b. B.B. 54a.

bitterly. He said, What can I do for you? For you did not establish your title properly.

(b. B.B. 54a)

Since it was in the hands of the court to confirm or deny title to the land, the judges were able to effect their view of the law, even though it ran contrary to popular practice. In this case, the woman had assumed she owned the tree, and until someone challenged her in court, no one assumed to the contrary. Hence it stands to reason that most people identified usufruct with possession. The rabbis did not, and when they came to apply the Mishnaic law, they were able only through *force majeure* to sustain their decisions. Doubtless in time, the people became better acquainted with these laws, as indeed they would have had to in order to avoid chaos in economic affairs.

The rabbis encouraged the people to avoid purchasing disputed lands, but to seek a clear title. As we have seen, Samuel applied the verse, 'And did that which is not good among his people' (Ezek. 18.18) to one who buys a field about which are disputes. Such disputes could easily arise, for example, when the Persians allocated title to whoever paid the delinquent taxes on a piece of property. The Jewish owner could keep alive his claim to the land by protesting to the Jewish court.[1] The frequency of cases involving improvement of land is seen in the following:

> R. Naḥman in the name of Samuel said, In three cases the improvements are assessed and payment made in money, [to settle the debt of] the first-born to the ordinary son, of the creditor or of the widow who collected her ketuvah to orphans, and of the creditors to the vendees .... Samuel said, A creditor collects the improvements ... *Cases arose daily* where Samuel ordered distraint even of the improvement touching the carriers ...

(b. B.B. 110b)

In the third case, if the debtor sold his land, the vendee may lose it to the creditor, but must be compensated for his improvements. The range of laws which were actually enforced quite obviously extends far beyond the few cited here; what is significant in those noted above is that cases *are* cited, in which the rabbis, speaking quite without guile, refer to decisions and precedents.

Cases of claim for loss or damages came quite regularly to the rabbinical courts, and these were discussed in legal study in the academies. For example:

---

[1] b. B.B. 39b, for example.

A certain person borrowed an axe from his neighbor and broke it. He came before Rav, who said to him, Go and pay [the lender] for his sound axe . . .

(b. B.Q. 11a)[1]

Abbuha b. Iḥi . . . bought a garret from his sister, and a creditor came and took it away from him. He appeared before Mar Samuel, who said, Did she write you a guarantee? No. Then, if so, go in peace. So he said to him, Is it not you, Sir, who said that [omission of a clause] mortgaging the debtor's property is due to an error of the scribe [and therefore not actionable]? He replied, This applies only to notes of indebtedness but it does not apply to documents of buying or selling, for a man may buy land for a day.

(b. B.M. 13b)

Normally, the litigants were given a choice of arbitration or litigation.[2]

The rabbis' judgments were carefully studied, and abstract legal principles were derived, sometimes wrongly, from their decisions:

R. ʿAnan in the name of Samuel said, An orphan's money may be lent at interest. R. Naḥman objected, Because they are orphans are we to feed them with forbidden food? What happened [in the case you have in mind, that you issue such a dictum]? He replied, A cauldron belonging to the children of Mar ʿUkba [who were orphaned] was in Samuel's care, and he weighed it before hiring it out, and weighed it when receiving it back, charging for its hire and for its loss of weight. But if a fee for hiring existed, there should be no charge for depreciation, and if there was a charge for depreciation, there should be no fee for hiring. [Hence, interest is involved]. He replied, Such a transaction is permitted even to bearded men, since he [the owner] stands the loss of wear and tear, for the more the copper is burned, the greater the depreciation.

(b. B.M. 69b)[3]

Hence it is clear that R. ʿAnan had no tradition whatever about Samuel's opinion, but only a story from which he deduced a saying. Since he did not indicate, in his original formulation, that he was transmitting his own interpretation of Samuel's view, it stands to reason that other such sayings in Samuel's name in fact were derived from his actions or court decisions. It is significant, I think, that such instances emerge only in matters of civil and commercial law, rather than, for instance, cultic or agricultural law. The legal sayings of the

---

[1] See also b. B.M. 96b.
[2] b. Sanh. 6b.
[3] Compare b. Git. 52a.

rabbis on dormant matters, such as the cult, or on areas of law which were mostly matters of theoretical discussion, such as agricultural tithing, did not give rise to any such speculation on the basis of action, as indeed they could not. It was where the law actually governed daily affairs that the rabbis' actions were subjected to close scrutiny.[1] We have a similar example for Rav:

> It was stated, If one enters his neighbor's field and plants it without permission, Rav said, An assessment is made, and he is at a disadvan tage, and Samuel said, We estimate what one would pay to have such a field planted. Rav Papa said, There is no conflict, Samuel refers to a field suitable for planting [trees] and Rav to a field not so suited. Now this ruling of Rav was not explicitly stated, but inferred from a general ruling, for a man came before Rav. Go and assess it for him, he said. He demurred, But I do not desire it. He said, Go and assess it for him and he shall be at a disadvantage. But I do not desire it, he repeated. Subsequently he saw that he had fenced the field and was guarding it, and Rav said to him, You have revealed your mind that you desire it, Go and assess it for him, and the planter shall be at an advantage. (b. B.M. 101a)

Similarly, in a case of damages:

> It was stated, If one bailee entrusted to another, Rav said, He (the latter) is not liable, and R. Yoḥanan said, He is liable. R. Ḥisda said, This ruling of Rav was not stated explicitly but by inference. For there were certain gardeners who used to deposit their spades daily with one particular old woman. But one day they deposited them with one of themselves. Hearing the sounds of a wedding, he went out and entrusted them to that old woman. Between his going and his return, the spades were stolen, and when he came before Rav, he declared him not liable. Now those who saw this thought that it was because if a bailee entrusts to another, he is free, but that is not so. This case was different, seeing that every day they themselves used to deposit with that old woman . . . (b. B.M. 36a)

If we did not have the testimony of R. Ḥisda, we should have assumed that Rav held such an opinion, transmitted by the 'Amora' in the academy; but, in fact, he never expressed, and probably did not hold it. Such a case signifies that the actions of the rabbis were closely observed and widely discussed, a situation explicable, as I said, only if they in fact judged cases publicly. I have not attempted to cite *every* case of damages which the rabbis adjudicated; those given above provide sufficient evidence that their authority was effective and mostly unchallenged.[2]

---

[1] As in blessings over food, among the academicians, see below p. 274f.

[2] See for example, on the return of lost property, b. B.M. 24b; on damages

By contrast to the substantial number of civil suits, I know of not a single criminal action reported as a precedent, or described as a case under adjudication, in the time of Rav and Samuel, except for those cited above[1], in which 'a man wanted to show another's straw,' and another 'had intercourse with a Gentile woman.' These cases provide no significant exception, for they involved political, rather than merely judicial, policy, and do not prove that the rabbis judged criminal cases or executed the death penalty. On the contrary, the former was a case, at best, involving civil damages, which political circumstances transformed into something more serious. The latter entailed only flogging for immorality. In Parthian times, Jewish courts probably had the right to inflict the death penalty. In this period, they did not. We do not have the record of other cases, involving less serious penalties, which the rabbis judged. We know that there were Jewish courts, and that these courts did govern substantial matters, including significant civil and commercial litigations. We also have many sayings on criminal law by Rav and Samuel, but have no cases showing that they enforced their opinions in court-actions. Since, in a vast population, criminal cases must have arisen, we can reasonably assume that in this period the Jewish courts did not try them, but that the Sasanians mostly did.

IV. Laws of Personal Status

In matters of personal status, the view of the rabbis was enforced in courts, and therefore prevailed widely. The reason is the same: the public recognition of the legality of a marriage and the legitimacy of its offspring depended upon court action, not merely upon private acquiescence, and since the rabbis were in charge of the courts, their views gained ascendancy. We have seen above that in territories where people were indifferent to rabbinical laws, there was little the rabbis could do but prohibit marriage with the inhabitants, and where appropriate, declare the offspring illegitimate. In Babylonia however, the rabbis' power and authority were substantial, and their courts possessed great prestige. We have reports of many cases where they were consulted, or their laws put into effect, in matters of personal status, marriage, and divorce, and in the preparation of documents

---

ensuing from depreciation of the coinage, b. B.Q. 99b, B.Q. 103a, b. B.M. 44b (not a court case), unpaid debts, b. B.M. 77b, loss because of error in ritual slaughtering, b. B.Q. 99b, damages through negligence, b. B.Q. 48b, B.Q. 27b.

[1] See above, p. 30-35.

relevant to such affairs. Their dicta were widely discussed. I have no doubt, therefore, that the law on these subjects reflects practical, and not only theoretical, situations.

The rabbis issued public instructions in matters of marriage, though we do not know whether they were invariably obeyed. Benjamin (of Gazaca) publicly preached that intercourse with a virgin may be performed on the Sabbath, against the view of Samuel.[1] Similarly it was the view of Rav that a barren marriage must be annulled after two and one-half years, but we have not a single record of a case in which such a law applied.[2] The normal means of law enforcement in cases of personal status was flogging:

> Rav ordered the chastisement of any person who betrothed by cohabitation [rather than by a document or money-exchange], who betrothed in the open street, or who betrothed without previous negotiation: who annulled a letter of divorce; or who made a declaration against [the validity of] a letter of divorce; who was insolent towards the representative of the rabbis, or who allowed a rabbinical ban upon him to remain for thirty days and did not come to the court to request the removal of the ban; and of a son-in-law who lived in his father-in-law's house. The Nehardeans stated, Rav ordered the chastisement of none of these except him who betrothed by cohabitation without preliminary negotiation [because this was sheer licentiousness].
>
> (b. Yev. 52a, Qid. 12b)

It seems most reasonable to accept the view of the Nehardeans, because the other cases would have involved the flogging of people who probably acted in a way they thought right, without evil intent, except for those who did not heed the decree of a rabbinical court, and these may have been so numerous that floggings would have been required everywhere, bringing the law and the rabbis into disrepute.

The rabbis' medical knowledge brought respect for their judgments of the legitimacy of children:

> Is a man [whose stones are] punctured incapable of procreation? Surely a man once climbed up a palm tree and a thorn pierced his stones, so that his semen issued like a thread of pus, and he begat children. In that case, as matter of fact, Samuel sent word to Rav telling him, Institute inquires respecting the parentage of his children.
>
> (b. Yev. 75a-b)

Here we see a case in which the rabbis were able to deny, if they

[1] y. Ber. 2.6.
[2] b. Yev. 64b.

chose, the legitimacy of children, and the implication is clearly that such a declaration would have carried weight. Indeed, since such a child would have been unable to claim his inheritance in court, and since the rabbis would not recognize (for judicial purposes) his marriage to a legitimate Israelite, they had considerable power. Similarly, we cited above[1] the case in which a rabbi was consulted on whether the wife of a man believed to have drowned might remarry. These cases indicate without question that the rabbis exerted considerable power over marriage, divorce, and similar affairs.[2]

Their students, moreover, believed that their actions were worthy of emulation, even where the courts could not, or would not, require behavior in like manner. Thus we have the following account:

> Rav Kahana once went in and hid under Rav's bed. He heard him chatting with his wife, and joking, and doing what he required. He said to him, One would think that Abba's mouth had never sipped the dish before. He said to him, Kahana, are you here? Go out, because it is not proper. He replied, It is a matter of Torah, and I need to learn.
>
> (b. Ber. 62a)

The students' eagerness to learn and transmit the ways of their masters in time extended the influence of the rabbis to matters far beyond those which their courts adjudicated, so that their values, embodied in exemplary action among the masses, came to shape those of the entire community. But in this period, it was mainly through court action and the threat of court-inflicted punishment that they were able to affect public behavior.

They were concerned that people who did not know the law should not deal with matters of marriage and divorce, since the consequences could be quite serious:

> R. Judah in the name of Samuel said, He who does not know the particular nature of divorce and betrothal [laws] should have no business with them . . .
>
> (b. Qid. 6a, 13a)

For their part, they investigated the validity of betrothals:

> R. Jeremiah b. Abba said, The disciples of Rav sent to Samuel saying, Would our master instruct us? If a woman was *reported* to have been engaged to one man, and then another came and betrothed her

---

[1] P. 115-116, b. Yev. 121a.

[2] As y. Qid. 3.12, y. Yev. 4.15, may the child of an Israelite woman and an "Aramaean" man marry a Jew?

formally, what is to be done? He replied, She must leave him, but I want you to ascertain the facts and inform me . . .

(b. Git. 89b)[1]

A certain man betrothed a woman with a bundle of tow cotton. Now R. Shimi b. Ḥiyya sat before Rav and examined it. If it was worth a perutah, well, and if not, it was not a valid betrothal . . .

(b. Qid. 12a)

A certain man betrothed with a myrtle branch in the market place. R. Aḥa b. Huna asked R. Joseph, How is it in such a case? He replied, Have him flogged in accordance with Rav, and demand a divorce in accordance with Samuel . . .

(b. Qid. 12b)

These are three cases which indicate that the rabbis did look into the validity of betrothals, and executed the law. In a further case, we have a report which almost certainly reflected actual practice:

Samuel said, One is allowed to betrothe a woman during the [weekdays of] a festival, lest another anticipate him . . . . It means, the preliminary terms, as R. Giddal in the name of Rav stated, How much do you give to your son? So-much and so-much. How much do you give to your daughter? So-much and so-much. If they then stood up and pronounced the dedication they have acquired their legal rights. These are matters that are legally concluded by word of mouth.

(b. M.Q. 18b)

Samuel likewise decreed that one might betrothe even on the 9th of Av.[2] While no cases provide illustration of the enforcement of this decree, the language cited by Rav reflects actual daily speech, and Samuel's dictum certainly does not contradict what one would expect people to have done. On the other hand, the rabbis demanded considerably more reticent behavior with women than they could possibly have publicly required:[3]

R. Judah and Rav were walking on a road, and a woman was walking in front of them. Rav said to R. Judah, Lift your feet before Gehenna [Speed on]. But you yourself said, he replied, that with respectable people, it is well [for two men to be alone with one woman]. Who says that respectable people mean such as you and me, he replied? Then such as whom? Such as R. Ḥanina b. Pappai and his companions.

(b. Qid. 8a)[4]

---

[1] See below, p. 273, and Git. 81a.
[2] y. Beẓah 5.2.
[3] b. Qid. 80b, 81a, 81b.
[4] See b. Qid. 39a.

Similarly, Samuel said that even the voice of a woman constituted an invitation to license. Rav held

> We flog on account of *yiḥud* [being alone with a woman] but we do not excommunicate on its account.
>
> (b. Qid. 81a)

Since there was no actionable case likely to arise from such matters, unless they produced significant complications, we have no reason to believe that the rabbis actually did any such thing, because, as in former instances, their police power was inadequate to it.

The dissolution of a marriage tie, on the other hand, bore significant consequences. Property had to be transferred, and persons had to be designated as free to remarry. Hence court action was invariably required, for the preparation of a document of divorce, or for the provision of a ceremony of *ḥaliẓah*. Yet even in the latter case, the peoples' pattern of behavior took precedence over rabbinic opinion:

> Rabbah in the name of R. Kahana in the name of Rav said, If Elijah should come and declare that *ḥaliẓah* may be performed with a shoe that covers the foot, he would be obeyed. If he said that *ḥaliẓah* may not be performed with a sandal, he would not be obeyed, for the people have long ago adopted the practice of [performing it] with a sandal.
>
> (b. Yev. 102a)[1]

Furthermore, individual rabbis supervised the ceremony in accord with their own, and not the majority, view.[2] Divorces, on the other hand, were easier to regulate, since they required correct documents, and the rabbis were implacably meticulous in enforcing the law, as well they could be:

> There was a certain man who said, If I do not come back from now until thirty days, grant a divorce to my wife. He came back at the end of thirty days, but the ferry prevented his crossing the river. He called, See I have come back, see I have come back, but Samuel said, That was not regarded as having come back.
>
> (b. Ket. 2b, Git. 34a)

Similarly, they had to adjudicate unclear situations:

> R. Joseph the son of R. Manasseh of Dewil sent an inquiry to Samuel saying, Would our master instruct us: If a rumor spread that so-and-so, a priest, has written a *get* for his wife, but she still lives with

[1] Compare y. Yev. 12.1.

[2] b. Yev. 104a. Compare b. Ket. 54a, Rav's town followed his practice in marriage-contracts, and Samuel's his.

him and looks after him, what are we to do? He sent back, She must leave him, but the case must be examined. What are we to understand by this? Shall we say that we examine whether we can put a stop to the rumor or not? But Samuel lived in Nehardea, and in Nehardea it was not the rule [of the court] to put a stop to rumors . . .

(b. Git. 81a)

What is striking here is the ability of the rabbis to intervene in a matter which the people could manage for themselves. One did not *have* to have a bill of divorce written by a court-appointed scribe, for as we have seen in the above case, a man might write his own divorce and have it recognized. Nonetheless the rabbis were able in fact to regulate the matter, and the laws yielded cases which leave no doubt about their practical application.[1] They could compel a man to divorce his wife, if sufficient cause could be shown.[2] Their power did not rest merely upon popular acquiescence, but upon the coercive capacities of their courts, and the practical consequences of the decrees these courts might issue. The writing of such decrees by the court scribes was carefully supervised by the rabbinical judges:

R. Jeremiah b. Abba said, An inquiry was sent from the school of Rav to Samuel, Would our master teach us, If a man said to two persons, Write and deliver a bill of divorce to my wife, and they told a scribe and he wrote it and they themselves signed it, what is the law? [Are the words, THEY SHOULD WRITE in the Mishnah to be understood literally, or do they denote merely signatures?] He sent back word, She must leave [her second husband] but the matter requires further study . . .

(b. Git. 66b)

Rav said to his Scribes, and R. Huna to his, When at Shili, write at Shili, although information was given to you at Hini, and vice versa.

(b. B.B. 172a)[3]

There was a certain woman named Nafa'atha and the witness on the bill wrote it Tafa'atha. R. Isaac b. Samuel b. Martha in the name of Rav said, The witnesses have discharged their commission.

(b. Git. 63b)

They similarly supervised the writing of marriage-contracts:

The marriage-contract of R. Hiyya b. Rav was written by day and signed by night. Rav himself was present and made no objection.

(b. Git. 18a)

---

[1] Compare b. Qid. 44b, y. Git. 6.1 for such cases.
[2] b. Git. 88b, with a case in y. Git. 3.8.
[3] b. Git. 80a, b. Yev. 116a.

The presentation of documents and their proper verfication were likewise strictly regulated.[1]

The cases cited here do not, of course, nearly exhaust the great number of sayings relevant to personal status. My intention is not to present a profile of the law, but rather to suggest those areas of law, a profile of which would be congruent to social realities. As we saw at the outset, a legal saying by itself testifies quite inadequately, if at all, to the prevailing social conditions. Some sayings, however, are part of a corpus of enforced law, specifically those dealing with matters of commerce, transfer of property, marriage, divorce and the like, and that corpus of law did shape public life, and can provide a valuable resource for describing the life of the people. The sayings of Rav, Samuel, and their adult contemporaries, however, constitute only a small portion of that resource, which accumulated over a period of three hundred years, and it would be misleading to isolate their sayings for such a purpose. I hope in time to attempt a more comprehensive portrait than is possible within the narrow chronological limits set for this study.

v. Laws on Religious Life

The Bible shaped the religious life of the masses. The rabbis did not need to urge the people to keep fundamental, biblically-ordained laws. This they did because they believed it was what God wanted them to do. Popular practice required rabbinical supervision of the *ways* the commandments were to be carried out. On matters where biblical laws and rabbinical interpretations were perfectly clear, well known, and widely accepted, there the rabbis merely guided, without need of coercion of any kind, the affairs of the people, who brought them their queries. Where rabbinical injunctions were more severe, or in some way not widely known or accepted, the rabbis had to rely upon a measure of coercion, as best they could. For the most part, however, more than they coerced, they were *consulted* by the people, because they were believed to know precisely the way the law should be obeyed, and they did not have to resort to floggings, excommunication, and the like, in commonplace areas of the law. This is not to suggest that the masses were quite so meticulously observant as the rabbis would have liked, nor that in some even elementary matters the law was easily enforced. We have seen that

[1] See for example b. Git. 6a.

R. Aḥai b. R. Josiah had to excommunicate a whole village because of Sabbath violations, and many married contrary to the law. Tension between a class of religious virtuosi and the masses of their followers is certainly not an uncommon phenomenon in the history of religions. Because they knew the Bible, the Jewish masses, however, provide an example of a community which, on the whole, proved amenable to the guidance of their leaders, even when they modified long-established customs, if they could base such actions on exegeses of Scripture. It was, in the end, the school-house which guided, and the academy which defined, obedience to the law.

The three kinds of laws most rigorously obeyed were those of Kashrut, menstrual separation, and the Sabbath. In all three, we find that the rabbis were frequently consulted, but it was mainly in Sabbath observance that they resorted to flogging. The rabbis could not supervise every kitchen in Babylonia, and therefore had, mostly, to wait to be consulted about the law, or to enforce it out-of-hand in the butcher shops if they could. When they were consulted, they could, of course, issue decrees which the people, if they wanted to do the right thing, might carry out. The laws governing the cessation of intercourse during a woman's menstrual period likewise could not be enforced except by voluntary action, for if the rabbis could not inspect every farm and every kitchen, they most certainly could not supervise every bedroom. The cases we shall examine indicate, however, that the people did consult them with frequency, and thus conscientiously sought to obey the menstrual tabus. The Sabbath, on the other hand, was publicly observed, and if it was broken, that, too, took place in public. The rabbis did not have to wait to be consulted; they aggressively punished Sabbath breaking, and the people doubtless expected them to, because of well-known biblical precedents. The cases we have, likewise, indicate that the rabbis used physical coercion to ensure proper Sabbath observance in their communities. We do not know how the Sabbath law was observed in areas not under rabbinical supervision. We have, however, numerous inquiries on the part of students, whose Sabbath observance would have carried the rabbis' influence far beyond the limits of their supervision. By contrast, the synagogue liturgies were not invariably conducted according to rabbinical opinion. The rabbi had no special function in synagogue affairs. He did not preside over the service, nor was his presence necessary for its conduct. As we shall see, accepted and ancient synagogue practices were sometimes far beyond the supervision or contrary to the will of the rabbis.

As in many other matters, the fundamental laws of ritual slaughter were widely observed, while details varied from place to place. For example, two teachings of Rav contradict one another:

> R. Huna in the name of Rav said, If the femur of a bird was dislodged, it is permitted. Rabbah b. R. Huna said to R. Huna, But the rabbis who came from Pumbedita reported the statement of R. Judah in the name of Rav, If the femur was dislodged it is prohibited [terefah]. He replied, My son, every river has its own course.
>
> (b. Ḥul. 57a)

> Rav once happened to be at Tatlefush[1] and overheard a woman asking her neighbor, How much milk is required for cooking a rib of meat? Said Rav, do they not know that meat cooked with milk is forbidden? He therefore stayed there and declared the udder forbidden to them.
>
> (b. Ḥul. 110a)

Since Rav apparently found an obedient audience, it cannot be concluded that the people were hostile to observance of these laws. They simply did not know the rabbinic exegesis on Exodus 34.26. The rabbis differed among themselves, moreover, on details of the food laws, and these differences may have been based upon varying local customs, traditions, or view of what the facts in the case required:

> It was stated, If [hot] fish was served on a [meat] plate, Rav says, It is forbidden to eat it with milk sauce. Samuel says, It is permitted to eat it with milk sauce. [The issue is whether it imparted a flavor]. This ruling of Rav . . . was not expressly stated by him, but was inferred from the following incident. Rav once visited the house of R. Shimi b. Ḥiyya, his grandson. He felt a pain in his eyes, so they prepared an ointment on a dish. Later on he was served with stew in this same dish, and he detected the taste of the ointment in it. He remarked, Does it impart such a strong flavor? [Thus even an indirect taste is of consequence.] . . . .
>
> (b. Ḥul. 111b)

On the other hand, Samuel served fish upon a meat plate with milk sauce. Similarly, the proper manner of ritual-preparation of meat was debated, and people acted according to the opinion of one or another of the rabbis:

> Bar Piuli was standing in the presence of Samuel and porging [removing the sciatic nerve] a side of meat. He was only cutting away

[1] Obermeyer 298.

the surface. Samuel said to him, Go down deeper, Had I not seen you you might have given me forbidden meat to eat. He was alarmed, and the knife fell out of his hand. Samuel said, Do not be alarmed, for he who taught you this taught you according to the view of R. Judah . .
(b. Ḥul. 96a)

Numerous cases came before the rabbis for practical decision;[1] as we noted above, the exilarch expected that his rabbinical judges would deal with such cases.[2] If they were present, they would also give an opinion where it was not solicited:

Rav said, Meat which has disappeared from sight is forbidden. This rule of Rav was not expressly stated, but was inferred from the following incident. Rav was once sitting by the ford of the Ishtatit[3], when he saw a man washing the head of an animal in the water. It fell out of his hand, so he went and fetched a basket, threw it into the water, and brought up two heads. Said Rav, Is this what usually happens? And he forbade him both heads. R. Kahana and R. ʾAssi asked Rav, Are only forbidden heads found here, and not permitted ones? He replied, Forbidden ones are more frequent. [It was a jetty frequented by gentiles]. Rav was once going to his son-in-law R. Ḥanan, when he saw a ferry boat coming towards him. He said to himself, When the ferry boat comes to meet one, it is a good omen. He came to the door, and looked through the crack, and saw the meat of an animal hanging up. He then knocked at the door, and everybody came out to meet him, even the butchers. Rav did not take his eyes off the meat, and said, If that is how you look after things, you are giving my daughter's children forbidden meat to eat, and Rav did not eat of that meat.
(b. Ḥul. 95b)[4]

The rabbis therefore held much higher standards than the people, but there can be very little question that the people obeyed the basic laws, because they learned them in the Bible.

While most laws of ritual purity were inapplicable in Babylonia,[5] the biblical prohibition of intercourse with a menstruant was certainly observed by the people. The rabbis were consulted on the meaning of vaginal stains and excretions:

Shila b. Abina gave a practical decision following Rav [that a woman in labor during eleven days of *zibah* who discharged some blood is unclean]. When Rav's soul was about to depart to its eternal rest, he

---

1 b. A.Z. 68b, b. Ḥul. 44a, 53b.
2 b. Ḥul. 58b, Pes. 76b.
3 Obermeyer 300.
4 See y. Sheqalim 7.2.
5 See Funk, *op. cit.*, I, 70, Ginzberg, *Law and Lore*, 13.

> said to R. ʾAssi, Go and restrain him, and if he does not listen to you try to convince him . . . .
>
> (b. Nid. 36b)[1]

Further, the rabbis aggressively enforced the law when evidence reached them that it had been broken:

> . . . When a certain sac was submitted to Mar Samuel, he said, This is forty-one days old, but on calculating the time since the woman had gone to perform her ritual immersion until that day and finding that there were no more than forty days, he declared, This man must have had intercourse during her menstrual period, and having been arrested, he confessed.
>
> (b. Nid. 25b)

As I said, the rabbis did not have to wait for consultations on Sabbath observance, nor did they need to resort to calculations to discover when it had been violated. Sabbath observance was public and communal, and the rabbis vigorously enforced its laws. Their own Sabbath observance was closely watched, and emulated by the disciples.[2] Two kinds of violations were easily punished, first, those involving publicly-observed work on the Sabbath:

> Certain gardeners once brought water [on the Sabbath, from the public to private domain] through human walls [the men forming them were aware of the purpose] and Samuel had them flogged. He said, If the rabbis permitted human walls where the men composing them were unaware of their purpose, would they also permit such walls where the men were aware of the purpose?
>
> (b. ʿEruv. 44b)

Secondly, the setting up of Sabbath limits (*ʿeruvin*) to permit carrying within a specified village or courtyard was a public action, and easily supervised:

> [Come and hear of the case of a certain alley in which Eibu b. Ihi lived.] He furnished it with a sidepost (for an *ʿeruv*) and Samuel allowed him his unrestricted use. R. ʿAnan subsequently came and threw it down. He exclaimed, I have been living undisturbed in this alley on the authority of Samuel. Why should R. ʿAnan b. Rav now come and throw the sidepost down!
>
> (b. ʿEruv. 74a)
>
> R. ʿAnan was asked, Is it necessary to lock [the door of an alley] or not? He replied, Come and see the alley gateways of Nehardea which

[1] For other practical decisions see y. Nid. 2.5, 2.7, b. Nid. 66a, 65a, 25a.

[2] As b. ʿEruv. 102a, b. Shab. 146b, y. ʿEruv. 6.8, a question asked by disciples to Samuel; b. Beẓah 16b, Samuel permits another to rely upon his *ʿeruv tavshilin*.

are half-buried in the ground [and cannot be moved from their open positions and locked] and Mar Samuel continually passes through these gates and yet never raised any objection . . . When R. Naḥman came, he ordered the earth to be removed . . . There was a certain crooked alley in Nehardea upon which were imposed the restriction of Rav and the restriction of Samuel . . . .

(b. ʿEruv. 6b)

In these cases, the rabbis could easily order that the Sabbath-limit conform to the law, or simply construct the *ʿeruv* they approved of.[1] In their travels, likewise, they lectured on Sabbath law,[2] and outlying towns wrote and asked for advice:

The citizens of Bashkar[3] sent a question to Levi: What about setting a canopy [on the Sabbath]? What about cuscuta in a vineyard [is it prohibited on account of 'mixed seeds']?[4] What about a dead man on a festival [can you hold a funeral]? By the time it arrived, Levi had died. Said Samuel to R. Menashia, If you are wise, send them (a reply). So he sent word, As for a canopy, we have examined it from all aspects and do not find any aspect by which it can be permitted . . . Cuscuta in a vineyard—Rav said, He who wishes to sow cuscuta in a vineyard, let him do so. As for a corpse, he sent word, Neither Jews nor Arameans may occupy themselves with a corpse, neither on the first, nor on the second day of a festival.

(b. Shab. 139a)

It is significant that most of the cases illustrating the enforcement of Sabbath law relate to the statutes of *ʿeruvin*, and not, for the most part, to those of Sabbath work itself, except the case cited here and the one, dating from Arsacid times, about the men excommunicated by R. Aḥai b. R. Josiah. Given the complexity of those laws, and the conditions of life, one cannot easily assume that no Sabbath-law violations required attention, nor that only the relatively complex laws of *ʿeruvin* produced questions. The simple inquiry from Bashkar reflects, quite to the contrary, that people did not know very basic laws, and doubtless they were unaware of other such laws, without being instructed by the rabbis unless they sent inquiry, or having received a pastoral visit from one of the rabbis. For the most part, except for public actions in which the law was unequivocal, the rabbis could not easily enforce their will. Rav, for example, "saw a man

---

[1] b. Beẓah 16b, Samuel's Father used to set the *ʿeruv* for all of Nehardea.

[2] y. ʿEruv. 1.4, Rav happened to come to a certain place; b. ʿEruv. 6a, Rav at Damharia, near Sura; 100b, Rav at Afsatia.

[3] Obermeyer, p. 91.

[4] See above, p. 260-262.

sowing flax on Purim, and he cursed him, so the flax would not grow."[1] The rabbis' prestige far outweighed their coercive power, for people believed in their curses. On the other hand, Samuel's father was asked whether, if a man is compelled by force to eat unleavened bread [on Passover] he has performed his religious obligation to do so,[2] and he replied, that he had, which suggests that force was used in religious matters, yet not by the rabbis in this instance. It stands to reason, therefore, that the people themselves enforced religious law as they understood it; everyone knew that one should eat unleavened bread on Passover, and it might easily happen that villagers might force one of their number to do so. As we have seen, the rabbis relied on flogging and on the ban to ensure proper observance:

> Rav and Samuel both said, We impose the ban [for violation of] the two festival days of the diaspora.
>
> (b. Pes. 52a)

Such means were effective only in a context of general obedience, in which the people for the most part wanted to do the right thing, and required supervision and encouragement, and in the case of minor recalcitrance, a limited measure of coercion.

While the rabbis laid down many laws about proper mourning customs, we have only the case of the inquiry from Bashkar, about festival law, to illustrate popular adherence to their views. On the other hand, the following teaching was probably not invariably obeyed:

> R. Judah in the name of Rav said, When a person dies in town, all the townspeople are forbidden from doing work.
>
> (b. M.Q. 27b)

We have no example of punishment meted out for failure to observe that law. The rabbis' views on proper mourning procedure were most easily enforced among their own students, and I believe that it was *only* among the disciples, in this period, that meticulous observance of rabbinical enactments on mourning was found. We have questions addressed to the rabbis only from their students,[3] and the single case of law enforcement deals with a student:

---

[1] b. Meg. 5b.
[2] b. R. H. 28b.
[3] b. M.Q. 21a, Rabba b. Bar Ḥana is instructed by Rav.

> A certain student of Samuel had intercourse [during a bereavement]. Samuel heard about it and was angry with him, and he died . . .
>
> (y. M.Q. 3.5)

(Such a matter could easily become public at a ritual bathhouse.) I have no doubt whatever that the people observed mourning rites, but there is no ground to assume that these rites followed rabbinical enactments:

> [Mishnah: A Person should not stir up wailing for his dead nor hold a lamentation for him thirty days before a feast]. Why just thirty days? R. Kahana in the name of R. Judah in the name of Rav said, It once happened that a man saved money to go up for a feast [to Jerusalem] when a [professional] lamenter came and stopped at his door and the wife took her husbands savings and gave them to him, so he was prevented from going . . . .
>
> (b. M.Q. 8a)

This case, which happened in Palestine, suggests that popular mourning practices were well-established, and the rabbis would have had difficulty modifying them.

Synagogue liturgies were likewise very ancient, and the people had long conducted synagogue affairs without rabbinical supervision. Even though such matters were public, and therefore easy to regulate, the tenacity of ancient customs was such as to prevent the rabbis, who had no sacerdotal function, from effecting their will. For example, we cited above the following story:

> Rav once came to Babylonia, and noticed that they recited the Hallel on the New Moon festival. At first he thought of stopping them, but when he saw that they omitted parts of it, he remarked, It is clear that it is an old ancestral custom with them.
>
> (b. Taʿanit 28b)

We have, further, the following remarkable account:

> Rav happened to be at Babylonia during a public fast. He came forward and read in the scroll of the Law. Before commencing he made a blessing, but after finishing he made no blessing. The whole congregation [afterwards] prostrated themselves, but Rav did not . . . . Why did he not fall on his face? There was a stone pavement, and it has been taught (Lev. 26.1), 'Neither shall ye place any figured stone in your land to bow down to it,' meaning, upon it ye may not bow down in your land, but you may prostrate yourselves on the stones in the temple. If so, why did only Rav refrain from prostrating himself? The entire congregation should not have done so? It was in front of Rav. But could he not have gone among the congregation and fallen on his face? He did not want to trouble the congregation . . .
>
> (b. Meg. 22a-b)

> Was there not a synagogue 'which moved and settled' in Nehardea, and in it was a statue [of a king] and Rav and Samuel and the father of Samuel used to go in there to pray . . .
>
> (b. R.H. 24b)

These three cases (in addition to Dura) offer striking evidence that the rabbis did *not* govern synagogue life, did not approve aspects of it, and yet participated in it, and contributed to the liturgy. Their influence in the synagogue depended upon their prestige; they had no effective legal authority to change practices they did not like. Since the masses of the people had accustomed themselves to their current ways, the rabbis could not resort to a decree of excommunication, nor could they flog an entire congregation. In the end, however, their reputation as holy men gave them considerable influence:

> When Rav died, R. Isaac b. Bisna decreed that none should bring myrtles and palm-branches to a wedding feast to the sound of a tavla [bell], yet he [a certain man] went and brought myrtle and palm-branches at a wedding to the sound of the tavla, so a snake bit him and he died.
>
> (b. Shab. 110a)

Under the circumstances, it is likely that many would obey the rabbi, rather than risk his curse or some worse result. On the other hand, no legal system could depend for enforcement upon the vagaries of curses, snakes, and barren flax-seeds. The many stories in which a rabbi's curse was sufficient to bring down punishment upon the head of a recalcitrant sinner reveal that in such cases, it was only the curse, and not flogging, or an act of excommunication acceptable among the masses, that was probably available for enforcing the law. The laws, the breaking of which was punished by rabbinical curses, were most likely those which rabbinical courts could not otherwise cope with, or which were not subject to popular inquiries addressed to the rabbis about proper observance. We have too much contrary evidence about very practical law-enforcement to conclude otherwise.

vi. The Rabbis' Influence

Talmudic law as we have it for this period must, therefore, be used with considerable caution to recover a picture of the conduct of daily affairs. Among the masses, ancient customs, dating in some instances without doubt to the very beginnings of the Babylonian Jewish settlement seven centuries earlier, exerted considerable influence, and the rabbis were able to effect their own policies only in limited matters. On the other hand, within their academies, their authority was unlimited, and as they trained the judges of the coming generation, and students went out to their villages throughout Jewish Babylonia and beyond, the legal doctrines of the rabbis radiated into the common life. This was not a process which was completed in one generation, nor was the transformation of the life of approximately 860,000 people effected by a few men alone. The laws on proper blessings, for example, were probably observed in this period mainly in the academies. The many dicta on the etiquette of saying grace, on the proper forms of benedictions over food, conditions for prayer, and the like, produced only one case reflecting conditions outside of the academy, but many within it:

> Once when R. Giddal b. Minyumi was in the presence of R. Naḥman, the latter made a mistake in the grace . . .
>
> (b. Ber. 49a)

> When Rav died, his disciples . . . sat discussing the question, When we learned 'reclining' is it to be taken strictly, as excluding sitting . . . R. Adda b. Ahava rose and turned the rent in his garment from front to back, and made another, saying, Rav is dead, and we have not learned the rules of grace after meals . . .
>
> (b. Ber. 42b-43a)

> Said Rav to his son Ḥiyya, My son, Snatch [the wine] and say grace . . .
>
> (b. Ber. 53b)

> Once Rav and Samuel were sitting at a meal, and R. Shimi b. Ḥiyya joined them and ate very hurriedly. Said Rav to him, What do you want, to join us? We have already finished . . . The disciples of Rav were once dining together, when R. Aḥa entered. They said, A great man has come to say grace for us . . .
>
> (b. Ber. 47a)

> R. Judah gave a wedding feast for his son. The guests said a *moẓi* (blessing over bread) before the dessert. He said, What is this *ẓiẓi* I hear! Are you saying '*moẓi*'? They said, Yes, because R. Muna in the name of R. Judah said, Over bread with dessert you say a *moẓi*, and Samuel said that the law follows R. Muna . . .
>
> (b. Ber. 42a)

These cases exemplify the practical reports on blessings. The rabbis similarly discussed how R. Judah the Prince recited the Shema,[1] how to behave during the Silent Prayer, and many other matters.

[1] b. Ber. 13b.

What is significant is that among the numerous cases, questions, and discussions of the actual behavior of individuals, we find only one instance in which a common person, not a student of the academy, was discussed, that of Benjamin the shepherd, cited above (b. Ber. 40b). Significantly, this incident with a common person reveals great leniency on the part of the rabbi, for the required form of the liturgy was not there prescribed. The difficulty Rav's students found with the elaborate laws of grace suggests that the common people would have found it quite impossible, without the elaborate education provided in the academies, to do precisely the right thing. If this is so for the commonplace act of blessing food, one may reasonably suppose that more difficult or unusual matters were quite remote from public comprehension, let alone observance. The kinds of cases which prove *beyond doubt* the efficacy of rabbinical authority were, as I have said, specifically those which came before them in their judicial capacity.

One cannot conceive that before the foundation of rabbinical academies, after the Bar Kokhba war, Babylonian Jewry possessed neither laws nor authoritative doctrines. During the six preceding centuries, as we have seen,[1] indigenous traditions were cultivated, both of law and exegesis, and of doctrine as well. It could not have been otherwise. Babylonian Jews married, bore children and educated them; divided their estates and litigated their affairs; celebrated the ordained festivals and the Sabbath; and pursued the many affairs which required legal adjudication and produced a rich corpus of precedents,[2] for many centuries before the appearance of the first rabbi in their midst. The process by which Babylonian Jewish life was modified to conform to the rabbinical doctrines based on the

[1] Vol. I, 148-63.

[2] I had earlier thought that it would prove useful to compare the legal traditions of Rav and Samuel, for it seemed to me that Samuel's traditions, being almost wholly indigenous, would produce a picture of the law as it existed before the third century, and hence of more ancient social realities. [See vol. I, 154]. Research for this chapter has shown me, however, that such a comparison would not yield the kind of information I had sought, since the 'Babylonian' interpretation of the law would not necessarily yield an adequate portrait of the common life of the people, which is the purpose of my inquiry. The Babylonian traditions are, of course, of interest for their own sake, and I have no doubt that legal historians will greatly facilitate our understanding of the Babylonian *Tannaitic* heritage through a systematic comparison of such teachings. But it is not possible invariably to conclude that Samuel's viewpoints reflect 'Babylonian' conditions, and Rav's, the 'Palestinian' ones, nor did such viewpoints automatically reveal how people actually lived.

Mishnah was a long and slow one. In this period, as we have seen, while very substantial areas of law came under rabbinical supervision, other important aspects of daily life remained outside it. At the very least, one may say that the contact between the people and the law did not yield a literature of inquiry, precedent, and law-enforcement pertaining equally to each type of law and every area of rabbinical concern, but only to specific limited ones. What is remarkable, on the contrary, is that anything changed at all in response to rabbinical influence, for the inertia of centuries made the process of social and legal change painful indeed. The cases we have examined suggest that it was mainly where the rabbis were able to apply very specific pressures, in the form of legal opinions which they could enforce through the courts, that matters changed. We do not know whose authority the rabbis replaced even in these matters. If, as I said, people required legal documents before the third century, we do not know who employed the scribes who issued them, for example, or who presided over litigations. There can be little doubt that a judiciary of some kind existed,[1] and the rabbis represented a continuation of the authority of earlier figures, even though they applied the Mishnah, a corpus of law originating not in Babylonia but in Palestine, in place of whatever ancient precedents and biblical exegeses had accumulated in Babylonia itself. I do not think, on the other hand, that the Babylonian antecedents could have been profoundly different, for they were very strictly based upon biblical exegesis, which permitted only a relatively narrow range of options on how to decide basic issues, though of course secondary questions would have proven complicated, and may have resulted in very different judgments in Babylonia from those in Palestine. The rabbis found it easiest to enforce those laws which the Bible itself laid down, most difficult to effect decrees which the Bible did not make explicit. One must therefore regard as limited the 'revolution' in Babylonian Jewish affairs, resulting from the development of the rabbinic academies. The academies produced judges, and men learned in traditions which in part must have been relatively new to Babylonia. They did not however bring 'the Torah' to Babylonia, nor was it

[1] But for Parthian times I am fairly certain these authorities were upper-class, assimilated Jewish grandees, who possessed both military power *and* a knowledge of law, as in the case cited in vol. I, 94, 98, 104, 131, 137, 153, from b. Git. 14a-b and y. Git. 1.5. They probably issued decisions based upon their indigenous legal traditions, formed through a legal exegesis of Sciiptures.

necessary to win the loyalties of the people to a new doctrine, but rather, to a renewed interpretation of a very old one.

One cannot ignore, finally the eschatological significance of law-observance. We noted above that the rabbis emphasized the conditional quality of redemptive promises. If Israel had kept the first Sabbath, or would now obey the will of their father in heaven, then no nation or race can rule over them. Similarly, Samuel taught that because Israel casts words of Torah to the ground, the heathen are able to make, and carry out, their decrees, and Rav Papa said, later on, that if the haughty will cease in Israel, then the *hazarapats* will cease among the Iranians. These words were not idle homilies, but rather provide the key to understanding why it was that the rabbis laid such emphasis upon law and upon the legal and social reformation of Israel. They possessed the "oral Torah," which, they believed, contained the true and exhaustive interpretation of the written, revealed laws, and as we have seen, they went to great lengths to enforce that law wherever and whenever they could. In the light of their view of history, we can understand the reason: it was through the complete realization of the Torah in Israel's life that they intended to bring the redemption. If Israel keeps the law, then they will no longer be ruled by pagan nations: this is the converse of Samuel's saying, and one which must be understood against his view that the Messianic time would be like the present one, except that the heathen would have no sovereignty over Israel. How better to respond to Sasanian rule, therefore, than to fulfil the Torah? If Israel did, the decrees of the pagans would be nullified, and *that very nullification* would signify for Samuel the advent of the age to come. The achievement of justice and morality, the protection of the rights of the poor and weak, the establishment of a serene and decent public order—these were crucially significant, because through them, as much as through prayer, Israel would carry out its side of the messianic contract. Prayer, study, and fulfillment of the Torah as a whole therefore represented in the end a very vigorous response to the cataclysmic events of the age, and from the rabbis' viewpoint embodied more powerful instruments than any other for the achievement of the better age for which Jews longed. Prayer, study, deeds—these three, but of greatest weight and consequence was the legal and judicial enterprise.

This was, quite obviously, the faith of the rabbis, but if had been theirs alone, I do not think we should have the evidences of law-enforcement that have come down to us. As I said, the Jews in Babylonia were a numerous group, possessing ancient customs and traditions. No matter how effective the exilarch's courts may have been, in the end they relied far more upon the acquiescence and cooperation of the people than upon force, and this was attained, I think, because the people were convinced that the rabbis were leading them in the right direction. Although we do not know how profoundly ancient practices were affected, we do know that they *were* modified; customary patterns of acquisition through usufruct represent a most tenacious body of precedents, and as we saw, these were challenged and changed by the rabbis. One thinks, by contrast, to the reaction, a century earlier, of the Jews of R. Aḥai b. R. Josiah's day, who, when excommunicated for a Sabbath violation, simply left Judaism altogether. By contrast, I know of no similar story in the period under study. And yet the rabbis' decrees were more far-reaching than earlier. I can think of one explanation only. The great number of Jews must have been convinced of the correctness of the rabbis' view that only through a grand reformation would redemption be reached. And if they accepted the rabbis' definition for substantial parts of the needed reformation, or at least, conformed to it, the reason may well have been that they hoped that by so doing, they would see the realization of the ancient hope of Israel, the time their lips would tire from saying 'Enough.'

CHAPTER TWO

THE RABBI AND HIS TORAH

I. The Role of the Rabbinate in Babylonian Jewish History

If the rabbi were merely a lawyer and judge, and the *yeshiva*, or rabbinical academy, merely a law school, then we might appropriately now turn to study the relationship between the rabbinical law codes and the affairs of the ordinary people (as we shall below). The rabbi was much more than a lawyer, however, and the academy was different from a law school. The rabbinate constituted a party or estate in Babylonian Jewish life, the only organized one so far as I can tell, and aimed at a radical reformation of the life of the Jewish people. It was prepared to effect such a reformation through whatever political agencies it could get its hands on. Its purposes however were far more than political, though at first the issues seemed merely to relate to law and, in some measure, sociology, devolving upon who should administer the internal affairs of the Jews, and what law should pertain.

Four forces shaped the history of Babylonian Jewry. First was the Sasanian government, which had power to do exactly as it liked with various groups in the empire, and proved it by the way it solved the Manichaean problem. The Manichaeans posed a severe threat to the Mazdean faith, for they appealed to the same groups upon which the Mazdean church was based, namely the Iranian component in the population of the western part of the empire. Seen by the Mazdeans as dangerous heretics, they could not be tolerated, but had to be expelled, and were driven out as soon as the Mazdean authorities were able to arrange it.[1] For our purpose, the fate of the Manichaeans

[1] Later on the Christians came to be thought of as a threat to the Iranian state, because of the conversion of the Roman emperors and the later establishment of Christianity. But in this period, no equivalent reason existed to persecute the Christians, who regarded the destruction of their churches as a terrible mistake, as we have seen. And yet, it was specifically the orthodox Christianity of the Byzantine Empire which was later treated as hostile by the Sasanian government. The Nestorians fled eastward, and found refuge in Iran. So I think it is clear that the Sasanian government knew who its enemies really were, and distinguished among various minority groups, tolerating, or even favoring, those who posed no threat to its interests.

illustrates what *could* have been done to the Jews, had the government so desired. But no reason to expel the Jews existed. It was perfectly satisfactory through a loyal agent to oversee their affairs, to collect their taxes, and to leave them pretty much to their own devices. Through the exilarchate the Sasanians proposed to attend to Jewish affairs, and it thus constituted the second major force in Babylonian Jewish history. As we have seen, it was its duty to govern the Jews and to carry out among them the policies of the Sasanian regime. Having agreed to do so, the exilarch was given a free hand. In his view, his authority was based upon his distinguished ancestry and upon the support quite naturally accorded to him by the Sasanian government. Even more than the Sasanians, he wanted only to keep the peace and maintain a stable and constructive control of Jewish affairs. The scion of David could ask no less of himself, or promise more to the people, than good government. To govern the people, he sought to apply to their affairs the one law they recognized and he with them as divinely ordained, namely, the Mosaic revelation.

In order to do so, he increasingly drew upon the personnel and leadership of the third force, namely the rabbinate. The rabbinical movement had first appeared in Babylonian Jewry after the Bar Kokhba War, when the refugees from Palestine established their schools in Nisibis and Huẓal, and there carried on the studies they had pursued in Palestine. The Nisibis group, formed by students of R. ʿAqiba, eventually returned to Palestine, but the Huẓal school, constituted by the leading students of R. Ishmael, remained in Babylonia, and trained some distinguished rabbis of late second-century Babylonia.[1] The exilarch of the period seems to have made use of these highly motivated lawyers in his administration, even though they could not have constituted the whole of it. Alongside were Jewish upper-class officials, who knew the traditions of Babylonian Jewry and were well acquainted with difficult legal issues. They were well-trained, though we do not knew in whose schools or according to what traditions. We know only that they were not educated as rabbis or in rabbinical schools. The one encounter between the rabbinical and the native groups reveals that the latter did not defer to the former, but held the rabbis strictly to their own view of what the law required.[2] By the beginning of the third-century, with the foundation of still another school by Rav, and the development of the Nehardean academy by

[1] Vol. I, pp. 128-135.
[2] *ibid.*, pp. 94-97.

Samuel, the non-rabbinical lawyers no longer could have mattered very much. We can only conjecture that so far as the exilarch was concerned, the graduates of the rabbinical academies proved quite satisfactory. Since the academies were run by men loyal to himself, he could not have found any reason to curb them, or even to take much interest in what was taught there. In Rav's and Samuel's day, the schools turned out men trained in the Mishnah, recently promulgated in Palestine by R. Judah the Prince, who were dedicated to enforcing that code among Babylonian Jews.[1] As the years passed, it became clear that they had other purposes as well, and the exilarch faced a new problem. He found that the lawyers and judges, administrators and teachers educated in the academies were not of one mind about their service to his government. A few of them openly defied his authority, and many apparently regarded his rule as founded upon inferior right. If it was the "Torah" that was to shape the life of Babylonian Jewry, then its rabbinical masters—and they alone were privy to the true meaning of Scriptures—should have the supreme rule, and ought not remain subservient to one who was supposedly their inferior in knowledge of Torah. Whether in fact the exilarch knew less about "the Torah" than they is no issue here. The fact is that they claimed he did, and preserved in their records numerous stories of how he had humbly studied the law with his own rabbinical employees. By the end of the third-century, however, the exilarch found that their subversion affected only slightly, if at all, the practical administration of his regime. Leading rabbis, some related to him, including Naḥman, Huna, Rabbah b. Abbuha, and others, were thoroughly loyal, and clearly rejected the pretensions of other academicians to have a say in the government, except upon the basis of exilarchic acquiescence.

The fourth, the largest, and least effective group, was formed by the ordinary people. As I have stressed, we have almost no direct knowledge of what they thought about their government and its agents. We have supposed[2] that they had traditions they believed to be both ancient and correct, and that these would not have conformed in significant ways to the views of the rabbis. But what was more important, they must have responded to the presence of a relatively new group, or class, of religious authorities in their midst in more varied ways than we can now discern. Some part of the ordinary people would have come very much under the influence of local authorities, as in the case of the Ne-

[1] Vol. II, pp. 251-287.
[2] e.g. Vol. II, p. 176.

hardeans and R. Naḥman, and the Pumbeditans and Rav Judah, in this period. Both of these towns, like Sura, were the sites of major academies, and one may suppose that where the academies were located, there rabbinic influence in one form or another was substantial. The many major towns in which rabbinical schools were not found, indeed in which even *rabbinical* courts may not have been permanently situated, must have been another matter entirely. But what made the rabbis an effective group was not alone the power of their courts. They formed a class of religious literati and theurges, distinguished by their behavior and carriage, conforming to rules of conduct not widely observed, or even heard of before the preceding century, but nonetheless claiming to set the standard for *popular*, and not merely elite, behavior. It was in the streets, as much as in the academies or courts, that the ordinary people were exposed to the rabbi.

These four 'forces,' the Sasanians, the exilarchate, the rabbinate, and the masses, cannot be compared to one another, for they constituted different entities. The Sasanian government in this period proved weak and not very effectual. Had it been stronger, it might have become aware of the danger to the lasting power of its agency, the exilarchate, posed by the rabbinate, and might have intervened not only when called upon as in the case of Geniva, but more vigorously and consistently, to eliminate such a threat. On the other extreme, I do not think the ordinary people constituted a party or a group at all. The foci of their life were the fields and marketplaces, the streets and the synagogue. Whatever leadership they had did not extend beyond the given town or village. They were not a 'movement' transcending local lines. Where they lived, there alone did they act. They were, so far as I can see, inert, a great mass to be twisted this way and that, but incapable of guiding or shaping its own growth except in response to events or powers more determined, better organized, and more dynamic than itself. The inertial force of tradition and culture rather than a particular theology or purpose shaped the life of the masses. But we can only guess what that tradition consisted of, beyond Scriptures. The middle groups—exilarchate and rabbinate—cannot be compared to one another. The former was a relatively small and self-contained administration, centered upon the person of the Davidic scion and his police and administrators, and based upon the authorization and active support of the imperial regime. The latter estate, not centered upon a single man, or dependent upon the recognition of the government, constituted a party based on schools, attracting through active proselytization in the academies and courts alike the support of growing numbers of Jews. These accepted their claim and therefore did the things one must do to carry it out: they went, or sent their children to the academies; they paid respect to the great men of the party; they supported its cause by observing its bans and honoring its decrees. As a party, the rabbinate could not easily be compared to the inchoate masses upon which it worked, or to the subordinated exilarchate, or to the imperial government. The people were not similarly coherent, the imperial government not so purposefully engaged or single-minded, the exilarch not equivalently motivated. Sporadic persecution would not destroy them, nor was such persecution undertaken to begin with. Occasional setbacks would not deter them. All the while, as the government ignored them, and the exilarch made use of some, perhaps many, of them, for its own purposes, the rabbinate continued to seek every possible means to win over to its particular viewpoint on politics and theology whomever it could, to educate in its schools, and through the exemplars it sent out from them, as many people as possible. So the established forces, the government and its Jewish administration, proved unequal to the task of opposing a fairly well-disciplined, coherent, and certainly well-organized party, which in time—though not in this period—subverted the latter and thus rendered the former's choices for the Jews quite irrelevant.

The study of the rabbinate must, therefore, precede the study of the ways in which the law (and that means, *rabbinical* law, for that is the only law we know about) shaped the life of the masses. What the rabbi was, the roles and functions he carried out in society, institutional and structural analogies in other parts of Babylonian society,[1] the nature of his leadership—these are the necessary themes of our study. Before we can appreciate the means by which the rabbis effected social change, in this case the reformation of the masses to conform to a pattern other than that which earlier prevailed, we first must carefully analyze the agents of that reformation.

The importance of this inquiry cannot be overestimated. From third-century Babylonia to nineteenth-century Europe, "rabbinic Judaism" was regarded as normative; its laws *were* Jewish law; its theology shaped the conceptions of the masses, and required the speculative defense of the philosophers; its enemies were designated heretics, and its devotees, the 'normative' and 'authoritative' exemplifications of

[1] See also Vol. II, pp. 147-150, comparing the rabbi to the Magus.

"Judaism." The rabbinate represents a singularly successful 'party.' In the history of mankind, one can find few 'parties' which achieved so lasting a success that until this very day, their conception of history and society dominates precisely the group which they intended from the beginning to shape and control. I can think of only one similarly successful group, and that is the Christians, who actively undertook to subvert, and then control, and finally to dominate, the Roman empire, and whose historical role provides an analogy to that of the rabbis. They are not wholly comparable, for the Romans persecuted the Christians, sporadically but ferociously, while the patriarchate in Palestine and the exilarchate in Babylonia actually employed the rabbis. The two parties however thrived by persistence and faith, and in time succeeded in winning the sovereignty to which they aspired, the one to the Roman world, the other to the rule of Israel. It is only in the past two centuries that either has had to face a significant challenge, when the values and ideals of each ceased to shape the groups whom they had dominated for so many centuries.

The survey which follows is intended to provide an insight into some aspects of academic culture, about which our sources provide abundant information. It is based upon a conflation of sayings of the chief figures in this generation. One thus hopes to attain a view of the trends and fashions of thought characteristic of this particular time. By isolating dicta said in it, and separating them from those said by earlier, or later figures, we should be able eventually to achieve a better portrait of a single generation than we now have. However, this is not an entirely satisfactory approach to the problem. It would be better if we had critical biographies of the great men of the time, which would permit us to compare the chief concerns and attitudes of many individuals, each thoroughly investigated by himself. Then by finding what issues and ideas engaged *all* or most of the central figures, we might come to a valid insight into the rabbinical culture of the time, and be able to compare it to earlier and later ages. We do not have such biographies, apart from the brief collections of dicta, and since, as I said,[1] it is not now my purpose to write them, I rely upon the less adequate evidence provided by drawing together discrete sayings and stories, in which one or another contemporary rabbi figures, for a portrait of a whole age. The only justification for this admittedly inadequate approach is the quite remarkable consistency of the rabbinic value-structure from

[1] See above, p. XVII.

earliest days to the end of Talmudic times and beyond. The literature reveals little movement or change. It is indeed only with great difficulty that we have been able to propose the historical relevance of one or another saying, and then only very tentatively. I do not know whether minds changed so little over a vast period of time. One would expect that the issues facing one generation would produce answers and raise new problems for the next, rather than yield such an abiding sameness of discourse. But that is how the literature seems to portray matters, and one can at this point hardly even conjecture about the reasons for it. Schools differ, as do rabbis, but within an amazing range of issues, the differences are on details, rather than on basic issues. Perhaps there were schools of thought, as Heschel showed with reference to R. ʿAqiba and R. Ishmael,[1] which disputed basic theological or legal questions. But I have not perceived in this time such schools set apart by really fundamental differences. For the most part, narrow disagreements revealed greater, more fundamental agreement.

At the same time, I cannot overemphasize that these values were academic. We do not really know what the people outside of the academy thought on the same matters. It is one thing to study the complex relationship between rabbis and ordinary men. It is quite another to say what the people believed concerning the classical issues here under consideration. The only written data we have come from the academies, appearing in a highly rigid and conventional structure. We can be certain that the people read the Bible, but we do not know whether they read it according to the rabbinic hermeneutic, according to some other, or according to discrete local traditions. It is for this reason that we here speak not at all of popular values of conduct, theology, liturgy, and exegesis, but only of those of the schools. Our evidence permits no other course. Law is quite another matter, as we shall see later on, for we have not only legal discussions and sayings, but also case reports which indicate how the law was applied to, and hence shaped, the common life. It is there that the culture of the academies and that of the people intersect, and in the interstices we are able to recover some insight into the relationships between the religious virtuosi and the masses. The rabbis were in constant communication with the masses, not only in the court, but also in the synagogue, in the streets, in the common life. The academies were not situated in the back-country, or, like monasteries, in inaccessible places. They were found in the towns

[1] Vol. II, pp. 232-236.

and villages where the masses of Jews lived. The rabbis were not seeking isolation, but communal leadership, and there is absolutely no equivalent in Babylonian Judaism to the Christian phenomena of anchoritism and encratism. The rabbi was a holy man, but he was never on that account a separatist. His political and administrative role forced him—and I think he wanted it that way—into a continuing relationship with those outside of his schools and unaccomplished in the sacred sciences. Furthermore, the rabbi exposited a book which everyone held to be revealed by God to Moses at Sinai. He was not, it is true, concerned merely to say what was written in it, but rather to exposit Scripture by reference to traditions supposedly revealed at Sinai along with the Scripture but unavailable to those who had not learned them in the academies. So he had at once a commonality and a speciality: Scripture in common, but exegesis and (mostly) eisegesis quite his own, the product of the academy and not of the street. The rabbi however aspired to transform the ordinary people into "rabbis."[1] It was this aspiration which most of all brought him into close and constant contact with the masses, forcing him to teach and to exemplify the truths he believed everyone should conform to. And it was this aspiration which so clouded the literature, that later on it was assumed that the religious attitudes of the rabbis were "normative," all others "heretical," and those of the common people to have been shaped by the rabbis. I do not think we can at the outset *assume* such an identity between virtuoso and common man. The evidence allows no final judgment whatever on what the people outside of the academies thought. While I should suppose that the rabbis were not wholly without success in influencing the people, I cannot estimate the degree of their success.

II. The Rabbi as a Holy Man

We have referred to the rabbinate as a party and estate. The partisan role of the rabbinate will later concern us. Here we shall seek a valid definition for the rabbinate as an estate, or a recognizable group within Jewish society. It is clear, first of all, that the rabbinate did not form a caste, for it was not only open to all who qualified, but also actively fostered the conformity of the masses to its paradigms. Everything demanded of the rabbi was *equally* expected of ordinary people. The

[1] Following Judah Goldin, "Of Change and Adaptation in Judaism," *HR* 4, 2, 1965, 288-292, esp. noting the qualifications stated, pp. 288-9.

rabbinate's social ideal, which stressed the transformation of the lives of *all* Jews and not merely those of the elite to conform to "the Torah," had nothing in common with the aspirations of a caste. Neither birth nor marriage could help a man to achieve status within the party, though both might naturally confer obvious advantages. Second, it is concommitantly clear that the rabbinate did not constitute an economic class, or occupy a single stratum within Jewish society. While many of the most important rabbis emerged from, or became part of, the upper classes, theirs were not intrinsically upper-class values or ideals. They recognized tensions between themselves and the rich and powerful classes. They greatly encouraged the education of poor students. Third, they were not a clerical group. They played no particular role in the liturgical or sacerdotal life of the Jewish community, nor did the synagogue afford them a special platform for their ideas, except when they preached there.[1] They contended in earlier times[2] with the priesthood, which did form a sacerdotal caste, but by this time, the priests were not a significant or influential group within Babylonian Jewry, according to the evidence available to us, but had long since accommodated themselves to a perfunctory and inconsequential place in ritual life alone. (We are not even certain whether they continued to receive priestly offerings, though at least a few did.)

One thing is perfectly obvious: It was not only as men learned in the law or Scriptures that the rabbis set forth their claim against those of the sons of Aaron and the seed of David. Had they possessed legal or exegetical learning alone, the superior genealogy of priest and Davidide alike in a community so obsessed with genealogy would have proved insurmountable. The priests had earlier had their legal traditions, believed by numerous Jews to be the proper guide to the application of revelation to the current age. (Before 70, they had also had a court, based in the Jerusalem temple, to issue *ad hoc* decrees as needed.)[3] The exilarch proved quite able to hire lawyers as bureaucrats, judges, and protagonists. Since none doubted that he had the most distinguished ancestry of all, the claim to superior learning alone could have meant little in the political economy of Babylonia. The rabbi both presented himself as, and was widely believed to be, a holy man, whose charisma weighed at least as heavily as his learning, and whose learning to begin with encompassed far more than a mere collection of ancient traditions

[1] See especially vol. II, pp. 177-180, 274-287.
[2] *Life*, pp. 33-63.
[3] *ibid.*, p. 45ff.

of Scriptural exegesis. What was extraordinary about him was his mastery of a body of theurgical learning, the power of which rendered him exceptionally influential in heaven and earth. This learning was called "Torah," but as we shall soon see, "Torah" comprehended more than merely the Scriptures revealed at Sinai or to the prophets, along with the oral traditions that had accompanied them. If rabbinical knowledge, or gnosis, proved an effective basis for public activities, it was because the rabbis could authenticate it by a wide variety of impressive proofs. No phenomenon above or below proved too hard for their understanding. They were neither wizards nor sorcerers, but their wisdom was such that they could interpret natural phenomena and consort with heavenly beings. They were not physicians, but possessed sound knowledge about healing. The substance and effects of their gnosis sufficiently impressed other Jews that they were seen, by virtue of what they *knew*, to have been transformed into extraordinary men. Against "Torah," genealogy and politics could scarcely contend, but one must stress, it was "Torah" based as much upon personal charisma[1] as upon knowledge of facts, even of mysteries, that characterized the rabbinical estate.

If prophecy was suspended, according to the Pharisaic tradition, at the time of Malachi, Elijah continued to make his appearances to the rabbis. These were not merely occasional, or for brief instruction. R. ʿAnan supposedly received frequent visits from Elijah, who was teaching him the Order of Elijah. When R. ʿAnan behaved poorly, Elijah refrained from visiting him. After the prayer and fasting of R. ʿAnan, Elijah resumed his visits, though now the visits frightened the rabbi:

> Thereupon he made a box for himself, and sat in it before him, until he concluded his Order with him. And that is why people speak of the Greater Order of Elijah, and the Lesser. (b. Ket. 105b-106a)[2]

Lest it be thought that such heavenly figures influenced lore, but not law, the following case, including legal dialectic, suggests otherwise:

> Rabbah b. R. Huna's view is in disagreement with the angel's. For an angel once found R. Qattina wearing a linen wrap. He said to him,

[1] I use the word to refer to the possession of extraordinary powers in general. I do not mean by it the capacity to arouse popular loyalty or enthusiasm through "a personal magic of leadership".

[2] See also b. B. M. 114a-b, p. 60.

> "Qattina, Qattina, a wrap in summer and a cloak in winter, and the blue fringes, what will happen to them [for neither garment required them]?!" He replied, "Do you punish an affirmative commandment [if a man is not liable for doing it]?" He replied, "When there is a time of wrath, we do."

The Talmudic discussion continued:

> Now if you hold that the commandment of fringes applied to the man, not merely to the garment, then we can understand why he is liable for not wearing them, but if you hold that it is incumbent upon the appropriate garment only, then he ought not to be liable! What is the law? It is the obligation of the man. I grant that the All-Merciful would punish one who wears [without fringes] a garment which is subject to fringes, but would He punish one who wears [without fringes] a garment not subject to it? So did he reply, "You justify yourself to free your soul from the commandment concerning fringes." (b. Men. 41a)

So the supernatural appearances affected legal as much as theological discussions, and the opinion of Elijah carried considerable weight in deciding the law.[1] Elijah similarly communicated good advice to various rabbis. For this generation, the following is representative:

> Said Elijah to Rav Judah brother of R. Sala the Pious, "Fall not into a passion and you will not sin. Drink not to excess and you will not sin. When you go forth on a journey, seek counsel of your Maker and go forth." (b. Ber. 29b)

This story is one of a great many depicting the teachings of Elijah to a rabbi. How are we to understand it? On the one hand, if people widely believed that the rabbis' teachings derived from a heavenly source, then their influence would have substantially exceeded what would otherwise have been accorded to them. So one may doubt that the rabbis themselves discouraged the people from believing it. On the other hand, I do not see any grounds to suppose that Elijah-encounters were a deliberate fabrication. What must have happened in such incidents is that a rabbi, living in a world in which people normally thought that demons or angels,[2] including Elijah, frequently appeared to men, interpreted an unusual encounter in the light of quite natural expectations. (We obviously do not know, however, who else met

---

[1] See also b. ʿEruv, 43a, Elijah was believed to appear in the academy before leading rabbis to repeat traditions, in this case R. Ḥisda and Rabbah.

[2] E.g. R. Huna, "Everyone among us has a thousand demons on his left hand and ten thousand at his right," based on Ps. 91:7.

Elijah or other angels, for the data are exclusively derived from rabbinical circles.)

It was when he was engaged in study that the rabbi's supernatural powers were mobilized. If he was repeating a tradition, with his lips moving, he might have been seen by outsiders to be mumbling an incantation or a magical formula, even though in fact the words he repeated were citations of the Mishnah or traditions from the earlier generation about its meaning. The act of learning was supposed to include movement of the lips, however, and to the minds of outsiders, it would have signified something very like incantation, particularly since the rabbi was, to begin with, accredited with supernatural power. The rabbis' act of study was thus believed to render them immune from the angel of death, a notion earlier applied by Rav to the death of King David.[1] Several accounts indicate that contemporary rabbis were endowed with similar powers:

> The angel of death could never overcome R. Ḥisda, for his mouth was never silent from rehearsing his learning. He went and settled on the cedar tree of the academy. The tree cracked. R. Ḥisda stopped [studying], and he overcame him. (b. M.Q. 28a)[2]

> R. Sheshet caught sight of him [the angel of death] in the market. He said, "Do you seize me here like a beast? Come to the house." (b. M.Q. 28a)

> Rava was seated at the deathbed of R. Naḥman, and saw him slipping away. R. Naḥman said to Rava, "Tell him not to torment me." Rava replied, "Are you not an important man?" He said, "Who is important, who is regarded, who is distinguished?" He said to him, "Appear to me [after death]." He appeared to him. He said, "Was it painful?" He replied, "Like removing a thread from milk, and [yet] if the Holy One blessed be He said to me, 'Return to that world where you were,' I should not want to because of the fright of it." (b. M.Q. 28a)

> R. Sheshet was once sitting in the 'synagogue which moved and settled' in Nehardea. The Shekhinah came [as frequently happened there] and he did not go out. The ministering angels came and frightened him. He said before Him, "Lord of the Universe, one who is afflicted, [R. Sheshet was blind] and one who is not afflicted—who gives way before whom?" He (the Lord) said to them (the angels), "Leave him alone." (b. Meg. 29a)

---

1 Vol. II, p. 205.

2 See also b. Mak. 10a.

> Rav Judah said, "If there is none to be comforted for a dead person, ten people go and sit in the place [where he died]." A certain man died in the neighborhood of Rav Judah. As there was none to be comforted, Rav Judah assembled ten men every day and they sat in his place. After seven days he appeared to him in a dream and said, "Your mind be at rest, for you have set my mind at rest."
>
> (b. Shab. 152a)

One recalls also the story of Rabbah b. Abbuha, who was taken to paradise by Elijah, and there enriched, for his robe retained so pleasant a fragrance that he was able to sell it for 12,000 denarii.[1] Gentiles were reported to respect rabbinical magic[2]; and to believe that the rabbis were good at necromancy.[3] We here see that the rabbis were also thought to be able to converse with Elijah and the angel of death, to come back from the 'world beyond' in dreams to converse with their disciples, to argue with the angels and with God himself. It is remarkable that despite such power, they were rarely if ever alleged to have used it in dealings either with one another or with the exilarch or with the Persian government, but rather with ordinary people alone. It is one thing to tell stories, which none could verify, about intercourse with angels, Elijah,[4] and the like, but quite another to claim that one's magical power helped overcome very practical difficulties with this-worldly authorities. What is important is that the rabbis were not ordinary men, but were widely believed to have other-worldly powers. Indeed, Samuel remarked of Rav Judah,

> "This man is not born of woman."
>
> (b. Nid. 13a)

Among the powers ascribed to them was the ability to control heat and fire. A fire did not spread to R. Huna's neighborhood, and people *assumed* it was because of his merit.

> In a dream it was made clear to them that this was far too small a matter to need R. Huna's merit, but it was because of a certain woman who would heat her oven and permit her neighbors to use it.
>
> (b. Ta'anit 21b)

---

[1] b. B.M. 114b, cited above, p. 60.
[2] Above p. 29, b. Ḥul. 105b.
[3] Above p. 34-35.
[4] But see vol. II, pp. 32-34.

> The daughters of R. Naḥman used to stir a cauldron with their hands when it was boiling hot ...
>
> (b. Git. 45a)[1]

The story goes on to tell how they were taken captive along with R. 'Ilish, to whom birds brought a message. He was unable to speak their language, but a fellow captive could, and it turned out that R. Naḥman's daughters were endowed with knowledge of witchcraft.

Rabbis could similarly issue an effective curse. A certain woman in R. Huna's vicinity lost a son and wept excessively. He cursed her so that all her other sons and she herself died for ignoring the rabbi's warning that if she wept her other six sons would die.[2] None of R. Huna's own children survived during the lifetime of R. Adda b. Ahavah, because Ḥoba, R. Huna's wife, acted contrary to R. Adda's view of the law.[3] Rabbis did not require the protection of walls. Rav Judah taught that everyone must contribute for the upkeep of a city's defenses, even orphans, but not the rabbis, "*for they do not require protection.*"[4] Rabbis could also make rain.[5]

In an age in which religion served the needs presently met elsewhere, it was quite natural for the rabbis to be regarded as interpreters of dreams. They themselves repeated the standard exegeses, handed on in their circles from earlier times, concerning the meaning of one or another symbolic dream or vision. Examples of the traditions on dream-interpretation are as follows:

> R. Ḥisda said, "Any dream but not one of a fast. A dream which has not been interpreted is like a letter which has not been read. A good dream is not wholly fulfilled, nor is a bad one wholly carried out. A bad dream is better than a good dream. The sadness of a bad dream is sufficient for it, and the joy of a good one is sufficient for it. A bad dream is harder than scourging."
>
> (b. Ber. 55a)

> R. Huna said, "To a good man, a good dream is not shown, and to a bad man, a bad dream is not shown."
>
> (b. Ber. 55b)

---

[1] See A. Guttmann, "Significance of Miracles for Talmudic Judaism," *HUCA* 20, p. 365.

[2] b. M.Q. 27b.

[3] b. Nazir 57b, b. B.Q. 80a.

[4] b. B.M. 108a.

[5] Below, pp. 120ff.

> A tanna taught before R. Sheshet, "He who sees a snake in a dream—his livelihood is prepared for him. If it bit him—[his livelihood] is doubled. If it killed him, he has lost his livelihood." R. Sheshet said to him, "Rather, all the more so that his livelihood should be doubled." But it is not the case. R. Sheshet saw a snake in his dream and it killed him [so he wished to give the matter a favorable interpretation].
> (b. Ber. 57a)

Similarly, R. Zera said that he did not emigrate from Babylonia to Palestine until he saw barley in a dream.[1]

The rabbis similarly interpreted the signs and omens of the times, and possessed a store of knowledge concerning the auguries of daily events, the right way to conduct humble affairs, and the ways of the world. For instance, R. Kahana said that a pot with two cooks is neither hot nor cold.[2] Rav Judah warned to make certain there is corn in the house, for strife is prevalent in the home only on account of corn, citing Ps. 147:14.[3] Knowledge of the natural world included the following:

> R. Zera met Rav Judah standing by the door of his father-in-law's house and saw that he was in a cheerful mood, so that if he would ask him all the secrets of the universe, he would disclose them to him. He asked him, "Why do goats march at the head and then sheep?" He said, "It is as the world's creation, darkness and then light." "Why are the latter covered and the former uncovered [without a tail]?" "Those with whose material we cover ourselves are themselves covered, and the former are not." "Why is a camel's tail short?" "Because it eats thorns [a long tail would get entangled]." "Why is an ox's tail long?" "Because it grazes in meadows and must beat off the gnats." "Why is the nose of a locust soft?" "Because it dwells among willows, and if it were hard, the locust's nose would be dislocated and it would go blind." "Why is a fowl's eyelid bent upwards?" "Because it dwells among the rafters and if dust entered (its eyes) it would go blind."
> (b. Shab. 77b)

R. Huna in the name of R. Mattena said that a leopard is formed from a white drop containing 365 colors.[4] These explanations of natural phenomena were not based upon Scripture, like many of the rabbis' moral sayings, but rather upon the folklore of the schools, which, one supposes, ultimately derived from the "wisdom of the

---

[1] b. Ber. 57a.
[2] b. B.B. 24b.
[3] b. B.M. 59a.
[4] Gen. R. 7:4.

ages." What is of interest is the reference of R. Zera to "the secrets of the universe," and the implication that these were not commonly spoken of, but preserved for particular times or students. It is striking that the wisdom of the rabbis comprehended such folkloristic etiologies, which, like the interpretation of dreams, far transcended the ordinary concerns of lawyers and judges.

It is quite clear, therefore, that the rabbi was believed to enjoy more intimate connections with God and the angels, and more searching knowledge of the 'mysteries' of the world, than ordinary people. Nonetheless, such knowledge alone would not have set him apart for special respect or veneration. It would, at best, have characterized him as a man of broad learning, a philosopher, but certainly not a "holy man." Much as people may have been impressed by what he knew about the natural world and dreams or about the Torah, they expected something more practical, namely mastery of occult, including healing arts. Without the ability to do extraordinary deeds, the rabbis would hardly have achieved a more significant status than merely that of unusually learned men. The ability to talk to Elijah, or to interpret and explain the phenomena of nature, was by itself hardly sufficient to relieve the rabbis of the obligation to pay for the defense of the cities in which they lived. If the rabbis required no protection, the reason had to do with something more than their learning.

III. Torah, Medicine, and Magic

The people looked to the "holy man" for healing, and when he was able to oblige, ascribed his skill to divine favor or heavenly wisdom. The earliest Christian missionaries to Adiabene and Edessa gained a hearing through their ability to perform miraculous cures. For example, when Pekidha, later the first Christian bishop of Arbela, who had been in the service of a Magus, met Addai, he was so impressed by his ability as a physician that he converted to Christianity.[1] Similarly, Mani was expected to act as the physician of the court.[2] Likewise many of the rabbis of this, as former generations[3] mastered medical traditions,

[1] See Appendix II, below, p. 354-357.

[2] See above, p. 9.

[3] See especially Saul Lieberman, *Hellenism in Jewish Palestine. Studies in the Literary Transmission, Beliefs, and Manners of Palestine in the I Century B.C.E.—IV Century C.E.* (N.Y. 1950), 180-93, on the natural science of the rabbis. See vol. I, pp. 141-2 and vol. II, pp. 126-150.

which were part of the normal paraphernalia of any "holy man," along with astrological knowledge (of which this generation produced almost no data[1]). That the holy men of various communities knew something about matters of health ought not to obscure the fact that a medical profession existed. The rabbi knew he himself was not a physician, who, as in other cultures, combined medicine with barbering and sundry other arts. So when a rabbi taught his disciples about matters of health, or prepared an ointment or salve, he did not do so because no one else would. Rabbinical medical 'practice' stressed two things, first of all, good advice about maintaining health, and second, occasional preparation of medicines to cure specific ailments. We rarely, if ever, hear of rabbis' actually letting blood or carrying out one of the other commonplace medical or surgical procedures. Medical knowledge, part of "Torah" and quite necessary for the enforcement of parts of the law, represented partially esoteric learning, which was not to be widely shared. I should thus understand the place of medicine in the schools. The ordinary people had different expectations. They were sick, and if the physicians could not help, why not turn to God, or to "holy men" who had a closer relationship to him—if Jews, they might have phrased it in terms of "learning"—than other people? After Rav died, people used to take the dirt from his grave and made it into poultices, for application on the first day of an attack of fever. If so, the person, and not merely the learning, of the rabbi must have been seen as "holy" by the plain people. So the people would have understood the rabbis' medical knowledge and traditions as signifying mastery of divine mysteries. The rabbis, by contrast, regarded medicine as a perfectly normal segment of "Torah."

The medical sayings of this generation were based in part upon observation and in part upon earlier traditions, and mostly concerned the maintenance of good health, rather than, as earlier, preparation of actual medicines and cures. We have already noted that R. Bibi knew how to prepare an ointment to lighten the skin.[2] Rav Judah, following Samuel, declared it permissible to paint an eye on the Sabbath;[3] R. Naḥman explained what gout is, basing his remark upon Ps. 25:14;[4] and R. Huna urged his disciples to take a bath:

[1] b. Pes. 12b, R. Adda b. Ahava; y. M.Q. 3.5, a student of R. Ḥisda's was ill, saw a comet and improved. Neither instance represents an astrological dictum.

[2] b. M.Q. 96b, see above, p. 29.

[3] b. A.Z. 28b. For other specific remedies, see b. Shab. 110b, R. Kahana cured R. Aḥa b. Jacob of jaundice; b. Shab. 67a, R. Huna on the remedy for tertian fever.

[4] b. Sanh. 48b.

R. Huna said to the disciples, "Masters, who do you make so light of this [ritual] bathing? Is it because of the cold? You can use baths." R. Ḥisda said to him, "Can ritual immersion be performed in hot baths?" He replied, "R. Adda b. Ahava is of your view."

(b. Ber. 22a)

Many of the sayings concerned proper diet in time of illness:

Rav Judah said, "The sting of a wasp, the prick of a thorn, an abscess, a sore eye or inflammation—for all these a bath-house is dangerous. Radishes are good for fever, and beets for cold shivers, the reverse is dangerous. Warm things for a scorpion [bite] and cold things for a wasp's, the reverse is dangerous. Likewise warm things for a thorn prick and cold for an eruption, the reverse is dangerous. Vinegar after letting blood, and small fish in brine after fasting, the reverse is dangerous. Cress after blood-letting is dangerous. Fever is dangerous for blood-letting, so also are sore eyes dangerous for blood-letting. The second day after fish for letting of blood, the second day after blood for fish: on the third day it is dangerous."

(b. A.Z. 28b-29a)[1]

Similarly, Mar ʿUqba said that an inferior white wine debilitates.[2] R. Ḥisda said,

"A broth of beets is good for the heart and good for the eyes, and all the more so for the intestines."

(b. Ber. 39a)

But, he added,

"Raw beet kills a healthy man."

(b. ʿEruv. 28b)

In evaluating the uses of various foods as medicines, the rabbis had to decide what might be used on the Sabbath, and what should be prohibited. So R. Sheshet taught,

"Cuscuta has no healing properties."

(b. Shab. 109a)

[1] Trans. A. Cohen (London, 1948), 142-3. For sayings of Naḥman, another student of Samuel, on the sun and similar matters, see b. Yoma 28b-29a. Other sayings about how to survive blood-letting emphasize the importance of avoiding a chill on that day. Rav Judah had a table made of juniper-wood broken up for a fire to provide some warmth on the day he was chilled after blood-letting, and making such a fire was permitted even on the Sabbath, see b. Shab. 129a. R. Naḥman drank a great deal on that day, *ibid.*

[2] b. Git. 70a, R. Ḥisda agrees. Rav Judah says, It is bad to get overheated in Nisan.

The attitude of the rabbis toward medical traditions was by no means consistent. Some, such as Samuel a generation earlier, had paid considerable attention to the observation of nature, and his students transmitted a wide variety of sayings about health and healing. Others, as in the following case, did not understand why health was a part of "Torah":

> R. Huna said to his son Rabbah, "Why are you not to be found before R. Ḥisda whose dicta are so keen?" "What should I go to him for," he replied, "since when I go to him he treats me to secular discourses. He tells me when one enters a privy he must not sit down abruptly, nor force himself overmuch, because the rectum rests on three teeth-like glands, and these might become dislocated and he be endangered." "He treats of health matters, and you call them secular discourses! All the more reason for going to him."
>
> (b. Shab. 81b)

Why the student should have regarded these things as worldly matters seems clear. He expected to study sacred writ and legal codes, and found that what most concerned ordinary people, such as matters of the bowels and the like, was the subject of the lectures. So he neglected the classes of one of the most distinguished rabbis of the day, his father's future successor in the Suran academy.

By contrast, some evidence suggests that medical teachings were held to be esoteric, and not to be publicized widely. This attitude characterized Rav Judah and his master, Samuel. It may be that the Pumbeditan academy took such things more seriously because of Samuel's emphasis upon them. The following is of special interest:

> Rav Judah said, "The soft part of a pumpkin [should be eaten] with beet; the soft part of linseed with *kutah*. But this may not be told to the *people of the land* [ignorant]."
>
> (b. Ned. 49a)

Why such information should not be shared with ordinary people I cannot say. One recalls that the rabbis told a story of how a gentile used an ointment similar to R. Bibi's, and killed his daughter. Similarly, Samuel held back part of his medical teaching from Ablat:

> Ablat found Samuel sleeping in the sun. He said, "O Jewish sage, can that which is injurious be beneficial?" "It is a day of bleeding," he replied. Yet it is not so, but there is a day when the sun is beneficial for the whole year, the day of the summer solstice, and he said to himself, "I will not reveal it to him."
>
> (b. Shab. 129a)

It may be that Samuel and Rav Judah regarded medical traditions as a secret lore, and since the people would have to consult the rabbi-doctors to obtain them, they were to serve as a means of extending rabbinical influence over the masses. Yet it is far-fetched to suppose so, for dietary and other information was not kept private,[1] and the rabbis were quite eager to convince people of the accuracy of their medical information. The story about R. Bibi would suggest it is important to consult a *rabbi*, and not to experiment without expert advice; that about Samuel and Ablat leads one to suppose that the rabbis should not tell everything to gentiles, however admirable. But why the people should not be allowed to know how to eat pumpkin and linseed pulp I cannot explain, unless they might eat too much and grow sick. If so, along with the information could go a specified limit, were that the only issue.

Samuel's students continued to discuss his sayings concerning sex, pregnancy, and birth. We have already noted[2] Rav Judah's citations, which indicate extreme hostility to women's company, combined with vivid concern for overcoming sexual desire. In general, the rabbis wanted people to marry young, at sixteen if not earlier. R. Ḥisda said that if one marries at less than 20, he begets children until 60, at 20, to 40, at 40, no more begetting at all.[3] R. Naḥman regarded dropsy as a manifestation of lewdness,[4] and the absence of pubic hair as a sign of impotence, unless the body steams.[5] Impotence was believed to result from sitting excessively long at lectures, R. Huna's long lectures being blamed for that of several rabbis.[6] R. Naḥman also stated that an unchaste imagination is more injurious than the sin itself.[7] R. Huna taught that the stock of a *mamzer* does not survive, which would encourage people to marry those "worthy" of them.[8] R. Ḥisda said that if a daughter is born first, it would be a good sign for children,[9] and R. Ḥisda warned that a foetus could survive if born in the seventh or ninth month, but not in the eighth.[10] All these sayings contain little

[1] See for example R. Ḥisda's saying on the very same page, None ask the fastidious of Huẓal how to eat porridge, the obvious implication being that if someone asked, he would be told, as R. Ḥisda proceeds to do.

[2] b. Qid. 70a-b, above, pp. 65-67, and see below, pp. 142-145.

[3] b. B.B. 119b.

[4] b. Yev. 60b.

[5] b. Yev. 80b.

[6] See below, p. 132.

[7] b. Yoma 28b.

[8] b. Yev. 18b, y. Yev. 8.3.

[9] b. B.B. 141a.

[10] Gen. R. 14.2; compare R. Huna, Gen. R. 20:6 on the opening of the uterus, Rav Judah, cited by Rava, b. Shab. 129a.

that Samuel had not already taught a generation earlier. Naturally, specific individuals became known for their specific cures, Mar ʿUqba and Yalta having their own nostrums for treating a sheared sheep, or a ewe in labor.[1]

M. Beer stresses,[2] however, that the rabbis' medical traditions were never intended to produce economic benefit. They knew about medical lore, but did not practice medicine. Their traditions were no different from those of an experienced midwife or husbandman. Such knowledge was acquired through experience and not medical study, with the exception of Samuel's, though he did not practice for a fee either. Not a single instance of a rabbi's accepting a fee for medical advice can be located, and, Beer rightly adds, the popular saying, 'A physician who cures for nothing is worth nothing'[3] indicates that others did accept fees. The medical teachings were a necessary foundation for their rabbinical leadership. As we have seen, none of the data pertaining to this generation indicates that the rabbis were credited with the ability to produce miraculous cures, though other miracles were ascribed to them. Medicine was part of wisdom, and nothing the rabbis said or did was meant to prove that they were "holy men." And yet, as I said, what the people expected from the rabbis, or understood by their actions, and what the rabbis themselves thought, were by no means one and the same thing. In a situation in which the "holy men" of other groups were credited with miraculous cures, the rabbis' knowledge and abilities must have been understood by the people in a similar way. The chief issue emerges in Rav Judah's saying, that prolonging prayer, eating, and sitting in the privy prolong a man's days.[4] The people would have wanted to know, How does a person achieve a long life? Hearing a rabbi say that one must pray, eat, and relieve himself slowly, ordinary men would have heard not merely a homily, nor only good advice, but a great 'insight' deriving from one who must be assumed to know what he was talking about.

Medicine constituted a subdivision of magic, to which we now turn. I have found it difficult to define precisely what one can mean by "magic." If magic refers to the use of means, such as charms, spells, incantations, or other occult acts, to exert supernatural power over

---

[1] b. Shab. 54b.

[2] *Maʿamadam HaKalkali veHaḤevrati shel ʾAmoraʾe Bavel* [The Economic and Social Status of the Babylonian Amoraim] (Ramat Gan, 1963) 114-18.

[3] b. B.Q. 85a.

[4] b. Ber. 54b, compare *Diq. Sof.* I, 279, Rav Judah in Rav's name.

natural forces, then one is forced to make theological judgments about what is a charm and what is a "genuine" prayer. If a man believes, for example, that a sacred rite, properly done in the right spirit, will produce a natural effect, then we can not properly distinguish—and I do not argue that it is necessary to begin with—between the Temple cult and the private hocuspocus of a local sorcerer. If prayer cannot be distinguished from incantation, or rite from enchantment, sorcery, or wizardry, then religion cannot be set apart from magic. And whether the purpose of that magic is to assure physical health or achieve material results of some other sort, such as success in love or on the race-track hardly matters. I am unable to follow the argument about whether magic precedes religion, or results from its decay.[1] The common contrast between magic and religion is based upon that distinction between the use of physical means to effect spiritual ends, and of spiritual means, such as worship; or it may be said that magic uses compulsion, and religion, petition. Goodenough phrased the alleged distinction as follows:

> ... it is held that magic, in contrast to religion, first, looks to physical ends, such as cure of the sick, avoidance of illness, escape from accident or financial failure, or success in love. Secondly, to do this it uses material means, such as fetishistic objects or rituals, or verbal charms written or spoken. Thirdly, these work by compulsion rather than by petition...[2]

Goodenough points out however that these characteristics are present in the so-called "higher" religions.[3] Physical ends are invariably a part of religion, including Judaism. Use of material means, including amulets, proper dress, holy objects, is hardly rare. As to coercion of the God, I think it is a matter of perspective. If the people are disappointed because they have adhered to the law, but the expected result has not come about, then that disappointment suggests the expectation that the doing of the law will work *ex opere operato*. So I share Goodenough's view that magic is a term of judgment,[4] not of classification:

---

[1] A. A. Barb, "The Survival of Magic Arts," in Arnaldo Momigliano, ed., *The Conflict between Paganism and Christianity in the Fourth Century* (Oxford, 1963), 100-125. Barb's data are of interest, but the distinctions he offers are theological and not phenomenological.

[2] *Jewish Symbols in the Greco-Roman Period* (N.Y. 1953), II, 155.

[3] *Ibid.*

[4] *ibid.* 159. Recent anthropological thought on the definition and nature of magic will be found in the eighteen reviews of Adolf E. Jensen, *Myth and Cult among Primitive Peoples*, in *Current Anthropology*, 6, 2, 1965, 199ff. It seems to me that greater clarity prevails among historians of religion. See also W. Schmidt, *The Origin and Growth of Religion* (trans. H. J. Rose, London, 1931) pp. 118-166.

> Most religious symbols seem to have had at first such direct power as we now associate with the words 'magic' and 'superstition,' and so long as they remain religious symbols, never entirely lose that direct operative power. When we deal with the so-called magical, then we deal with the use of material means (words or objects or forms) to induce or compel divine forces to serve human ends ...[1]

Yet one cannot ignore the fact that the *rabbis* distinguished between what they regarded as magic, and what they regarded as religion. In doing so, they differed not at all from the Greeks, who saw a distinction between white magic, or theurgy, and black magic.[2] So too Rav defined divination:

> "An omen which is not after the form pronounced by Eliezer the servant of Abraham [Gen. 24:14] or by Jonathan son of Saul [I Sam. 14:9-10] is not considered a divination [which is forbidden by Lev. 19:26]." (b. Ḥul. 95b)

That is to say, where the action to be taken *depends* upon the happening of a certain event, that is divination and is prohibited. But interpreting an event as an omen is not prohibited, and so the rabbis interpreted as *omens* but not as divination the arrival of a ferry-boat, or the random quotation of a Scriptural verse by a child.[3] Whether a valid distinction can be proposed between "mere" omens and divination I cannot say. What is important is that Rav and other rabbis saw such a distinction, and one may suppose, similarly distinguished between acceptable and unacceptable sorcery.

Professor Saul Lieberman notes[4] that charms were everywhere believed to be effective. "Even the foremost scholars of the time were not able to mark the definite limits between superstition and science."[5] They likewise accepted the validity of astrology, denying for theological reasons that it applied to Israel.[6] Of a magical act performed on a barren date tree, Lieberman says,

> The Babylonian rabbis were confronted with a practice current among peasants from time immemorial. They had either to uproot it

---

Professor H. H. Penner provided valuable insight into these matters, and called to my attention many important studies.

[1] *ibid.* 161.

[2] Barb, *op. cit.*, p. 101.

[3] b. Ḥul. 95b, and see above, p. 85.

[4] *Greek in Jewish Palestine, Studies in the Life and Manners of Jewish Palestine in the II-IV Centuries C.E.* (N.Y. 1942), 97-114.

[5] *ibid.*, pp. 100-101.

[6] *ibid.* pp. 97-100. See also vol. I, pp. 162, and vol. II, pp. 126ff.

> or to legalize it. They chose the latter because they have had some vague notion of its natural course, and especially because they were able to attach to this practice a genuine Jewish idea. They kept to the rule that there is no need to fight the superstition of the people when it is possible to transform it into true religion.[1]

How *consciously* they so acted I cannot say. The rabbis believed, as we have seen, that demons populated the world, that one thousand stood at each man's right hand, and ten thousand at his left, and they must have conceived the presence of billions of demons, each to be exorcised or neutralized. It is reasonable to suppose that the rabbis tried to attach a "Jewish" interpretation to various magical rites, but whether they did so because they no longer believed in, or actually disapproved of, the original "magical" understanding of the rite cannot be proved one way or the other. Indeed, "Judaizing" magic made it no less magical. As to "superstitions," Lieberman stresses that belief in sorcery (*k'shafim*) and in the power of incantation formulae could be denied only by rejecting the science of the age. Everyone believed in love charms, demons, the power of sorcery, and the like. The rabbis, Lieberman stresses, thus "used the 'scientific methods' of their time and place."[2] Knowledge of "Torah" endowed the rabbis with power that we should call magical, just as many of their medical traditions were attached to Scriptural exegeses. As I have said, they may sometimes have distinguished, as I can not, between magic and "Torah," but the evidence before us leaves little ground to repeat that distinction. Whether it was theurgy or black magic matters little to us. The only relevant issue is, Were the rabbis seen as magicians, and did they so understand *themselves*? It is to this issue that we turn.

It was mostly through the act of study that the rabbis achieved supposedly fantastic power, more than through acts of conformity to the commandments, or genealogy, or other merit. An exegesis almost a century earlier had made this clear:

> "For the commandment is a lamp and Torah is light" (Prov. 6:23). R. Menaḥem b. R. Yosi expounded, "The verse identifies the commandment with a lamp and Torah with light. Just as a lamp protects only temporarily so does a commandment protect only temporarily. Just as light protects permanently, so does Torah."

---

[1] *ibid.* p. 103.

[2] *ibid.*, 114. See also Max Kadushin, *The Rabbinic Mind* (N.Y. 1952) 158 n. 29, "Only he who is worthy can be the agent through whom a *Nes* [miracle] is performed. A similar effect produced by one who is unworthy is regarded by the Rabbis as an act of magic."

The parable was told:

> "A man walking in the middle of the night and darkness is afraid of thorns, pits, thistles, wild beasts and robbers, and also does not know the way. If he lights a torch, he is saved from thorns, pits, and thistles, but is still afraid of wild beasts and robbers and does not know the way. When the dawn breaks, he is saved from wild beasts and robbers, but does not know the way. When he reaches the cross-roads he is saved from everything."

So the commandment is the torch, and Torah the dawn. In this period, R. Ḥisda and R. Naḥman b. Isaac explained the third element in the parable, the 'cross-roads.'

> R. Ḥisda said, "It refers to a disciple of the sages at the day of his death." R. Naḥman b. Isaac said, "It refers to a disciple of the sages and his fear of sin ..."
>
> (b. Sotah 21a)[1]

The "Torah" represented as permanent protection as one could achieve in this life. Only at death is the end in sight. These words, and many like them, have normally been interpreted in a perfectly rational and mostly ethical sense, as metaphors by which the great value of intellectual mastery of Jewish tradition was to be measured. The obvious and natural meaning would therefore be, learning was illuminating and of great moral and 'spiritual' value. Here it is emphasized that both Torah-study and the commandments supplied "protection." In this period, Torah was much more than morally and spiritually "protective." It was a source of physical, worldly power. Rabbis needed no other protection than their Torah. We shall here examine data to prove that the *source* of such magical powers or protection was both knowledge of Torah *and* the very act of studying Torah. As to the latter, the death-scene of David, cited earlier[2], and of R. Ḥisda provide unequivocal evidence. So long as the sage repeated his lessons, so long indeed as his lips were moving, the angel of death could not overcome him. Hence the virtual repetition of 'words of Torah' had a kind of independent magical force, which would constitute an incantation formula of prophylactic power. Stories implying an intrinsic relationship between learning and magic include the following, cited earlier:

---

[1] For another treatment of the passage, see vol. I, 82-88.

[2] Vol. II p. 205.

R. Papa said to Abaye, "In the years of Rav Judah, the whole of their studies was limited to Neziqin [civil law] and we study all six orders [of the Mishnah], And when Rav Judah came to 'Uqzin, 'If a woman presses vegetables in a pot,' he used to say, 'I see here all the reflections of Rav and Samuel,' and *we* have thirteen versions of 'Uqzin. Yet when Rav Judah drew off one shoe [to fast] rain used to come, while we trouble ourselves and cry out loud, and nothing happens [lit. No notice is taken]." He replied, "The former generations used to be ready to sacrifice their lives for the sanctity of the name, and we do not."

(b. Ber. 20a)[1]

Rav Judah once saw two men using bread wastefully, and he said, "I should infer that there is abundance in the world." He set his eyes, and there was famine. The rabbis said to R. Kahana son of R. Ḥananiah, his attendant, "You who are frequently before him, arrange it so he goes out the door near the market." He did so, and went out to the market. He saw the crowd. He said to him, "What is this?" He said to him, "They stand around a bunch of dates which is up for sale." He said, "I should infer there is famine in the world." He said to his attendant, "Remove my shoe for me." He removed one, and rain came. When he reached to remove the other, Elijah came and said to him, "The Holy one blessed be He said that if you remove the other, I shall destroy the world."

(b. Ta'anit 24b)

The same story tells that R. Naḥman called a fast and prayed, but no rain came. He said,

"Take Naḥman and throw him down from the wall to the ground. His mind was weakened, and then rain came."

(ibid. 24a)[2]

R. Qattina said, "Rain is withheld only on account of neglect of Torah."

(ibid. 7b)

The standard means of producing rain was fasting and prayer, and that was how R. Huna and R. Ḥisda, called "the pious men of Babylonia" managed it, saying, "Let us assemble and pray, perhaps the Holy One ... may be reconciled and send rain."[3] Hence the saying concerning R. Naḥman, stressing his lack of humility as an obstacle to magical success, represents no striking evidence that learning and magic

[1] See above p. 21.
[2] See above, p. 62.
[3] b. Ta 'anit 23b.

had an integral relationship. But the comment of R. Papa to Abaye, and a similar comment of Rabbah presuppose a very different viewpoint. R. Papa and Rabbah both thought that the greater learning of their generation ought to have made them more effective rain-makers.[1] Rav Judah's generation knew less, and yet had more effective influence over the elements than did the next one, a paradox in the mind of their sucessors. Rav Judah was so influential, in fact, that Elijah had to warn him, because of God's impatience, to limit the gestures he made, lest the world be destroyed. It was therefore not their prayers that ought to have mattered, but their learning.

Should there remain any doubt of the integral relationship between the act of learning and magic, the following concerning R. Adda b. Ahava ought to eliminate it:

> R. Huna had wine in a certain delapidated house. He wanted to remove it. He went and brought R. Adda b. Ahava there, and he[2] continued his learning until he[3] cleared it out. After he left, the house fell down.
>
> (b. Ta'anit 20b)

The same collection relates that Rav and Samuel had high regard for R. Adda's merits, and R. Adda ascribed his long life to his personal kindness:

> "In my whole life I was never stern in my house, and I never walked in front of one who is greater than myself, and I never looked into dirty alley-ways, and I never walked four cubits without Torah and Tefillin, and I never slept in the school house, neither regularly nor accidentally, and I never enjoyed the shame of my fellow and I never called my fellow by his nick-name ..."
>
> (*ibid.*)

He was, furthermore, angry with R. Huna for endangering his life by making it depend upon a miracle. So one cannot say that the source of his magic was only his learning, but his merits, including his kindness to others. His faithfulness in study of the Torah however was certainly a part of it. R. Huna depended upon the magical effectiveness of that study to support the walls and roof of a house, as Rav and Samuel had earlier depended upon his merits to stay a shaky bridge. Whatever

---

[1] b. Ta 'anit 24b.
[2] R. Adda.
[3] R. Huna.

other sources of magic R. Adda b. Ahava may have enjoyed, and however little he trusted in them—as well he might—one of these sources certainly lay in his knowledge and act of study of the Torah.[1] It is quite fruitless, however, to distinguish between "study of Torah" or "knowledge of Torah" and other sources of magical power. R. Adda b. Ahava clearly made no such distinction. He had great merit, he thought, because he was a gentle husband, a modest student, a meticulous and pious person, who never walked without talking about "Torah" or wearing his phylacteries. He also never slept in school, or dishonored a colleague. So he was a model rabbi, and his magical successes were held up to others as the signs of the reward for his exemplification of the virtues of the academies. What is important is that because of such merits, he could hold up houses and bridges. "Torah," including *all* the requirements attendant upon those who studied it, produced that kind of power, and transformed an ordinary person into a "holy man," who could do things others could not.

The 'blessings' of Torah obviously were not limited to magical matters, such as rain-making or holding up a collapsing house. When, for instance, R. Huna said, "The language of the sages is blessing, wealth, healing," he referred to this-worldly dicta from which this-worldly benefits were to be derived.[2] When, on the other hand, R. Sheshet said that if one teaches Torah in this world, he will do so in the next as well, basing his comment upon Prov. 11:25, he meant quite literal assurance that the sages would continue after death to do pretty much what they did in this life.[3] Each saying requires its own interpretation. We cannot decide in advance to ignore, or explain away, evidences that the rabbis regarded 'Torah' in a way which later generations did not, but rather as a source for magical power over the natural world and mankind. The elements we have isolated as peculiarly magical concern the natural world, causing famines, bringing rain, casting an evil eye, and the like. But knowledge of Torah led also to control of history.[4] To set one segment of the power of Torah apart and call it magical therefore represents our *own* rationalistic reading of the other segments, for while no one believes that rabbis could make rain, it is not beyond "reason" that they could be seen quite "rationally" to

[1] See also y. Ta 'anit 3.11.

[2] b. Ket. 103a, and note Rav's blessing which supposedly enriched R. Huna, below, p. 127.

[3] b. Sanh. 92a.

[4] Above, pp. 17-24, and see my "Religious Uses of History," *History and Theory* V, 2, 151-172.

have hoped through Torah to run society and shape history. Yet I do not think we can so neatly distinguish the kinds or quality of this kind of *gnosis*. If one knew what the rabbis did, he was supposedly able to control reality, and it is futile to call one kind of control magical, and not another. It is only the modern religionist's prejudice in favor of the "rational" which causes any difficulties. For the earlier generations, as evidenced in the medieval commentaries upon these stories, there was none at all. If rabbis were sufficiently pious, worthy, and learned, they could do miracles. The things they could do were many, but the source of their power was one: learning, repeating, and exemplifying the words of Torah. So the rabbis were not ordinary people, for it was believed that they could talk with the dead, with angels and demons; they could go to heaven and come back; they could attempt even to overcome the angel of death, and given the right circumstances, could have hoped to succeed. Both for what they *were* and for what they *knew*, they were therefore exceptional men. Their claim to rule Jewry and their efforts to do just that in preference to any other group or individual found a more immediate and contemporary basis than their *understanding* of revelation in the power inherent in their gnosis, called Torah. Since they believed that their traditions were revealed by God, they would naturally have ascribed to heaven the corpus of knowledge which proved so useful in their hands.

One cannot suppose that the exilarchic rabbis were different from the academic rabbis in magical power. The story about R. Naḥman's inability to bring rain might have come from a circle critical of his "arrogance," for the story would easily provide a critical appraisal of R. Naḥman's boasts about his learning, fear of sin, and piety. But R. Huna, and especially, Rabbah b. Abbuha, were both associates of the exilarchate and capable magicians, and Rav Judah who was apparently distant from the exilarch and his circle was equivalently famed for his theurgy. So the stories about the several circles indicate that each group claimed for its most distinguished representatives extraordinary powers, and denigrated the powers of hostile rabbis. A convention in telling stories about *any* great rabbi thus required inclusion of such wonderful accounts.[1] Indeed, the effort to deny such an ascription to R. Naḥman—if that is what is here intended—and to stress his lack of humility as an impediment to his prayers' effectiveness, leads one to suppose that some miracle-stories were part of the broader polemic

[1] R. Yoḥanan held that to qualify for a seat in the Sanhedrin, one must be a master of sorcery! See b. Sanh. 17a.

discerned earlier. One would naturally stress the miraculous abilities of the central figure in one's school.

The major rabbis were *expected* to produce unusual feats, and their prayers were supposed to be answered. Whatever actually happened, no one supposes that angels came down, or that it rained because a rabbi took off his sandal. We may however regard it as a fact that some rabbis were widely believed to be magicians. I therefore see no reason whatever to suppose a self-conscious effort to "Judaize" what the people were already doing, but what the rabbis disapproved of in its popular form. Doubtless the rabbis like others made distinctions we can no longer apprehend between white, good and black, evil magic. It was all right to make rain by removing one's shoe and praying, and so they did. Omens were acceptable, but not divination. Whether they did so because the people expected them to, and because they hoped in so doing to render acceptable what in other forms was not, is no where indicated. The later generation envied their exceptional puissance, giving no hint whatever that they did not want exactly the same power. I find here no evidence at all of a generalized rejection of magic, nor of a conscious effort to clean up and employ what was more or less distasteful but required by the people or environment. R. Qattina, one recalls, did not want the people to follow the gentile necromancer. The reason had nothing to do with the biblical prohibition. He himself was better at it than the pagan. That was just the point: he, like other rabbis, could do just about anything that the pagan magicians, or holy men, were able to do, so the people had better not think that the pagans had more magical power than did the Jews. What this has to do with "transforming" the "superstition" of the people into "true religion" I cannot say.

Are we supposed, therefore, to conclude that the rabbis were essentially "Jewish magicians"? The answer must be a qualified negative. Any religious leader of the region would normally conform to the behavior-pattern of the "holy man," and so did the rabbis. But upon what aspects of their activities did the *rabbis* lay greatest stress? It was "Torah" that lay at the center of their being, though a "Torah" which was believed to endow the knower with unusual skills and knowledge. The rabbi did not study Torah in order to become a magician. The content of his studies did not concern sorcery or witchcraft. He studied a law-code and what had been said about it by earlier teachers. Everything else was secondary. If the rabbis did wonders, they were not chiefly wonder-workers, any more than they were primarily physicians or rain-makers or traders and merchants. These were by-products of their central concern for Torah. The rabbis were chiefly judges and lawyers, teachers and masters, and their lives were spent not in the marketplace, but mostly in the academy. It would be a gross misunderstanding to call the rabbis magicians, or Magi, in any narrow or precise sense. While they exhibited significant functional parallels to the Magi, the rabbis were not Magi, and the Magi were not rabbis.[1] They were separate and distinct religious leaders, just as the communities they led were quite different from one another. If there were *functional* parallels, it is because the society in which both existed expected and even demanded parallel *kinds* of leadership from men who gave evidence of proper qualification. I have stressed the wonder-working side of that qualification for leadership, but it would be an error to regard it as more than it was, namely, one among many, but not the most important, means by which a rabbi secured public acceptance. The chief means was his learning, of this there can be no doubt, but learning was accompanied by "deeds." The particular deeds men expected, however, we should now regard mostly as magical.

The academy was the place of Torah par excellence, above the synagogue, the shrine, and the numerous places and occasions of religious devotion. What happened there supremely mattered, had to be recorded, and handed down as Torah. The sayings of this generation reveal nothing but a perfect consistency with earlier ideas about study of Torah. The Deuteronomic curses (Deut. 28:48), that the sinning people would be "in want of all things," were understood by R. Ḥisda to mean a lack of wives, by R. Sheshet, a lack of attendants, and by R. Naḥman, a lack of knowledge.[2] Commenting upon Prov. 17:14, R. Hamnuna said that the first matter for which a man is called to account is whether he studied the Torah.[3] R. Sheshet held that a husband should even sell his wife's estate to buy a scroll of the Torah.[4] The sheer pleasure of study is reflected in the following debate:

> Every thirty days R. Sheshet would review his learning, and would stand and lean at the side of a doorway and say, "Rejoice my soul, rejoice my soul, for *you* have I studied Scripture, for *you* have I learned Mishnah."
>
> (b. Pes. 68b)

---

[1] See vol. II, pp. 147-151.
[2] b. Ned. 41a.
[3] b. Sanh. 7a.
[4] b. ʿEruv. 64a.

R. Sheshet was criticized:

> But that is not so, for R. Eleazar [b. Pedat, a Palestinian contemporary] said, "But for Torah, heaven and earth would not endure, as it is said, 'If not for my covenant by day and by night, I had not appointed the ordinances of heaven and of earth' (Jer. 33:25)." "In the first place [it is replied] when a man does it, he does so with himself in mind."
>
> (*ibid.*)

Jeremiah was understood to be saying that *if* the Torah is not studied by day and by night, then heaven and earth would pass away, so R. Sheshet's view seemed selfish, for he was concerned with his soul alone. Study of Scripture and Mishnah produced therefore both personal and cosmic benefit, bringing man's soul into the world to come, and sustaining the world. If such a view is magical, it is we who say so. But if I may articulate the distinction the rabbis seem to have seen, studying "Torah" sustained heaven and earth, brought power and joy to him who learned it, and eternal life to its sages. And "Torah" prohibited magic.[1]

IV. A Spade to Dig With?

It is quite natural to ask whether the rabbis sought to enrich themselves through their knowledge of Torah. Pharisaic tradition was uncompromising: One should *not* use the Torah as a spade to dig with, meaning that one should not receive recompense in any form for his learning. And yet we have striking evidence that several rabbis of this generation did become very wealthy men indeed, including Rabbah b. Abbuha, whose wealth seemed so sudden that a miracle was alleged to have brought it about, and R. Huna and R. Ḥisda. All were originally poor, for R. Huna said when a case came to him that the litigants would have to supply a man to draw water in his place and he would provide a judgment,[2] which, if meant literally, would suggest that he was a field-worker. R. Ḥisda at first was especially careful about his garments,

> When he walked among thorns and thistles, he would life up his garments, saying, "The body will heal but not the cloth."
>
> (b. B.Q. 91b)

[1] For a study of the Jewish elements of the Aramaic Incantation Bowls, see Irving Teitelbaum, Jewish Magic in the Sassanian Period (Dropsie College. Philadelphia, Doctoral Dissertation, 1964, unpublished).

[2] b. Ket. 105a.

Later on, both men became wealthy:

> R. Ḥisda said, "If I were not a beer manufacturer I should not have grown rich." What is the meaning of *sudna* [=brewery]? Said R. Ḥisda, "A pleasant secret [sod na'eh] and the exercise of charity."
>
> (b. Pes. 113a)[1]

> R. Huna was girdled in a string and standing before Rav. He said to him, "What is the meaning of this?" He replied, "I did not have [wine for] sanctification and I pawned my girdle and got some." He said to him, "May it be his will that you be smothered in silks." When he married off his son Rabbah, R. Huna, who was short, was lying on a bed and his daughters and daughters-in-law stripped silk from themselves and threw them on him until he was smothered in silk. Rav heard and was angry. He said, "Why did you not say to me, when I blessed you, 'The same to you'."
>
> (b. Meg. 27b)[2]

> R. Ḥisda said, "I washed with full handfuls of water and was granted full handfuls of prosperity."
>
> (b. Shab. 62b)

We are supposed to infer, therefore, that R. Ḥisda got rich because he washed his hands with full handfuls of water, and that it was Rav's blessing which brought great wealth to R. Huna. We do not know how R. Naḥman's wealth was explained. His father was a clerk in Samuel's court. By contrast he was famous for his luxurious way of living.[3] Whether it was because of his marriage, or for some other reason, the Talmud does not say. It seems to me obvious that Rabbah b. Abbuha and R. Naḥman grew wealthy through the exilarchate, and R. Huna and R. Ḥisda, through the academy. It was through appointment to the staff of the former, or to the headship of the latter, that the four men under discussion grew wealthy. Beer[4] stresses, however, that other rabbis grew rich as well, mainly in commerce rather than in agriculture, but the striking rise in economic status noted of four chief figures in this generation is due entirely to their political role. (Appointment to the academy probably brought with it considerable endowment,

---

[1] On the wealth of R. Ḥisda, see Weiss, *op. cit.*, III, 163-4; Yavetz, *op. cit.*, VII, 114-17, also b. M. Q. 28a. See also b. Shab. 140b, when he was poor, he did not eat vegetables.

[2] On the wealth of R. Huna, see Weiss, *op. cit.*, III, 161-2, and Funk, *op. cit.*, I, 111.

[3] See above, p. 72.

[4] *op.cit.*, 47-51.

Beer notes.[1]) Such social mobility was uncommon in Iranian society, as Christensen points out.[2]

At the same time, a position in the rabbinate in general led to wealth. First, it was regarded as a pious act to leave sums of money to rabbis in one's will, or to marry one's daughter off to a rabbi, and this advice was directed especially toward wealthy but uneducated people. Second, the rabbis enjoyed certain market-privileges which made it possible for them to profit. Since the markets were under their supervision, it was fairly easy for them to enforce these privileges for their fellows' benefit. Beer notes the following factors[3]: first, traders would include sages in the profits of their ventures; second, sages were permitted to display and sell their wares in the marketplace before others were allowed to do so, a privilege which could not have been granted willingly, but must have been effected by the rabbinical supervisors of the markets themselves; third, the sages, Beer holds, were free of taxes and hence able to market their produce more cheaply than others[4]; fourth, the sages were revered, and hence named as guardians of ownerless, or orphans' property, from which they derived access to liquid capital; and finally, the sages were mostly in commerce, and not in agriculture, and it was commerce which was the chief source of wealth.

With such advantages at their hand, it is no wonder that the sages were able to support themselves adequately and to set aside leisure time for study of the Torah. It was indeed a circular process. Because they were sages, they acquired certain advantages in economic life. Because of these advantages they were able to devote themselves to learning. But on what basis was the rabbinical advantage founded? Beer points out that ordinary people did not willingly *grant* these privileges. The sages gained them for themselves. How did they rationalize their acquiring such privileges? A fourth century source suggests a neat rationalization: Just as the priests were formerly free of taxes, so now the sages inherited their position:

> Just as a priest takes first, so a sage takes first
>
> (Ned. 62a)[5]

---

[1] *ibid.*, 50.

[2] *L'Iran sous les Sassanides*, 311ff., "C'était un principe fermement établi de la politique sassanide, que personne ne derait aspirer à un ranq plus haut que celui qui lui était destiné par sa naissance." (p. 312)

[3] *op. cit.*, 78-86.

[4] *ibid.* 81. We shall return to this matter in volume IV.

[5] On the rabbi as priest, see Judah Goldin, "Of change and Adaptation in Judaism," *HR* 4, 2, 1965, p. 277 n. 31, and my *Life*, pp. 50, 62.

That explains why the sages thought they ought to claim privileges of this sort. But why did the people accept that claim, or at least, acquiesce in it? They were, first of all, forced to by the Jewish regime itself, which enforced the privileges of its own rabbinical agents. It was, Beer stresses, one of the factors which kept the exilarchate and the rabbinate in a close alliance, for the one reenforced the other. I think a second fact must be considered as well. If a trader included a sage in his business venture, he must have hoped to derive some 'benefit,' material or spiritual, from such a partnership, since otherwise he might as well have given money to charity, rather than going through the trouble of making a sage his partner. Whatever distinction between material and spiritual 'value' may be drawn in later times, in this period I see no reason to set them apart. Rather, the inclusion of a holy man had an obvious advantage, for he would bring to the venture the protection of heaven, and indeed, the many times the rabbis praised kindness to the rabbinate would lead us to suppose that they encouraged just such a notion. Similarly, as I said, the sage was made guardian of the capital of others, which he was able to use for his own benefit in investment, because of his position in society, as a holy man to be trusted and revered. Furthermore, the teachings of the sages encouraged them to go into the most profitable ventures, namely commercial ones, as we have already seen in connection with Rav's advice to his son.[1] So in a very real sense, the "Torah" as they read it was indeed a source of wealth, for it provided very sound economic information indeed. The sages thus profited—after the fact or before it—from their place in society, from the value-system they advanced in Jewish life, and from the beliefs people entertained concerning them. One cannot divorce charismatic qualities from their economic implications. If one is revered, he is trusted. If he is trusted, he will be given economic opportunities denied others. Similarly, if he is believed to be a holy man, then others who want to benefit from his particular fortune will make him a partner in their ventures, as happened, or seek to marry their daughters off to him, or otherwise to win his, and thereby, heaven's favor. One cannot ignore the very practical advantages which accrued to the sage, therefore, because of his theological, or, more narrowly, magical, abilities.

It is futile to ask, Were the sages then using 'the Torah as a spade to dig with?' I think it clear the sages gained very substantial economic

[1] Vol. II, p. 14. But their sympathies lay elsewhere, I think with the land-owning classes. It was simply that commerce seemed to them a quicker way to wealth.

benefits from their learning, and still more directly, from their reputations and from the fantasies that other Jews attached to them. The rabbis certainly were convinced that what they enjoyed was right and proper, congruous to their duties (for they were able to study if they engaged in business, but otherwise not so easily), and appropriate to their position in the divine economy. I cannot say whether or not the sages connived at using their charisma for economic advantage. In their value-system, material prosperity was not the highest value, but rather a means to other, holier ends. But that means *they* gained, and others did not, through the respect that "Torah" lent to their reputation in society. I think it nicely symbolic that Rabbah b. Abbuha's rise to sudden wealth—used, to be sure, to supply the needs of his students—was ascribed to a trip to Paradise. There can be no more adequate portrayal of what people believed: Heaven favored the sages, and that favor resulted in considerable wealth to some of them. I see no reason to differ from so accurate, if fanciful, an account.

v. The Education and Conduct of a Sage

The sages had their own distinctive words for various objects, use of which marked a man as a member of the rabbinical estate. Rav Judah had ridiculed R. Naḥman's language, which, he thought, was neither rabbinical nor ordinary.[1] The transformation of customary verbal usages was only one of the many affectations produced by the schools. Rabbis dressed differently, wearing phylacteries at all times.[2] Indeed to become a sage, one had to undergo a considerable education and training, education in the traditions of the academy, and training in the customary behavior which would in time transform the neophyte into a disciple, and later even into a master. Entry into the rabbinical estate required, therefore, a long preparation, as the novice learned to conform to the expected behavior-and thought-patterns characteristic of those who held such a station in the community. After a man had achieved his place within the schools and was recognized as a disciple, he would therefore adhere to their values and attitudes, and outsiders would be able to discern from his behavior and appearance, as much as from his knowledge of Scriptures and the legal code and ability to

---

[1] Above, pp. 65-67.

[2] On a distinctive rabbinical mantel, see L. Blau, in *HUCA* 3, 1926, p. 210. See also E. R. Goodenough, "The Greek Garments on Jewish Heroes in The Dura Synagogue," in A. Altmann, ed., *Biblical Motifs* (Cambridge, 1966), 221-237.

reason, his membership in the inchoate society of the religious virtuosi.

According to the following, considerable numbers attended the academies:

> When the rabbis left the school of Rav [*mibe Rav*, alt. = school house] they left behind 1,200 rabbis; from the school of R. Huna, 800. R. Huna would speak through thirteen *'amora'im*. When the rabbis stood up from their sessions at R. Huna's and shook out their cloaks, a cloud of dust arose and obscured the daylight, so that they would say in the west, they have arisen from the session of R. Huna the Babylonian ...
> (b. Ket. 106a)

The rabbis left behind were those who were fed by the academy itself, and hence this account supposes many more students than the 1,200 or 800 who were left after the sessions. The story goes on to relate diminishing numbers, and since it begins with Elisha, who had 2,200 to feed, it purports to indicate the decline in the generations, so the exact figures can mean little. That R. Huna required many to repeat his words in shouting to a vast throng, and attracted huge numbers of students, is striking, for these details are omitted in the account of Rav's time, as well as that of the generation afterward. They interrupt the numerical structure of the generations' declining, from 1,200 to 800 to 400 to 200, and would suggest that people thought R. Huna did attract a very large audience indeed.

What were the requirements of the academies? It should be stressed, first of all, that unlike other possessors of mysteries, the rabbis were eager to bring as many as they could into the academies, and openly to share almost everything they knew. I do not think there is a more vivid contrast between the rabbinical movement as a salvific, or mystery community, and other such movements of the age. Whether or not the esoteric traditions on Ezekiel's vision of the chariot and the Works of Creation were taught in this period only to the initiated and worthy few or more widely we cannot say.[1] But the rabbis were seeking a popular hearing, and they wanted nothing more than to be heard and understood everywhere. Since theirs was an exclusivist message, unlike that of the salvational cults, and since they were attempting to set Israel apart from the gentiles, one may see here a paradox: the mysteries in general were *not* exclusivist, for it was common for a man to be initiated into any number of cults, *but* they were secretive, in that the

[1] Though I think only a few disciples were allowed to study those traditions. See below, pp. 151-153.

central cult and rite were supposed never to be revealed to outsiders, so that beyond the fact of initiation we know absolutely nothing about them. By contrast, the rabbis made it perfectly clear that no Jew, least of all among their followers, may participate in anyone else's cult, but they were completely open, or mostly so by contrast with the mystery cults, about the method and message of salvation. What accounts for the difference is the differing focus. The rabbis were concerned to transform all the Jews into "Israel," as they understood and defined it, and hence both the exclusivism and the openness, indeed the aggressive publication of their teachings. They needed both to set the Jews apart, and to transform them, so exclusivism and exotericism went side by side.

Learning was carried on through three processes, hearing a public lecture, memorizing sayings and discussing them, and observing the masters. R. Huna's public lectures were supposedly so long that Rabbis Abba b. Zabda, Giddal, Ḥelbo, and Sheshet all became impotent through sitting through them.[1] (It was believed that failing to discharge one's natural functions would render a person impotent, and hence the rabbis ascribed their childlessness to the requirements of the academy.[2]) R. Huna stressed the importance of learning a little at a time,[3] and R. Ḥisda that "Torah can only be acquired with mnemonic signs."[4] Constant repetition of what was already learned was essential:

> R. Naḥman said, "... It is harder to remember well something old than to memorize something new, and the mnemonic sign is, Cement from old cement."
>
> (b. Yoma 28b)

As soon as the student had heard a tradition, he was supposed to repeat it:

> R. Huna said, "What is the meaning of the text, 'The flock settled therein, thou prepared in thy goodness for the poor, O God' (Ps. 68:11)? If a man acts like a wild beast that treads its prey and eats it—or drags it and eats it—his learning will endure, but otherwise it will not. If he so acts, the Holy One blessed be He will himself prepare a banquet for him, as it states, 'You prepared in your goodness for the poor' (Ps. 68:11)."
>
> (b. ʿEruv. 54a)

[1] b. Yev. 62b, 64b.

[2] b. Bekh. 44b.

[3] b. ʿEruv. 54b, also A.Z. 17b, 19a—based on Prov. 13:11, and R. Sheshet, based on Prov. 12:27.

[4] *ibid.*

Constant effort was required, and though some rabbis thought that the night was created only for sleep, R. Ḥisda said, in declining to do so, "Days are coming which are long and short, and I shall then have time to sleep."[1] Group study was encouraged; R. Eleazar b. Pedat sent word from Palestine that one should study in community.[2] But memorizing and discussion should cease in a filthy place. One should not recite or even meditate upon "matters of Torah" in an alleyway,[3] or in other unclean places, as in the following:

> Rava said, "When we were following R. Naḥman [to the privy], if he had a book of *aggadah*, he would give it to us. But if he wore *tefillin* he did not give them to us, saying, 'Since the rabbis have permitted them, they will guard me [against the demons of the privy].'"
>
> (b. Ber. 23b)

Rav Judah advised that serious study be preceded by lighthearted conversation.[4] Students from all classes were welcome to come to the academies, but R. Eleazar urged the rabbis to encourage the children of the poor, and the academies provided for their upkeep. Nothing can more clearly illustrate the classless nature of the rabbinical movement. Rich and poor alike were eagerly recruited, and provision for the poor was everywhere arranged.[5]

Two kinds of skills were admired, though not by the same people: excellent memory and sharp reasoning. Of Samuel it was said, "Better is one grain of sharp pepper than a whole basket full of pumpkins."[6] The following are good examples of academic discourse involving both skills:

> R. Ḥisda said, "This matter I heard from a great man, and it is R. Ammi: 'The daughter-in-law is only forbidden on account of the daughter-in-law,' and when the Chaldeans [=astrologers] told me, 'You are going to be a teacher,' I thought, If I should become a great man, I should reason it of my own knowledge, but if I should become a teacher of children, I shall ask the rabbis who come to the synagogue. Now I explain it of my own knowledge ..."
>
> (b. Yev. 21b)

---

[1] b. 'Eruv. 65a.
[2] b. Ned. 81a, compare b. Shab. 17b.
[3] b Ber. 24b, R. Adda b. Ahava.
[4] b. Shab. 30b.
[5] See below, p. 217.
[6] b. Yoma 85b.

Rava used to praise R. Aḥa b. Ya'akov before R. Naḥman, as a great man. He said to him, "When he comes to you, bring him to me." When he came, he said to him (R. Naḥman to R. Aḥa), "Ask me something?" He asked him [a complicated question]. While he was pondering the matter, he further asked ... He (R. Naḥman) replied, "Leave me alone, for I am still imprisoned by your first question ..."

(b. B.Q. 40a)

Abimi was studying [the tractate of] Menaḥot at the school of R. Ḥisda ... R. Naḥman met him and asked, "How does one take out the handful?" "Out of this vessel," he replied....

(b. Men. 7a)

Abaye said to a certain rabbi who used to arrange the Mishnah before R. Sheshet, "Have you heard the meaning of [a certain word]?" He said, "So did R. Sheshet say ..." Abaye said, "Therefore a rabbinical student who heard something but does not know what it means should ask someone who is frequently before the rabbis, since he is certain to have heard it from some great man."

(b. Meg. 27a)

R. Ḥisda's reflection, before he had found his place in the academies, is significant. If he achieved greatness, he would be able to reason things out on his own, but if not, he would have to ask others. The description "a great man," which appears in these accounts in both Hebrew and Aramaic, clearly means a man able to reason subtly, and R. Ḥisda regarded that ability as a mark of his greatness. R. Naḥman similarly sought to check the skill of R. Aḥa by answering his most difficult question, but it turned out that the question proved so difficult R. Naḥman himself was stumped.[1] At the same time, studies with a given rabbi would concentrate on a certain tractate, and R. Naḥman's question concerning the meal-offering stressed proper acquisition of, and capacity to exposit, a particular tradition. Abaye's saying, with reference to R. Sheshet's student, indicated the confidence he felt in the resources of the academy, for there could have been no difficulty which *someone* would not have information to illumine; since Abaye was a great logician, it was the tradition, and not the reason for it, which he required and received.

The actual method of the academies, therefore, had nothing whatever to do with magic, as I said, and the "Torah" of the rabbis was not essentially other than a legal tradition, which had to be studied by the

[1] It is quite obvious, by our earlier analysis (above, pp. 61-75) in what circles such a story would have been told.

classical legal methods. The rabbis were expected to act as did other holy men, but they themselves most respected legal learning and the capacity to reason about cases. The consequences transcended the law. Not everyone would achieve such a skill any more than everyone could make rain, R. Ḥisda recognized, and the academies doubtless attracted many who could only memorize and repeat what they knew. The whole process of learning, and not merely its creative and innovative aspect, however, was regarded as sacred, for the words themselves were holy. The following exposition of the school of R. ʿAnan describes the process:

> "What is the meaning of the Scripture, 'You that ride on white asses, that sit on rich cloths, and that walk by the way, tell of it' (Judges 5:10). Those that ride on asses are the sages who go from city to city and from province to province to study Torah. 'White'—means that they make it clear as the noon hour. 'Sitting on cloths (MDYN),' means that they judge a case truly. 'And that go,' refers to masters of Scripture. 'On the way'—these are masters of Mishnah. 'Tell of it' refers to masters of Talmud, all of whose conversation concerns matters of Torah.
>
> (b. ʿEruv. 54b)

Found in the Song of Deborah, this verse about the victory of Israel over the Canaanites was seen by the rabbis as a description of the triumph of the Lord in the wars of the Torah, a frequent image of rabbinical Judaism, as in monasticism, and the consequent celebration by the people of the Lord. That people included many whose talents were limited, but who, added all together, could constitute, and celebrate, the Lord's triumph. Some, like itinerant philosophers, would wander in search of teachings; others had a great skill at clarification; others were able and selfless judges; still others merely knew Scripture, or Mishnah, or Talmud, but spoke of nothing else. Here is the integrated, mature vision of the academies: a whole people devoted to Revelation, each in his way and according to his talent. Nonetheless, R. Naḥman expressed contempt for a merely learned man, one who had memorized great quantities of classical traditions, calling him a mere 'sack of books,' and declining to present a eulogy at his funeral.[1] Whether or not such a story, which conforms to the traditions about R. Naḥman's hauteur, is historical or not, it reveals a commonly held view, one of contempt for mere knowledge of the traditions unaccompanied by personal charisma of some kind, whether expressed in

[1] b. Meg. 28b.

brilliance of reasoning or unusual powers of another sort. It was not only what one knew that mattered, but also what he could do with what he knew, whether his actions were narrowly magical, or parabolic in quality. "The Tanna repeats and does not know what he is saying, the Magus mumbles and does not know what he is saying," so went a proverb quoted by a fourth-century rabbi.[1] The Tanna of the Babylonian academy, that is, the man who had memorized the Tannaitic traditions of the academy, was not a figure to win broad public admiration. All those who did, in this period as in the preceding one, were noteworthy for their miracles, or for their public actions as judges and administrators, or for their insight as logicians, or for their medical and astrological learning, or for their knowledge of Scripture and its contemporary meaning. These were *rabbis*. The rest were mere bystanders, useful though their learning was. The observance of the strangely formal etiquette and language of the academies, the emphasis upon where to walk by a master, how to observe him, how to serve him, and the like—these are the significations of membership in the rabbinical estate, and mastery of the traditions was by itself insufficient.

Three qualities were demanded of the student: base humility, dignity, and good hygiene. In commenting upon Num. 21:18, R. Mattena said, "If a man makes himself like a wilderness, in which all are able to tread, his learning endures in his hand, but if not, his learning will not endure."[2] He should not call his teacher by name.[3] Rav Judah said that one who walks at his master's right hand is a boor.[4] An ordinary man—not a sage—is distinguished by his pushing himself in front of others, R. Kahana taught.[5] The personal dignity of a student of the sages was of equal importance:

> R. Huna was once carrying a spade on his shoulder when R. Ḥana b. Ḥanilai wanted to take it from him. He said, "If you usually carry in your town, take it, but if not, do not take it. I do not want to be paid respect through your degradation." (b. Meg. 28a)

A disciple could excommunicate another person for a matter of his personal dignity, according to the same master.[6] Good personal hygiene

[1] b. Sotah 22a.
[2] b. 'Eruv. 54a.
[3] b. Sanh. 100a. See also b. 'Eruv. 67b, Rav Judah explained the rules for objecting to a master's teaching.
[4] b. Yoma 37a, Ḥul. 91a. See also b. Sotah 46b, R. Sheshet and R. Kahana on how far one must accompany his friends.
[5] b. Meg. 12b, with reference to Est. 1:16.
[6] b. M.Q. 17a.

was included in the traditions handed on to disciples. He should not live where vegetables are not obtainable, R. Huna taught.[1] R. Ḥisda provided an enchiridion of proper behavior:

> R. Ḥisda said, "When a scholar buys vegetables, let him buy long ones, for one bunch is like another [in thickness], and so the length [comes] of itself."
>
> R. Ḥisda also said, "When a scholar buys canes, let him buy long ones; one load is like another, so the length [comes] of itself."
>
> R. Ḥisda also said, "When a scholar has but little bread, let him not eat vegetables, because it whets [the appetite]." R. Ḥisda also said, "I ate vegetables neither when poor nor when rich. When poor, because it whets [the appetite]; when rich, because I say, Where the vegetables are to enter, let fish and meat enter!"
>
> R. Ḥisda also said, "If a scholar has but little bread he should not divide [his meal]." R. Ḥisda also said, "If a scholar has but little bread he should not break [bread]." [What is the reason?—Because he does not do it generously.] R. Ḥisda also said, "Formerly I would not break [bread] until I had passed my hand through the whole of my wallet and found there as much as I needed."
>
> R. Ḥisda also said, "When one can eat barley bread but eats wheaten bread he violates, 'Thou shalt not destroy' (Deut. 20:19)."
>
> R. Ḥisda also said, "When a scholar has no oil, let him wash with pit water, [which is like oil]."
>
> R. Ḥisda also said, "If a scholar buys raw meat he should buy the neck, because it contains three kinds of meat."
>
> R. Ḥisda also said, "When a scholar buys linen [underwear], he should buy it from the Nehar Abba and bleach it every thirty days, and I guarantee that it will relieve him [from buying another] for a full year."
>
> R. Ḥisda also said, "A scholar should not sit upon a new mat, because it destroys the garments."
>
> R. Ḥisda also said, "A scholar should not send his garments to his host for washing, for this is not in good taste, lest he see something and he come to despise him."
>
> R. Ḥisda advised his daughters, "Act modestly before your husbands: do not eat bread before your husbands, do not eat greens at night, do not eat dates at night nor drink beer at night, and do not ease yourselves where your husbands do, and when someone calls at the door, do not say 'who is he' but 'who is she?'"
>
> (b. Shab. 140b)[2]

R. Ḥisda similarly taught,

> It is forbidden for a *ḥaver* to eat at a meal which has no [designated] name.
>
> (y. Demai 4.2)

[1] b. 'Eruv. 55b.

[2] Trans. H. Freedman (London 1948), pp. 710-11.

A sage had to be forebearing:

> R. Huna tore up silk in the presence of his son Rabbah, to see whether he was temperamental.
>
> (b. Qid. 32a)

This mixture of advice on good diet, wise marketing, careful husbanding of one's resources, modesty, and proper behavior with women could, one supposes, have been of profit to anyone and not merely a sage's disciple. But so acting would *mark* one as a disciple. In these ways, the disciple was supposed to distinguish himself from commonplace people, and display a greater sense of cleanliness and intelligence than was thought to be characteristic of the masses. By so doing, the sage would show himself to be shrewd, economical, clean, and not boorish but humble. He was moreover careful to give full credit and respect to others. R. Sheshet was angered when one of his traditions was cited not in his name.[1] It was important to honor the sage, for, R. Mattena taught in the name of R. Ḥisda,

> "A father who forgave disrespect—that disrespect is forgiven. But a sage who forgave disrespect—that disrespect is not forgiven."
>
> (b. Qid. 32a)

The "forgiveness" here referred to is in Heaven, and the meaning is that Heaven would exact recompense for disrespect paid to sages, whether the sage did so or not.

The schools were supposed to educate men in the proper way of living. R. Adda bar Ahavah's merits quite naturally included constant rehearsal of words of Torah. But they also included never walking in front of his betters, never looking into dirty alley-ways, never calling his colleagues by nick-names, and the like. One must therefore characterize the dicta on how a disciple and a rabbi should behave as *ritualistic*. Just as one speaks of Torah and keeps the commandments, so he follows the patterns here adumbrated with the same result. It was part of the *ritual* of being a sage to behave modestly and hygienically, not to waste material blessings, to respect one's colleagues, and the like. By contrast to the medical traditions, which were mostly commonplaces, the teachings on etiquette are clearly quite separate from those which other, ordinary men obeyed. Conformity to them was part of the authentication of the sage, assuredly as significant as his ability to answer difficult questions or discuss legal traditions.

---

[1] b. Bekh. 31b.

It was customary to give the rabbis personal service. Each was accompanied by an attendant, whose doings were observed for evidence as to the master's legal opinions.[1] R. Sheshet, one recalls, regarded the attendant as a necessity of life, probably because he was blind.[2] But the attendant benefitted as much as the master, for he gained the opportunity at close hand to observe the law as it was embodied by living men. The traditions of those who had so served were preserved:

> R. ʿAnan b. Taḥlifa told, "I was once standing before Samuel when they brought him a dish of mushrooms, and if he had not given me some, I should have been exposed to danger [for hunger pangs]."
> (b. Ket. 61a)

Courtesy to the attendant was encouraged, for supposedly Elijah conversed with a rabbi who gave his attendant a taste of every kind of dish which was served, while he did not converse with one who gave only one kind.[3] I should suppose that such a story is meant to encourage masters to feed their attendants generously, which leads to the inference that some did not, and had to be warned that Elijah would not look kindly upon their inconsideration.

One cannot imagine that the growth of the Babylonian academies now led to the proliferation of laws on how the students should behave. These parietal rules were all known in Tannaitic times, and many of the discussions here cited are continuations of earlier ones. As in the emphasis upon study and the centrality of Torah, one can discern little development or change within the rabbinic circles. What characterized second century Palestinian academies was similarly expected in the Babylonian ones a century and more later. Ideas of right and proper conduct changed very little over a long period of time. The figure of the sage seems one perfect constant in rabbinic Judaism. From earliest times, the sage was supposed to be a "living Torah," symbolized at the death of R. Huna by the desire of the rabbis to place a scroll of the Torah on his bier, as the rabbis believed had been done for King Hezekiah "who had done what was written in the scroll."[4] R. Ḥisda however cited evidence that R. Huna would not like it. (Then R. Abba preached, "Our master was worthy that the Shekinah would rest upon him, but Babylonia prevented it." R. Naḥman b. Ḥisda, or R. Ḥanan

[1] Compare b. Beẓ. 22a, such an assumption was not always correct.
[2] See also b. ʿEruv. 65a, he would entrust him to wake him up from sleep.
[3] b. Ket. 61a.
[4] b. B.Q. 17b.

b. Ḥisda objected, "'And the word of God was unto Ezekiel the priest son of Buzi in the land of the Chaldeans by the river Chebar'(Ezek. 1:3)." His father touched him with his sandal and said, "Have I not told you not to bother people? What is meant by *'aḥyo hayah*?' That it was while he was still in Palestine.")

On the other hand, an academician who did not keep the rules would be punished severely, for he could bring a bad name upon the schools as a whole. Thus we have the following account:

> A certain rabbinical novice had a bad name. Rav Judah said, "What shall I do? To put him under the ban [is impossible because] the rabbis require him. If I do not place him under the ban, the name of Heaven will be profaned." He said to Rabbah bar bar Ḥana, "Have you heard of a tradition of what to do in such an instance?" He said to him, "So said R. Yoḥanan, 'What is the meaning of the Scripture 'For the lips of the priest will guard knowledge, and Torah will be sought from his mouth, for he is an angel of the Lord of hosts' (Malachi 2:7)? If the rabbi is like an angel of the Lord then should Torah be sought from his mouth.'" Rav Judah excommunicated him. Later on, Rav Judah grew weak. The rabbis came to inquire after his health, and that person came with them. When Rav Judah saw him, he laughed. The man said to him [Rav Judah], "It is not enough that he banned that man [me], but he is also laughing at me!" He replied, "I am not laughing at you, but when I go to that world, I am rejoicing to think that even to such a person as yourself I have not shown unwarranted favor." Rav Judah died. The man came to the school house and said to them, "Free me [of the ban]." The rabbis said said to him, "A man of the importance of Rav Judah is not here to set you free, but go to R. Judah the Prince [in Palestine] to seek absolution." He went before him. He [the patriarch] said to R. 'Ammi, "Go examine his case. If he requires absolution, absolve him." R. 'Ammi looked into the case, and considered absolving him. R. Samuel bar Naḥmani arose on his feet and said, "If a maid-servant in the house of Rabbi [Judah the Prince] could ban and have the sages respect her ban for three years, how much the more so one imposed by our colleague Judah!" R. Zera said, "From the fact that this venerable sage has come before us, who has not come before us for so many years, one should infer that we must not absolve him." They did not grant him absolution. He left the school house in tears, and as he went along, a hornet came and stung him in the penis and he died. They brought him up to the cave of the pious, but they [the deceased] did not admit him. They brought him to the cave of the judges, and they received him ...
>
> (b. M.Q. 17a)

What is striking in this story is the willingness of Rav Judah to excommunicate a student whose knowledge was important to the academy. Having made for himself a bad name, the student could not hope to be tolerated, even though Rav Judah congratulated himself on his death-bed for not giving in to pressure to show the boy special favor. We do not know what he did to make a bad name, but it hardly matters.[1] The important fact is that even though tempted to do otherwise, Rav Judah was willing to enforce the rules of the academy, and so to protect its good name in the most trying circumstance. The remainder of the story carries the usual earmarks of rabbinical legend. The rabbis in Palestine were tempted to make a (from the narrator's perspective) wrong decision, whereupon a miracle happened, and a rabbi who was absent for some years suddenly made his appearance and warned otherwise. Then the student got his comeuppance in an appropriately miraculous way. The providential incident resulted in the death of the sinning student.[2] Presumably other, equally important students were thus warned that however much they were needed in the academy, or whatever outside influence protected them while there, they had better toe the line, because the heads of the academies would not be intimidated, and the Palestinian patriarch, indeed, Heaven itself, would not forebear. What academic politics necessitated the telling of such a story we can hardly guess. What is important for our interest is its emphasis on the inexorability of rabbinical punishment for disciples' infractions of their code.

Much was expected of the sage, but great was his reward. He could in time himself become a "living Torah," as useful as Scriptures themselves for finding out what was right action and what was not. Everything he said and did would then be studied by future disciples, and perhaps by people outside of the academies as well, and so it was important that he behave with perfect conformity to the academic rituals, required attitudes, speech and dress, and ideals of private and public conduct. The stakes were high, because the rabbis believed that their teachings constituted the will of God for Israel, and their actions would demonstrate in a worldly way the demands of Heaven. The "imitation of God" through adherence to the commandments was asked of all Israel, but the rabbis believed that the sage's behavior would exemplify for the rest of the Jews just what that broader ideal required. The sage almost as much as the divinity must therefore be understood as the primary paradigm. If he was a "living Torah," then his deeds were illustrative of revelation itself, and following them, the

[1] If the punishment fit the crime, then the crime must have been sexual.
[2] And suggests he was guilty of sexual sins.

Jews would truly conform to the heavenly expectations. So what we have called 'academic etiquette' must in their minds have represented a very different, and more solemn dimension of behavior. We recall once again the consequence of R. Adda b. Ahavah's right actions: he could do wonders not vouchsafed even to other rabbis, and enjoyed the constant favor of heaven. These were by no means of inconsequential rewards for avoiding unclean places and not calling colleagues by nicknames.

Whatever the claim to represent "a living Torah," the rabbis' attitudes toward women must have owed more to their environment than to Scriptures. Like the Christian and Manichaean ascetics,[1] they expressed an extreme fear of licentiousness of any kind. We recall Samuel's warning that even hearing a woman's voice is potentially a source of licentious action, and Rav Judah's refusal to shake hands or come into contact in any way with R. Naḥman's wife. Similarly, R. Ḥisda told his daughters not to eat even with their *husbands*, nor to use the same sanitary facilities, nor to come into contact with other men even by accident. R. Sheshet forbade a disciple of the sages to talk with a woman in the street, and R. Ḥisda forbade talking even with one's own wife in the street.[2] R. Sheshet similarly held that whoever looked at the little finger of a woman is as if he gazed upon her private parts.[3] R. Sheshet and R. Kahana were just as wary of bestiality as of licentiousness.[4] Even close relatives were regarded as potentially dangerous:

> R. Aḥa b. Abba happened by R. Ḥisda, his son-in-law, and took the daughter of his daughter and seated her on his lap. He said to him, "Does not the Master know that she is betrothed? ..."
>
> (b. Qid. 81b)

Commenting on R. Joshua b. Levi's saying, "Beware of your wife with her first son-in-law," R. Ḥisda explained that it was on account of licentiousness, and R. Kahana, on account of money.[5] R. Qattina said that standing in the middle of a marital bed is like standing on a woman's belly.[6] Nor was age a factor, as in the following:

---

[1] Below, pp. 195-200.

[2] b. Ber. 43b.

[3] b. Shab. 64b, compare the saying of Rav Judah, b. Ber. 10a, and R. Sheshet on the hair of a woman, b. Ber. 24a.

[4] b. Qid. 81b.

[5] b. Pes. 113a.

[6] b. Shab. 140b.

> R. Ḥisda's wife made her toilet before her daughter-in-law. R. Ḥina b. Ḥanina sat before R. Ḥisda and said, "The Mishnah applies to a young woman, but not to an elderly woman." R. Ḥisda replied, "By God! Even to your mother, grandmother, or even at brink of grave, as the saying goes, 'At sixty as at six, the sound of the timbrel makes her move.'"
> (b. M.Q. 9b)

But it was women, more than men, whom the rabbis regarded as eager for immoral action whenever possible.[1] The obvious fact is that the sages had a very vivid expectation that sexual desire would arise under almost any circumstances[2]:

> R. Isaac said, "Whoever says Rahab, Rahab at once has a seminal emission." R. Naḥman said, "I do so and nothing happens to me." He replied, "I refer to someone who actually knows her."
> (b. Meg. 15a)

In stressing the repression of illegal sexual temptations, the rabbis made provision for legal intercourse, by marrying their children at the earliest possible time, and by seeing to it that everyone got married. R. Ḥisda said,

> "I am superior because I married at sixteen, and had I married at fourteen, Satan would have had no control whatever over me."
> (b. Qid. 30a)

R. Huna instructed R. Hamnuna to marry, refusing to agree with R. Ḥisda that he was a "great man" unless he would take a wife.[3] We have already discussed[4] the enigmatic saying of Rav in his travels, "Who will be mine for a day"; R. Naḥman did the same.[5] This strange procedure would seem contrary to everything the rabbis stood for, for the normal safeguards for a woman, including a marriage-contract and the like, do not seem here to have been provided; since a considerable sum was required at divorce, it seems a rather expensive procedure. Perhaps that is the very point, that the rabbis were so concerned not to transgress sexual prohibitions of any kind that they went to enormous expense properly to marry and divorce a woman even for a one-day marriage. But the text does not say so. It merely says that some noted rabbis would announce that they were available for a quick marriage.

---

[1] R. Kahana, b. Qid. 81a.
[2] But compare R. Giddal, speaking of himself, b. Ber. 20a.
[3] b. Qid. 29b.
[4] Vol. II, pp. 129-130.
[5] b. Yev. 37b, Yoma 18b.

It is not strange that the rabbis were eager to secure proper marital relationships and avoid improper ones, but the extremes to which they went, the highly sexual view they held of all human relationships, the ascription of sexual desires of a most unusual sort even to themselves, along with absolute prohibitions against contact of the seemingly most innocent kind with a woman of any age or condition,—these reflect more than a reasonable, social concern for proper sexuality. They imply the view that anyone, at any time, and under any circumstance, is prepared forthwith to engage in sexual relations, and the most rigid and effective barriers must be everywhere erected to prevent it. It remains for a psychologist to interpret these data in the proper context. I do not think it suffices to explain them as a reaction against the "oriental" milieu. They also characterized Babylonian Christians and Manichaeans. One cannot suppose that they represented a rabbinical prohibition against local Iranian, Greek, or Semitic practices the rabbis would have regarded as "obscene." The Palestinians were equally firm, and many of the above discussions and sayings are attached to congruent Palestinian ones. Indeed, the rabbis earlier had specifically praised the modesty of the Persians, which they commended to their followers.[1] Whether or not an integral relationship exists between religious nomism and sexual puritanism remains to be investigated. One thing seems perfectly clear: the rabbis' view of women was entirely normal for *their* setting, held in monastery and academy alike, in fact by all sorts of "holy men," though *not* by the ordinary people. That ordinary people behaved differently is suggested by R. Naḥman's comment, that Manoah was a boor because he walked behind his wife (Judges 13: 11),[2] with the obvious implication, in fact spelled out elsewhere, that sages did not walk behind, but in front of, women, so as not to gaze upon them and be led to unchaste thoughts. So the dicta on women were a part of the code of the sage. On the other hand, the sages tried to enforce them wherever they could, and to maintain public standards of decency, as in the following case:

> There was the case of R. Adda b. Ahava who saw a heathen woman wearing a red head dress in the street. Thinking that she was an Israelite, he rose and tore it from her. It turned out she was a heathen and they fined him 400 zuz. He said to her, "What is your name?" She replied, "Mathun." "Mathun," he said "that makes four hundred zuz."
>
> (b. Ber. 20a)

---

[1] Vol. I, p. 152.
[2] b. Ber. 61a, 'Eruv. 18b.

I do not think that ordinary people would have found something intrinsically immoral, even actionable, in the woman's dress, for it is clear that the Persian court did not, but rather fined the rabbi for gross assault. What is significant is that the rabbi thought the woman was a Jew, which suggests two things. First, not all Jews conformed to the rabbinical sex-ethic. Second, the rabbis were prepared to do something about it, as best they could, and when they achieved sufficient power, they most certainly would not regard "their" view of proper sex morality as applicable only to a small circle of illuminati, but rather to the life of the whole people.

Patterns of behavior among the men of the academy proved no more similar to those of ordinary people. Given the insistence upon humility and utmost deference in student years, one need hardly be surprised that once a sage achieved significant recognition, as leading authority, head of an academy, or a judge, he paid close attention to matters of his own honor and personal respect. What he had given so long he now expected to receive, and he mostly did. Problems were raised by the touchy relationships among sages of the same generation, however, and we hear loud echoes of these disputes. Part of the tension was professional:

> When R. Ḥisda and R. Sheshet would meet, R. Ḥisda's lips would tremble at the mastery of Traditions of R. Sheshet, and R. Sheshet would tremble in his whole body at the dialectical skill of R. Ḥisda ...
> (b. ʿEruv. 67a)

When scholars absented themselves from R. Ḥisda's sessions, he excommunicated them. They had complained that he could not answer their questions.[1] But more serious quarrels broke out for personal insults:

> R. Ḥisda asked R. Huna, "What is the law concerning a student whose master requires him?" He said to him, "Ḥisda, Ḥisda, I do not need you but you need me!" For forty years they were angry with one another and they did not meet. R. Ḥisda observed forty fasts because R. Huna was disturbed, and R. Huna kept forty fasts because he had suspected R. Ḥisda ...
> (b. B.M. 33a)

[1] b. Qid. 25a. See also b. Zev. 96b, R. Isaac b. Judah left Rami b. Ḥama to study with R. Sheshet, and when the former complained, R. Isaac explained that he was not so well-informed as R. Sheshet.

While a disciple was not supposed to judge cases during the lifetime of his master, R. Ḥisda did so during R. Huna's lifetime, as did *his* student R. Hamnuna before his death.[1]

R. Sheshet, whom Rava called "a hard man, hard as iron,"[2] was referred to as "a suckling who perverted the way of his mother," because he did not listen to her plea for mercy on a student; R. Aḥadboi b. Ammi had asked him questions in a mocking way, and he was insulted. The result was that R. Aḥadboi lost his speech and forgot his learning.

> His mother came and wept before him, but he paid no attention to her cries. At length she said, "Behold these breasts from which you sucked." Then he prayed for him and he was healed.
>
> (b. B.B. 9b)

Rav Judah was no different:

> Zutra b. Tuviah was repeating his lesson before Rav Judah. When he came to this verse, 'And these are the last words of David' (II Sam. 23:1), he said to him, "*Last*—One would infer that there were earlier ones. What were they?" He was silent and said nothing. He [the student] repeated, "*Last* implies that there were earlier words. What were they?" Rav Judah said to him, "What is your view? That if someone does not know the explanation of this verse, he is not a great man?" He realized he had taken the matter to heart, and treated himself as under ban for one day.
>
> (b. M.Q. 16b)

Rav Judah would similarly summon those who absented themselves from his sessions, sending Adda his attendant to seize those who were missing.[3]

These stories have their parallels in the traditions of earlier generations. One is struck, here as elsewhere, by the perfect continuities in academic behavior patterns and values, extending over a period of two hundred years and more. Whether or not laws were changed for Babylonian conditions, there can be no doubt that academic etiquette and relationships remained quite constant. It stands to reason that those who not only studied a given text, but observed men who were carefully trained to emulate, even to imitate, their master's gestures, would,

---

1 b. 'Eruv. 62b-63a.
2 b. Men. 95b.
3 b. Shab. 148a.

when they rose to eminence, exact the same kind of consistent standards of behavior. Indeed, it is quite natural to suppose that the combination of studying texts conveying certain values of behavior and observing men who embodied them would permit very little alteration from one age to the next. The rabbi is a remarkably unchanging figure. Rav had insisted that a student must feel bitter toward his master. The pitiless behavior ascribed to R. Sheshet and the arrogant attitude of Rav Judah, are in the same spirit. One notes also that the rabbis' displeasure was believed to produce dire personal consequences. Mocking a teacher could result in worse things than a day of excommunication. The lot of the students could not have been an easy one. On the one hand, they were required to memorize, with as little inquiry as possible, a considerable heritage. On the other, they had to watch every movement to conform to the ritualistic patterns expected of a student of the sages. It is this rigorous and rigid pattern of education which partially may account for the conservatism, timelessness, and consistency of academic values.

And yet, students did come to the academies, and willingly undergo the training imposed there. Most of them did not achieve fame or high position. What explains the willingness of young men to put themselves into the hands of the sages of their day? The reverence, fear, and humility required of the students were called forth, I should suppose, by a combination of facts. First, study in the academy obviously resulted in a better opportunity in Jewish society than otherwise. Second, the sages were the subject of numerous stories, some of which we have here noted, concerning their holiness and magical influence over the natural world. Students would accept the conditions of the academies, and they knew no other so far as we can tell, to sit at the feet of such extraordinary men. Indeed, one may suppose that behind the literature of rabbinical miracles, stories of the anger and wrath of one rabbi against another, of the implacability of this one for that one, and the like—behind these stories must lie an expectation that that is what a sage *would* be like. Third, the sage did allege that he and he alone knew the will of God for Israel and mankind, and could claim to authenticate that knowledge in the several ways we have considered heretofore. And many must have believed him.

The values of a society emerge most readily in its educational institutions, but in the case before us, we do not know enough to assess how widely academic values were accepted among the masses. We are so well informed about the academies and the rabbis, their sayings and doings, that it is easy to forget what a small segment of a great society is revealed in these sources. The mother of R. Sheshet must represent another viewpoint entirely, one which would have looked with little admiration upon the excessive pride of the sage and self-abasement demanded of the disciple. The popular saying comparing the meaningless mumbling of the Magus with the repetition of the sage,—both not knowing what they said—tells us that some, at least, thought the whole affair ludicrous. So we are reminded once again of Professor Lieberman's view, that rabbinic literature reflects a continuous war between the rabbis and the masses. It was the rabbis' intention to transform the Jews into a "kingdom of priests and a holy people," a kingdom whose laws they alone had mastered and could administer, and a people which found its "true" identity in the very laws and doctrines which the academies possessed. The *yeshiva* represented the locus for a new polity, an imperium founded not upon language, culture, and power, but rather upon learning and conformity to the Scriptures as the rabbis read and exemplified them. The language of the academies differed, in ways thought significant, from that of the streets, the culture—the patterns of behavior toward women, masters, disciples—was not the same, and power was embodied not by politics but by the men who could both teach what God wanted, and demonstrate it. What was at issue? Why did the rabbis conceive it so important that through their schools they should constitute, then shape a new society? A hint derives from the following:

> R. Hamnuna said, "Jerusalem was destroyed only because they neglected the school-children ['s education]," (citing Jer. 6:11). Rav Judah said, "Jerusalem was destroyed only because scholars were despised therein" (citing II Chron. 36:16).
>
> (b. Shab. 119b)

One could duplicate these sayings many times. Jerusalem was destroyed, the rabbis held, because *their* values were not sufficiently rooted in the lives of the people, because children were not educated, because sages were not honored. So Jerusalem would *not* have been destroyed had sages found proper respect, had the schoolchildren been given their education. These words cannot be understood as mere homilies; their spirit recurs in many variations and contexts, and what the rabbis meant was clear and concrete. By their teaching, by the respect they exacted from the people, they would so reconstitute the Jewish community that it would never again suffer destruction. They were engaged in an effort to reshape the history of the Jews, by applying the revealed lessons of former times, hoping to wipe out the shaky foundations of the Jewish polity, and solidly and firmly to reconstruct them. Their theology demanded no less. God had said that if the Jews kept the Torah, he would bless them, and if they did not, he would punish them. They had been punished, so it was clear that they had not properly kept the Torah. The rabbis, heirs of a party now more than five centuries old and nearing success, thought that the reason the Jews had been "punished" was that they had not kept the Torah as God had intended it to be kept, namely, according to the traditions of their party. It was such a theological understanding of Jewish history which led the rabbis to seek to reform Jewish society.

The normal life of Babylonian Jewry did not require the creation of such a new society. The Jews were a stable, separate group under no pressure to "cease" to exist. They had their established traditions, believed to date back to the beginnings of their community more than nine hundred years earlier. In the millet-system of Sasanian society, they were a recognized, distinct, and self-governing ethnic community. The rabbis and the society of their academic institution represented an unnatural presence among the Jews. We turn now to consider part of the configurations of that presence, specifically the theological, liturgical, and exegetical traditions which formed a substantial segment of rabbinical culture in this period.

VI. Theology

The inner tension of their theological inquiry lay in the rabbis' conviction that although God could not be wholly known, yet he could be known in some measure. R. Huna stressed the former, and R. Naḥman the latter:

> 'Lo these are but parts of his ways, and what blemish of aught is heard of him? But the thunder of his mighty deeds who can understand' (Job 26:14)? R. Huna said, "Whatever things you see are but parts of the ways of the Holy One, blessed be He, as it says, 'Lo these are but parts of his ways ...'' 'But the thunder of his mighty deeds who can understand?' R. Huna said, "When thunder goes forth in its full force no creature can understand it. It is not written, 'none understands,' but 'who can understand' [implying that *some* may understand]." Said R. Huna, "If you cannot comprehend the essential nature of thunder: can you comprehend the essence of the world? If a man tells you, 'I can comprehend the essential character of the universe,' say to him, 'For

what is the man that comes after the king' (Qoh. 2:12)? After the king of the universe, the supreme King of kings, the Holy One blessed be he." R. Naḥman said, "This may be compared to a thicket of reeds which no man could enter, for whoever entered therein lost his way. What did a clever man do? He cut down and entered, cut some more and penetrated further, thus he entered the clearing and went out. Then all began to enter through his clearing ..."

(Gen. R. 12:1)[1]

R. Naḥman referred specifically to Solomon, who "pondered the words of the Torah and investigated them," and made it possible for others properly to understand the Torah:

As soon as Solomon arose all began to comprehend the Torah.

(Song R. 1.1.8)

The same context indicates that Solomon was especially praised for his ability to create parables and to discourse in public. R. Huna's comment, that whatever men see are "but parts of the ways of the Holy One," stressed the panentheism of the rabbis, that the world everywhere exhibits the marks of its maker. At the same time he held that men cannot comprehend the essence of the world. They may, R. Naḥman responded, be helped by especially clever people, who, proceeding step by step, penetrate into the mysteries of creation and find their way back. It was the theophany at Sinai, particularly the thirteen attributes of Ex. 34:6, which revealed all that the rabbis were willing openly to say about divine qualities:

Rav Judah said, "A covenant has been made with the thirteen attributes that they will not be turned away empty-handed, as it says, 'Behold I make a covenant' (Ex. 34:10)."

(b. R.H. 17b)[2]

R. Huna and Rav Judah similarly stressed divine love and compassion:

R. Huna contrasted: "It is written, 'The Lord is righteous in all his ways' and then it says, 'And gracious in all his works' (Ps. 145:17). At first he is righteous, but at the end, gracious."

(*ibid.*)[3]

---

[1] Trans. H. Freedman, (London, 1961) 87. See also Qoh. R., 2.12.1., and Song R. 1.1.8, and J. Theodor and Ch. Albeck, ed., *Midrash Bereshit Rabba* (Jerusalem, 1965) I 97-8. One recalls the discussion between R. Qattina and the heathen magician, above, p. 34f., on the meaning of thunder.

[2] b. Ḥag. 13b.

[3] See also b. Shab. 53b, Rav Judah says that the natural order of the world is set aside for man's needs.

> Rav Judah said, "The Merciful One wants the heart."
>
> (b. Sanh. 106b)

Rav Judah's first saying would suggest that the 'attributes' were independent of the Godhead, and could supplicate for mercy on their own.

R. Naḥman's comment calls to mind the existence of two esoteric metaphysical traditions handed on from earliest times in Pharisaic-rabbinic academies concerning the mysteries of creation (Ma'aseh Bere'shit) and those of the Chariot (Ma'aseh Merkavah), the latter a form of pleroma-mysticism. In these arcane doctrines, the rabbis carried on speculation, which they hid from the masses as best they could, about the nature of the Godhead, of the aeons intervening between the highest heaven and the earth, of the shape and measurements of God (Shi 'ur Qomah) and the like. A Jewish form of the widespread astral mysticism, the Merkavah tradition was represented by one saying of Rav Judah, that the *ḥashmal* referred to by Ezekiel in his vision were "living creatures speaking fire." Rav Judah similarly said that the thickness of the firmament is one-tenth of a day's journey, a saying that relates to the Shi'ur Qomah tradition.[1] It was as leading student of Rav and chief tradent of his mystical sayings that Rav Judah would have acquired such teachings as these. He similarly made a statement we may identify with the tradition on Creation:

> Rav Judah further said, "At the time that the Holy One blessed be He created the world, it went on expanding like two clues of warp until the Holy One blessed be He rebuked it and brought it to a standstill, for it is said, 'The pillars of heaven were trembling, but they became astonished at his rebuke.' (Job 26:11)."
>
> (b. Ḥag. 12a)

Rav had made a comment on that verse, transmitted by Zutra b. Tuviah, that God had created the world by a rebuke, and so Rav Judah's comment extends the teaching of his master on the same verse, by drawing forth from the Scripture a metaphysical implication. R. Naḥman and Rav Judah were the only teachers of this generation to do more than repeat the traditions of the earlier one on Creation and the Chariot. An exoteric saying on creation was:

---

[1] b. Pes. 94a, see further in the same place for R. Yoḥanan b. Zakkai's Shi'ur Qomah sayings, which indicate that Rav Judah's tradition is part of the same corpus.

> Rav Judah said, "The Holy One ... created this world only that they might fear him, as it is said, 'And the God made it so that they may fear him' (Qoh. 3:14)."
>
> (b. Shab. 31b)

The contrast between the Creation saying and this one is of interest. The former concerns the mysteries of how the world came into being, the latter the response required of the people to creation. The latter saying seems to me not a part of the Creation mysteries at all, but one which would have suited any public occasion. R. Naḥman left two sayings relevant to the Creation tradition, first, that the sun's orb was created from the earth,[1] the other a reference to the legend, based upon Job 4:9, that when God wanted to bring a flood, he took two stars from Pleiades and did so, and when he wanted to stop it, he took two stars from the Bear. He will, R. Naḥman said, one day restore them to her, a comment based on Job 38:12, 'And 'Ayish will be comforted for her children.'[2]

The sacred history of Israel, which provided for the rabbis of the preceding generation paradigmatic evidence on the meaning of events in their own days,[3] elicited comments in this time which indicate only the persistence of the classical patterns, but no obvious effort to utilize them for contemporary purposes. R. Naḥman held that Israel would be redeemed in splendor on account of Abraham's faith.[4] Before Israel sinned, the Shekhinah dwelt with each individual, but afterward it departed from them, R. Ḥisda said.[5] He also held that the earthly sanctuary was modeled upon the heavenly one.[6] R. Huna wept at verses which reminded him of the love of God and the estrangement of Israel:

> When R. Huna came to this verse he wept, "'And you shall sacrifice peace offerings and eat there (Deut. 27:7).' The slave whom his Master longs to see should become estranged from him! For it is written, 'To what purpose is the multitude of your sacrifices to me, says the Lord (Is. 1:11).'"
>
> (b. Ḥag. 4b)[7]

---

[1] Assuming that R. Naḥman's saying, "Even the sun's orb was created from the earth," based upon Job 9.7 (Gen. R. 12.11) is part of the Creation-Mystery tradition.

[2] b. Ber. 59a.

[3] Vol. II pp. 57-64.

[4] Song R. 4.8.2, based on Gen. 15.6.

[5] b. Sotah 3b, on Deut. 23:15 and Deut. 23:4.

[6] Midrash on Psalms 30:1.

[7] He makes a similar comment, in the same place, on Ex. 23:17 and Is. 1:12.

R. Sheshet held that the light of testimony (Lev. 24:3) was meant as a sign to the world that the Shekhinah is present in Israel.[1] R. Naḥman commented, on the basis of Ex. 19:16, that Israel is so stiffnecked that God *had* to show them miracles.[2] By contrast R. Qattina said that even in the time of the destruction of the Temple, men of faith did not disappear from Israel.[3] Rav Judah held, as we saw, that Jerusalem was destroyed only because scholars were despised there, basing his comment on II Chron. 36:16. 'They mocked the messengers of God and despised his words and scoffed at his prophets until the wrath of the Lord arose against his people until there was no remedy.' His comment was an extension of Rav's, which he cited, that one who despises a scholar has no remedy for his wounds.[4] R. Qattina said that this age would last for six thousand years, and would be desolate for one thousand, quoting 'And the Lord alone shall be exalted in that day' (Is. 2:11), a day being a thousand years (Ps. 90:4)[5]. So the great moments in sacred history elicited the conventional comments, made many times before: Israel's merit derived from Abraham's faith; before the Golden Calf, Israel enjoyed intimacy with God; the sanctuary was a cosmic model; its light testified to God's presence, and its destruction was a cosmic calamity. Jerusalem was destroyed because 'the messengers of God'—strikingly, seen by Rav Judah to be *disciples of the sages*—were mocked. This age had to come to an end, and at the end of days, God alone would be exalted. Nothing here had not been said by previous generations, nothing would not be repeated later on. It is this classicism that is most striking in rabbinic theology. This generation seems quite interchangeable with any other so far as its view of the divinity and of sacred history is concerned.

The rabbis held a mostly mechanistic view of sin and punishment. Men are fully responsible for their own actions, and bring upon their

---

[1] b. Shab. 22b.

[2] Ex. R. 42.9.

[3] b. Shab. 119b, b. Ḥag. 14a. The proof text is Is. 3:6. Such a midrash would be useful in polemics against Christians, who held that the destruction in 70 represented the end of Israel's period of grace, but in fact it is a dispute between R. Qattina and Rava, who held that Jerusalem was destroyed only because men of faith ceased therein. There seems to me no chronological problem in supposing Rava and R. Qattina in dispute, at the end of the latter's life and the beginning of the former's career. Since R. Qattina's statement is quoted as a criticism of Rava's, however, it may have been made independently. But that does not by itself prove a polemical intent.

[4] b. Shab. 119b.

[5] b. R.H. 31a.

heads a just recompense. R. Huna interpreted Lam. 1:14. "When my hands are at my own disposal," to mean, "I bear my own responsibilities."[1] He similarly said that once a man has transgressed and repeated his transgression, it is as if that transgression is permitted to him.[2] R. Ḥisda stressed the inexorability of punishment, saying that all gates are locked except the gates through which pass the cries of those who are wronged.[3] The rabbis could not accept with equanimity any seeming injustice, which might imply that the wicked really prospered:

> R. Huna said, "What is the meaning of the verse, 'Wherefore do you look when they deal treacherously and hold your peace when the wicked swallows up the man that is more righteous than he' (Hab. 1:13). Can the wicked swallow up the righteous? Is it not written, 'The Lord will not leave him in his hand' (Ps. 37:33), and further, 'There shall no mischief befall the righteous' (Prov. 12:21). You must therefore say: He swallows up one who is merely 'more righteous than he' but he cannot swallow up the perfectly righteous man."
>
> (b. Ber. 7b)[4]

Hence whatever happens cannot be unjust or inappropriate. Each sin has its punishment, each good deed its reward. And these were spelled out. R. Qattina said that the sustenance of a scoffer is reduced.[5] Children died because of the neglect of the commandment concerning fringes, R. Kahana thought.[6] R. Ḥisda said that Gehenna is deepened for him who puts his mouth to folly.[7] We have the following account as well:

> Once 400 jars of wine of R. Huna turned sour. R. Judah brother of R. Sala the Pious, and some say, R. Adda b. Ahava, and other scholars came to visit him. They said to him, "You ought to examine your actions." He said to them, "Am I suspected in your eyes?" They replied, "Is the Holy One, blessed be He, suspected of judgment without justice?" He said to them, "If anyone has heard anything against me, speak out." They replied, "We have heard that the master does not give his tenant his (lawful share of) vine twigs." He replied, "Does he leave me any? He steals them all." They said to him, "That is exactly what the proverb means, 'If you steal from a thief you also have a taste of thievery.'" He said to them, "I pledge myself to give it to him." Some report

---

[1] Lev. R. 14:10.

[2] b. ʿArakh. 30b, Sotah 22a, Qid. 20a, 40a, an exegesis of Prov. 24:21. Compare b. Sukkah 52b, on Hos. 4:12 vs. 5:4.

[3] b. B.M. 59a, on Amos 7:7.

[4] See also b. Meg. 6b.

[5] b. A.Z. 18b, an exegesis of Hos. 7:5.

[6] b. Shab. 32b.

[7] b. Shab. 33a, based on Prov. 22:14.

that thereupon the vinegar became wine again, and others that the vinegar went up so high that it was sold for the same price as wine.

(b. Ber. 5b)

The central issue was, Does God do anything unjustly? This the rabbis could not affirm, so it was quite natural to seek reasons in ethical or moral misbehavior for any misfortune. One cannot ignore the end of the story: the vinegar gained its original price for R. Huna. So the rabbis believed that reward was as inexorable a consequence of right action as punishment for bad, attested in the following:

R. Huna said, "He who is accustomed to light the (Sabbath) candle has sons who are disciples of the sages. He who is careful concerning the *mezuzah* merits a beautiful house. He who is careful concerning fringes merits a beautiful cloak. He who is careful concerning the sanctification of the Sabbath day merits and fills kegs of wine." R. Huna was accustomed to learn and teach at the door of R. Abin the carpenter. He saw that he was accustomed to light many lights. He said, "Two great men are coming forth from here." There went forth R. Idi bar Abin and R. Ḥiyya bar Abin.

(b. Shab. 23b)

R. Huna saw a certain man drinking water before *Havdalah*. He said to him, "Are you not afraid of choking? For it was taught in R. ʿAqiba's name, He who tastes anything before reciting *Havdalah* shall die through choking..."

(b. Pes. 105a)

Punishment may well be postponed, however, 'until the measure is filled,' R. Hamnuna held.[1] The main principle was that man is wholly responsible. R. Huna provided Scriptural proofs from the three parts of Scripture to prove that in the way in which a man wants to go, he is led. He was hereby supporting Rav's teaching to the same effect.[2]

Things did not always work out that way. The righteous suffered, the sinner did not, and sometimes he prospered. The rabbis' understanding of the inexorable relationship between sin and punishment had to take account of such facts, which were already commented upon in the Scriptures that formed their consciousness. In this generation, we find three explanations. The first is revealed in the following story:

'None that go to her return, neither do they attain the paths of life' (Prov. 2:19). But if they do not return, how can they attain [the paths of

---

[1] b. ʿArakh. 15a, Sotah 9a, based on Job 20:22.

[2] b. Mak. 10b.

> life]? This is what it implies, And if they return, they will not attain the paths of life. Is this to suggest that whoever separates himself from heresy (*minut*) dies? And behold, there was a women who came before R. Ḥisda and said to him, "The least of all light sins which she [I] did was that her [my] younger son is the child of her older son." R. Ḥisda said to her, "Prepare a shroud for her [yourself]." But she did not die. Now since she refers to her act as the lightest, it is to be inferred that she was also guilty of heresy [and yet did not die]. She did not altogether renounce her evil-doing, which is why she did not die.
>
> (b. A.Z. 17a)

The implication is that she had not repented fully, lived out her years, but would suffer in the afterlife. Hence any situation which seemed irregular could be explained by reference to posthumous punishment. The suffering of a good man was explained as follows:

> Rava in the name of R. Seḥorah in the name of R. Huna said, "If the Holy One blessed be he is pleased with a man, he crushes him with painful sufferings, as it is said, 'And the Lord was pleased with him, hence he crushed him by disease' (Is. 53:10). Now you might think this is so even if he did not accept them with love. Therefore it is said, 'To see if his soul would offer itself in restitution' (ibid.) Even as the trespass-offering must be brought by consent, so also sufferings must be endured with consent. And if he did accept them, what is his reward? 'He will see his seed prolong his days,' and more than that, his knowledge of Torah will endure with him ..."
>
> (b. Ber. 5a)

So, it was thought, God would punish him whom he loved in this world, and he would merit a good portion in the world to come. Third, God by his grace might forego the punishment truly merited, as R. Huna said, "How little does he whom God supports need to grieve or trouble himself."[1]

Atonement took the form of suffering or repentence. Such penitence required confession of sins, though R. Sheshet regarded as shameless one who publicly specified them.[2] One proved himself truly penitent if he had the opportunity to repeat his original sin on two occasions and he avoided the temptation:

> Rav Judah specified, "With the same woman, at the same time, in the same place."
>
> (b. Yoma 86b)

---

[1] b. Yoma 22b.
[2] b. Sotah 7b.

One might repent because of love or fear of God, or because of suffering, as in the case of R. Huna cited above, Rav Judah taught.[1] But confession without penitence was of no avail. Rav Adda b. Ahava compared one who sinned and confessed, but did not repent, to a man holding a reptile and immersing himself.[2] R. Huna applied Jer. 22:10 to one who repeats his sins without penitence.[3] R. Naḥman said that public sins have to be made known to others, but ritual transgressions may be confessed to God alone.[4] One form of atonement is exile, which suffices to attain pardon for three things, Rav Judah taught, with reference to Jer. 31:8-9.[5]

The neat symmetry of rabbinic thought is here represented by one or another of the rabbis. Behind the discrete sayings lies a single and unified conception, which finds expression in detail. The convictions of this generation reveal sameness and abiding unity, in which the orderly ideas of divine justice and mercy, reward and punishment, are set forth each in its own way and with its own qualifications. One cannot help but feel astonishment that ideas first expressed hundreds of years earlier changed so very little, grew not at all, yet had lost none of their interest. R. Huna's warning about choking if one ate before a certain prayer cited a rabbi now dead for more than one hundred years. In the meantime, either people did choke to death in a way attributable to that cause, or they did not. Had they choked to death, it would have been appropriate to comment on it, "Be careful, because at such and such a time, someone died, illustrating the warning of R. ʿAqiba." Had they not choked to death, that too should have evoked some comment, perhaps about the unreliability or lack of empirical basis for R. ʿAqiba's observation. What is striking is the silence about what may or may not have *actually* been observed to happen. Observation and empirical testing were not outside of the rabbis' intellectual framework. When, one recalls, someone said that there are no Christians among the star-worshippers, the immediate comment was, "But behold, we see them every day!" Here however sayings and observations concerning not the world above or the age to come but the streets and present-day life were not similarly subjected to the obvious tests of reliability and accuracy.

---

1 b. Yoma 86a, with reference to Jer. 3.14.
2 b. Taʿanit 16a, with reference to Prov. 28:13 and Lam. 3:4.
3 b. M.Q. 27b.
4 b. Yoma 86b.
5 b. Sanh. 37b.

The conservatism of the academies seems to me illustrated best in theological data, for, as we shall see, while there was considerable legal innovation in this generation, ideas seem not to have changed very much. I cannot propose an adequate explanation. If one supposes that the Scriptures fixed the one, they should have rendered the other permanent as well. If the processes of learning through memorization and closely supervised discussion, exemplification and conformity to the behavior of others, rendered theology formal and unchanging, they also ought similarly to have affected law. I can see one difference only. While theological ideas were relevant mainly in the academies, where the teachers and students talked pretty much as had former generations about the same Scriptures and theological problems, the law pertained outside the schools as well. With the growth of rabbinical authority over the common life, over the litigations and complex daily relationships of the towns and villages, the changing quality of common life posed to the law new issues, raised for it new dilemmas, and called forth from it new responses based upon innovation both in theory and in practice. Everyday affairs seem to have had no similar impact upon academic culture standing by itself. What sufficed to explain the suffering of the righteous and the prosperity of sinners, to account for the failure of the evil man to exhibit the recompense for his actions, to instruct in the way to atone for sin and the way to avoid it altogether—such traditions could not have undergone much alteration. Those who learned and taught them did so, I think, mostly among themselves, and though they strove to influence others, it was only in matters of law that they had to face the realities of the common man's situation. The rabbis' orderly explanations for what in any generation must have seemed to ordinary people a very disorderly moral economy reflect, I think, the neat preference of the academy, rather than the chaotic problems of the streets.

VII. Liturgy

Both rabbi and ordinary person believed that God and angels heard and answered prayers, though preferably those said in Hebrew, according to the following authorities:

> Rav Judah held that one should not ask his needs in Aramaic, and R. Yoḥanan said that if he did, he would not be heard by the angels, who do not understand Aramaic.
>
> (b. Shab. 12b)

Since the language of the ordinary people was Aramaic, the insistence of the rabbis upon the Hebrew language required the support of such a warning: If you want the help of the angels, you had better pray in a languate they understand. Nonetheless, while numerous formal differences between academic and popular prayer will become evident, one can hardly distinguish between the prayerful spirit of the academies and the piety of the streets. In both instances, prayer was regarded as a puissant act. The teachings of the rabbis concerning prayer stressed proper attitude, dress, and conduct, but these teachings could not have run contrary to popular sentiment. Since the rabbi was seen as a holy man, the way in which he prayed and the effectiveness of his prayers would have elicited popular emulation and credulity. Rav Judah would dress himself before he prayed; R. Sheshet would, at the appropriate places, "bow like a reed and rise like a serpent."[1] The earlier rabbis' manner of prayer was remembered, and so it was with this generation. The most propitious time for prayer was the Ten Days of Penitence between the New Year and the Day of Atonement, so R. Naḥman taught in the name of Rabbah b. Abbuha.[2] R. Ḥelbo in the name of R. Huna said that the afternoon prayer was of special importance, "for even Elijah was heard only while offering his afternoon prayer," and that if one hopes to be heard in prayer, he should be filled with fear of God.[3] R. Ḥisda held that if one appeals for mercy for his fellow, he does not need even to mention his name.[4] R. Huna advised:

> Whoever has a fixed place for his prayer has the God of Abraham for his helper, and when he dies, people will say of him, "Where is that pious man, where is that righteous man, one of the disciples of our father Abraham."
>
> (b. Ber. 6b)

He also taught that one should not pray at the rear of the synagogue, or leave it by taking large steps.[5] The prohibition to pray at the rear of the synagogue was based on Ps. 12:9, "the wicked walk around," and one may surmise that some people did not pay much attention at public prayers, and so required warning to do so. Ideas on the proper manners in praying were mostly derived from I Sam. 1.10ff., R. Hamnuna inter-

---

[1] b. Ber. 30b, 12b. On kneeling, see b. Ber. 34b, R. Sheshet and R. Naḥman.

[2] b. Yev. 105a, with reference to Is. 55:6, and b. R.H. 18a with reference to I Sam. 25:38.

[3] b. Ber. 6b, with reference to I Kings 18:36-7, and Qoh. 12:13.

[4] b. Ber. 34a.

[5] b. Ber. 6b, not to pray at the rear as in Ps. 12:9. See also R. Ḥisda, y. Ber. 5.1, based on Prov. 8:34; R. Huna, b. Ber. 62b, re Ezek, 46:9.

preting Ḥannah's prayer to mean that one must direct his heart heavenward, that he must frame the words distinctly with his lips, that a drunken person is forbidden to say the *Tefillah*, and the like.[1] So the etiquette of prayer was shaped by exegesis of Scripture. What the rabbis held to be seemly and proper was seen by them not merely as their own opinion, but ordained by prophets and handed on in the Tradition. Part of the etiquette of the academies certainly pertained to the manner in which prayers were said, including the formation of a proper quorum.[2] Violation of that code, here as in other details, would stamp a man a boor. But the rabbis' frame of reference was not academic, rather extending to the synagogues of ordinary people.[3]

A number of rabbis composed prayers. R. Sheshet's prayer after fasting was as follows:

> "Lord of the aeons, It is fully revealed before you that in the time when the Temple was standing, a man would sin and offer a sacrifice, and they would present of it only the fat and blood, and it would make atonement for him, and now, I have sat in a fast and diminished *my* fat and blood. May it be pleasing before you that my fat and blood, which have been diminished, be seen as if I have offered it to you on the altar, and may you be reconciled to me."
>
> (b. Ber. 17a)

Mar ʿUqba contributed the following prayer for a time of crisis:

> R. Ḥisda in the name of Mar ʿUqba said, "Even in the hour that you are as filled with wrath concerning them as a pregnant woman, may all their needs be before you." Some say, R. Ḥisda in the name of Mar ʿUqba said, "Even in the time that they are transgressing matters of Torah, may all their needs be before you."
>
> (b. Ber. 29b)[4]

---

[1] b. Ber. 31a.

[2] y. Ber. 4.6, R. Naḥman on the importance of saying one's prayers in a quorum; b. Ber. 48a, Rav Judah is asked about whether eight or seven might constitute a proper quorum. Note also the following, in which the rabbis compare themselves to the ark or to the Sabbath:

> R. Huna said, "Nine and ark make ten." R. Naḥman said to him, "Is the ark a man?" "I mean," said R. Huna, "that when 9 look like 10 they may be joined together." R. Ami said, "Two and the Sabbath may be joined together." Said R. Naḥman to him, "Is the Sabbath a man?" What R. Ammi really said was that two scholars who sharpen one another in knowledge of *halakhah* may count as three. R. Ḥisda gave an example, "For instance, I and R. Sheshet." R. Sheshet gave an example, "For instance, I and R. Ḥisda."
>
> (b. Ber. 47b)

[3] But see below, pp. 176-179.

[4] For minor variations, see *Diq. Sof.* I, 152.

Rav Judah's Tanna recited the following:

"If a man was standing and saying the *Tefillah* and he broke wind, he waits until the odor passes and begins with the following prayer, 'Sovereign of the Universe, You have formed us with various hollows and vents. Well do you know our shame and confusion, that our latter end is worms and maggots.' And he begins from the place where he stopped."

(b. Ber. 24b)

This prayer is not described as composed by Rav Judah, but rather as recited before him by the Tanna of his school. It was not widely known, and may have been originally written in his academy. We have several compositions attributed to, or cited by, Rav Judah:

What is the blessing of betrothal? Both Rabin b. R. Adda and Rabbah b. R. Adda in the name of Rav Judah say, "Blessed are you, O Lord, our God, king of the universe, who has sanctified us by his commandments and commanded us concerning forbidden relations, forbidding to us betrothed women and permitting us a woman through marriage by means of canopy and sanctification." R. Aḥa b. Rabba in the name of Rav Judah completed it as follows: "Blessed are you, Who sanctifies Israel by the wedding canopy and sanctification."

(b. Ket. 7b)

The passage continues:

[Our Rabbis taught: The blessing of the bridegrooms is said in the presence of ten people all seven days.] Rav Judah said, "That is only if new guests come." What does one say? Rav Judah said, "Blessed are you, O Lord, our God, king of the world, who has created all things for his glory... the creator of man... who has made man in his image, in the image of the likeness of his form, and has prepared for him out of himself an eternal building [Gen. 2:22, 3:20]. Blessed are you O Lord, creator of man. May the barren greatly rejoice and exult [Is. 54, 61:10, 57:5] when her children will be gathered in her midst in joy [Is. 54: 1-3]. Blessed are you, O Lord, who makes Zion rejoice through her children [Is. 62:3–4]. May you make these beloved companions greatly to rejoice even as in ancient times you delighted your creatures in the Garden of Eden. Blessed are you, O Lord, who delights the bridegroom and the bride. Blessed are you, O Lord our God, king of the universe, who made joy and gladness, bridegroom and bride, rejoicing, song, mirth and delight, love, brotherhood, peace and friendship. Quickly, Lord our God, may there be heard in the cities of Judah and in the streets of Jerusalem the cry of joy and of gladness, the cry of the bridegroom and the bride, the cry of the singing of bridegrooms in their canopies, and of youths from their feast of song.[1] Blessed are you, O Lord, who delights the bridegroom with the bride."

(b. Ket. 7b-8a)

[1] Re Jer. 33:11, see R. Huna, b. Ber. 6b.

For the Day of Atonement, two confessions were cited:

> What is the Confession... Rav Hamnuna said, "My God, before I was created I was unworthy, and now that I have been created, it is as if I were not. I am dust in my life, and more so in my death. Behold I am before you like a vessel filled with shame and humiliation. May it be pleasing before you that I should not sin, and my former sin erase in mercy but not by suffering."
>
> Rav Judah said, "Our iniquities are too many to count, and our sins too numerous for numbering."
>
> (b. Yoma 87b)

Rav Judah's betrothal blessing follows the form, now more widely accepted than ever, of the *Berakhah*. The brief reference to "his" confession may indicate merely that such was the prayer, among many available, which he selected; or that he composed the brief sentence, contrasting to the confession of Rav Hamnuna. The blessing for betrothal seems more clearly ascribed to Rav Judah, in which case one wonders whether a blessing was said for betrothal before his time, or whether he was in fact adding to the betrothal ceremony. Rav Judah also provided a text for the blessing of the new moon:

> Rav Judah gives it thus: "Blessed... who created the heavens with his word, and all their hosts with the breath of his mouth. He appointed unto them fixed laws and times, that they should not change their way. They rejoice and are glad to do the will of their maker. They do his work truthfully, for their action is truth. The moon he ordained that she should renew herself as a crown of beauty for those whom he sustains from the womb, and who will be renewed in the future, and magnify their maker in the name of the glory of his kingdom. Blessed are you, O Lord, who renews the moons."
>
> (b. Sanh. 42a)

R. Ḥisda cited a prayer for the traveller:

> R. Jacob... in the name of R. Ḥisda said, "Whoever sets out on a journey should say a prayer for the journey. What is it? 'May it be your will, O Lord my God, to lead me forth in peace, and direct my steps in peace, and uphold me in peace, and deliver me from the hand of every enemy and ambush by the way, and send a blessing on the works of my hands and cause me to find grace, kindness, and mercy in your eyes and in the eyes of all who see me. Blessed are you, O Lord, who listens to prayer.'"
>
> (b. Ber. 29b)

R. Ḥisda held, according to R. Jacob, that the prayer should be said at the moment that he starts out, but it is permissible to say it until he has gone a parasang. He should say it standing still, though R. Sheshet said he may say it while moving. We have the following story:

> Once R. Ḥisda and R. Sheshet were going along together, and R. Ḥisda stood still and prayed. R. Sheshet asked his attendant, "What is R. Ḥisda doing?" He replied, "He is standing and praying." He said to the attendant, "Put me in position also that I may pray. If you can be good, do not be called bad" [praying while standing still is better].
> (b. Ber. 30a)

The earlier generation had invested considerable energy in the definition of various blessings and prayers to be said on the occasion of enjoying food or natural phenomena, the so-called 'blessings of enjoyment.'[1] It was Samuel who laid down that anyone who enjoyed any worldly benefit without a benediction was guilty of sacrilege. The forms of these blessings were on the whole well established by this time,[2] though Rav Judah's father still made use of the Kaddish-formula for giving thanks for rain.[3] Precise definitions for the required blessings were provided in much earlier times, and Rav and Samuel had concentrated upon mainly secondary matters, proving, for instance, that even fragrances should be blessed, and saying what that blessing ought to be. They likewise discussed what blessing was required for relatively complex foods, in which several species were combined, each of which separately would have its own formula of blessing.

The Scriptural warrants for the liturgies of blessing now were discussed. Rav Judah said that the blessing after a meal was to be inferred from Deut. 8:10, "And you will eat and be satisfied and bless..." The blessing before reading the Torah was supposedly required by Deut. 32:3, "When I call upon the name of the Lord, give greatness to our God."[4] Rav Judah cited a saying of Rav, that Jeremiah (9:11) condemned the failure of blessing the Torah before public reading.[5] His providing Scriptural warrant for such a blessing suggests that it was still widely neglected, and required support. R. Naḥman traced the history of the grace after meals:

> "Moses ordained for Israel the blessing 'who sustains all' when the mannah descended. Joshua ordained for them the blessing over the

1 Vol. II pp, 167-76.

2 y. Ber. 9.2, Gen. R. 13:15, Midrash on Psalms 18:16, with reference to Job 36:27.

3 Vol. II p. 170.

4 b. Ber. 21a. Compare b. Ber. 48b.

5 See below, p. 170, and b. B.M. 85a-b. On academic study, R. Ḥiyya b. Ashi reported that Rav required such blessings, see y. Ber. 1.5, and b. Ber. 11b.

> land when they entered Palestine. David and Solomon ordained the blessing 'who builds Jerusalem', David requiring 'For Israel your people and for Jerusalem your city' and Solomon, 'for this great and holy house.' 'He who is good and does good' was ordained when the slain of Betar were given over for burial, for R. Mattena said, 'On that day on which the slain of Betar were given over for burial they decreed in Yavneh 'who is good and does good', 'who is good', that the bodies did not moulder, and 'who does good,' that they were given over for burial.'"
>
> (b. Ber. 48b)[1]

R. Naḥman b. Isaac held that the final blessing was *not* ordained by the Torah, but seemed unaware of R. Mattena's teaching.[2]

In defining 'blessings of enjoyment' and those pertaining to the commandments, this generation continued to explore the highly uncommon issues left unresolved by the earlier masters, but advanced not at all the identification and discussion of new or different questions. One finds only a little innovation, but rather the completion of the tasks assumed by earlier sages. For instance, while it was well known that wine required a blessing, Rav Judah added that even sour wine required the same blessing, against R. Ḥisda who denied it.[3] Such was a secondary issue indeed, as was Rav Judah's decree about the blessing said over wine on the Sabbath day.[4] Rav Judah decreed that a blessing was required when hunting out the leaven before Passover, but it was only Rava, in the next generation who defined just what the blessing should be.[5] Rav Judah said that a prisoner who is set free should say the blessing, "Blessed are you ... who does acts of grace,"[6] and accepted the following blessing after the recovery of a person from illness:

> Rav Judah was ill and recovered. R. Ḥanan of Bagdad and other rabbis went to visit him. They said to him, "Blessed be the All-Merciful who has given you back to us, and has not given you over to the dust." He said, "You have freed me from the obligation of giving thanks."
>
> (b. Ber. 54b)

R. Hamnuna, one recalls[7] decreed blessings on seeing "the wicked

---

[1] See also y. Ber. 1.5, 7.1, b. B.B. 121b, b. Taʿanit 31a.

[2] b. Ber. 46b, he derives it from a legal decree of the Tannaim that it was not of Sinaitic origin, ignoring R. Mattena's earlier saying about the slain of Betar.

[3] b. B.B. 95b.

[4] b. B.B. 95b.

[5] b. Pes. 106a.

[6] b. Pes. 7a. On blessing the Ḥanukkah light, see Rav Judah, y. Suk. 3.4, and below p. 254.

[7] b. Ber. 57b, see above, p. 34.

Babylon," and he further held that one who sees a crowd of Israelites should say, "Blessed is he who discerns secrets."[1] R. Naḥman supplemented the Tannaitic blessing over Jewish graves, which was "Blessed is he who fashioned you in judgment, fed and maintained you in judgment, and in judgment gathered you in, and in judgment will one day resurrect you," as follows:

> "And who knows your number. He will one day revive and establish you. Blessed is he who resurrects the dead."
>
> (b. Ber. 58b)

These concluding words, which complete the blessing decreed in earlier times, add two ideas, first, that God knows how many dead there are, and second, that the prayer should close with a blessing. They contain nothing new, but complete the old formula in a manner thought to be more suitable.

The specific "blessings of enjoyment" ordained at this time include that over wheat flour when eaten raw, for which Rav Judah required, "who creates the fruit of the ground," while R. Naḥman held the blessing should be, "by whose word all things exist."[2] (The limiting influence of the earlier generation is here seen in Rava's warning to R. Naḥman, "Do not argue with Rav Judah, since R. Yoḥanan and Samuel would agree with him ..."[3]) R. Sheshet required the blessing for pepper to be "by whose word all things exist," while Rava held that no blessing was necessary, since it is not food.[4] Rav Judah debated with R. Kahana on the blessing for a pulp made of flour, honey, and oil boiled in a pot, and for pounded grain, the former requiring "by whose word" and the latter "who creates various kinds of foods."[5] R. Sheshet said that if the pulp-mixture contains crumbs of bread even less than an olive, then one must say, "who brings bread out of the earth."[6] In most of their discussions, the rabbis were forced simply to interpret the decrees of the former generations. Rav and Samuel had disagreed on the blessing of *shatita*, a flour of dried barley and honey. R. Ḥisda said they do not really disagree, but the blessing of one is over the thick kind, while that of the other is over the thin.[7] R. Ḥisda similarly ex-

---

[1] b. Ber. 58a.
[2] b. Ber. 36a.
[3] *ibid.* But it is probably R. Naḥman b. Isaac.
[4] b. Ber. 36b.
[5] *ibid.*
[6] b. Ber. 37b.
[7] b. Ber. 38a.

pounded the teachings of Rav on the blessing over boiled vegetables, and R. Naḥman, those of Samuel on the same matter.[1] R. Huna held that if turnip tops are cut into large pieces, one must say, "who creates the fruit of the earth," but if into small, "by whose word all things exist," while Rav Judah required the former blessing for both.[2] R. Ḥisda and R. Hamnuna disagreed on the order in which various kinds of fruit, served together, should be blessed.[3] R. Huna and R. Naḥman disputed about another detail with R. Sheshet:

> If figs and grapes were set before them in the midst of a meal, R. Huna said that they require a blessing before (eating) but not afterward [since the grace after meals suffices], and R. Naḥman agreed. R. Sheshet required a blessing both before and after.
>
> (b. Ber. 41b)

R. Ḥisda in Zeiri's name said that all incense required the blessing "who creates fragrant wood" except for musk, which, coming from a living creature, requires the benediction, "who creates various kinds of spices."[4] Rav Judah chose the blessing for Palestinian balsam oil.[5] He likewise required a blessing for spring fever:

> If one goes in Nisan and sees the trees sprouting (leaves) he should say, "Blessed is he who has not left anything out of his world, but has created in it pleasant creatures and pleasant trees for man's enjoyment."
>
> (b. Ber. 43b)

In a similar spirit, R. Sheshet required that the blessing "who creates fragrant herbs" be said over violets.[6] On the other hand, spices and incenses used to drive away bad odors required no blessing, according to R. Huna.[7]

The corpus of blessings reveals little innovation. Rav Judah, the most creative liturgist of this generation, really was merely developing Rav's legacy when he set forth blessings for prisoners who were freed or those who recovered from an illness, for Rav had found Scriptural warrant for such blessings, and it was simple enough to continue in the same way to define new ones based upon other current situations.[8] Similarly Rav and Samuel had reasoned from known principles in

[1] b. Ber. 38b. There are numerous examples in other matters as well.
[2] b. Ber. 39a.
[3] b. Ber. 41b.
[4] b. Ber. 43a.
[5] *ibid.*
[6] b. Ber. 43b.
[7] b. Ber. 53a.
[8] See b. Ber. 54b, and Vol. II pp. 169-70.

setting forth the blessings for foods whose benediction had not earlier been defined, and the current generation did exactly the same thing. R. Naḥman merely completed a Tannaitic benediction. The discussions of blessings for pepper, flour-honey-oil pulp, and the like centered on tertiary matters, left open by the earlier masters probably because they were inconsequential to begin with. The blessing for turnip-tops cut into small pieces vs. that for turnip-tops cut into large pieces hardly constituted a very important issue. The later generation invented remote and arcane issues for new discussion, the primary and important ones having been settled long ago. So I should conclude that these are strictly academic issues; the work of the rabbis in settling them would have had little to do with the needs of the masses, for whom large turnips and small ones would have logically demanded the same blessing, if any, and for whom the issue of which order of blessings a varied menu demanded would have meant nothing whatever. The blessings for the budding trees in spring and for violets remind us that the rabbis were deeply sensitive to the grandeur of nature, and eager to respond to its blessings with an appropriate benediction. So did the nomistic system gather force. Rav and Samuel had discussed mostly secondary matters, laying down no new principles, but spelling out the old ones. They had devised the logical methods, and explained the principles by which such benedictions would be assigned. They themselves had said nothing about the blessings for basic foods, as these had been well known for generations. By the end of the third century, even the most unusual and uncommon foods had already been discussed,[1] and the following generation had very little to say about the definition of blessings.

The same situation pertained to the grace after meals. Grace was, as we have seen, believed to have been decreed by Moses, Joshua, and David and Solomon, with a Tannaitic addition of a century and a half earlier also noted. Rav and Samuel had discussed such matters as these: What do you do if you leave out an important paragraph of the grace? What if one forgot to mention the festival on a festival day? Or the New Moon in the *Tefillah*?[2] What to do if one has entirely forgotten to say grace? These laws were taught in the academy, most frequently when the masters and disciples were eating. So the students learned from both the sayings and the actual practice of their masters. For this

[1] See also y. Ber. 7.2, b. Pes. 115a, R. Huna and R. Ḥisda on blessings over vegetables.

[2] On forgetting other prayers, see R. Naḥman and R. Sheshet, y. Ber. 4.4.

generation, few new issues remained. One was, What does one do if he forgot to say a blessing *before* he ate? Rav Judah taught that he puts the food to one side of his mouth and says the appropriate blessing.[1] I can think of no more striking example of the progression of legal issues through the generations. The former masters inquire what one must do if he forgets the *entire* grace, and the latter, if he forgets to say only the preliminary benediction. Other questions reveal a similar relationship. But the main effort was merely to review, not to improve upon, what the earlier masters taught:

> Rabbi Zeira was sitting behind R. Giddal and R. Giddal was sitting before R. Huna, and he (R. Giddal) was sitting and saying, "If he forgot and did not mention the Sabbath in the grace, he says, Blessed be he who gave Sabbaths for rest..." R. Huna said to him, "Who made this statement?" He replied, "Rav."
> (b. Ber. 49a)

Several other such citations of Rav's dicta by R. Giddal to R. Huna and R. Naḥman are here noted as well.[2] The sayings of Samuel were also spelled out by R. Huna and R. Ḥisda, on whether several groups may divide and form their own quorum for the purpose of saying grace.[3] Concerning the invitation to grace, R. Naḥman taught that one may count a child who is under age if he knows to whom the benedictions are addressed.[4] The act of saying grace continues, according to R. Naḥman until the conclusion of the call, and according to R. Sheshet, up to the end of the first paragraph of blessing.[5] Of particular interest at this time were laws pertaining to the "cup of blessing," wine which was consumed at the end of the grace. R. Naḥman in the name of Rabbah b. Abbuha said that it must contain a quarter of a *log* of wine.[6] Rav Judah "crowned" the cup with disciples, meaning that he required his students to sit about him when he said the blessing. R. Ḥisda surrounded it with cups.[7] The matter caused difficulty for R. Naḥman:

[1] b. Ber. 50b. For a discussion in this time of forgetting the grace afterward, see also b. Ber. 50b, R. Ḥisda was asked about it, For the requirement to say a blessing over thunder, see y. Ber. 9.2. R. Ḥisda holds that it is sufficient to say it once a day. But he does not contribute the *requirement* to say such a blessing, or the actual text of the blessing, both of which were, by this time, ancient. On a detail of the blessing over a new house, see R. Huna's comment on the Mishnah requiring it, b. Ber. 59b.

[2] And see b. Ber. 49b.

[3] b. Ber. 50a.

[4] b. Ber. 47b.

[5] b. Ber. 46a.

[6] b. ʿEruv. 29b.

[7] b. Ber. 51a.

> ʿUllah was once at the home of R. Naḥman. They ate, and he said grace, and handed the cup of blessing to R. Naḥman. R. Naḥman said, "Please send it to [my wife] Yalta." He said to him [that it was not necessary, and] Yalta meanwhile heard [that he refused to do so]. She got up in anger and went to the wine-cellar and broke four hundred jars of wine. R. Naḥman said to him, "Please send her another cup." He sent it with the message, "All that wine can be counted as a blessing. [That is, all the wine of the flask from which it has been poured]." She replied, "Gossip comes from pedlars and vermin from rags."
> (b. Ber. 5a-b)

The grace after meals posed complications, therefore, and the students in the academies, eating with their masters, were frequently corrected in the proper procedures concerning it.[1] Rav Judah, at the wedding feast for his son in the house of R. Judah b. Ḥabiba, informed the guests that the blessing "who brings forth bread from the earth" is not required over the dessert.[2] Before Rabba b. bar Ḥana made his marriage feast for his son, at the home of R. Samuel b. R. Qattina, he first informed his son:

> "The bridegroom may not break bread until the guests have finished responding Amen." R. Ḥisda said, "The majority of the guests..."
> (b. Ber. 47a)

R. Huna told Rabbah his son to be quick about snatching the cup of blessing to say grace, as did other rabbis.[3] Those whose fathers were not sages, or who did not frequent the academy, would doubtless not have known very much if anything about the etiquette of saying grace.[4]

The Sanctification of wine in honor of the Sabbath had been discussed mostly in peripheral terms by Rav and Samuel, for example, whether the Sanctification of the Sabbath could be recited over a substance other than wine. Rav held that it must be said over wine suitable for the altar, that it must be a quantity of "at least a mouthful," and the like. This generation continued to discuss such matters. R. Ḥisda (a beer manufacturer) asked R. Huna whether it was permitted to recite the Sanctification over beer. R. Huna replied that he had asked Rav, and that Rav had asked R. Ḥiyya, and that R. Ḥiyya had asked Rabbi

---

[1] R. Naḥman reports Rabbah b. Abbuha's teaching on erring by saying the weekly grace on the Sabbath, b. Ber. 21a.

[2] b. Ber. 42b.

[3] b. Nazir 66b. For Rav, see also Vol. II, p. 173.

[4] See also y. Ber. 7.1.

Judah the Prince, the answer being no.[1] R. Huna taught that the Sanctification may be said only where the meal was eaten:

> R. Huna recited the Sanctification and his lamp was upset, so he carried his utensils up to the marriage chamber of Rabbah his son, where a lamp was burning, recited it again, and then ate something, which proves that he holds the Sanctification is only where the meal is eaten.
>
> (b. Pes. 101a)

R. Ḥisda held that such a rule applied for a change of place from one house to another, but not from one place to another in the same house.[2] One may not recite more than one Sanctification over the same cup of wine, R. Huna said in R. Sheshet's name, while later on R. Naḥman b. Isaac explained the reason, that one may not perform religious duties in a wholesale fashion.[3] Here again one notes that if the issues facing the earlier generation were secondary, those of this one were still more remote.

A question that continued to trouble the later rabbis was whether one had to recite a blessing before study of the Torah. R. Huna held that for the reading of Scripture it is necessary to do so, but for the study of exegesis (midrash) no benediction was required. R. Ḥiyya b. Ashi reported that Rav would first wash his hands, say a blessing, and then go over the passage of the day. The benediction which was required had been set by Samuel:

> Rav Judah in Samuel's name said, "...who has sanctified us by your commandments and commanded us to study the Torah." R. Yoḥanan used to conclude, "Make pleasant therefore we beseech you, O Lord our God, the words of your Torah in our mouth and in the mouth of your people the house of Israel, so that we with our children and the children of your people the house of Israel may all know your name and study your Torah. Blessed are you, O Lord, who teaches Torah to your people Israel." R. Hamnuna said, "...Who has chosen us from all the nations and given us your Torah. Blessed are you, O Lord, who gives the Torah." R. Hamnuna said, "This is the best of all blessings."
>
> (b. Ber. 11b)[4]

The fact that a later figure, R. Hamnuna (or R. Huna) was able to compose a blessing despite the availability of those of Samuel and R. Yohanan suggests that no formula had achieved wide acceptance. But

---

[1] b. Pes. 107a.

[2] b. Pes. 102b.

[3] b. Pes. 102b.

[4] Rabinowicz, *Diq. Sof.*, I, 51, reads in place of R. Hamnuna, R. *Huna*.

as we have seen, where the academies had mostly agreed to a given formula, it was no longer possible to vary or change procedures, and only newer and more remote issues would permit variation.

A good insight into the academic problems of this generation is revealed by the reports of Rabbah about questions discussed at R. Huna's school, along with the answers he provided from Mishnaic or other Tannaitic traditions: Is it necessary to mention the New Moon in the prayers of the New Year? Does the blessing of the season ("who has kept us in life... and enabled us to reach this season") have to be recited on the Near Year and on the Day of Atonement or not, since the holidays are not described in Scripture as festivals? (Rav Judah answered the question by reference to Rav's and Samuel's dictum, that it was not required except on the three festivals). Does a student who kept a fast on the eve of the Sabbath have to complete it (as he would were the fast to fall on an ordinary day)?[1] These questions were not new, for, as the discussion makes abundantly clear, the principles required for answering them had been discussed in earliest Tannaitic times, even by the Schools of Shamai and Hillel; or were discussed, in directly pertinent form, in the Mishnah or in *beraitot.* The dialectic of the discussion would lead us to suppose that even the Tannaim had debated these very points. The question on the fast on the eve of the Sabbath, for example, elicited no reply from R. Huna, who had no ruling on the subject, nor did Rav Judah. Rabbah thereupon said that they should reason it out for themselves, which they did by reference to the 9th of Av. Yet immediately afterward is cited a *beraita* in which Rabbi Judah the Prince reports that in his presence, R. Aqiba and R. Yosi had debated the same principle, and by inference one may suppose that R. Gamaliel had laid down an appropriate rule on the matter, which was further discussed by R. Joshua and R. Yoḥanan b. Nuri. It is therefore striking that the later generation knew nothing of the matter, and specifically admitted that in the absence of other traditions, they would have to reason it out on their own. Later on, R. Joseph and Abaye also discussed it, and they referred to Rav Judah's inability to reply to Rabbah. One may therefore suppose that the real limitation of the preceding generation's discussions is this: where traditions were available to solve problems, such sayings were quite naturally consulted, but otherwise, the newer generation had an opportunity to make its own decisions. In this instance one can hardly conclude other-

[1] b. ʿEruv. 40a-b.

wise than that the Babylonian academies of R. Huna and Rav Judah simply did not know the Palestinian discussions of a century earlier, while later on, the data on these discussions became available to the editor of the Talmud.

In any event, the contribution of this generation becomes evident. Theirs was mostly a task of completion and application, rather than of formulation and innovation.[1] What the Tannaim had not made clear, Rav and Samuel mostly did, and by the end of the third century and the beginning of the fourth, the liturgical laws were fixed for the most part, and required little new effort. Evidence may be derived from a review of who participated, or was cited, in a Talmudic chapter on liturgy, namely, that in which the various blessings are discussed in detail. What we find is that while Rav and Samuel, and their disciples, R. Naḥman, R. Huna, Rav Judah, and others, for the most part provide *specific* laws, the *following* generation (Rava, Abaye) tends to discuss earlier Amoraic sayings and stories about their practices, or objects to Tannaitic teachings on the basis of other such teachings, or for the most part, derives new principles from earlier Tannaitic teachings. But they do *not* lay down further detailed laws. We have already surveyed the sayings of the second generation, and it is clear that the rabbis of that time mostly continued to do what their masters had done, that is, to define unclear areas of law, or decree blessings for those now remote and ever more obscure items which had earlier been ignored. In the following age, a new approach characterized the sayings of the sages, for they for the most part no longer either composed new prayers or transmitted the teachings of old masters, but now engaged in an intense, dialectical discussion of the material already in their hands. They raised objections or they contrasted one Tannaitic saying with another, or they compared such sayings against the reports of the actions of Amoraic masters. The generation under study saw its task as completing the work of the old, rather than of striking out in such new and unexplored directions.

Two other parts of the liturgy were the focus of attention in this period, as they had been earlier: the recitation of the *Shema*ʿ, and the repetition of the *Tefillah* (Eighteen Benedictions). In both instances, the disciples of Rav and Samuel continued in a straight line the inquiries of their masters, raising few new issues, and these mostly peripheral

---

[1] I suppose that a saying originated with the teacher in whose name it is cited. E.g., if a saying was cited by Rav Judah in the name of Samuel, it is credited to Samuel.

and tertiary. The requirement to recite the *Shema'* morning and night was a very old one, and the text of the *Tefillah* likewise had long ago been established. Precisely the questions discussed by Rav and Samuel were still pursued in this period. For example, Rav and Samuel had debated whether one might recite the *Shema'* in a place where urine was to be found. Samuel said that one ought not so long as it moistens the ground, and Rav, so long as the mark was discernible.[1] Rav Judah extended the matter:

> Rav Judah said, "If there is *doubt* about [the presence of excrement] it is forbidden. If there is doubt about urine, it is permitted..." R. Hamnuna said, "The Torah forbade reciting the *Shema'* only *before* a stream [of urine]."
>
> (b. Ber. 25a)

Similarly, if there was excrement on one's flesh, or if his hand was inside the privy, R. Huna said that he might recite the *Shema'*, while R. Ḥisda forbade it. If there was a bad odor emananting from some specific place, R. Huna said that one must move four cubits away to recite the *Shema'*, and R. Ḥisda said he was to move four cubits from the place where the smell ceases to be apparent. *Beraitot* supported R. Ḥisda's position.[2] R. Sheshet was asked about an odor which has no identifiable source:

> He replied, "See the mats in the school house. Some sleep on them while others study."
>
> (b. Ber. 25a)

The same problem was raised concerning wearing *tefillin* in a privy. R. Zevid, or Rav Judah, taught that one may restrain himself and continue his *Tefillah* if he can.[3] But if he must use the privy, and no regular one is available, R. Sheshet said that he may immediately remove his *tefillin* and make use of the place where he finds himself.[4] Rava reported concerning R. Naḥman that he would wear his *tefillin* in the privy for protection.[5]

Rav Judah was asked whether one may place his *tefillin* under his pillow, and he cited a saying of Samuel.[6] He was similarly asked whether, if two were sleeping in one bed, they were permitted to turn

---

[1] Vol. II, p. 178.

[2] b. Ber. 25a. Compare R. Huna and R. Ḥisda in b. Yoma 30a.

[3] b. Ber. 23a.

[4] b. Ber. 23a. R. Adda b. Ahavah similarly held that one may pray his *Tefillah* in the bath-house, b. Shab. 10a.

[5] *ibid.* against demons.

[6] b. Ber. 24a.

their backs to one another to recite the *Shema*ʿ, to which he replied again with a saying of Samuel.[1] On his own account, he forbade reciting the *Shema*ʿ in the presence of a naked gentile.[2] He required the first part of the *Shema*ʿ to be said standing.[3] In all, the principles of Rav and Samuel—and these antedated *their* time as well--were applied to new and ever more subtle questions,[4] but nothing much was changed nor were new principles enunciated.

The *Tefillah* had earlier been discussed by Rav and Samuel in such a way as to emphasize, in the spirit of the *Tannaim*, the exceptional sanctity of that prayer.[5] The recitation of the eighteen benedictions was seen as a direct confrontation with God, in which man praised, beseeched, and thanked the Creator for both public and personal blessings. An example of the way in which the later generation was limited in its study of the laws on the *Tefillah* is the following:

> [Mishnah: Even if a snake wound itself around his foot he should not break off.] R. Sheshet said, "This applies only in the case of a serpent, but if it is a scorpion, he breaks off..." (b. Ber. 33a)[6]

The limitation of Mishnah commentary permitted very little innovation, but rather a further setting of distinctions and search for ever narrower limitations. R. Huna similarly was quoted as saying in his own name a law on what to do if one erred in reciting the *Tefillah*, elsewhere quoted by him in Rav's name.[7] Rav Judah taught that one should beseech for his private needs during the middle blessings, and not at the beginning or the end.[8] One recalls that Rav Judah's Tanna recited a special prayer which was to be said if one was interrupted by personal need during the recitation of the *Tefillah*.[9] R. Huna gave a law pertaining to a man's entering the synagogue and discovering that the congregation was in the midst of the *Tefillah*.[10] R. Adda b. Ahava also

---

1 *ibid.*

2 b. Ber. 25b, Shab. 150a.

3 b. Ber. 13b.

4 E.g. b. Ber. 24b, R. Huna said, "If one's garment is wrapped around his waist (and his upper body is uncovered) he may recite the *Shema*ʿ." A Tannatic beraita taught the same. Similarly (b. Ber. 25a) if a man forgot and entered the privy wearing his *tefillin*,he covers them with his his hand until he finishes.

5 Vol. II, pp. 177-8.

6 See b. Ber. 14a, R. Sheshet objects, by citing a Mishnah, to a dictum of Rav and Samuel.

7 b. Ber. 34a vs. y. Ber. 5.3.

8 b. Ber. 34a.

9 b. Ber. 24b, see above p. 161.

10 b. Ber. 21b.

provided an exegesis to prove that a man praying by himself is not supposed to say the Sanctification.[1] But the practice long antedated his exegesis. Similarly R. Huna interpreted the Mishnah, that one who raises his voice in his *Tefillah* is a man of little faith, to apply to one who can otherwise direct his heart, but should he be unable to direct his heart through whispering (or silence), he is permitted to raise his voice.[2] He taught that one may eat nothing before saying the Additional *Tefillah* (*Musaf*) where required.[3] R. Kahana said that one who prays in a valley is regarded as arrogant.[4] R. Zera reported that he heard in R. Hamnuna's school that if one sneezes in saying his prayer, it is a good sign for him, "for as he is given relief below, so they give him relief above."[5] Rav Judah advised that if one is standing and reciting the *Tefillah* and spittle collects in his mouth, he should cover it in his robe, or in his scarf.[6] Many of these sayings represent mere repetitions of earlier ones. For instance, R. Huna's condemnation of raising one's voice in saying the *Tefillah* unless it is absolutely necessary merely repeats a saying of R. Judah the Prince, reported in the same place. At best, R. Huna was liberalizing R. Judah's flat prohibition. Others provide good counsel, not to pray in a valley, to be glad if one sneezes during prayer, what to do if one needs to expectorate, and the like. The *Tefillah* and most of the laws concerning its recitation were fixed, and there was little left to do but to collect odds and ends, and record them.

Rav and Samuel had discussed the proper order of the blessings of *Havdalah*, about which Samuel's father had already inquired of R. Judah the Prince in Palestine.[7] They had decreed that one must stand near enough to the light to make use of it if he should want to. Rav Judah's practice in conformity to this rule was recorded.[8] The Palestinian customs continued to concern the Babylonians, for when ʿUllah visited Pumbedita, Rav Judah sent his son R. Isaac to see how he recites the *Havdalah*.[9] R. Ḥisda defined what the Tannaim had meant by glowing coals, "over which a blessing may be made."[10]

The rabbis also set forth the rules of the priestly benediction. R. Ḥis-

[1] b. Ber. 21b, based on Lev. 22:32.
[2] b. Ber. 24b.
[3] b. Ber. 28b.
[4] b. Ber. 34b.
[5] b. Ber. 24b.
[6] *ibid.*
[7] Vol. II, pp. 174–5.
[8] b. Ber. 53b
[9] b. Pes. 104b
[10] b. Ber. 53b

da held that the precenter who signals the priests to proceed must be an Israelite. He also said that if only one priest was present, the precenter calls "Priest" rather than "Priests," but R. Huna differed:

> "Even though there is only one priest, he calls 'priests' for he is calling upon the *tribe*, so that no one may say, 'Such-and-such a man is an adulterer and a murderer and he yet blesses us!' The Holy One blessed be he has said, 'And who blesses you? I bless you...'"
>
> (y. Git. 5.9)[1]

R. Ḥisda who was a priest said that the blessing to be recited by the priest before raising his hands in the priestly benediction is as follows: 'Blessed are you, O Lord, our God, king of the universe, who has sanctified us with the sanctity of Aaron and told us to bless your people Israel with love.' R. Ḥisda appointed Rabbana 'Uqba as lecturer, and the latter exposited the prayer of the priest before his ascent, as follows, "Lord of the universe, we have performed what you have decreed for us, now fulfil with us what you have promised us, 'Look down from your holy habitation, from heaven'" (Deut. 26:15). R. Ḥisda also laid down other rules on the proper recitation of the priestly benediction by priests and congregation alike.[2] R. Huna said that a man whose eyes run should not lift up his hands in the priestly benediction, on which we have the following comment:

> But was there not such a man in the town of R. Huna? The townspeople were accustomed to him.
>
> (b. Meg. 24b)

The accepted practices of the people thus limited the ability of the rabbi to legislate about synagogue practice.

Our interest transcends the question of whether or not this generation made significant contributions to the development of Jewish liturgy. What is of greater interest is, What kind of religion is to be inferred from the prayers and rules of praying here considered? One needs first to note the ways in which the rabbis and the ordinary people together shared a common faith. These become most obvious in the compositions[3] of prayers. The rabbis' prayers centered upon four

---

[1] See also y. Ber. 5.4, Naḥman and R. Ḥisda.

[2] b. Sotah 39a–b

[3] Or citation with approval, for it is not completely clear to me that some of the prayers noted above were actually composed by Rav Judah, R. Ḥisda, and others who stated them. It may be that these prayers were available, and were selected from a number of alternate liturgies by the rabbis who said them, or in whose presence they were stated. But whatever their origin, the prayers do come under

major images, first, the Temple and its cult, second, the wrath of God which was revealed in an hour of crisis, third the humility and helplessness of man, and finally, the corpus of ideas and symbols embodied in the sacred history of Israel. The spiritual situation of both rabbis and the masses may be described as follows: 'We are absolutely worthless, and are now deprived even of the former ways of finding favor with You. Once there was a Temple, and we could offer sacrifice there, but now it is no more, so we must give the sacrifice of our flesh and blood. But who are we to propitiate, who are of no consequence and have no future? We are nothing, except that we are *Israel*, the children of men you loved, and bearers of the revelation you delivered. And so, even in the most private moments of life, we are not alone, but are surrounded by the merits of the fathers and the presence of memories of the sacred moments of our history. Nor are we hopeless, because we look forward to the fulfillment of the promises made to the prophets in olden times. So we are sanctified in all which we do out of love and loyalty to you. In the hour of our greatest private joy, at the marriage canopy, we remember both the public sorrow and the coming joy of Zion, and recall not only its destruction, but what was said by Jeremiah when it was destroyed, that it will be rebuilt. So if we are sinners, we lie in the hands of a God of great mercy. Even the passage of the seasons, which we witness regularly month by month, testifies to your enduring sovereignty. Just as the moon keeps your laws, so do we, and just as it testifies to the greatness of its maker, so would we. So when we find ourselves in a time of danger, we turn to you and beseech your blessing.' I see no detail in which ordinary people would have either not comprehended, or not believed in the faith of the rabbis as here expressed. While the prayers concerning study of the Torah and the discussions of proper procedures in the academies or of benedictions may not have been understood by the people, the spiritual situation revealed by the rabbis' prayers was precisely congruent, so far as I can tell, to theirs. They too were "Israel," and they revered the Scriptures, and remembered its lessons. They too longed for the coming of the Messiah, and though unable to express their yearnings in the evocative and noble language of the rabbis, they could surely have adopted the rabbinical liturgies without the least difficulty.

The precise and detailed discussions of how and when to pray, the proper blessings to say over one thing or another, the conditions for

---

discussion at this period, and the approval of the rabbis, if that is all it was, suggests that the compositions were congruent to the spirit of the age, or of the schools.

interrupting prayer and the like—these represent, as I said, a more narrowly academic concern.[1] I doubt that ordinary people were much bothered by the issues posed to the masters, nor did the instruction imparted to the disciples reach a broad audience. To learn the proper way of saying grace proved terribly difficult for many students, and outsiders could scarcely have comprehended all the rules. Indeed, knowing and keeping them was one of the important significations that a person had entered the rabbinical estate. Yet one must not suppose that the issues of the common faith were divorced from the rabbinical discussions, or that the legalistic rabbis really had no very vivid spiritual life. The prayers they composed testify to the contrary. But so too does the seriousness with which they considered the whole matter of prayer. It was precisely *because* they believed as fervently as ordinary people in prayer that they thought one should pray with at least the decorum and respect shown to an earthly king of kings, and that they seriously inquired into the proper and improper procedures for praying. In this sense, the rabbis' laws do represent the continuation of popular faith: if the people believed that prayer mattered, then the rabbis—who were, after all, lawyers—set out the rules of conduct and procedure which would conform to such a belief.

Above all, I am struck by the intensity of Rav Judah's prayers concerning the Messianic kingdom. In the liturgy for the marriage ceremony, the center of attention focused upon the coming joy of Zion, which was even now prefigured by the delight of bridegroom and bride. Just as the one loved the other, and rejoiced in that love, so in time would God again espouse Israel in Zion, and rejoice in her. The most private joy of life was thus seen to be paradigmatic for the most public event of coming history. As we have noted,[2] it was the Messianic hope which became most vivid in times of difficulty. If the academic discussions of when the Messiah might come and who he might be seemed less fervent than earlier, still the very deep and abiding longing for his coming characterized master, disciple, and outsider alike. However they might accommodate themselves to the conditions of the current life, the Jews saw it as merely transitory and impoverished. In time to come, the advent of the true and permanent age would inaugurate a time of fulfillment and completion. However private, personal, and ahistorical seem the prayers and discussions of these years, they must be seen against the broader framework of faith

[1] Vol. II, pp. 159-180.

[2] *ibid.*, pp. 52-57, and above, pp. 23-24.

in which they found a place. Within the humble affairs of Israel's life here and now, one might, though darkly, discern the shadowed reflections of a great illumination that was to come. Both in and for that light, Jews prayed.

VIII. Scriptural Exegesis

Practically everything the rabbis said and did was intended as a vivid exegesis of Torah, oral or written. One therefore can hardly distinguish between remarks on various non-legal passages, which we shall consider here, and the sayings cited above and below in which Scriptures are provided as proof-texts for ideas and imperatives alike. In the narrower realm of strict exegesis, we shall see, as earlier, that no very significant advances were made. Rav had composed what seems to me to be a history of the kingship of Saul, David, and Solomon, very much in the manner of the classical historians, fabricating dialogue and using verses in Samuel, Kings, Chronicles, Proverbs, and Psalms to provide the biblical basis for an extended account of the Messianic house.[1] In this generation, practically no similar broadly historical account was produced, nor were the numerous imaginative comments of the earlier generations greatly improved upon. As in other ways, this was a generation of completion. A great legacy of law and lore had come down to the disciples of Rav and Samuel, and they spent most of their scholastic energies in the task of reducing it to some order and preparing it for transmission to future ages. In the process, they themselves found little to add to what had already been said. But that was not the point. Innovation meant less than true apprehension of what had already been discovered or revealed. No higher achievement existed than to learn and do what others had already handed on. The purpose of the rabbis in studying Scripture was not to say something new, but rather to learn better what had been commanded of old. They wanted more than anything else to transform themselves into biblical-men, to embody the "Torah," or to become true disciples of those who did. If along the way, they turned to new forms of exegesis, as we shall see happened, so much the better. But ultimately what would be "new" was the way living men would assume ancient obligations in a new

---

[1] Vol. II pp. 201-206. On Rav's later influence, see Ẓuri, *Darkhei Halimud*, p. 3ff. Whether or not Rav's 'history of the Messiah' had contemporary implications I cannot determine.

time, and this had little to do with exegetical innovation, though in fact some new insights were bound to emerge therefrom.

Original[1] sayings on the book of Genesis pertained to the stories of Creation and Adam and Eve,[2] the flood, Abraham, and the Joseph narrative. The exegetical fashion of this time is best illustrated by the following:

> Rav Judah contrasted two texts: "It is written, 'And God created man in his own image' (Gen. 1:27) and also, 'Male and female he created them' (Gen. 5:2). In the beginning God thought of creating two, but in the end he made only one."
>
> (b. Ket. 8a)[3]

The contrasting of two texts and the resolving of supposed contradictions or inconsistencies between them were a commonplace exegetical device in this period, as we shall see again.[4] In this instance, the text seems to imply either two creations or one, and the intent is therefore unclear. Rav Judah clarified the matter by supposing a change in divine intention. He also said that Adam's bullock was a unicorn.[5] R. Ḥisda interpreted the use of "built" with reference to the creation of Eve (Gen. 2:22) to mean that she was built in the shape of a storehouse, wide below and narrow above; just as the one contains produce, so the other contains the embryo.[6] R. Ḥisda also said that he built more chambers in her than in man.[7] R. Huna said that Eve was called Adam, with reference to Is. 44:13.[8] He also said that Cain and Abel fought over the additional (female) twin that was born with Abel.[9] Stressing the appropriateness of the punishment of the generation of the flood, R. Ḥisda pointed out that it was with hot passion they sinned and by hot water were they punished.[10] Beasts with which bestiality had been committed were not accepted by the ark, R. Ḥisda said, with reference

[1] By 'original' I mean only that a given saying is reported first in the name of a tradent of this generation. I do not mean to infer that no one else ever said it, or that the sage could not have learned it by reference to, or by inference from, an earlier saying.

[2] Others are cited above, pp. 161-162.

[3] In the name of R. Abbahu in b. ʿEruv. 18a and Ber. 51a.

[4] See Bacher, *Agada*, 52-6 on the tripartite proofs, "from Torah, Prophets, and Writings," and below, p. 190.

[5] b. Ḥul. 60a, on the basis of Ps. 79:32.

[6] b. ʿEruv. 18a. See the blessings of Rav Judah, cited above, p. 161, for the same inference.

[7] Gen. R. 18:3.

[8] *ibid.* 21:2.

[9] *ibid.* 22:7.

[10] b. Sanh. 108b, with reference to Gen. 8:1 and Esther 7:10.

to Gen. 7:2. Rav Judah taught that God promised Abraham to create for him a new creation.[1] R. Ḥisda in a parallel comment said with reference to "After I have waxed old, I have had youth" (Gen. 18:12).

> "After the flesh is worn, and the wrinkles have multiplied, the flesh was rejuvenated, and the wrinkles were smoothed out, and beauty returned."
>
> (b. B.M. 87a)[2]

R. Naḥman in the name of Rabbah b. Abbuha said that Sarah had no womb.[3] R. Adda b. Ahava said that Jacob warned his sons against cold and heat, which are in the hands of heaven.[4] R. Ḥisda explained that Joseph's brothers did not know him (Gen. 42:8) because he did not have a beard when they sold him to Egypt.[5] R. Naḥman explained (Gen. 46:1) that Jacob went by way of Beer Sheva because he wanted to cut down the trees which Abraham his grandfather had planted there.[6] It was the vision of Jacob's face which calmed the ardor of Joseph when confronted with Potiphar's wife, according to R. Huna.[7]

The 'daughter of Levi' referred to in Ex. 2:1 would have been one hundred and thirty years old. Rav Judah explained that she is called a daughter because the signs of virginity were reborn in her.[8] R. Naḥman interpreted the 'watchnight' (Ex. 12:42) to refer to a night which is guarded from devils.[9] R. Adda b. Ahavah said it was with agreement that Moses ascended the mountain and likewise descended.[10] The *mem* and *samekh* engraved in the tablets stood by a miracle, R. Ḥisda said, for the centers of the two letters, if normally written as the rabbis would have inscribed them, would have fallen out.[11] Beẓalel made three arks, Rav Judah taught.[12] He also said that the tribe of Levi did not participate in the incident of the Golden Calf (Ex. 32:26).[13] R. Ḥisda

[1] Tanḥuma Ḥayye Sarah, ed. Buber I, 119.
[2] Trans. H. Freedman, (London, 1948) p. 502.
[3] b. Yev. 64b.
[4] b. Ket. 30a, re Gen. 42:4.
[5] b. Yev. 88a.
[6] Gen. R. 94:4, Song R. 1.12.1.
[7] Gen. R. 87:7, re Gen. 39:11. See also Midrash Samuel 5:16, R. Huna in the name of R. Mattena.
[8] b. Sotah 12a.
[9] b. Pes. 109b. Hence the night of Passover is secure from demons.
[10] b. Shab. 86a.
[11] b. Shab. 104a, Meg. 3a.
[12] b. Yoma 72b. And R. Hamnuna said that the decree that all would die in the wilderness (Num. 26:65) in that generation did not apply to the Levites. See also R. Huna, y. Pe'ah 1:1, on Beẓalel in Ex. 35.
[13] *ibid.* 66b.

interpreted Lev. 20:25, with reference to violence and oppression, that oppression referred to a continual deferment of payment, while robbery referred to outright refusal to pay.[1] R. Mattena understood Lev. 25:9, "and thou shalt proclaim" to require the usual manner of proclamation.[2] Eldad and Medad (Num. 11:26) prophesied concerning Gog and Magog, according to R. Naḥman.[3] Cozbi (of the same event) falsified her father's teaching, R. Sheshet taught.[4] "The Lord shall open unto you his good treasure" (Deut. 28:12) means that when Israel does God's will and is settled in its own land,[5] then rain comes down from a good treasury, but otherwise, it does not.[6]

These comments present a striking contrast to those of Rav and Samuel on the Pentateuch.[7] They are, first of all, mostly unrelated to one another, sparse and fragmentary. We find no equivalent to the continuous commentaries ascribed to Rav and Samuel concerning several sections of the Pentateuch. Since many of the earlier generation's comments were transmitted by Rav Judah and others of his time, one might suppose that the later rabbis mostly concentrated upon organizing and transmitting the teachings of the preceding masters. Neither theology nor homily dominates here, but rather, an occasional comment intended to respond to an occasional question. Specific words, or obvious questions, elicited most attention. What does the text mean in saying that "Eve was built?" Why did Cain and Abel fight? Were *all* beasts admitted into the ark? What was the 'watch-night' guarded *from*? Were the Levites guilty along with all Israel? What was the content of the prohecy of Eldad and Medad? If Cozbi's name recalls the Hebrew root 'to falsify,' then what did she do to deserve the name? The sermonic comments, such as R. Ḥisda's on the 'good treasure' are few and far between. One may rightly suppose that for this generation, the chief interest in the non-legal passages of the Pentateuch was mostly to expound what the given text said, rather than, as in Rav's and Samuel's case, to extend and expand upon it. Rav's genius in enhancing the narrative by additional speeches in the manner of the Greek historians was not handed on; very few similar accounts were provided by the following generation.

[1] b. B.M. 111a.
[2] b. R.H. 34a.
[3] b. Sanh. 17a.
[4] b. Sanh. 82b.
[5] b. Shab. 64b.
[6] b. B.B. 25b.
[7] Reviewed in vol. II pp. 187-198.

Apart from the exilarch's question to R. Huna on Joshua 7:24,[1] the only strictly exegetical comment on the book of Joshua and Judges concerned the 'concubine of Geva' (Judges 19:2), R. Ḥisda holding that her husband had terrified her and hence brought on a great calamity, which proves that a husband should not intimidate his household.[2] R. Naḥman said that Ḥulda was a descendent of Joshua.[3] He supposed that Rahab had converted to Judaism and married Joshua. He also held that haughtiness does not befit women, which is proved by Judges 4:6 and II Kings 22:15.[4] Such comments, using the text as a proof or pretext for some antecendent thought, indicate less about what R. Naḥman understood Scripture originally to have meant than how he now found it useful.

Exegesis could lead to complications:

> 'Saul was one year old when he began to reign' (I Sam. 13:1). R. Huna said, "Like an infant of one year, who knew not sin." R. Naḥman b. Isaac objected, "Perhaps like an infant, filthy with mud and excrement?" He thereupon was shown a frightening vision in his dream, and said, "I beg your pardon, bones of Saul son of Kish." He again saw such a vision in his dream, and said, "I beg your pardon, bones of Saul son of Kish, *king* of Israel."
>
> (b. Yoma 22b)

The belief that such things could happen would have led to considerable caution in commenting on the biblical heroes. R. Sheshet found in II Sam. 3:39 proof that impudence is sovereignty without a crown.[5] R. Ḥisda said that Michal had a child on the day she died (II Sam. 6:23).[6] R. Ḥisda reconciled II Sam. 6:13 and I Chron. 15:26, 'at six paces, he sacrificed an ox and a fatling' vs. 'they sacrificed seven bullocks and seven rams' to indicate that at each six paces, an ox and a fatling were offered, and at each six sets of six paces, the offering of sevens.[7] R. Huna similarly ironed out the contradictions between II Sam. 7:10, 'to afflict them,' and I Chron. 17:9, 'to exterminate them,' saying that at first the intention was merely to afflict, but at the end, to exterminate them.[8] David's execution of "justice and righteousness" (II Sam. 8:15)

---

[1] Cited above p. 82.

[2] b. Git. 6b. Note also R. Kahana on Jud. 21:12, how did they know the 400 virgins were virgins, b. Yev. 60b.

[3] b. Meg. 14b. based on II Kings 22:14 and Jud. 2:9.

[4] *ibid.*

[5] b. Sanh. 105a, see above, p. 71.

[6] b. Sanh. 21a.

[7] b. Sotah 35b.

[8] b. Ber. 7b.

was discussed by Rav Judah and R. Naḥman. According to Rav Judah, if a person was guilty but could not pay his fine, David would provide the money, hence, "justice (= charitableness) and righteousness." R. Naḥman said that such would have encouraged deceit. Rather, David made the guilty party give up the stolen object.[1] The counter-posing of two elements of one Scripture, or two separate Scriptures was not new in this generation. Samuel, cited by R. Papa above, was portrayed as discussing the matter with R. Ḥisda, and there are other such examples of this kind of exegesis dating from the earlier generation.[2] But it seems to me that while the repertoire of Rav and Samuel was considerably broader, that of this generation laid special emphasis precisely upon such scholastic exegesis. There are numerous instances in which R. Huna, or R. Ḥisda, or R. Naḥman, would pose one Scripture as a challenge to another, and iron out the apparent contradiction, but few examples, as I said, of the creative historiography of Rav in the earlier time. The arts of logical distinction and penetrating analysis of questions uncovered in apparent contradictions of a given text were ever more intensively cultivated.[3]

On II Sam. 21:8, "but the king took two sons... and the five sons of Michal..." R. Huna answered the question, Why just these? He said that all the surviving descendants of Saul were made to pass before the ark, and those whom it retained were condemned to death.[4] Araunah (II Sam. 24:22) was a resident alien, R. Naḥman said.[5] Rav Judah and R. Naḥman debated the meaning of "twelve officers" who provided food for the king, one holding that a single officer supervised the others, the other that there was a special officer in charge of provisions during the intercalated month.[6] R. Hamnuna explained the meaning of I Kings 5:12, that Solomon spoke three thousand proverbs and one thousand five songs, to mean that he uttered three thousand proverbs for every single word of Torah, and one thousand five reasons for every teaching of the scribes.[7] R. Ḥisda derived from I Kings 8:59, "the judgment of

[1] Deut. R. 5:3.

[2] E.G. vol. II p. 192, re Gen. 39:1 and 41:45, etc.

[3] For another such example, see, R. Huna, I Chron. 14:12 vs. II Sam. 5:21, in b. A.Z. 44a. The Books of Samuel and Kings and Chronicles provided an especially rich field for such harmonizations, for obvious reasons, but I do not think that these were the center of academic interest in preference to other Scriptures on that account. See also b. Sanh. 21b, Rav Judah on I Kings 5:6 vs. II Chron. 9:25.

[4] b. Yev. 79a.

[5] b. A.Z. 24a.

[6] b. Sanh. 12a, re I Kings 4:19.

[7] b. ʿEruv. 21b.

his servant [Solomon] and the judgment of his people," that when the king and community appear together for trial, the king is judged first.[1] R. Huna interpreted the meaning of "land of Kabul" (I Kings 9:13) to mean, "a land whose inhabitants were smothered (mekubalin) with gold and silver."[2] R. Naḥman held that Jeroboam's learning was flawless[3] but his conceit was his downfall.[4] supplying Jeroboam's reasoning in preventing the Israelites from making pilgrimages to Jerusalem: If the people see that Rehoboam sat in the Temple court (a privilege reserved for the house of David) while he *stood*, they would conclude that Jeroboam was merely his subject. If he sat too, he would be guilty of rebellion against royal authority. So his scholarship led him to perdition. These comments do not yield a whole or full portrait of David, Solomon, or other great heroes of First Temple times. While we have not exhausted every comment on the books of Samuel and Kings, most of those omitted deal with the explanation of an occasional word or phrase. None would significantly alter the picture to be gained from this brief survey. It is striking that no one further sought the potential insights made available by Rav's methods and approaches.[5] It is as if all he left were sayings and stories, but no new *way* of reading these or other Scriptures.

An exception to the rule is provided by R. Hamnuna's discussion of the relationships between Isaiah and Ḥezekiah:

> R. Hamnuna said, "What is the meaning of the Scripture, 'Who is as the wise man? And who knows the interpretation of a matter' (Qoh. 8:1)? Who is like the Holy One blessed be he who knows how to effect a reconciliation between two righteous men, between Ḥezekiah and Isaiah. Ḥezekiah said, 'Let Isaiah come to me, for we find that Elijah went to Ahab' (I Kings 18:2). Isaiah said, 'Let Ḥezekiah come to me, for so we find regarding Jehoram son of Ahab that he came to Elisha' (II Kings 3:12). What did the Holy One blessed be he do? He brought suffering upon Ḥezekiah and said to Isaiah, 'Go and visit the sick,' as it is said, 'In those days was Ḥezekiah sick unto death, and Isaiah the prophet son of Amoz came to him and said to him, So says the Lord, Set your house in order for you shall die and not live.' (Is. 38:1) ...He [Ḥezekiah] said to him, 'Why all this?' He [Isaiah] replied, 'Because you did not engage in being fruitful and multiplying.' He said, 'The reason was that I saw by the Holy Spirit that there would go forth from me

[1] b. R.H. 8b, 16a, see also b. A.Z. 2b.
[2] b. Shab. 54a.
[3] b. Sanh. 102a, re I Kings 11:29.
[4] b. Sanh. 101b, I Kings 12:26 and 28.
[5] Vol. II pp. 199-217.

unworthy children.' He said to him, 'What have you to do with the secrets of the All-Merciful? What you were commanded you should have done, and what is pleasing to the Holy One, blessed be he, let him do.' He [Ḥezekiah] said to him, 'Then give me your daughter. Perhaps my merit and your merit combined will produce from me virtuous children.' He replied, 'Already has the decree concerning you been issued.' He said, 'Son of Amoz, Finish your oracle and get out. So I have received from my father's father's house, that even though a sharp sword is hanging over one's shoulder, he should not restrain himself from praying for mercy...' Forthwith 'And Ḥezekiah turned his face to the wall and prayed unto the Lord' (Is. 38:2)." (b. Ber. 10a-b)

This comment, in the manner of Rav, is quite exceptional. For the most part, exegesis was close and prosaic. R. Huna said that Sennacherib made ten marches in one day, with reference to Is. 10:28-31.[1] Sennacherib had been so advised by his soothsayers:

"If you proceed to attack now, you will conquer it." So the journey that should have taken ten days he made in one, When Jerusalem was reached, mattresses were piled up until he climbed up and could see the whole of Jerusalem. When he saw it, it looked small, "Is this the city of Jerusalem for which I set all my troops in motion and conquered the whole country? It is smaller and weaker than all the cities of the nations which I have subdued by my might..."

He gestured contemptuously toward the Temple on Zion and the Court. The astrologers again urged an immediate attack, but he said the people were too worn out. That night the angel of the Lord slew his army.[2] R. Ḥisda contrasted two verses in Isaiah (Is. 24:23 and 30:26), one of which spoke of the moon's and the sun's being ashamed, and the other, of the light of the moon's shining like that of the sun. The former he applied to the world to come, the latter, to the days of the Messiah.[3] Commenting on "With him also that is of a contrite and humble spirit" (Is. 57:15), R. Huna and R. Ḥisda differed:

One says that it means, the contrite is with me, the other, that I am with the contrite. (b. Sotah 5a)

The exilarch asked R. Huna the meaning of Is. 58:13, ['and you will call... the holy of the Lord honored']. He replied, "This refers to the Day of Atonement, on which is neither eating nor drinking, so the Torah prescribed that it be honored with clean garments."[4]

[1] b. Sanh. 94b.
[2] *ibid.* 95a.
[3] b. Pes. 68a, Sanh. 91b.
[4] b. Shab. 119a.

No substantial exegeses of Jeremiah are extant, apart from those implied by Rav Judah.[1] R. Ḥisda made three comments on Ezekiel. He explained Ezek. 4:10, "And thou shalt eat it as barley cakes" to mean "in fixed quantities," on account of the siege.[2] Second, the law forbidding an uncircumcized priest from performing the sacrificial service derives not from the revelation of Moses, but from Ezekiel 44:9; it had been a tradition, for which Ezekiel provided a Scriptural basis.[3] Third, Ezek. 48:19 proves that in the world to come, the king will get an extra portion of the land of Israel.[4] The vision of the four craftsmen (Zech. 2:3), was explained by Rav Ḥana b. Biznah in the name of R. Simeon the Pious as follows: "The Messiah son of David, the Messiah son of Joseph, Elijah, and the Righteous Priest." R. Sheshet objected to this explanation, but to no avail, and admitted that he had no place in circles studying expositions of Scriptural lore.[5] The thirty pieces of silver (Zech. 11:12) signify the thirty righteous men of the world, according to Rav Judah.[6] Rav Judah explained the name of Hosea's wife, Gomer, "That they wished to finish off (GMR) the wealth of Israel in her time."[7] R. Mattena explained Hab. 3:2:

> R. Mattena said, "'He stood and measured the earth, he beheld'... What did he see? He saw the seven commandments which were accepted by all the descendants of Noah, and since (some) rejected them, he rose up and exiled them from their lands..." (b. B.Q. 38a)

Rav Judah and R. ʿEna debated the meaning of Ps. 11:3, "When the foundations are destroyed, what have the righteous accomplished?" One said, "If Ḥezekiah and his followers had been destroyed, what would the righteous have achieved?" The other said, "If the Temple had been destroyed, what would the righteous have achieved."[8] Both followed the contemporary interpretation which held that the Scripture referred to Is. 22. Rav Judah interpreted Ps. 18:26, 'With the merciful you show yourself merciful' to apply to Abraham's relationship to God. When he was merciful, frank, or subtle, the Holy One was similarly predisposed.[9] Rav Judah said that Ps. 44:23 referred to

[1] Above p. 161.
[2] b. ʿEruv. 81a.
[3] b. Taʿanit 17b, Yoma 71b, Zev. 18a.
[4] b. B.B. 122a.
[5] B. Suk. 52b.
[6] b. Ḥul. 92a.
[7] b. Pes. 87b.
[8] b. Sanh. 26b.
[9] Lev. R. 11:5.

Hannah and her seven sons.[1] R. Mattena explained the *shor par* (bullock) of Ps. 69:32 as an ox which is full grown.[2] R. Hamnuna counterposed Ps. 119:11 and Ps. 40:10, both of which he thought pertained to Ira the Jairite, the former when he was alive, the latter when he was dead.[3] A verse in Ps. 119 elicited a *Shiʿur Qomah* exegesis:[4]

> R. Ḥisda cited the exposition of Mari b. Mar, "What is the meaning of the Scripture, 'I have seen an end to every purpose, but your commandment is very broad' (Ps. 119:96)? This statement was made by David but he did not explain it. So said Job, but did not explain it, and similarly Ezekiel. [So the exact magnitude remained unknown] until Zechariah b. Iddo came and explained it. It was made by David but he did not explain it, for it is written in Scripture, 'I have seen an end... but your commandment is very broad.' Job similarly said, 'The measure thereof is longer than the earth and broader than the sea (Job 11:9).' Ezekiel likewise, 'And he spread it before me and it was written within and without, and there was written therein lamentations and meditation of joy and woe' (Ezek. 2:10). 'Lamentation' refers to the retribution of the just in this world, for so it is said, 'This is the lamentation wherewith they shall lament' (Ezek. 32:16), and the latter refers to the reward of the righteous in the hereafter... But Zechariah b. Iddo came and explained it, for it is written, 'And he said to me, What do you see? And I replied, I see a folded roll, the length is twenty cubits and the breadth ten cubits' (Zec. 5:2), and when you unfold it, it is twenty by twenty, and since it is written, 'It was written within and without,' what will be its size when you split it? Forty cubits by twenty. But it is written, 'Who has measured the waters in the hollow of his hand and meted out heaven with the span' (Is. 40:12). It follows that the entire universe is equal to one three thousand and two hundreds part of the Torah.
>
> (b. ʿEruv. 21a)

R. Giddal derived from Ps. 119:106 the rule that one may take a vow to keep the commandments.[5] Commenting on Ps. 126:5, 'Those that sow in tears reap in rejoicing,' Rav Judah said, "When the ox is ploughing on his forward journey he weeps, but on his return he eats the young green from the furrows."[6] R. Ḥisda said that 'Hallelujah' marks the end of a chapter of Psalms.[7] Apart from a few citations in other connections, I have found few consequential exegeses of Proverbs.[8]

---

[1] b. Git. 57b. Note Rav Judah on Ḥanukkah, below, p. 254.
[2] b. R.H. 26a.
[3] b. ʿEruv. 63a.
[4] See above, p. 149ff.
[5] b. Tem. 3b.
[6] b. Taʿanit 5a.
[7] b. Pes. 117a.
[8] R. Sheshet on Prov. 3:16, b. Shab. 63a.

R. Zera in the name of Rav Judah, or R. Ḥisda, or R. Mattena proved from Job 22:28 that a righteous man can annul the decree of God.[1] R. Hamnuna said that a sick man returns to the days of his youth after he is healed, on the basis of Job 33:25.[2] When the south wind blows, it stills all other winds, R. Taḥalifa son of R. Ḥisda said in the name of his father, on the basis of Job 37:17.[3] Rav Judah explained the meaning of a word in Job 38:31.[4] The deliverance referred to in Lam. 1:14 was, R. Ḥisda said in the name of Mar ʿUqba b. Ḥiyya, from a bad wife with a large marriage-settlement.[5] Comments on the Esther Scroll were narrowly exegetical. 'Mordecai returned to the gate of the king' means, R. Sheshet said, that he returned to his sack-cloth and fasting.[6] R. Huna said that Qoh. 11:9, 'Rejoice young man' was spoken mostly by the Evil Impulse.[7] Ezra 10:19 teaches, R. Ḥisda said, that all had intercourse with designated hand-maids.[8] The blessing of Ezra (Neh. 8:6) was, R. Giddal said, 'Blessed be the Lord, the God of Israel, from everlasting to everlasting' (I Chron. 16:36).[9] R, Mattena said that he recited, 'The great, might, and awful God' (Neh. 9:32).[10] 'And they cried with a loud voice to the Lord...' (Neh. 9:4). Rav Judah (or R. Jonathan) said this is what they cried:

> "Woe, woe it is that [idolatry] which destroyed the Sanctuary, burned the Temple, slew the righteous, and exiled Israel from their land, still is among us. Have you not set it among us so that we may be rewarded [for resisting temptation]. But we want neither the temptation nor the reward for resisting it." They fasted for three days asking for mercy, and their sentence fell from heaven, with the word 'truth' inscribed upon it. The figure of a fiery lion's whelp issued from the Holy of Holies, and the prophet said, "That is the tempter of idolatry." While they held it fast, a hair fell out, and his roar of pain was heard four hundred parasangs. They cried, "What shall we do? Perhaps

[1] y. Taʿanit 3.10.
[2] b. Ned. 41a.
[3] b. Git. 31b. Compare b. B.B. 25b, R. Ḥisda says that the north wind makes gold flow, on the basis of Job 37:22 and Is. 46:6.
[4] b. Ber. 58b.
[5] b. Yev. 63b.
[6] b. Meg. 16a. Other relevant comments are R. Ḥisda, b. Meg. 15b, R. Naḥman on the crowning of Mordecai, b. Meg. 12b, and R. Ḥisda, that at first Ahashueros ruled seven, then, twenty, then one hundred provinces, b. Meg. 11a. This last is a reflection of a dispute of Rav and Samuel, see Vol. II, 57-64, 288-290.
[7] b. Shab. 63b.
[8] b. Ker. 11a.
[9] b. Yoma 69b. In Palestine, R. Giddal's exegesis was corrected according to the antecedent question of Abaye.
[10] *ibid.*

> Heaven will pity him." The prophet answered, "Cast him into a lead pot, and cover it with lead to absorb his voice," as it is written, "And he said, This is wickedness, and he cast it into the midst of the ephah... (Zech. 5:8)." Then they said, "Since the time is ripe, let us pray that the tempter of Sin [may likewise be delivered]." They did so, and it was. They imprisoned it for three days. After that they looked for a newly-laid egg for an invalid in all of Palestine, but could not find one. Then they said, "What shall we do? Shall we pray that his power be partially destroyed? Heaven will not grant it." So they blinded it with rouge. This was so far effective that one does not lust for incestuous relations.
>
> (b. Sanh. 64a)[1]

R. Ḥisda proved from II Chron. 19:11 that at first officers were appointed only from the Levites.[2] Two exegeses on the Song of Songs continued the earlier tendency to relate various scriptures to study of the Torah and practice of the commandments.[3]

Other noteworthy kinds of exegesis are, first, the exegeses of "threes," that is, triplicate analyses, or triplicate proofs of a given proposition, based upon Pentateuch, Prophets, and Writings. These are exemplified in the following:

> A certain Galilean lectured before R. Ḥisda, "Blessed be the All-Merciful who gave a tripartite Torah to a tri-partite people through a third-born on the third day of the third month."
>
> (b. Shab. 88a)

Israel consisted of priests, Levites, and Israelites; Moses was born after Miriam and Aaron.

> Rabbah b. R. Huna in the name of R. Huna[4] said: "From the Pentateuch, Prophets, and Writings it may be shown that on the way a man wishes to go he is led."
>
> (b. Mak. 10b)

The proofs are Num. 22:12 and 20; Is. 48:17, and Prov. 3:34. A second type of exegesis consisted in proving "from Scripture" or "from the Torah" that a well-known truth or obvious fact was revealed from heaven. That approach was very hoary. When Rav came to Babylonia, Samuel sent Qarna to test him in just such a way.[5] It was apparently a popular pastime:

---

[1] But compare the account in b. Yoma 69b, in R. Giddal's name.

[2] b. Yev. 86b.

[3] R. Ḥisda in Mar ʿUqba's name on 5:11, b. ʿEruv. 21b, and R. Ḥisda on 7:14, *ibid.* See vol. II pp. 222-229.

[4] Or, Rabba b. B. Ḥana in the name of R. Huna, or R. Huna in the name of R. Eleazar b. Pedat.

[5] Vol. II p. 128, "How do we know blood is red?" (= II Kings 3:22) etc.

The men of Papunia asked R. Mattena "...Where is Moses indicated in the Torah?" He replied, "In the verse, 'For that he also is flesh' (Gen. 6:3)".[1] "Where is Haman in the Torah?" "In the verse, 'Is it from tree' (Gen. 3:1)".[2] "Where is Esther indicated in the Torah?" "'And *I will surely hide* my face' (Deut. 31:18)".[3] "Where is Mordecai indicated in the Torah?" "In the verse, 'Flowing myrrh', as in the Targum *mira dakia*. (Ex. 30:23)".

(b. Ḥul. 139b)

This is obviously an example of "Purim-Torah," in which the most fantastic plays on words or far-fetched questions were brought forward. An equally jocular inquiry is that of Yalta to R. Naḥman her husband, matching prohibitions with Scriptural permissions: Everything Scripture prohibits also has an equivalent permission, blood is forbidden but liver permitted and the like.[4] One recalls also the ability of the rabbis to provide Scriptural warrants for popular apothegms. A further example, produced by this generation, is as follows:

R. Aḥa b. R. Huna in name of R. Sheshet said, "This Scripture bears out the popular saying, 'A full stomach is a bad sort,' as it says, 'When they were fed they became full, they were filled and their heart was exalted; therefore they have forgotten me' (Hos. 13:6)." R. Naḥman derived it from here, 'Then thy heart may be lifted up and thou shalt forget the Lord' (Deut. 8:14).

(b. Ber. 32a)

A good example of the kind of Scriptural discussion of this time is provided by the following account:

R. Naḥman said to R. Isaac: "What is the meaning of the verse, 'For the Lord has called for a famine, and it shall also come upon the land seven years' (II Kings 8:1). What did they eat during that time?" He replied, "So said R. Yoḥanan, 'In the first year they ate what was hoarded in the houses, in the second, what was in the fields...?" Further R. Naḥman asked R. Isaac, "What is the meaning of the verse, 'The Holy One is in the midst of thee, and I will not come into the city' (Hos. 11:9). [Surely it cannot be that] because the Holy One is in the midst of thee, I shall not come into the city." He replied, "Thus said R. Yoḥanan, 'The Holy One... said, I will not enter the heavenly Jerusalem until I can enter the earthly Jerusalem.'" "Is there then a heavenly Jerusalem?" "Yes, for it is written, 'Jerusalem, thou art built as a city that is compact together' (Ps. 122:3)."

(b. Ta'anit 5a-b)

[1] The numerical value of the Hebrew 'for that also' is equivalent to that of Moses's name.

[2] Esther 7:10, a play on the Hebrew "is it from" and the name of Haman.

[3] *astir*.

[4] b. Ḥul. 109b.

So the conversation continued, on the meaning of Jer. 10:8 explained by reference to Jer. 10:15, I Samuel 8:1, explained by reference to I Samuel 15:11, etc., and in each case, R. Yoḥanan's teaching was cited to solve the problem raised by R. Naḥman.

IX. Summary

We have now considered three aspects of the rabbinate: the rabbi as lawyer, magician, and academician. Earlier the rabbis appeared to constitute a party of lawyers, judges, and teachers of the law, which for apparently theological reasons aspired to displace the established Jewish authority, the exilarchate, and to substitute their claim to political power, based upon knowledge of "the whole Torah," for his, based upon Davidic ancestry and imperial support. But it quickly became apparent that the rabbinate transcended its partisan guise. The rabbi also seemed to be a "holy man," who possessed considerable personal charisma and was believed able to do miraculous deeds. In our review of rabbinical theology, liturgy, and exegesis, we have seen the rabbi as a school-man, whose intellectual life was shaped by earlier generations. He enjoyed considerable latitude in providing alternative answers to classical questions, but raised few really new issues concerning the basic studies of the academy, asked few genuinely innovating questions. He found a snug place within the previous interpretive tradition. His teachers—and theirs—were presumed to have shown the way, raising all possible logical questions, leaving nothing basic for the later generations to contend with. Any other presumption would have indicated a disbelief in the fundamental wisdom of the masters.[1]

So like other "holy men," the rabbi played political, religious, and cultural roles. Just as the Magus was involved in the administration of the local community, in the maintenance of cultic life, and in the study and teaching of Mazdean beliefs and possibly, by this time, Scriptures, so too was the rabbi. While the Magus, however, never aspired to overthrow or subvert the Sasanian dynasty, but only to serve as a significant and influential part of its administration and to constitute its religious arm, the rabbis wanted independently to exercise quite direct and substantial power over the Jewish community. I do not think that in this period, such a difference was readily to be discerned, for it was only

[1] See Edward M. Gershfield, "The Value of Comparative Law," *Conservative Judaism* 21, 1, 1966, 49-56, esp. p. 51.

Geniva who apparently acted according to such aspirations. The lines were nonetheless drawn and the direction of rabbinical policy quite clear. On the one side were rabbis such as Naḥman and Rabbah b. Abbuha, who would correspond to Kartir, "the soul-savior of Bahram." These would represent the closest parallel to the leading Magi. On the other were R. Sheshet and those who shared his disdain for, and suspicion of, the exilarch. To these I see no clear counterpart among the Magi.

As we shall see, a more significant parallel is to be drawn to the Christian "religious," the monastic figures who dominated the Christian faith east of the Euphrates and shaped its character. Unlike the Christian monks, however, it was the aspiration of the rabbi *not* to form a separate society. He kept to himself very little. He did not live in a tight little eschatological community, confidently awaiting the day on which the sinners would know that he was right and they were wrong. He did not, for all his sense of forming part of an elite, look upon the rest of the community as outsiders or less 'elect' than himself. At many important points he shared the fundamental convictions of the broader community. What he most wanted was to teach the people how to live up to these convictions as *he* understood them. So if he was not a sectarian, the reason was that he aspired to a wider influence than others. He wanted all the Jews to become rabbis. He asked *nothing* of himself that he felt inapplicable to others, and nothing of others that did not pertain to himself. Herein lies a paradox of the rabbinical "estate." On the one hand, it was separate and, by its own standard, superior. On the other, it hoped to obliterate the distinctions between the rabbinate and other Jews, and believed that every Jew was equally able to achieve "superiority." So its aspiration to political power, at once so partisan and subversive of existing authority, represented a perfectly natural extension of its self-understanding. It was through politics that people might be changed. Through the courts and collaboration with the regime that set them up, the most effective influence might be attained. Indeed, when one seeks to locate the points of contact between the rabbi and the town, he finds them less in the marketplace, synagogue, or in the streets, though the rabbis did not avert their eyes from what happened there, than in the lawcourts. The court is most usefully to be compared to the U.S. Southern county court, that is to say, not only a place of litigation, but also of administration of all manner of affairs. To direct the court represented the most convenient and efficient way of doing what the rabbinate wanted. And yet, as I have emphasized, what the rabbinate wanted was not to *control* others, who would permanently remain essentially outside its circle, but rather to win others to the viewpoint of its estate, to transform the community into a replica of the academy. The rabbi wanted to bring all Israel closer to their "Father in Heaven", and his traditions provided a very full program on how to do so—and what to do then.

The ultimate issue, therefore, was not politics, but piety: What must one do to serve God in heaven? Piety was manifested by right action in society, and right knowledge of what right action consisted of, by continual study and reflection upon revelation which defined right from wrong, and by acts of devotion. If the rabbi was the object of divine or angelic favor, that was not authenticated by the miracles he supposedly could perform, though these clearly mattered to everyone, but, in the end, by the rightness of the ideals he advanced in Jewish society. Such was admittedly *his* viewpoint. And in studying the history of Babylonian Jewry in this or any other period, we know for certain only that viewpoint. As we turn to consider the relationship between the culture of the academies, and the life of the people, we may well keep in mind the conviction of Rav Judah:

> Rav Judah said, "He who would like to be a man of piety (*ḥasida*) should carry out the matters of *torts* (*neziqin*)."
>
> (b. B.Q. 30a)

That is to say, the real issues of faith are truly settled in the civil courts and by law. Doubtless ordinary people would greatly have differed, for their concerns would have centered quite naturally upon the private anguish of common people in any generation: how to sustain life, provide for children, die an easy, dignified death, and achieve "immortality," or a "portion in the world to come," or in some other way to triumph over personal extinction. But paradoxically it was this most private and personal concern which opened the heart of the ordinary man to the message of the rabbis, for they claimed they knew how to attain that last, least accessible hope, through "Torah."

CHAPTER THREE

THE LIFE OF THE SCHOOLS

I. Introduction. The Rabbi and the Image of God

The rabbis' traditions represent the rabbis as that group in Babylonian Jewry which decided what was normative in all social and cultural affairs. The results of our inquiry into the effective influence and power of the rabbinate suggest, to the contrary, that the rabbis formed an important, but not dominant element. They may have constituted the sole well-organized creative force in cultural life, and they did try to control Babylonian Jewry. They succeeded in taking over the courts and in using them for their own purposes. But they did not wield the only effective power, whether political or cultural, within the Jewish community. The exilarchate held most political power, which it parcelled out to the rabbis for specific purposes. The masses of the people, inchoate and inert, could not easily be moved, and in some crucial ways certainly did not conform to the rabbis' demands. The schools were far from coextensive with Babylonian Jewry, let alone with the Jewries of the other Sasanian satrapies. Because of the nature of our sources, however, the two themes upon which Babylonian Jewish history centers are, first, the relationship between the rabbis and the ordinary people, and second, the configuration of the rabbi as a religious figure, of the schools as a cultural phenomenon, and of the rabbinical movement as a historical force.

Had later history worked out otherwise, we might have a wholly different picture of Babylonian Jewry. To take two hypothetical cases: If in post-Sasanian times, the exilarchate had vanquished the rabbinate in its struggle for the control of Babylonian Jewry, the exilarch and not the rabbis would have shaped the consequent legal and theological literature. That literature would surely not have consisted of a great commentary upon the Mishnah, but, one may guess, of a collection of legal rules and precedents as preserved in the exilarchic court archives, and stories about various exilarchs.[1] In a word, it would have been not

[1] The contrast between Babylonian stories about the exilarch in relationship to the Parthians and Sasanians, and Palestinian ones about the Patriarch and the Romans, is noteworthy. Since the exilarch lost control of the transmission of legal

a Gemara, but a Mishnah, the Mishnah of the legal head of Judaism in the Sasanian territories, or Babylonian satrapy at any rate, just as the preserved Palestinian Mishnah is that of the legal head of Judaism in the Roman territories. When the influence of Babylonian Jewry began to be felt in other parts of the world, for reasons largely irrelevant to the rightness or wrongness of anyone's theology or law, the exilarch would have loomed not only as the dominant figure in earlier times, but more important, as the single most significant source of right doctrine and law in the present age. It is possible that the great theme of Judaism might not have been "the Torah" and how to effect its laws in everyday life, but rather, the Messiah, and how to extend his power through the rule of his earthly surrogate, the heir of David and holder of the sceptre of Judah (Gen. 49:10). The exilarchic view of Jewish history might have preserved an account of a useful but dangerous group of heretics and fanatics, known in olden times for their abilities to work wonders and for their loyalty to a law-code now forgotten, superseded, or ignored, the Palestinian Mishnah. In writing the story of "normative Judaism" of "Mar ʿUqba's age"—and no longer,

---

and other traditions, he was unable to secure the inclusion of accounts of his dealings, successful or otherwise, with Iranian governments. Therefore all we have are the rabbis' traditions about *their* dealings with the Persians, Samuel and Shapur, R. Ḥama and Shapur II, and so forth. I earlier supposed that Samuel had in fact represented the exilarch before the Persian government, and hence to him was attributed the saying that "the law of the kingdom is law." However, it is equally plausible to suppose that later tradents deliberately excluded the participation of Mar ʿUqba I or some other exilarch of the day in those dealings. Similarly, the Jewish representative to Ardavan V was supposedly Rav, and not Huna I, about whom we know a bit more than other exilarchs. In Palestine, by contrast, we have a rich corpus of "Rabbi Judah and Antoninus" stories, revealing the patriarch in a quite honorable and influential position at the Roman "court." Since the patriarch had considerable control over the formation of Palestinian traditions, he was able to provide for himself a far more favorable press than the exilarch received. We may conclude that had the exilarch preserved his power over the schools in the decisive centuries in which the Babylonian Talmud was formed, he would have been able to include stories similar to those told in Palestine about his counterpart. The fact that such stories were not included does not prove that the exilarch was a mere figurehead, only that he failed to retain control of those who later on decided who earlier had counted, and who had not. So literary and political factors help us understand why the patriarch appears as a pious, learned, noble figure, while the exilarch was "not a religious figure at all", or was "a mere tool of the Persians," or was "not pious," etc. Modern historians generally swallow these characterizations without bothering to chew on them. But the contrast between the patriarch and the exilarch is a striking instance of how different history would seem to us if we had either some additional Jewish data, or only data from other than rabbinical circles. Hence the mental experiment here attempted.

"Talmudic times"—the historian would pay approximately as much attention to the rabbinate as he now pays to the exilarch. He would stress the rabbinate's submission to the exilarch, who decided all important questions. The result would be an appendix and oblivion. It would carry us far afield to speculate on the consequent shape of Judaism, its theology, law, and history, which would have resulted from exilarchic revision and transmission of the sources.

If, to consider a second possibility, neither the exilarchate nor the rabbinate had flourished, if the Sasanians had refused to deal with *any* recognized Jewish authorities whatever, another kind of history might have emerged. It would be the history of a mass of Jews, living according to ancient customs and traditions, without particular impact upon Judaism in other times or other parts of the world. Like the Jews of Afghanistan, Bokhara, or Samarkand, Babylonian Jewry would have represented an ethnological curiosity. Its customs would have been interesting, along with its magic, astrological beliefs, sorcery, and laws. Its surviving ancient legends would have been written down by anthropologists, but neglected by historians. Such was the historiographical fate of Kurdish (Adiabenian) Jewry, which did survive to this century.[1] Its customs constitute mere relics, not the basis of "the law" for all "good Jews." With neither politics, law, nor theology to attract the attention of later historians, lawyers, and theologians, Babylonian Jewry would similarly have survived, much like its ancestors of Achemenid, Seleucid, and Arsacid times, mostly as a blank page in history, sometimes as the object of rather hesitant speculation. In either case, the rabbis would have been no more clearly remembered than were the preliterary prophets of ancient Israel. Their deeds might have been recorded, but their doctrines would surely have been forgotten.

In fact, however, the rabbis won out. The literature which issued from their schools became normative for all European Judaism. It has therefore shaped our picture of their times. For this reason we have to stress what other kinds of sources might have taught us, and how they

[1] Perhaps Moses Xorenaẓi's account of pre-Christian Armenian history might approximate the historiographical traditions we should have, had the Jews produced such a figure at about the same time. A still more striking comparison would be to the Mandaean writings, "an extraordinary farrago of theology, myth, fairytale, ethical instruction, ritual ordinances, and what purports to be history. There is no unity or consistency, and it is not possible to give a succinct summary of their teaching," so C. H. Dodd, *The Interpretation of the Fourth Gospel* (Cambridge, 1953), p. 115.

might have shaped our picture of historical reality. This we must do especially because the schools provide a strangely impoverished view of history. Heirs of Scriptures which found in historical politics a partial revelation of divine judgment or intentions, the rabbis might have derived chastisement, reasons for hope, and theological information, from worldly happenings. Yet they paid remarkably little attention to contemporary events. Shapur II is barely mentioned, and Julian not at all, in the literature of the schools. The exilarch appears only when he said or did something of interest to the lawyers. The fate of the Jewish people was timeless, never specific or concrete. Even the academic politics involved in selecting the head of an academy was barely recorded, except in terms so veiled that only searching interpretation enables us to guess what may have taken place. Petty day-to-day "events" such as the meeting of one master with another, an occurrence in the school-house, a contretemps in the marketplace—these are reported, but only incidentally. Mishnaic and Biblical exegesis, legal and theological speculation based upon such exegesis, predominated in the literature to the near-exclusion of everything else. What we can say about the schools therefore concerns less what happened in or to them, than the broad, static phenomena they seem to reveal.[1] We can, therefore, barely describe what took place in Abaye's school, who came or went, what was said on a given occasion, and why. But we know a good deal about the opinions held in that school and in others and about the roles the rabbis seem to have played in the larger society of Jewry.

One important body of opinions is preserved in the stories told about various rabbis, especially the wonders of learning and magic ascribed to them. These stories contain clear, incontrovertible, and factual testimony not as to what the rabbis did, but as to what disciples believed, and thought it important to say, about them. This is what matters when we are told that Rabbah was taken up to heaven because the heavenly academicians required his advice, and the rabbis received letters from heaven informing them when to start and when to cease their mourning for Rabbah. I see no value in speculating about naturalistic explanations for such fabulous tales. Even if we could plausibly argue that the storyteller actually was talking about some earthly phenomenon or meant to convey a "rationalistic" idea in folkloristic terms, we should not as

[1] While I have made a number of suggestions about the phenomenon of the rabbi as a religious figure, as in Vol. III, pp. 95-194, I hope eventually to treat that topic more comprehensively within the context of the history of Judaism in this period.

historians have gained much. The account is all we have as fact, and no interpretation or philology can add very much to the historical information it contains. The historical question, second, is for us relatively unimportant. We are reasonably sure that the stories are false, and we cannot discover just how they originated. What is both important and reliable is the picture they give of the religious life of the schools.

That picture is strangely unchanging. We have now studied four generations in succession, counting the present ones, of Babylonian masters, those of Rav and Samuel, of Ravs Judah, Huna, Sheshet, and Naḥman b. Jacob and finally, of Rabbah and R. Joseph, Abaye and Rava. I find it difficult to think of a type of miracle-story unique to any single generation. I cannot point to a genre of story introduced in a later period and not found earlier, as the summary-tables make clear. The literature exhibits stability not only when legal issues but also when most other kinds of data are presented. (The magical powers characteristic of the Babylonians were usually attributed to the Palestinians as well.) It seems *a priori* likely that academic ideas and values broadly and generally changed over a period of two hundred years, but no considerable changes are reflected in the preserved material. It therefore seems likely that evidence of changes has been eliminated by the editors, and that our pictures of the life of the schools, drawn from this material, will picture the life of *the editors'* schools, not the original rabbis'.[1] Be that as it may, what we have before us, therefore, is a mass of uniform data about the rabbi, his life, legal and theological traditions. We must now examine the picture of "the rabbi" which emerges from these data.

The Rabbi and the Image of God. What is most striking about the schools is the conception that in them lived holy men, who more accurately than anyone else conformed to the image of God conveyed by divine revelation through the Torah of Moses "our rabbi." The schools were not holy places in the sense that pious people made pilgrimages to them, though they did,[2] or that miracles were supposed to take place there, though many miracle-stories were told in a scholastic setting. The schools were holy because there men became saints. They became saints by learning the lessons and imitating the conduct of the masters. In doing so, they conformed to the heavenly paradigm, the Torah, believed to have been created by God "in his image," revealed at Sinai, and handed on from prophets to sages, to their own teachers. In the

[1] See above, pp. 114-119.
[2] On the institution of the *Kallah*, see below, pp. 384-386.

schools, sainthood was achieved through study of Torah and imitation of the master. What sainthood consisted of, how Torah was studied and what were its consequences—these are the issues of our present inquiry.

Obedience to teachings of the rabbis surely led not merely to ethical or moral goodness, but to holiness or sainthood:

> Abaye said, "Whoever carries out the teachings of the sages is called a saint (*qadosh*)."
>
> (b. Yev. 20a)

That disciples were called saints is also seen in the following:

> "Even though he loves the peoples, all his saints are in your hand, and they are cut at thy feet. He shall receive of your words" (Deut. 33:3).... R. Joseph learned, "These [saints] are the students of the Torah who cut their feet going from town to town and country to country to study Torah. 'He shall receive of your words' alludes to their give-and-take in [discussing] the words of the Omnipresent."
>
> (b. B.B. 8a)[1]

So discussion of legal traditions, rather than ascetic disciplines or long periods of fasting and prayer, was the way to holiness.[2] If the masters and disciples obeyed the divine teaching of Moses "our rabbi," as they surely supposed they did, then their society, the school, would replicate on earth the heavenly academy, just as the disciple would incarnate the heavenly model of Moses "our rabbi."[3] We must take

---

[1] Cited above, p. 86.

[2] b. Meg. 16b. R. Joseph held that study of Torah was superior to the saving of human life.

[3] See especially Wayne A. Meeks, *The Prophet King. Moses Traditions and the Johannine Christology* (Leiden, 1967, Supplements to Novum Testamentum XIV), pp. 176-215. Meeks's excellent discussion of "Moses-piety" provides the background for these remarks. See also Moses Hadas and Morton Smith, *Heroes and Gods. Spiritual Biographies in Antiquity* (N.Y., 1965), for an account of the aretalogical literature on the "divine-man," a figure of pagan antiquity contemporary with the rabbis, and both as miracle worker and "living law", analogous to them. In this regard, the numerous insights of Mircea Eliade greatly help us to understand our data, which simply constitute a further illustration of Eliade's analyses.

Of greatest interest is Ludwig Bieler, ΘΕΙΟΣ ΑΝΗΡ, *Das Bild des "göttlichen Menschen" in Spätantike und Frühchristentum* (I, Vienna, 1935, II, Vienna, 1936). In suggesting that the rabbi may be analogous to the *theîos anēr*, I do not mean to imply that any specific rabbi known to us conformed in all respects to the ideal-type described by Bieler. On the contrary, the characteristic birth-legends, name-magic, personality-traits, and life-style may not be located in stories about any single rabbi. Nonetheless, the rabbis as a group seem to me to exhibit most of the important and relevant characteristics. If we had a richer hagiographical literature produced in the rabbinical schools, we might well have a fuller account

very seriously indeed the facts that the rabbis believed Moses was a rabbi, God donned phylacteries, and the heavenly court studied Torah precisely as did the earthly one. We may see these beliefs as projections of rabbinical values onto heaven, but the rabbis believed that they themselves were "projections" of heavenly "values" onto earth. That

---

of individuals according to the canons and conventions of divine-man literature. The rabbi certainly functioned in the Jewish context much as did the "divine-man" in other settings. On the other hand, when one compares the story of R. Yoḥanan ben Zakkai, as it might have been compiled, he finds many of the expected qualities and characteristics, though not all of them; see my *Life of R. Yoḥanan ben Zakkai* (Leiden, 1962).

See also the excellent discussion of Jesus as divine-man in Rudolf Bultmann, *The History of the Synoptic Tradition*, trans. John Marsh (Oxford, 1963), pp. 209-244, and in the supplementary section, pp. 419-424. I am less persuaded by Bultmann's conclusions, pp. 368-374, than by his analysis, especially in the light of Smith and Hadas, cited earlier.

On rabbinic and Christian miracle-stories, see also Martin Dibelius, *From Tradition to Gospel*, trans. B. L. Woolf (N.Y., 1935), pp. 133-151. Of special interest is Dibelius's discussion of when a "case" is actually a case-story, and when it is merely a narration in *case-form* of a legal doctrine. Dibelius discusses (p. 138) the story of the goat who ate the dough, and consequently died, judged by Rava (b. B.Q. 48a, cited above, p. 248). He says that the story might be true, but correctly points out that it is not told *because* it is true, but "because Rava had to decide this case just the same whether it was true or only possible." But, Dibelius adds, we have many hypothetical examples which have not developed into story-form, and so he concludes that this case was handed down as a happening "and thus probably was originally a happening." On b. Ned. 91b, cited above p. 198, see p. 139. Dibelius comments also on b. Sanh. 65b, Rava made a man and sent him to R. Zera, cited below, p. 358. He points out that it is a strikingly short account, standing without introduction, and very briefly told. He supposes "that an old, vivid report has been artificially shortened and put into the Talmud." On the miracle stories, Dibelius points out that such tales generally sought to prove that God exercises providence; but some were told simply to glorify certain rabbis or holy places. Dibelius says (p. 148) that miracle-working rabbis generally were puissant at praying. While I think he is not entirely wrong, what is more striking, as we shall see, is the intrinsic relationship between great learning, *not* prayer, and magic. He also states, "Miracles are not recorded of the great teachers of the law amongst the rabbis, but of others whose fame in the school is smaller." While he is certainly right of the early Tannaim, he is most certainly wrong concerning the third- and fourth-century Amoraim. See Table XXIII, below, p. 398-9, for a review of the evidence.

A further discussion of the historicity of case reports in ancient legal texts, germane both to the legal material studied above, and to the magical stories under consideration here, is John Crook, *Law and Life of Rome* (Ithaca, 1967), pp. 15-18. Crook points out that while we do not know whether legal situations are real or imaginary, we may circumscribe the range of uncertainty. First, references to specific dates or events are important. Second, even if imaginary, with the use of stock names showing that a case was invented for purposes of discussion, the relevance to practical situations is undeniable. Specific names or situations are more often than not patently real, and these do not differ in character from those discussed under stock names.

is not to suggest that the rabbis thought of themselves as consubstantial with the divinity.[1] They carefully preserved the distinction between the master of Torah and the giver of the Torah.

But they did believe that those whose lives conformed to the image of God, the Torah, participated in God's holiness and also in his power, and this was attested by their ability to create men and resurrect the dead, to control angels and demons, and to perform other spectacular miracles, as we shall see.

II. The Masters in the Time of Shapur II

Talmudic historians have provided rich accounts of the lives and teachings of various rabbis.[2] Our purpose here is simply to allude very briefly to the chief results of their studies. Since the focus of this account vastly differs from that of "Talmudic history," little will be achieved by rehearsals of earlier inquiries or by reopening issues debated by Talmudic historians, on which I find nothing to contribute.

R. Sherira's Traditions: In the *Letter of R. Sherira Gaon*, we find the following information, beginning before the death of R. Ḥisda in 309 [610]:

> And Rabbah and R. Joseph had been in Pumbedita together with Rav Judah [who had died in 299]. Each one said to the other, "You rule", but neither would accept upon himself the mastership as [academic] head...[3] Rabbah [finally] accepted the headship [of the Pumbeditan academy] and ruled twenty-two years, and died in 320 [631]...[4] And in these years, when Rabbah b. Naḥmani was in Pumbedita, Rabbah b. Ḥiyya was teaching Torah in Sura. And after Rabbah b. Naḥmani, R. Joseph ruled in Pumbedita two and a half years, and died in 323 [634]. And after him, Abaye ruled for thirteen years, and died in 338 [649]....[5] And after Abaye, Rava ruled in Maḥoza which was near [or,

---

[1] On the "ancient passion to 'be like God'", see Shalom Spiegel, *The Last Trial. On the Legends and Lore of the Command to Abraham to Offer Isaac as a Sacrifice: The Akedah*, translated by Judah Goldin (N.Y., 1967), pp. 83-4, and p. 83., n. 25.

[2] They have not, however, produced an adequate history of the Babylonian rabbinical academies. See vol. III, p. 213, n. 1, for reference to existing works.

[3] R. Sherira here refers to the passages in b. Hor. and b. Ber., cited above, pp. 91ff, and on the astrological prediction which moved R. Joseph to decline see below, pp. 330ff.

[4] R. Sherira summarizes the story of Rabbah's death, cited above, p. 41f.

[5] R. Sherira here refers to the fund which was kept by the several heads of the Pumbeditan school.

> thought of as a single academy with] Pumbedita[1]... And the years of Rava's rule were fourteen, and he died in 352 [663]. And in all the years of Rava, there was only one academy, in Pumbedita, and after Rava, they were divided into two schools. R. Naḥman b. Isaac [headed that] in Pumbedita for four years, and he died in 356 [667], and R. Papa, in Nersh, near Sura. He ruled there for twelve years, and died in 376 [687].[2] And after R. Naḥman b. Isaac there ruled in Pumbedita a number of *geonim* [including] R. Ḥama [who] died in 377 [688]... And after him, R. Zevid ruled in Pumbedita, and he died in 385 [696].[3]

R. Sherira thus concentrated upon naming the heads of the several schools. It is clear that some sort of reorganization of the schools took place, for there seems to have been an interruption in the succession of the Suran academy between Rabbah b. Ḥiyya and R. Papa's assumption of the headship at Nersh, which was identified with Sura as Maḥoza was with Pumbedita. Moreover the identification of Nersh with Sura and Maḥoza with Pumbedita is unexplained. Why the head of one school was regarded as head of another nearby I cannot say. In any case, the schools known earlier, Nehardea, Sura, Maḥoza, and Pumbedita, along with Nersh, were the only Babylonian schools extensively represented in the traditions in our hands. What others existed and what happened in them we do not know. Moreover, since almost all of the preserved material concerns the heads of these few schools, we know very little about ordinary rabbis or disciples in these schools, except in relationship to the heads as sons or major disciples.

Rabbah b. R. Huna, son of the distinguished head of the Suran academy, was educated by his father and by R. Ḥisda. He taught at Sura, where he was also communal judge. Weiss holds that the Suran academy was then in a period of decline.[4] Other sons of leading masters of the earlier generation included R. Isaac son of Rav Judah, and the sons of R. Naḥman and R. Naḥman b. R. Ḥisda.[5]

---

[1] See I. Y. Halevy, *Dorot Harishonim* II, p. 248a=495. Halevy says that the Pumbeditan and Maḥozan schools were thought of as a single academy. He discusses this passage at some length, and holds that only after the death of Rava were the schools divided and under separate masters. See also Z. Yavetz, *Sefer Toledot Yisrael* VIII, pp. 69-70.

[2] I suppose that his independent rule of Nersh began, therefore, in 364.

[3] *'Iggeret R. Sherira Gaon*, ed. B. M. Lewin, Sephardic tradition, pp. 84-90. I found no significant variations in the French tradition.

[4] On Rabbah b. R. Huna, see Yavetz, *op. cit.* VIII, pp. 2-4; J. H. Weiss, *Dor Dor veDorshav* (Vilna, 1904), pp. 172-173; A. Hyman, *Sefer Toldot Tannaim veAmoraim* (London, 1910), III, pp. 1071-1074; Graetz, *op. cit.*, II, pp. 583-584. On Rabbah in Palestine, see Funk, *op. cit.*, II, p. 97.

[5] Yavetz, *op. cit.*, p. 4. Hyman, *op. cit.*, on R. Isaac b. Rav Judah, II, pp. 792-793, on R. Naḥman b. R. Ḥisda, III, p. 941.

Rabbah b. Naḥmani, a priest, studied at Sura with R. Huna. He and his colleague, *R. Joseph b. Ḥiyya*, studied with R. Naḥman, Rav Judah, and R. Sheshet as well. Yavetz holds that R. Joseph's chief master was Rav Judah, and Rabbah's, R. Huna. Rabbah allegedly went to Palestine and studied with R. Yoḥanan, though only for a short time. We have already discussed the succession of Rav Judah at Pumbedita, and noted that Rabbah did succeed almost immediately upon Rav Judah's death, and held the post until his death in 320. Until R. Ḥisda's death in 309, Rabbah subjected himself and Pumbedita's school to the higher authority of Sura. Afterward, however, Pumbedita "took precedence," Yavetz states. R. Joseph was a wealthy man, with large landholdings. We shall note below his translation of Scriptures. His sons R. Nehemiah and Mar studied with Rava, their father's disciple.[1]

Interchange with Palestinian schools: Two leading students of Rav Judah, Rabbi Abba and Rabbi Zera, settled in Palestine in this period. Like ʿUlla in the time of R. Huna and Rav Judah, others went back and forth between Babylonian and Palestinian schools, and brought with them the traditions of each center to the other. R. Dimi, Rabin, R. Isaac b. R. Joseph, and R. Samuel b. Judah were among this group. (R. Dimi's first trip took place while R. Yoḥanan was still alive, that is, before 279.) All were born in Babylonia and educated there. They were consequently able to transmit Babylonian traditions to the Palestinian schools, as well as the converse. Their influence in Babylonian studies was substantial, for they made possible the inclusion of Palestinian Amoraic traditions of the third century in the later Babylonian corpus. Yavetz holds that the phenomenon ceased after the conversion of Constantine.[2]

Abaye and Rava: Abaye, also a priest, was raised by his uncle Rabbah b. Naḥmani, and regarded Rabbah's wife as his mother. He cited many of her medical traditions. His studies were mainly with Rabbah and R. Joseph, although he had some traditions from Rav Judah and other masters of the preceding generation. He became rich later in life, probably because of his appointment as head of the school of Pumbedita. Rava b. R. Joseph b. Ḥama, by contrast, was born to considerable wealth. His father also was a rabbi. Rava studied with R. Joseph, and

[1] Yavetz, *op. cit.*, pp. 4-18; H. Graetz, *op. cit.*, II, pp. 575-583; Weiss, *op. cit.*, pp. 167-172; Funk, *op. cit.*, II, pp. 28-34; Halevy, *op. cit.*, II, pp. 432-447; on Rabbah, Hyman, *op. cit.*, III, pp. 1062-1071, on R. Joseph, II, 742-750.

[2] Yavetz, *op. cit.*, pp. 34-39; Weiss, *op. cit.*, p. 173; Funk, *op. cit.*, pp. 25-27; Halevy, *op. cit.*, II, pp. 455-473. For Rava's complaint about the treatment of Babylonians in the Palestinian schools, b. Men. 52a.

married the daughter of R. Ḥisda. Abaye and Rava also studied with R. Isaac b. ʾAvdimi (Eudymos) and Rabbah b. Mari.[1]

Other Contemporaries of Abaye and Rava: We have already mentioned R. Zera, who studied with R. Joseph, migrated to Palestine, and returned in the time of Rava and Abaye. Another returnee was R. Abba b. R. Mattenah. Palestinian-born rabbis who came to Babylonia included R. Ḥezekiah and R. Huna, students of R. Jeremiah, as well as R. Yosi b. Abin, R. Yosi b. Zevida, R. Ḥana, R. Ammi and R. Abba. R. Papa b. Samuel lived in Pumbedita and held court there. Other Babylonians of the period were Rava b. R. Ḥanan who was brought up by Rabbah with Abaye, and later lived in Artabana, near Pumbedita; R. Manasiah b. Taḥalifa; and Rami b. Ḥama. R. Adda b. Abba was Rava's student. R. ʾIdi and R. Ḥiyya, sons of R. Abin of Sura studied with R. Ḥisda, and remained in Sura.[2]

R. Naḥman b. Isaac: His father was apparently not of the sages' estate, but his mother was the sister of R. Aḥa. Rabbinic stories of his youth suggest that she was particularly pious and eager to influence him to study in the rabbinical schools. Like Rava, he studied with R. Naḥman b. Jacob. He may have lived for a time in Derokert, but spent much of his life in Pumbedita, whose school he headed from 352 to 356.[3]

A Decline in the Schools? J. H. Weiss and Z. Yavetz both comment upon the obvious phenomenon that, apart from heads of academies, remarkably few rabbis and disciples were mentioned by name or cited very often in the traditions produced in this period. Weiss holds that in the time of Abaye and Rava, because of "Persian persecution" and the "decline of the generations," fewer students came to study, and achieved less than in former times. By contrast, Yavetz says that on account of "the brilliance [of the achievements] of Abaye and Rava,"

---

[1] Yavetz, *op. cit.*, pp. 39-64; Weiss, *op. cit.*, pp. 174-178; Graetz, *op. cit.*, pp. 583-593; Funk, *op. cit.*, on Rava, pp. 66-77; on Abaye, pp. 34-40; Y. L. Maimon, *Abaye ve Rava* (Jerusalem, 1965), in particular, on Abaye's life, pp. 15-22, on Rava's, pp. 236-244; Halevy, *op. cit.*, II, 473-480; Hyman, *op. cit.*, on Rava, III, pp. 1039-1057, Abaye, I, pp. 74-87.

[2] Yavetz, *op. cit.*, pp. 64-70; on R. Adda b. Abba, pp. 77-78; on R. ʾIdi and R. Ḥiyya b. Abin, pp. 78-80. See also Hyman, *op. cit.*, R. Zera, I, pp. 386-398; R. Papa b. Samuel, III, 1029; R.ʾ Idi b. Abin, I, 140-141, R. Ḥiyya b. Abin, II, 437-441.

[3] Yavetz, *op. cit.*, pp. 71-77; Weiss, *op. cit.*, pp. 179-180; Graetz, *op. cit.*, p. 593; Funk, *op. cit.*, II, pp. 86-88; Hyman, *op. cit.*, III, 941-945. We shall consider R. Naḥman b. Isaac as head of the school more fully in Vol. V. See especially Y. S. Ẓuri, *The Reign of the Exilarchate and the Legislative Academies* (in Hebrew, Tel Aviv, 1939).

all others of their time paled by comparison. Rabbah and R. Joseph had more students than we know about. Indeed, it seems to me that only those who headed academies were able to leave significant bodies of sayings, so no judgment is possible about either the decline or the extraordinarily splendid accomplishments of the other rabbis of the age.[1]

It is striking that many of the leading rabbis were related to one another or were children of distinguished teachers and heads of schools of the earlier generation. Rabbah b. R. Huna falls into the latter category. Rabbah b. Naḥmani was Abaye's uncle. Rava was married to R. Hisda's daughter, who had previously wed two other rabbis. The chief figures not only studied with the same masters, but knew one another in their childhood. While the rabbinic movement seems to have achieved very wide influence, if the literature is at all representative, its leadership seems to have remained in the circles of a small number of schools, and within these schools, in the hands of relatively few families, often of priestly origin. On the other hand, R. Joseph explained that it was not the rule for sages to raise their sons as sages so that people should not be able to say that the Torah is merely their inheritance.[2] So it may be that the heads of the schools, about whom our information is abundant, more regularly succeeded in raising their sons as masters of rabbinical traditions than did others.

III. The Way of Torah (I): Learning

At the center of the academy activities was the enterprise of learning. The rabbis regarded their studies as the most consequential and sacred element in the life of Israel. Rava said that when a man died and was brought to judgment, he would be asked six questions, as follows: "Did you deal with other people in good faith? Did you set aside times for Torah? Did you beget children? Did you look forward to salvation? Did you engage in the dialectics of wisdom?[3] Did you penetrate into the heart of things?"[4] Of the six 'cardinal rules,' therefore, three involved academic matters. In the rabbinic tradition it thus was as important to study the Torah as it was to contribute to the mainte-

---

[1] On the schools in this period, see Funk, *op. cit.*, II, pp. 22-41; Weiss, *op. cit.*, III, pp. 179-180; Yavetz, *op. cit.*, VIII, 68-69.

[2] b. Ned. 81a.

[3] So H. Freedman for PLPLT BḤKHMH.

[4] b. Shab. 31a.

nance of civilization and to obey the ethical laws about proper conduct in business. We cannot regard these words as mere platitudes. If the rabbis regarded study of Torah as intrinsically important, the reason must be that that study had immediate consequences. As we saw, these consequences included the creation of saints and the formation of a holy community. Why study, and not some other, equally sacred action, was seen as leading to saintliness is clear: the holy man was a replica of the "image of God," as I said, or of Moses "our rabbi," and the community of the saints was an earthly copy of the the academy on high.[1] God and the angels studied Torah. Study, as the memorization, repetition, and discussion of legal and other traditions, was, in effect, a peculiar form of incantation. As repeating the words of an incantation formula, so repeating words of Torah gave a man access to supernatural power and the ability to work wonders on earth. It was therefore important to describe precisely the manner in which one studied Torah, for the ritual actions used in that study, as well as the mastery of the content of Torah, were of no small consequence.

Praise of the act of study was repeated from one generation of masters and disciples to the next. So Rava said in an exegesis of Song 7:12:

> "What is the meaning of the Scripture (Song 7:12f.), 'Come, my beloved, let us lodge in the villages, let us get up early to the vineyards, let us see whether the vine has budded, whether the vineblossom is opened, and the pomegranates are in flower. There will I give you my love.' 'Come my beloved'—The congregation of Israel says before the Holy One, blessed be he, 'Lord of the World, Do not judge me like those that dwell in cities, who are masters of thieving, lewdness, vain and lying oaths.' 'Let us go to the field'—'Come and I shall show you the disciples of the sages who occupy themselves in the Torah in the midst of poverty.' 'Let us lodge in the villages'—Read not 'villages' (KFRYM) but infidels (KWFRYM). Come and I shall show them to you. You bestowed upon them goodness, and they denied you. 'Let us get up early to the vineyard'—These are the synagogues and schools. 'Let us see whether the vine has budded'—These are the masters of Scripture. 'Whether the vine-blossom is opened'—These are the masters of *Mishnah*. 'Whether the pomegranates are in flower'—These are the

[1] Yet I see here a certain circularity. Study because Moses was "our rabbi," and we must be like him. Yet that begs the question. What made the rabbis suppose that what was important about Moses was his mastery of Torah? The greater likelihood is that the myth of Moses "our rabbi" came into being to explain the everyday certainty of rabbis that Moses had to be like them. In other words, the myth came to explain, or account for, the highly ritualistic behavior of the rabbis themselves. See below, p. 309, n. 2, for further comment.

masters of *gemara*. 'There will I give you my love'—I shall show you my glory and my greatness, the praise of my sons and daughters."
(b. 'Eruv. 21b)

Further exegeses in praise of Torah as Israel's chief ornament included the following:

Rava said [with reference to Song 8:10], "'I am a wall' refers to the congregation of Israel. 'My breasts are like towers' refers to synagogues and houses of study."
(b. B.B. 8a)

Referring to Qoh. 10:9, "Who quarries stones shall be hurt therewith, and who cuts wood is warmed thereby"], Rava said, "'He who quarries stones....' refers to masters of Mishnah, and 'he who cuts wood...' refers to masters of *gemara*."
(b. B.B. 145b)

This was therefore the rabbis' vision of the true Israel, a community wholly devoted to study of Torah, embodying and exemplifying its lessons. It was, indeed, study which separated Israel from the nations and constituted its chief glory.

The sages thought that study weakened a man and diminished his strength. Rava said that by "the sick," rabbis are meant.[1] Many disciples, moreover, spent long periods of time away from their wives and children, suffered poverty and even starvation in order to continue their learning. Rabbah's and Rava's exegesis recognized these facts:

'And black as a raven' (Song 5:11)—Rabbah explained [the Scripture to refer to] "him who for their sake [for Torah] blackens his face like a raven [suffers hunger for the sake of learning]." Rava explained it to refer "to him who can be as cruel to his children and family as a raven [by abandoning them for the academy]."
(b. 'Eruv. 22a)

The following stories present contrasting viewpoints. On the one hand, a rabbi who neglected to come home once a year and so caused his wife to weep was therefore miraculously killed as punishment for her tears. On the other, Rava implacably refused to permit his son to return home after a three-year absence, bitterly saying that he returned for an improper motive and should continue to devote himself wholly to the school:

R. Reḥumi frequented the school of Rava in Maḥoza. He used to come home annually on the eve of the Day of Atonement. Once his

[1] b. Ned. 59b.

tradition engrossed him. His wife waited expectantly, "He is coming soon, he is coming soon." He did not come. Her heart was broken and she began to weep. He was then sitting on a roof, which collapsed under him so he was killed.

(b. Ket. 62b)

R. Joseph son of Rava was sent by his father to school before R. Joseph. He arranged for him to study six years. When three had passed, he came home at the eve of the Day of Atonement, saying "I shall go and see the people of my house." His father heard, took a weapon and went out to meet him, saying "You have remembered your whore!"... They were so perturbed that neither ate a meal before the fast.

(b. Ket. 63a)

Since students were thus supposed regularly to stay away for extensive periods of time,[1] the school took the place of home and family, constituting a new locus of existence, and providing a new father and a new bride, the master and the Torah, respectively. So becoming disciples radically transformed the students' way of living. They were expected not merely to acquire knowledge, but rather to devote their whole being to a singular mode of life. The school therefore represented a new society superimposed upon the conventional one, requiring total devotion even at the most extreme sacrifice. Since Jewish tradition had characteristically affirmed sexual and family life, it was hardly possible for the rabbinical schools to demand celibacy. Expecting the student to separate himself from wife and family for most of the year, however, came to much the same thing. So long as he returned home to procreate from time to time, it was sufficient. Otherwise, his life was lived in a world quite separate from that of women and ordinary folk. Through such separation, the rabbinical movement effectively created a new personality, not merely a learned man.

The rabbinical traditions preserved many sayings about how one should go about his studies, how to memorize rapidly and retain what was learned, and how to concentrate closely, as in the following:

R. Naḥman b. Isaac said, "Legal study requires as much clarity as a north wind day." Abaye said, "If my mother told me, 'Bring me the *kutḥa*', I would not have been able to repeat [Tannaitic traditions]." Rava said, "If a louse bit me, I could not repeat."

(b. 'Eruv. 65a)

---

[1] R. Reḥumi's sin was merely his failure to return for a single, annual visit. He was not punished for being away the whole year, only for failing to return home once during it.

Abaye said, "... a disciple should not begin his session in the evening of the thirteenth breaking into the fourteenth [of Nisan] lest his studies draw [absorb] him away and he neglect his religious duty..."

(b. Pes. 4a)

R. Naḥman b. Isaac said that because he learned little by little, he was able to retain his learning.

(b. 'Eruv. 54b)

Rava said, "One can only study that part [of Torah] which is his heart's desire.... Let one by all means learn even though he may forget or does not fully understand all the words which he studies..."

(b. A.Z. 19a)

Rava said, "A man should always learn Torah and then meditate on it."

(b. Ber. 63b)

That is to say, a person should first listen to the teacher, and then discuss what he has taught. Rava said that one should appoint fixed times for the study of the Torah (as an exposition of Prov. 7:4). He also observed that the Torah will not be found with the proud, and therefore warned against taking pride or showing expansive self-esteem on account of knowledge of Torah.[1] Rava derived from Ps. 21:3 that one should study out loud.[2] So the techniques of study of Torah were highly developed. One had to concentrate upon repeating traditions, and the slightest interruption would prevent it. The disciple's powers of concentration were such that he might even forget to do other religious duties, just as R. Reḥumi had forgotten about his wife at home. It was best to repeat one's tradition out loud, to learn little by little, and to choose materials one found interesting. But what was most important was *that* one study, and whatever he actually learned was of secondary interest. Thus Rava said one did not have to understand everything he memorized. Rabbis nonetheless made great efforts to understand and retain what they had learned. R. Joseph fasted forty times to ensure that "the Torah" should stay with him.[3] When R. Joseph fell ill and forgot his traditions, Abaye his disciple restored them to him.[4] Why fasting should have been thought to be mnemonically significant I cannot say, since it was a ritual, rather than an intellectual, action.[5] R. Joseph may have felt that he would receive heavenly

---

[1] b. 'Eruv. 54b, 55a.

[2] b. 'Eruv. 54a.

[3] b. B.M. 85a.

[4] b. Ned. 41a. For an example, see b. Nid. 39a.

[5] We shall see, below p. 359, how Abaye made use of magic to increase his mastery of Torah.

assistance in retaining his learning if he were by fasting to show himself sufficiently pious.

It is reasonable to suppose that where the rabbinical schools were located, the resident masters possibly supervised local primary education as well. Abaye and Rava discussed the training of children before they came to the advanced schools:

> Abaye said, "Mother told me, 'At six to Scripture, and ten to Mishnah, and thirteen to a full fast, and for girls, at twelve...'"
>
> (b. Ket. 50a)

> Rava [discussing the ordinance for universal education ascribed to Joshua b. Gamala] said that each teacher was to have twenty-five students; if there are fifty, then two teachers are to be appointed; if forty, then an assistant is appointed at communal expense. He also recommended that if one has a choice between two teachers, one of whom moves quickly but makes mistakes, and the other of whom moves slowly but without mistakes, one appoints the faster one, for mistakes correct themselves in time.
>
> (b. B.B. 21a)

Doubtless sensible advice such as this would have guided educational practices wherever rabbinical influence was effective.

IV. The Way of Torah (II): Conduct

The rabbis held that study of the Torah must lead to a reformation of the disciple's entire way of living. Ordinary folk should be able readily to recognize that a man was a disciple. Deportment testified to the status of a disciple at least as authoritatively as his ability to quote rabbinic traditions. As a group, the rabbis and disciples constituted an estate[1] within the Jewish community, enjoying special privileges and bearing special responsibilities. Entry into that estate was attained not through birth, although some rabbis were the children of masters of the early generations. It was not reached through social or economic status, for most of the disciples came from the poor classes,[2] and only the heads of schools consistently achieved great wealth. Political preference did not help, for the exilarch could not appoint ordinary people to the rabbinate, but probably had to accept the qualifications first achieved and recognized in the schools. One entered the rabbinical estate not only by learning, but by imitation of the rabbis, resulting in

[1] See vol. III, pp. 95-102.
[2] Compare pp. 390-391, below.

the acquisition of clearcut patterns of behavior and personal bearing, which thus became signs of membership. To be a disciple thus represented a highly ritualistic and formal way of living, in which one's manner of speaking, eating, walking, and of greatest consequence, conduct with certain other similarly designated figures, took on religious consequence.[1]

We may discern two reasons for the rabbis' stress upon the significance of rabbinical deportment-rituals, one political and sociological, the other religious. If the ordinary folk were expected to obey the rabbi and copy his patterns of behavior, people must immediately recognize that he was a holy man, not like themselves but obedient to supernatural disciplines. Just as the Christian monks and nuns achieved such a holy status by their exceptional asceticism, often leading to sacred vagrancy, so the rabbis did by their constant repetition of words of Torah, by their extraordinary deference to their masters, as well as by their speech, clothing, way of walking, behavior with women, and the like. An important source of the rabbi's influence over ordinary people thus was the strange and awesome behavior which both set him apart and attested to his singular character and was thought holy. Second, the ritualistic pattern of behavior was meant to conform to the heavenly archetype, as we have noted. If the rabbi was not an ordinary man, his way of living as much as his intellectual resources and his theurgical capacities testified to that fact.

Three kinds of advice are found, given by the rabbis first to ordinary people, second to their own children, and third to their disciples. One cannot, therefore, interpret all sayings indiscriminately as pertaining only to the life of the schools. The rabbis themselves recognized the limits of their effective counsel. Not all of their sayings revealed values and ideals unique to the schools. Advice to children included the following:

> Rava said to his children, "When you are cutting meat, do not cut it upon your hand. Do not sit upon the bed of an Aramaean woman. Do not pass behind a synagogue when the congregation is praying."
>
> (b. Ber. 8b)

Such advice would have been equally useful to disciples or ordinary folk. The following saying of Abaye, on the other hand, was directed toward the common society, and meant to shape ordinary conduct:

---

[1] See vol. III, pp. 102-110, 130-149.

A pearl in the mouth of Abaye [was], "A man should always be subtle in reverence [quoting Prov. 15:1], and increase peace with his brothers and relatives and with everybody, even with a stranger in the market place, so that he may be beloved above and cherished below and acceptable to everyone."
(b. Ber. 17a)

Abaye thought that if a man pleased people on earth, the heavenly court would be pleased with him as well. Hence if one wanted to do the things which would win heavenly favor, he would be wise to start with man, made in the image of God and therefore a useful source of information about the responses and desires of heaven. By contrast, the third sort of advice pertained most directly to the life of masters and disciples:

A pearl in the mouth of Rava was, "The purpose of wisdom is repentence and good deeds, that a man should not study [Scripture] and repeat [his Mishnaic learning] and then rebel against his father, mother, master, and someone greater than himself in wisdom and in years, as it is said, (Ps. 111:10), 'The beginning of wisdom is the fear of the Lord, and good understanding have all they that do thereafter.' It does not say, '*that do*,' but 'that do *thereafter*', implying that one should do them for their own sake and not for ulterior motives. If one does them for ulterior motives, it would be better for him had he not been created."
(b. Ber. 17a)

The excessive pride engendered by study was a problem for the schools, not primarily for the streets or for family life.

While the rabbis surely wanted the whole community to conform to their values, it was mainly to the schools that they directed their attention. There they tried as best they could—and that was very well indeed—to enforce conformity to the ideals of their movement. They recognized, as in Rava's saying above, that mastery of rabbinic traditions could lead to arrogance and pride, and more broadly, to hypocritical behavior, for learning alone did not qualify a disciple, but only learning joined with "deeds," that is, the total configuration of his daily conduct. So Rava warned:

'And this is the law which Moses set [SM] before the children of Israel', (Deut. 4:44) ... Rava said, "If he uses it properly, it is a life-giving drug [SM ḤYYM] to him, but if not, it is a [SM MWT] deadly drug."
(b. Yoma 72b = b. Shab. 88b)

Rava said [with reference to Ex. 25:11], "Any disciple of the sages whose inside is not like his outside is no disciple of the sages." Abaye ... said, "He is called an abomination..."
(b. Yoma 72b)

Abaye also found occasion to warn against hypocrisy. A way of living which stressed mastery of holy books and performance of ceremonial actions could easily be made a facade behind which various vices could flourish. The content of Torah consisted of more than legal prescriptions about property damages and divorces, for it included a great many rules of moral conduct. The disciples therefore had to be warned repeatedly against failing to live up to the "whole Torah." Part of that warning consisted of threats of the bad consequence of failure. Even more germane to the student's deepest concern, Rava interpreted Ps. 1:3-4 to mean that a student's deeds must be consistent with the Torah, so that his study will be of lasting benefit.[1] Improper behavior could lead to one's forgetting what he had learned, surely a disaster for the disciple. Further:

> Rava said (as an exegesis of Ps. 21:3) that a worthy student is rewarded by being granted without even asking what he desires, but an unworthy student has to ask [in prayer] for what he wanted.
>
> (b. ʿEruv. 54a)

> Rava contrasted these verses, "My doctrine shall drop as the rain" and "My speech shall distil as dew" (Deut. 32:2), [and said], "If a disciple of the sages is worthy, he is like dew, and if not, drop him like rain."
>
> (b. Taʿanit 7a)

So it is clear that Rava and other masters ascribed great importance to proper conduct and motivation.

Discipline within the schools themselves was easily maintained, first of all by the powerful personalities of the masters, second by the coercive influence of the environment, and third, in the case of most recalcitrant disciples, by means of flogging and excommunication, as in the following:

> R. Nathan b. ʾAsyaʾ went from school to Pumbedita on the second day of the Festival of Pentecost. R. Joseph put him under the ban. Abaye said to him, "Why not punish him with flogging?"...
>
> (b. Pes. 52a)

(A second tradition holds that R. Joseph had him flogged, and Abaye asked why he had not banned him instead.) For a disciple excommunication was a serious matter. He was thereby excluded, or ostracized, from all social relationships. Normal life in school was impossible. Ordinary people, such as the butchers of Huẓal,[2] might ignore a rabbi-

---

[1] b. A.Z. 19b.

[2] Vol. III, p. 225.

nic decree of excommunication. One whose life was bound up with the community of the school could not. R Papa said that he should be rewarded because he had never excommunicated a rabbinical disciple.[1] Others made no such claim. If ordinary people failed to honor the teachings of the sages, and these teachings had no reference to court litigations, the rabbis could at best threaten or curse them:

> "And much study is a weariness of flesh" (Qoh. 12.12). R. Papa b. R. Aḥa b. Adda in the name of R. Aḥa b. ʿUlla said, "This teaches that one who ridicules the words of the sages will be condemned to boiling excrement." Rava demurred...
>
> (b. ʿEruv. 21b)

Excommunication of ordinary folk was less effective than in the scholastic community. On the other hand, however unworthy a disciple might be, one should still pay attention to the traditions he has acquired, as Rava said:

> Rava expounded, "What is the meaning of the Scripture, 'I went down to the garden of nuts, to look at the green plants of the valley...' (Song 6:11). Just as the nut, though caked with mud and dirt,—still its contents are not discarded, so a disciple of the sages, though he may have sinned,—still his Torah is not discarded."
>
> (b. Ḥag. 15b)

The traditions were not measured by the personality of the one who repeated them, but had their own integrity.

Rabbinical attitudes toward sex revealed extraordinary stress upon chastity and modesty.[2] The assumption was that under almost any circumstance, any man, unless prevented by powerful self-control, would engage in sexual relations with any woman. It was a primary requirement for rabbinical status, therefore, that a man should avoid even looking at a woman, as Abaye's saying revealed:

> Abaye said that a disciple of the sages is not in the habit of taking note of a woman's appearance. Therefore when he goes to betroth stet a woman, he should take an ordinary person [ignorant—lit. *ʿam haʾareẓ*] with him so that another [woman] will not be substituted [at marriage] for the one [with whom arrangements had been made].
>
> (b. B.B. 168a)

Abaye also instructed the rabbis that when they go through the streets of Maḥoza to reach the fields, they should not look to either side,

---

1 b. M.Q. 17a.
2 See vol. III, pp. 276ff.

lest women may be sitting on the sides of the road, for it is not proper to gaze at them.[1] The reason for Abaye's warning was that he believed disciples, being away from their homes, had a much greater desire for promiscuous sexual relations than ordinary people, as in the following story:

> Abaye said that the evil inclination acts against disciples of the sages most of all. Abaye heard a certain man say to a certain woman, "Let us arise and go on the road." He said, "I shall go and keep them away from a forbidden [sexual] action." He followed after them three parasangs in a swamp. When they separated from one another, he heard them saying, "Our company is pleasant, but the way is long." Abaye said, "If it were I [lit.: if it were the one who hates me], I should not have been able to restrain myself." He went and leaned against a post and was troubled. A certain old man came and taught him, "Whoever is greater than his fellow, his desire [impulse, *yiẓro*] is also greater."
> (b. Suk. 52a)

Abaye had intended to prevent the couple from engaging in sexual relations, thinking that as soon as they got into the fields, they would take the opportunity, regardless of the danger of being caught. So he marveled that they were able to keep away from one another till they had gone the long distance into the swamp, where they were (they thought) safe from observation.

Strict rules, moreover, governed sexual relations between a disciple and his wife. They must take place in darkness and complete privacy, which could not be taken for granted in the relatively crowded housing of Babylonia. Rabbah b. R. Huna would even drive away wasps from his curtained bed, Abaye, flies, and Rabbah, or R. Papa, would chase away mosquitoes.[2] The reason for the prohibition of sexual relations in the day-time or in a lighted room was that the demons might be attracted and cause trouble.[3] What is interesting is that the rabbis taught their disciples how to avoid demons and made it a specific mark of rabbinical status that various anti-demonic prophylaxes be taken. We shall note below that the people of Maḥoza were condemned by the rabbis for having sexual relations in day-light.[4] From the rabbinical perspective, they not only behaved lewdly, but also foolishly ignored

---

[1] b. Ber. 62b.

[2] b. Nid. 17a.

[3] The prohibition against sexual relations in the light or in day-time, Trachtenberg says, "goes back to the Talmudic apprehension that the demons who are driven off by light may also perversely be attracted by it." See Joshua Trachtenberg, *Jewish Magic and Superstition* (Repr. N.Y., 1961), p. 86.

[4] p. 388.

rabbinical counsel on avoiding demons. Some sayings, such as Abaye's, that a woman is made joyful by her husband with fine clothes[1] and Rava's, that a man is required to have intercourse with his wife,[2] were directed at ordinary people, not merely at disciples. On the other hand, carefully avoiding a glance at a woman obviously was expected only of sages, and marked them as such.

Torah was supposed to produce circumspection not only in sexual matters, but in other aspects of conduct as well. It was expected to help a man to overcome his natural impulses to anger, pride, arrogance, bad temper, and cruelty, and to produce excellent self-control, shaping a self-contained person.[3] That is not to suggest that only disciples of sages were supposed to exhibit such qualities. Rava said that a person who was merciful, bashful, and benevolent may be sure that he was of the seed of Abraham the patriarch.[4] To be sure one was of the seed of Abraham meant certainty that the merit of the forefathers would protect one against evil, so it was a significant and practical promise. Everyone should be kindly, modest, and quiet, but it was the disciple, above all, who had better exhibit these qualities.

The disciple should kindly treat younger novices in the school house:

> R. Naḥman b. Isaac said, "Why are words of Torah likened to a tree [Prov. 3:18, 'It is a tree of life']? To teach that just as a small tree may kindle a larger one, so with disciples of the sages, the younger ones sharpen the minds of the older ones."
>
> (b. Ta'anit 7a)

He should also give himself and his learning freely to all men:

> Rava b. R. Joseph b. Ḥama explained (Num. 21:19), 'And from the wilderness...' to mean, "When one makes himself like the wilderness, which is free to all, Torah is presented to him as a gift ... And once he has it as a gift, God gives it to him as an inheritance ... and if so, he ascends to greatness. But if he exalts himself, the Holy One blessed be he casts him down ... And should he repent, the Holy One ... will raise him again..."
>
> (b. Ned. 55a)

Rava warned that a disciple must be careful to respect himself as a master of Torah, but not too much so:

---

[1] b. R.H. 6b, see b. Qid. 34b.
[2] b. Pes. 72b.
[3] On personality-traits of the "divine-man," see Bieler, *op. cit.*, I, pp. 49ff.
[4] Kallah Rabbati 55a, see also b. Yev. 79a, Beẓ. 32b.

> Rava said, "[A disciple] who is haughty deserves excommunication, and if not, he also deserves excommunication..."
>
> (b. Sot. 5a)

Like R. Naḥman, with the same dubious humility, R. Joseph said he himself was humble:

> [Mishnah: When Rabbi (Judah the Prince) died, humility and fear of sin ceased.] R. Joseph told the Tanna, "Do not include the word humility, because there is I."
>
> (b. Sot. 49b)

Bad temper was a disgrace, and signified that a disciple was a sinner. On the other hand, bad temper might be explained away as the result of the 'inflammation' of Torah:

> Rabbah b. R. Huna said, "He who is temperamental, even the Divine Presence is unimportant in his eyes." ... R. Naḥman b. Isaac said, "It is certain that his sins outnumber his merits..."
>
> (b. Ned. 22b)

> Rava said, "This disciple of the rabbis is like seeds under a hard clod. Once he sprouts, he soon shoots up. A disciple of the rabbis who rages does so because Torah inflames him, as it is said, 'Is not my word like fire, said the Lord' (Jer. 23:29)."
>
> (b. Ta'anit 4a)

One must not show excessive merriness, Rabbah told Abaye.[1] Above all, the disciple of the sages must refrain from publicly shaming or embarrassing anyone. So David replied to those who tormented him, saying that while he was guilty of a sin [with Bath Sheba] which would put him out of *this* world, those who ridiculed him for it would lose their portion in the world to come:

> Rava expounded, "What is meant by the verse, 'But in my adversity they rejoiced and gathered themselves together ... they did tear me and ceased not' (Ps. 35:15). David said before the Holy One, blessed be he, 'Lord of the Universe, It is fully revealed before you that if they had torn my flesh, my blood would not have poured out on the ground [he had blanched white at their insults]. Not only so, but even when they study the laws of leprosy and tents they say to me, 'David, What is the punishment of one who has intercourse with another man's wife,' and I say to them, 'His death is by strangulation and he has a portion in the world to come, but one who shames his fellow in public has no portion in the world to come.'"
>
> (b. B.M. 59a)

---

[1] b. Ber. 30b.

Not only social ethics and personality but also matters of etiquette signified that a man was a disciple of the sages. For example, a disciple must not take advantage of peoples' hospitality, and must drink wine in the proper manner:

> It was taught in a Tannaitic tradition, "Every disciple of the sages who feasts much in every place ... brings an evil name upon himself..." What is that name? Abaye said, "He is called a heater of ovens." Rava said, "A tavern dancer." R. Papa said, "A plate licker."
>
> (b. Pes. 49a)

> Rava said, "Wine and fragrant spices made me wise..."
>
> (b. Yoma 76b)

> Rava said, "A disciple of the rabbis who has not much wine should swallow it in quaffs." Rava used to gulp down the cup of blessing.
>
> (b. Suk. 49b)[1]

A striking example of the rigid, ritualistic etiquette expected of rabbis is provided by the following conversation, which took place between R. Huna b. R. Nathan and R. Naḥman b. Isaac, when the former visited the latter:

> [R. Naḥman b. Isaac] asked him, "What is your name?" He replied, "*Rav* Huna." He said, "Will the master sit upon the couch?" He [forthwith] sat down. They gave him a cup of wine. He took it at the first [invitation] but drank it in two [gulps], and he did not turn his face away. He [R. Naḥman b. Isaac] asked him, "Why did you call yourself *Rav* Huna?" He replied, "Because that is my name." "Why, when you were asked to sit on the couch, did you sit down?" "Because whatever the householder invites one to do, he should do." "And why, when they gave you a cup, did you take it on the first invitation?" He replied, "Because one may show reluctance to an unimportant man, but not to an important one." "Why did you drink it in two gulps"? R. Huna replied, "As it has been taught [in Tannaitic tradition], 'He who drinks his cup in one gulp is a gourmand, in two shows good breeding, in three is arrogant.'" "Why did you not avert your face?" "Because we have learned [in a Tannaitic tradition], 'A bride turns her face away' [but other people do not]."
>
> (b. Pes. 86b)

R. Huna had sufficiently mastered traditions both to act correctly and to explain his actions *according to rabbinic rules*. Hence he was truly a disciple of the sages. The rabbinic movement held many traditions on humble actions such as drinking wine, on titles, or on modes of ad-

---

[1] Note also b. Ber. 35b, Rava's custom of drinking much wine to improve his appetite.

dressing other people. These traditions, as much as general teachings about humility, compassion, and shyness or circumspection, were to be obeyed as signs of a person's mastery of Torah.

The important rabbis, heads of schools and teachers of great reputation, naturally were thought to exemplify the etiquette of Torah, and so their actions in humble situations were carefully observed and reported later on. The rabbis' deeds were no less authoritative than Tannaitic teachings, for it was presumed that a rabbi would know what he was doing in all circumstances, and so could be relied upon. While R. Huna could cite Tannaitic warrant for what he had done, he might as well have said that he had seen such-and-such a master do the same thing so he had adequate precedent for his behavior. We find reports of how the great masters engaged in sex relations,[1] how long they slept and hence thought it proper to sleep by day,[2] how they observed the rites of fasting,[3] and mourning,[4] how they made their market purchases of vegetables and meat,[5] where they kept *tefillin*,[6] how they dealt with fullers,[7] and how they relieved themselves:

> Rava used to go as far as a *mil* to relieve himself in the day-time, but at night he said to his attendant, "Clear me a spot in the street of the town."
>
> (b. Ber. 62a)

> Rabbah had the bricks [of the privy] placed for him east and west, and Abaye changed them to face north and south [so the back would not face the Temple in Jerusalem]. Rava explained [that one should wipe oneself with the left hand] because the Torah was given with the right hand [with reference to Deut. 33:2].
>
> (b. Ber. 61b, 62a)

> Rava said, "More numerous are those slain by delayed calls of nature than as victims of starvation..."
>
> (b. Shab. 33a)

Thus every aspect of daily life was to be subjected to Torah. Indeed, Torah transformed quite natural functions into formalized, ritual actions.

---

[1] Above, p. 300.
[2] b. Suk. 26b, Abaye and R. Joseph.
[3] b. Ta'anit 12b, Abaye and Rava.
[4] b. M.Q. 23a, Abaye and Rava.
[5] Rava's instructions to his attendant, b. Ber. 44b.
[6] R. Hamnuna son of R. Joseph concerning Rava, b. Ber. 24a.
[7] b. Shab. 19a, Abaye's dealings with the fuller.

Relations between disciple and master, and among the disciples as a community, naturally produced the most specialized forms of Torah. Ordinary people might be expected to observe and imitate the rabbis' etiquette, and take to heart their teachings about how to preserve good health.[1] On the other hand, only disciples were responsible to honor their particular teacher in the extreme forms of humility and perfect submission demanded by the protocol of the schools. To outsiders, Jewish and non-Jewish alike, the rites of discipleship must have seemed alien. Indeed, they heightened the sense of participating in a special, sacred community, which must have set the rabbinical estate apart from the ordinary society of Jews. This was made quite implicit:

> Rava was serving the drinks at his son's wedding. When he offered a cup to R. Papa and R. Huna b. R. Joshua, they stood up before him. When he offered it to R. Mari and R. Phineas b. R. Ḥisda, they did not stand up. He was offended, and exclaimed, "Are these rabbis and the others not rabbis?"
>
> (b. Qid. 32b)

The implied argument is that the others are rabbis no less than these, yet the others stood before me, therefore these, in spite of their rabbinical rank, should have stood also. It was a mark of the rabbinical estate to pay great deference to the master. At the heart of their sense of exclusiveness was that very deference shown to the teacher, as in the following instances:

> Abaye used to rise as soon as he saw the ear of R. Joseph's ass approaching.... [But a sage should not trouble the people]. Abaye said, "We have a tradition that if [the sage] takes a roundabout route [to avoid bothering people and causing them to rise in his honor] he will live a long time." Abaye took a roundabout route.
>
> (b. Qid. 33a)

> Mar Zutra b. R. Naḥman was once going from Sikara to Maḥoza, while Rava and R. Safra were going to Sikara, and they met on the way. Thinking they had come to meet him, Mar Zutra said, "Why did the rabbis trouble themselves to come so far?" R. Safra replied, "We did not know our master was coming. Had we known, we should have put ourselves to more trouble than this." Rava said to him, "Why did you say so? You have upset him." He replied, "Otherwise we would be deceiving him..."
>
> (b. Ḥul. 94b)

> When Rava would take his leave of R. Joseph, he would go backward so that his feet were bruised and the threshhold of R. Joseph's

[1] See below, pp. 363ff.

house was stained with blood. R. Joseph was told what Rava had done, and he said to him, "May it be the will (of Heaven) that you raise your head above the whole city."

(b. Yoma 53a-b)

Abaye and Rabin were once going along the road. The ass of Rabin took precedence over that of Abaye and he did not say to him, "Let the master go ahead." Abaye said, "Since this one of the rabbis came up from the west, he has grown proud." When they came to the door of the synagogue, Rabin said to him, "Will the master enter?" He replied, "Until *now* I was not a master?" He replied...

(b. Ber. 47a)

A master must not only rebuke his erring disciple, Rava held, but he must also accept correction when given in the proper form and spirit.[1] R. Huna instructed his son Rabbah that he must not spit before his teacher.[2] Rava did not hesitate to punish a disrespectful disciple:

R. ʾAvyaʾ visited Rava. His boots were muddy with clay, but he sat down on a bed before Rava. Rava was annoyed and wished to try him [so he asked various difficult questions, which R. ʾAvyaʾ was able to answer.] R. Naḥman b. Isaac commented, "Blessed be the All-Merciful that Rava did not put R. ʾAvyaʾ to shame."

(b. Shab. 46a-b)

Punishment was not always so mild. When R. Papa felt himself denigrated by the students of Rava, he cursed them. Rava insulted a disrespectful disciple:

When Rava suffered a loss, Abba b. Martha ... went to the house. Rava sat on an upright couch, while Abba sat on an overturned one. Rava said, "How lacking in sense is this disciple of the rabbis."

(b. M.Q. 26b)

R. Huna b. Manoaḥ, R. Samuel b. ʾIdi, and R. Ḥiyya of Vestania used to frequent Rava['s classes]. When Rava died, they came before R. Papa. Whenever he told them a tradition which did not seem reasonable to them, they would hint [make gestures] together. He was saddened [lit.: his mind weakened]. In a dream this Scripture was read to him, "And I shall cut off three shepherds" (Zech. 11:8). The next day when they took leave of him he said to them, "May the rabbis go *in* peace" [a greeting addressed to the dead].

(b. Taʿanit 9a-b)

R. ʾAvyaʾ was once ill and did not go to hear R. Joseph's lecture. On the next day when he came Abaye tried to appease R. Joseph. He

[1] b. B.M. 31a, as an exegesis of Lev. 19:17.
[2] b. Ned. 49b.

asked R. ʾAvyaʾ, "Why did the master not come to the lecture yesterday?" R. ʾAvyaʾ gave the excuse, "I felt weak and was not able." He said, "Why did you not take some food and come?..."

(b. Ber. 28b)

R. ʾAvyaʾ's excuses made it clear that there were sound legal grounds for his refraining from eating and thus not attending the lecture.

Great respect was paid to a master when he died.[1] Funeral orations were preserved, including the following, which was recited at the death of Rabbah b. R. Huna by "a certain child" (in the translation of H. M. Lazarus [London, 1948, p. 159]):

A scion of ancient stock from Babylon came
With records of prowess in combat and fame
Twice numerous pelican and bittern from far
Came for the ravage and ruin in Shinear.
When [God] views his world with displeasure
He seizes souls in exacting measure.
Awaiting their coming as new brides, with delight
And, riding on Araboth in empyrean height,
He welcomes the souls of the pure and right.

(b. M.Q. 25b)

At the death of R. Zera, the following was recited (in Lazarus's translation, p. 163):

The land of Shinear was his home of birth
The land of glory reared her darling to fame
"Woe is me," said Rakath in lament
For she has lost her choicest ornament.

(b. M.Q. 25b)

When great rabbis died, it was believed that the natural world marked the loss. So when Rabbah and R. Joseph died, "the rocks of the Euphrates kissed each other, and when Abaye and Rava died, the rocks of the Tigris did the same" (b. M.Q. 25b).

It was no less important for disciples to treat one another respectfully and to avoid bitter personal animosities on account of disagreements over matters of law or tradition:

Rava said, "Two disciples who live in the same city and are not forebearing to one another in legal matters provoke [heavenly] anger and bring it [upon themselves]..."

(b. Taʿanit 8a)

---

[1] On miracle-stories in connection with the death of the θεῖος ἀνήρ, see Bieler, *op. cit.*, I, pp. 45ff.

Where a master was present, a disciple should not give practical decisions of any kind, for that would imply he held his own judgment superior to that of his master, or regarded consulting the master as superfluous. Such a sign of pride could not be endured, except in special circumstances, as in the following:

> Rava said, "When it is a question of preventing a person from committing a transgression, it is quite proper [for a disciple to give a legal decision] even in his master's presence ... Rava ruled, "In the presence of one's master, it is forbidden [to give a legal decision] on penalty of death. In his absence, it is forbidden also, but no penalty of death is incurred..."
>
> (b. ʿEruv. 63a)[1]

The master, on the other hand, bore equally grave responsibilities to his disciples. Rava held that if a student did not progress, it was his teacher's fault. Rabbah tried to put his students at their ease before he taught them:

> Rava said, "If you have seen a student whose studies are as hard to him as iron, it is on account of his master who does not show him a pleasant face..."
>
> (b. Taʿanit 8a)

> Before Rabbah would begin [his discourse] for the rabbis, he used to say something humorous, and they were cheered, Then he sat in awe and began reciting his tradition.
>
> (b. Shab. 30b = b. Pes. 117a)

Abaye likewise said:

> "May I be rewarded, for when I saw a disciple complete his tractate, I made a holiday for the rabbis."
>
> (b. Shab. 119a)

When taking leave of one another, the rabbis of Pumbedita would say the following blessing, according to Rabbah:

> "May he who gives life to the living give you a long, good, and sweet life."
>
> (b. Yoma 71a)

How shall we account for the profound, ritualistic deference to be paid to the rabbi? First, the rabbi stood in the same relationship to the student as did the father, to whom great respect was due. But second, while the father brought his son into this world, "his rabbi brings him into the world to come." That is to say, the rabbi provides the disciple

[1] For Abaye's view of the same matter, see b. ʿEruv. 62b.

with the key to eternal life, preparing him to gain entry into, and to participate in the studies of, the heavenly academy. Most important, however, the Pharisaic-rabbinic tradition held that the Oral Torah was exemplified, not merely taught, by the rabbi. The teacher was the living Torah, a form or vehicle of divine revelation. To sit in his presence, hear his words, accompany him, all the while observing his actions, was to receive a revelation no less authoritative or sacred than that given to Moses at Sinai.[1] Hence no reverence was too great, no deference too profound. If gentiles paid honor and reverence to their kings and emperors, how much the more so should Jews, but especially the disciples, revere and honor their rabbis, the worldly exemplifications of revelation, therefore of the will and the image of the King of Kings. The forms of that respect, no less than prayers or festival observances or other pious practices, therefore represented a religious ritual. It was a ritual based upon, or expressive of,[2] the rabbinical myths about Moses "our rabbi", the heavenly academy and its study of Torah, and God's image as conveyed in oral and written revelation at Mt. Sinai and handed on thenceforward to prophets, sages, and now, to the rabbis.[3]

v. The Rewards of Torah

The reward of studying and living up to the lessons of Torah was both this-worldly and other-worldly. First of all, study was its own reward, a joy:

---

[1] See b. Mak. 22b, Rava said it is stupid to stand up before a Scroll of the Torah but not before a rabbi, who had authority to alter its content by his interpretation. The passage is cited below, p. 388.

[2] I do not mean to imply the opinion that the myth of the rabbi preceded the various rituals of *being a rabbi* or of signifying that one is a member of the rabbinical estate. It is more probable that the rabbinical rites preceded the formation of the myth of Moses "our rabbi," which would have come only afterward as a way of explaining the religious signification of the earthly phenomena already quite well known and widely established. But if so, that development must have been completed substantially before the arrival of the first rabbis in Babylonia, in the first and second centuries A.D. An inquiry into the transformation of the wise man, philosopher, or sage of Proverbs or Ben Sira into the rabbinical lawyer and holy man of the first century A.D., and of the myths and stories told to explain him, would be interesting for historians of religion.

[3] Bieler, *op. cit.*, I, pp. 36ff., stresses that miracle-stories pertained not only to the divine-man, but also to his master. In this connection, we have no important variation in the case of leading rabbis, concerning whose masters many unusual fables were told. But the reason was not to single out any particular rabbi. Rather, it was characteristic of the rabbinical movement as a whole that all major authorities were accredited with exceptional and often supernatural talents.

> Rava said, "All human beings are carriers.[1] Happy are they who are worthy of being carriers of the Torah [lit.: our light]."
>
> (b. Sanh. 99b)

As in Abaye's case, the completion of studying a tractate of the law was the occasion of special joy:

> R. Papa and R. Huna b. R. Joshua once came before Rava. He asked them, "Have you mastered a certain tractate?" They replied, "Yes." "And are you a little richer?" "Yes," they replied, "For we have bought a small piece of land." He exclaimed, "Happy are the righteous to whom things happen in this world according to the work of the wicked of this world!"
>
> (b. Hor. 10b)

Rava said that the righteous who enjoy this world in the way the wicked do are happy, but the wicked who enjoy this world according to the way of the righteous are unhappy. The reason was that the wicked enjoy this world, but the righteous suffer in it. Hence his question, "Are you a little better off?" When the disciples said that they had gotten richer in real estate, he commented that they had enjoyed this world the way the wicked do, so they were particularly fortunate. The presupposition of the question was therefore that the rewards of Torah are mostly other-worldly, and so will come later on. The sages however, also believed themselves the recipients even in this world of heavenly favor, concern, and special love:

> R. Naḥman b. R. Ḥisda held that even the angel of death loves the disciple of the sages.
>
> (b. A.Z. 35b)

When they went to the heavenly world, yet more awaited them:

> R. Naḥman b. Isaac said [expositing Jer. 23:19] that the disciples of the sages wrinkle themselves over the words of Torah in this world, but the Holy One blessed be he will reveal a secret to them in the world to come...
>
> (b. Ḥag. 14a)

Moreover, Rava said that the rabbis are descended from Levi or Issachar.[2] So they enjoyed not only the reward of learning, but also special merit derived from the patriarchs. It was quite natural, there-

---

[1] DRPTQY: Jastrow, I, 322, "mail bags." See also *'Arukh*, III, p. 161. Neither provides a satisfactory explanation.

[2] b. Yoma 26a, as an exegesis of Deut. 33:10, 11.

fore, for them to believe that their traditions brought supernatural blessings of many kinds.[1]

The rewards of Torah proved to be quite practical and material as well. First of all, the sage enjoyed a special status within society. Whether or not people obeyed the laws as he exposited them, they certainly paid him respect as a holy man. R. Joseph stated explicitly, as had R. Naḥman before him[2] that it was knowledge of the Torah that made him different from ordinary men:

> R. Joseph would order that a third-born calf be prepared for him on *Shavu'ot* [Pentecost, which commemorates the revelation of the Torah]. He said, "But for this day, how many Josephs are there in the market-place?"
>
> (b. Pes. 68b)

Among the many honors paid to the sage were unusual mourning rites,[3] exceptional regard at public celebrations,[4] as well as widespread reputation:

> Rava said, "If one studies Torah indoors, Torah proclaims his merit abroad."
>
> (b. M.Q. 16b)

> R. Joseph said, "We have a tradition that a rabbinical disciple does not suffer poverty." But lo, we see that he does? Even so, he does not go begging.
>
> (b. Shab. 151b)

Since people believed rabbis were holy men, they tried to win their favor by entertaining them in their homes, giving them gifts of considerable value, and making them partners, with little or no investment of capital, in business ventures. The rabbis did everything they could to encourage people to lavish hospitality on rabbis. Abaye said that a blessing follows immediately upon entertaining scholars.[5] Rava stated quite explicitly:

> "He who is kind to rabbis has rabbis for sons. He who cherishes rabbis will have rabbis for sons-in-law. He who reveres rabbis will himself become a rabbinical disciple. And if he is not fit for this, his words will be listened to like those of a rabbinical disciple."
>
> (b. Shab. 23b)

---

[1] b. Zev. 45a, Abaye said to Rava that expositing even a useless law was worthwhile because one would receive a reward for doing so.

[2] Vol. III, p. 61.

[3] As in the case of R. Joseph, b. Ber. 19a, and see above, pp. 41f., 307.

[4] B. Ket. 17b, Abaye noted that at the wedding of a disciple, the mother of the groom poured oil on the heads of the disciples attending the wedding feast.

[5] b. Ber. 42a, with reference to Gen. 39:27 and Gen. 39:5.

While the masters did not normally receive salaries for teaching, they could nonetheless attain material benefit on that account, as in the following story:

> R. Shimi b. Ashi asked Abaye to allow him to sit before him [as a student]. Abaye replied, "I need my time for my own studies." "Then," R. Shimi asked, "Let your honor teach me at night." Abaye replied, "I have to take care of irrigating my field then." Said the other, "I will irrigate for your honor by day, and you teach me by night." Abaye agreed...
>
> (b. Git. 60b)

What is important here is that in exchange for teaching, Abaye received services of a field-worker. Rava, moreover, received free labor without teaching:

> Rava's brother, R. Seʿorim used to seize people of poor reputation and make them draw Rava's litter [GWHRQʾ]. Rava approved what he had done, for it has been taught, 'If you see a man who does not behave in a proper fashion, how do we know that you may make him your slave?...'
>
> (b. B.M. 73b)

R. Seʿorim's action had nothing to do with a court penalty. It was in fact quite outside normal legal procedures.

The fourth-century rabbis moreover made use of their position as masters in the schools and as judges in the courts both to achieve personal gain and to discriminate in favor of others of the rabbinical estate. The following story is the most striking instance:

> The proselyte ʾIssur had twelve thousand *zuz* [on deposit] with Rava. The conception of his son R. Mari was not in holiness [it took place before his conversion to Judaism] though his birth was. He was at school. Rava said, "How could Mari gain possession of this money? If as an inheritance, he is not entitled to inherit anything. If as a gift, the gift of a dying man has been given the same legal force as that of an inheritance, and whoever is entitled to an inheritance is entitled to a gift but otherwise he is not ..." R. ʾIka son of R. ʾAmmi objected, "Why? Let ʾIssur acknowledge that that money belongs to R. Mari, who would then acquire it by virtue of such an admission." Meanwhile such an acknowledgement [actually] came from the house of ʾIssur. Rava was annoyed, and said, "They teach people what claims [to make] and so cause loss to me."
>
> (b. B.B. 149a)

Rava's intent was apparently to seize the inheritance of a disciple through a legal technicality. The disciple was the child of a convert to

Judaism, and because he was conceived before his parents' conversion, he was not entitled to inherit his father's wealth. We know that Jews were generally aware of that rule, and certainly took advantage of it when they could.[1] They did so with judicial support and approval. Rava hoped, therefore, to hold on to R. Mari's father's money—a huge sum—but was prevented when the convert found a way around the law. Israel W. Slotki[2] argues that the whole discussion was merely "for instructional purposes." It was Rava's method "of impressing these subtle laws upon his students' minds. No one at the academy suspected for one moment that the master would in all earnestness desire to retain the money he held as a deposit from one who obviously confided in him. Had Rava been in earnest, he would not have spoken publicly about such a matter when he well knew that Issur was still alive...." I am not persuaded by Slotki's argument or by his interpretation of Rava's saying, "They teach people what to claim," as an ironical statement.[3] As we shall see, there is considerable evidence of the attitude of the schools about benefiting from rabbinical status. There are numerous other examples of Jews' defrauding proselytes. We have no reason whatever to suppose that it then was even regarded as reprehensible behavior.[4] The plain sense of the story is that Rava hoped to hold on to twelve thousand *zuz* which had been deposited with him by an unsuspecting proselyte, and that he would have done so had the proselyte not found out how to prevent it. Whoever told him, it was not Rava.

Other examples of court favoritism of rabbis over ordinary folk included the following:

> Rava stated, "May I be rewarded for whenever I saw a disciple come to me with a lawsuit, I did not lay my head on the pillow before I saw points in his favor."
>
> (b. Shab. 119a)

> Rabbah b. R. Huna said, "If a disciple of the sages and an illiterate person have a litigation, we persuade the disciple to sit, but to the illiterate we say, 'Sit', and if he stands, it does not matter ... If a disciple of the sages and an ignorant person have a litigation, the disciple should

[1] See for example vol. II, pp. 264-265.

[2] Trans., (London, 1948), pp. 645-646, n. 14.

[3] In fact, 'Issur did not depend upon R. 'Ika's saying, for the story makes it clear that it was a quite independent action which did not depend upon what was said in the school house. Someone, not in Rava's school, must have told 'Issur what to do, according to the story as we now have it.

[4] See vol. II, p. 264, and III, p. 306, for cases in which the courts sustained such actions against proselytes' estates.

not come first and sit down, because it will look as if he is setting forth his case ... If he knows some testimony and it is undignified to him to go to the judge who is his inferior to give testimony before him, he need not go..."

(b. Shev. 30b)

R. Joseph interpreted, "In righteousness shall you judge your neighbor" (Lev. 19:15) to mean, "He who is *with you in Torah and commandments*—try to judge him favorably."

(b. Shev. 30a)

It was the disciple or rabbi who was "with the judge in Torah and commandments," and R. Joseph's meaning is quite clear. In the light of the sayings of Rava and Rabbah b. R. Huna, one need not doubt that wherever possible, the rabbinical litigant was given an advantage in court. Moreover, rabbis were not required to come to court at all, if they could get away with enforcing their "rights" outside of litigation:

R. Joseph said that a disciple of the rabbis may enforce his own rights in a matter where he is quite certain [on the law]...

(b. M.Q. 17a)

(Rabbinical disciples did not have to ask masters to examine their slaughtering knives, but were permitted to examine their own.[1] In this matter, the reason was not "favoritism" but merely sufficient knowledge.)

Two concrete economic privileges were enjoyed by the rabbis, in addition to their unsuccessful claim to be free of the poll tax.[2] First, according to the following, they did not have to pay certain other tolls:

A collector of bridge tolls [bazbana][3] once came before Abaye, and said, "Let the master give me his signature so that when rabbis come and present to me an authorisation [from you] I will allow them to pass without paying the toll..."

(b. B.B. 167a)

Abaye was apparently able to certify disciples so that they did not have to pay a bridge toll, at least here. Of far greater economic consequence was the rabbis' privilege of selling their produce in the market before other people:

Rava said, "A disciple of the sages may assert, 'I am a disciple of the sages. Let my business receive attention first [deal with my case first

---

[1] b. 'Eruv. 63a.

[2] Above, pp. 39-44, 85-91.

[3] Bazbina = bazbana, Jastrow, I, 152, "collector of bridge tolls." '*Arukh* II, p. 32.

in a shop or marketplace],' as it iswritten, 'And David's sons were priests' (II Sam. 8:18). Just as a priest receives first, so does a scholar."
(b. Ned. 62a)

We have already noted examples[1] in which rabbis demonstrated their knowledge of Torah and so received the right to sell their produce at advantageous prices.[2] The exilarch supported that privilege.[3] Moreover, the rabbis were not slow to make that claim, and did so by announcing their status:

> Rava said that a man may reveal his identity [as a rabbi] where he is unknown, [as an exegesis of I Kings 18:12.] (b. Ned. 62a)

I think it is beyond question that revealing one's identity as a rabbi could result in considerable economic advantage.

The rabbis were not wholly unjustified in claiming economic privileges. They served the public interest and generally did so without regular compensation. They had to devote valuable time to teaching disciples, judging cases, and supervising public life. The exilarch clearly supported their right to special market-privileges, for one thing, and he doubtless regarded those privileges as a means of compensating rabbis for their services. Otherwise he would have had to tax the ordinary people to pay salaries. By contrast, honor in this world, and heavenly rewards in the next, the enjoyment of public respect and hospitality, the indirect economic advantages derived from the public's belief that rabbis were charmed or could bring blessing (it was the same thing)—these benefits could not be so easily rationalized.

VI. Theology

The study of Torah in rabbinical schools followed highly rationalistic lines. Its method was based upon strict logic, and made extensive use of practical reason. The rabbis however lived in a world in which supernatural beliefs and phenomena were everywhere taken seriously. They believed in God. They believed in prayer as an effective action, so words could affect the physical world. They believed in angels, demons, astrology, and heavenly revelations. These constituted the supernatural environment, and produced an expectation that miracles

---

[1] Vol. III, p. 65.

[2] On the social position of the rabbis, see especially Beer, *Ma'amadam*, pp. 150-185; on market privileges, p. 80, and also his "Rashut HaGolah," *Ẓiyyon* 33, 1963, p. 21.

[3] b. B.B. 22a.

could and would be done through divine favor. Consequently, the essentially rational structure of the Babylonian Talmud, a legal commentary, is filled with teachings on supernatural subjects and stories of miracles. These teachings and stories we have now to examine, and we begin with the general world-view from which they derived, with what may be called, loosely, "rabbinic theology."

We have no evidence that an individual sage ever prepared a systematic, abstract treatise on theological issues, for example in the manner of Aphrahat. Whether or not various individual sages conceived an orderly, consistent view of God, sin and atonement, eschatology, and divine judgment, we simply do not know.[1] The reason is that most sayings germane to theological issues were transmitted in the conventional form of discrete comments, or in the context of arguments or dialectical discussions, or, most generally, as exegeses of various Scriptures. We know therefore what opinions some people held, but we do not know how they put together these opinions into a systematic account of fundamental issues. Most of the comments available to us were transmitted because they were regarded by later tradents as authoritative, and hence we may suppose they represented general opinion held in one or another school.

A part of that opinion was surely shared outside of the circles of the rabbis and their disciples. But an important part was held to be the secret doctrine of the schools, and not all men, not even all disciples, were permitted to know what it said. In the secret theological doctrines of the schools were four elements: first, the secret name of God himself, second, traditions concerning creation and the divine 'chariot' as envisioned by Ezekiel, third, the configuration of heaven and of God, and finally, the mystery of the coming of the Messiah. These elements were to be confided only to the worthy few, never to ordinary folk. They were handed on from one generation of schoolmen to the next, and the traditions on creation and the chariot in particular were by now at least three centuries old, if not older.[2] Knowledge of the pronunciation of the Tetragrammaton was illustrated in the following:

---

[1] This is not to say that one cannot show a few individuals to have held self-consistent positions. Heschel's discussions of R. Akiba and R. Ishmael have already been cited (vol. II, pp. 232-236). Until further detailed and analytical accounts of other major rabbinical masters have appeared, however, we can hardly come to a general conclusion.

[2] See my *Life of R. Yoḥanan b. Zakkai*, pp. 96-104, and the literature cited there. For Babylonian evidences of these traditions, see vol. II, pp. 180-188, and vol. III, pp. 149ff.

> Rabbah b. Bar Ḥanah said in the name of R. Yoḥanan, "[The pronunciation of] the Four-lettered Divine Name is confided by sages to their disciples once in seven years." ... Rava thought to lecture upon it at the [public] session. A certain old man said to him, "It is written (Ex. 3:15), '*le'allem*' [to be kept secret]."
>
> (b. Pes. 50a)

It is clear that only rarely were even the most worthy disciples to be told about the four-lettered name. Why Rava thought of lecturing about it publicly I cannot say. The accounts of the chariot and of creation were traditions which individuals received from masters only in exceptional circumstances. Not all the masters knew the whole tradition, and they would not share even with one another what they knew:

> R. Joseph was studying the 'Work of the Chariot', while the Elders of Pumbedita [= Rav Judah and R. 'Ana'] were studying the 'Works of Creation'. The latter said to him, "Let the master teach us the 'Works of the Chariot.'" He replied, "Teach me the 'Works of Creation.'" After they had done so, they asked him to keep his word. He replied to them, "We have learned concerning it, 'Honey and milk are under your tongue' (Songs 4:11). The things that are sweeter than honey and milk should be *under* your tongue'" ... They replied to him, "We have already studied as far as 'And he said to me, Son of man' (Ezek. 2:1)." He replied to them, "These are the very 'Works of the chariot' . "...
>
> (b. Ḥag. 13a)

R. Joseph thus indicated that they had, in fact, a more substantial knowledge of the Works of the Chariot than they realized. But he apparently did not contribute to their knowledge beyond what they already knew. Rava seemed to know something of the *Shi'ur Qomah* tradition, which contained the measurements of the heavenly firmament and of God. The following statement is handed on in the context of *Shi'ur Qomah* sayings:

> Rava said, "The world is six thousand parasangs (in diameter) and the thickness of [the second] heaven (*raqi'a*) is one thousand parasangs..."
>
> (b. Pes. 94a)

The heavens were divided into seven parts. The lowest was *Vilon*, and the next, much brighter still, was *Raqi'a*. Certain meteorological splendors were explained as taking place when *Vilon*, the lowest, was torn asunder so the next firmament appeared, R. Huna b. R. Joshua said.[1] Above all sat God enthroned on high, the brightest of all phe-

[1] b. Ber. 58b.

nomena. So although the righteous were arrayed in front of him, each with a glow of his own, God outshown them all:

> Rava said, "What is the meaning of the Scripture, 'And his brightness was as the light. He had rays coming forth from his hand, and there was the hiding of his power' (Hab. 3:4)? To what are the righteous compared when in the presence of the Shekhinah? To a lamp in the presence of a torch."
>
> (b. Pes. 8a)

Among the righteous, thirty-six were permitted to see the face of the *Shekhinah*, or Presence of God, but many others were also able to perceive it:

> Abaye said, "The world must contain not less than thirty-six righteous men in each generation who receive the face of the *Shekhinah*, for it is written, 'Blessed are all they that wait *lo* [for him]' (Is. 30:18), and the numerical value of *lo* is thirty-six." But Rava said, "The row [of the righteous] immediately before the Holy One ... consists of eighteen thousand, for it is written (Ezek. 48:35), 'There shall be eighteen thousand round about.'" There is no difficulty. Thirty-six see him through a bright speculum [= mirror, ʾYSPQL-RYʾ], but eighteen thousand see him through a dim one...
>
> (b. Sanh. 97b = b. Suk. 45b)

No disciple could have doubted that the righteous were those who conformed to the rabbinical rules and mastered rabbinical teachings and traditions.

Since God was conceived of in the image of rabbinical man, it was a natural supposition that God wore *tefillin*. So R. Naḥman b. Isaac and R. Ḥiyya b. Abin discussed what was written in the parchment of those divine *tefillin*. The reply was, "And who is like your people Israel, a singular nation on earth" (I Chron. 17:21).[1] Rabbah b. R. Huna held that men are obliged to touch their *tefillin* every hour, as a reminder of God.[2] God for his part would thus have been constantly reminded of the singularity of Israel. We have already noted that Abaye thought that the *Shekhinah* was present in Babylonia in certain ancient synagogues.[3]

The following story indicates a more philosophical view of theology:

---

[1] b. Ber. 6a.

[2] b. Yoma 7b.

[3] b. Meg. 29a, see also *Ozar HaGeonim* V, part i, p. 53. See above, p. 151. Note also b. Zev. 119a, R. Joseph said there were three divine residences, at Shiloh, Nob-Gibeon, and Jerusalem.

> Abaye and Rava were sitting before Rabbah. He said to them, "To whom do we say a blessing?" They replied, "To the All-merciful." "And where does the All-Merciful dwell?" Rava pointed to the roof. Abaye went outside and pointed to heaven. He said to them, "You are both going to be rabbis."
>
> (b. Ber. 48a)

So the principles of immanence and transcendence were ascribed to the two disciples in their youth, with the comment that both were correct.

Eschatological issues were similarly discussed mostly in the privacy of the school. Great historical events would naturally arouse popular unrest, as people looked forward to a heavenly resolution of earthly tensions in the coming of the Messiah.[1] We have noted the report that a Messianic pretender won widespread popular attention when he revealed himself and assembled the people for a return to Zion.[2] The rabbis' discussions supposed that some knew the solutions of the mysteries—When the Messiah would come, how long the world would last, and what would be the pattern of redemption. They therefore paid attention to whatever information they could get:

> R. Ḥanan b. Taḥalifa sent to R. Joseph, saying, "I once met a man who had a scroll written in Hebrew in Assyrian [square] characters. I said to him, 'How did you get this'? He replied, 'I hired myself as a mercenary in the Roman army and found it in the Roman archives. In it is written that 4291[3] years after the creation the world will be orphaned. Afterward, some of the years will be spent in the war of the great sea monsters [TNYNYM], some in the war of Gog and Magog, and the remaining will be the Messianic era, while the Holy One ... will renew his world only after seven thousand years.'"
>
> (b. Sanh. 97b)

The supposition was that among the holy books taken by the Romans when they conquered Jerusalem and put away in their archives was a text which reported the secret of when the world would come to an end. The rabbis believed that great cataclysms would precede his coming. R. Joseph, however, doubted that the cataclysms were accurately described:

> Abaye said, "We hold [a tradition that] Babylonia will not see the travails of the Messiah..."
>
> (b. Ket. 111a)

---

[1] See vol. II, pp. 52-57, and vol. III, pp. 23-24, 176-179.

[2] Above, pp. 32-3.

[3] 531 A.D.

[Our rabbis taught, "In the seven year cycle at the end of which the son of David will come—in the course of these years there will be various calamities, including dearth of rain, famine, death of saints, forgetfulness of Torah, and wars."] R. Joseph objected, "But so many septennates have passed and he has not yet come!" Abaye replied, "Were there the heavenly sounds in the sixth and wars in the seventh? Have the troubles come in the proper order?"

(b. Sanh. 97a)

In any case, the suffering of the Messiah's coming was much feared.[1] Since the rabbis were thought to be saints, some supposed they would not have to undergo these sufferings, being protected by their study and good deeds:

Rabbah said, "Let him [the Messiah] come, but let me not see him." R. Joseph said, "Let him come, and may I be worthy of sitting in the shadow of the saddle [or, dung] of his ass." Abaye asked Rabbah, "Why do you not wish to see him? [You will be spared because of your study and good deeds from the pangs of the Messiah]." He replied, "I fear lest sin [neutralize these advantages, so I may suffer]."

(b. Sanh. 98b)

None of these eschatological sayings reveals anything about world history in that day. No specific historical event elicited comment on its meaning in terms of an anticipated eschatological pattern. No equivalent to Aphrahat's Fifth Discourse, which is an effort to explain the Byzantine-Iranian wars of the age, appeared in the sayings attributed to contemporary rabbis.

The public side of rabbinic theology concerned sin, suffering, atonement, and divine mercy. Sin was caused by the 'evil impulse,' which God had formed:

R. Naḥman b. R. Ḥisda said that the word *vayyiẓer* ('And the Lord God *formed* man,' Gen. 2:7) is written with two *yods* to show that God created both inclinations, the good one and the evil one.

(b. Ber. 61a)

Nonetheless the wicked are guilty, not merely fated to do evil by their star. Though he said all things depend on the stars, Rava held:

---

[1] Note also b. Nid. 61b, R. Joseph held that the commandments would be abolished in the hereafter, presumably since people would no longer need to pile up merits. See the excellent article by Professor Judah Rosenthal, "Ra'yon Bitul HaMiẓvot b'Eskatologya HaYehudit," *Meyer Waxman Jubilee Volume*, (Chicago, Jerusalem, and Tel Aviv, 1967), pp. 217-233.

"This their way is their confidence [kesel]" (Ps. 49:14). Rava said, "The wicked know that their way is to death, but they have fat on their loins [kislam]."
(b. Shab. 31b)

That is to say, their loins, the seat of understanding, are closed, and that is why they sin. Abaye held a deterministic view:

"We have learned that a good man does not become evil."
(b. Ber. 29a)

Most people are neither wholly wicked nor wholly righteous:

[Ordinary people are swayed by both inclinations, as proved by Ps. 109:31]. Rava said, "People such as we are ordinary." Abaye replied, "The master leaves no creature a chance to live." Rava further stated, "The world was created only for the wholly wicked and for the wholly righteous [—this world for the wicked, the next for the righteous]."
(b. Ber. 61b)

It was Abaye's view that the rabbis were not ordinary, but able to free themselves of the snares of the evil impulse. Rava described the progress of the evil impulse. He showed from II Sam. 12:4 that first the evil impulse is called a passer-by, then a guest, and finally a man [an occupier of the house].[1] The worst sins were those of speech:

"Life and death are in the hand of the tongue" (Prov. 18:21). Rava said, "He who wants life [can find it] through the tongue, and he who wants death [can find it] through the tongue."
(b. ʿArakh. 15b)

The rabbis were certain that if a person suffered, it was in consequence of some sin or other. No suffering could escape explanation as punishment for sin. The presupposition of the following story was that premature death as well as suffering came on account of sin:

Rava said, "I used to think there is no truth [QWŠTʾ][2] in the world, but one of the rabbis, ... who would not lie for all the money in the world, told me he once came to a place called Truth, where no one lies [lit.: alters his word] and no one dies before his time. He married and had two sons with her. One day his wife was sitting and washing her hair. A neighbor came and knocked at the door. Thinking it would not be polite [to say what she was doing] he called out, 'She is not here.' His two sons died. People came and questioned him. He told what had happened. They said, 'We ask you to leave this town and do not incite death against us.'"
(b. Sanh. 97a)

---

[1] b. Suk. 52b.

[2] On *kušta* in Mandaean texts, see Edwin Yamauchi, *Mandaic Incantation Texts* (New Haven, 1967) p. 38, and n. 86.

Premature death meant death below the age of sixty, in the view of Rabbah and R. Joseph.[1] Sickness was similarly presumed to be a sign of heavenly displeasure. R. Isaac b. Rav Judah said that one should beseech mercy that he not become sick, for if he becomes sick, he would be asked to "show his merit" that he be restored to health.[2] Rava held that if one suffers, he should accept it in joy, as a sign of his submission to heaven.[3] Suffering was, after all, an occasion for overcoming sin. Nonetheless, no one really hoped that he would have to atone through suffering. So after Rava prayed, he recited the following:

> "My God, before I was created I was unworthy, and now though I have been created it is as if I were not created. I am dust in my life, all the more so after death. Behold I stand before you like a vessel full of shame and humiliation. May it be your will, O Lord my God, that I shall no more sin, and as to sins I have already committed before you, wipe them away in your mercy, but not by means of suffering or illness."
>
> (b. Ber. 17a)

(This was also the Confession of R. Hamnuna on the Day of Atonement, and may have been a prayer existing from earlier times.) God's wrath was seen to pass quickly. Abaye said that God was angry during one of the first three hours of the day, when the comb of the cock is white and when the cock stands on one foot.[4] When he exacts payment of Israel, God exacts it only a little at a time, Rava said in commenting on Job 30:24 and Ezek. 21:32.[5] Above all, he was merciful to those who submit to his will:

> Rava expounded, "'Go now and let us reason together, the Lord shall say' (Is. 1:18). It should say 'Come now,' not 'Go now,' and 'says' rather than 'shall say.' In time to come, the Holy One, blessed be he, will say to Israel, 'Go now to your forefathers and they will convince you.' And they shall say before him, 'Lord of the world, to whom shall we go? To Abraham ... who did not seek mercy for us?' 'To Isaac? ... To Jacob who also did not seek mercy for us. To whom then shall we go now? Let the Lord state it.' The Holy One shall answer them, 'Since you have made yourselves utterly dependent [lit. suspended] upon me, 'Though your sins be as scarlet, they shall be white as snow' (Is. 1:19)."
>
> (b. Shab. 89b)

---

[1] b. M.Q. 28a, When R. Joseph became sixty, he was very happy.

[2] b. Shab. 32a. Note also b. B.Q. 91a, Rava said that recovery from an illness was likewise the result of heavenly favor.

[3] b. Ber. 60b.

[4] b. Ber. 7a.

[5] b. A.Z. 4a.

In criticizing the doctrine of the merits of the forefathers and patriarchs, Rava stressed that they were not sufficiently concerned or effectual; so only God could truly grant mercy. One could encourage him to do so through several means. First of all, one could show himself worthy of mercy:

> Rava said, "How do we know that if one solicits mercy for his fellow man while he himself needs mercy, he will be answered first?..."
>
> (b. B.Q. 92a)

Similarly, compassionate action would follow from waiving one's rights:

> Rava said, "One who fails to exact punishment [of his neighbor] has all his sins forgiven."
>
> (b. Meg. 28a)[1]

The third, and most effective means, was to demonstrate one's perfect submission to God, by keeping the commandments not as an act of favor toward heaven, but because one sees himself as obligated by Heaven to do so. R. Joseph, who was blind and therefore not obligated to keep many of the commandments, said that one who kept the commandments because he was commanded to do so was better off than one like himself who did so merely because he wanted to, without such heavenly-imposed obligation.[2] Best of all was to keep the commandments "for their own sake," as in the following:

> Rava contrasted the scriptures, "'For your mercy is great *to* the heavens' (Ps. 57:11) and 'For your mercy is great *above* the heavens' (Ps. 108:5). It is to be explained thus: Those who perform commandments for their own sake find God's mercy great above the heavens, but those who do the commandments with an ulterior motive find God's mercy great [merely] to [but not above] the heavens."
>
> (b. Pes. 50b)

Nonetheless, many pious actions did supposedly produce rewards for specified sacrifices:

> R. Zera said, "The reward of attending a lecture is given on account of the running." Abaye said, "The reward of attending a *Kallah* is given on account of the crowding." Rava said, "The reward of repeating a tradition is given on account of the understanding of it."
>
> (b. Ber. 6b)

---

1 b. R.H. 17a, Yoma 23a, Yoma 87b, and here, as an exegesis of Micah 7:18.
2 b. B.Q. 87a, Qid. 31a.

Rabbinic theology thus consisted of two main elements, first, mostly secret doctrines pertaining to the being and essence of God, the mysteries of history and redemption, and the like. These doctrines were studied in the schools, and rarely if ever taught, or even alluded to, outside of them. Second, the rabbis publicly offered a self-consistent and comprehensive view of man's relationship to God. Man must submit to God's will and demonstrate his submission through observing the commandments. If he sins by not doing so, he will be held responsible. Punishment will follow in this world through suffering, but suffering must be gladly accepted, for it insures that one has at least begun atonement here, and hence need worry less about the world to come. If people sin and nonetheless prosper, or if they do not sin and yet suffer, an easy explanation was available. The wicked enjoy this world, but in time to come will pay a terrible penalty. The righteous suffer now, but in time to come will enjoy a great reward. This neat account sufficed for the orderly conceptions of the schools, but probably not for the disorderly life of the streets.

We cannot ignore other equally important elements of rabbinic theology. Demons, witchcraft, incantations, revelations through omens, dreams, and astrology, the efficacy of prayers and magical formulae, rabbinical blessings and curses, the merit acquired through study of the Torah and obedience to both the commandments and the sages—all of these constitute important components of the rabbinic world-view. A comprehensive account of the rabbis' view of this world and those above and below and of the invisible beings that populate space and carry out divine orders would yield a considerably more complicated theology than that briefly given here. Its main outlines, however, would not be much modified, for magic, angels, demons, and the rest mostly represented the way the rabbis thought matters worked themselves out; that is, they constituted the technology of the rabbis' theological world-view.[1]

VII. The Life of Prayer

Over the seen and unseen worlds alike, God presided, and he was to be approached through prayer. The rabbis believed that God sat enthroned above the seventh heaven, surrounded by his heavenly court.

[1] It seems to me a useful way of relating the two kinds of data, but I offer the distinction only tentatively, for I cannot prove that the rabbis saw different functions for different sorts of metaphysical and supernatural information. Abaye, for example, did not distinguish between his incantation and his prayer, p. 325.

One recalls that the court above was busy studying Torah (and therefore, required the opinion of Rabbah b. Naḥmani). It also attended to man's wants, when asked or otherwise, according to his merits and its compassion. It was just as important properly to phrase a prayer to heaven as it was properly to inscribe a court document on earth. Hence much discussion focused upon the laws of praying, how properly to enunciate various prayers,[1] the appropriate time, place, circumstance, gesture, and spirit.[2]

Abaye's incantation-like prayer before entering the privy, against the demons of the place, contrasts with his benediction of Heaven afterward:

> [Before entering he should say:] "Guard me, guard me, help me, help me, support me, support me, wait for me, wait for me until I go in and come out, for that is the way of mankind." When he goes out, he should say, "Blessed is he who formed man in wisdom and created in him various orifices...."
>
> (b. Ber. 60b)

The prayer before entering the privy therefore was a formula to secure angelic protection and to drive away demons. The blessing upon leaving was addressed to God. Satan was believed to listen to prayers, just as God did, and therefore Abaye prohibited a certain prayer, because one had to be careful not to say a prayer to heaven which might be heard and answered by Satan in a malevolent manner.[3]

Since prayer went up to heaven, Rava did not order a fast on a cloudy day, citing Lam. 3:44, "Thou hast covered thyself with a cloud so that no prayer can pass through."[4] R. Naḥman b. Isaac said one should take special care properly to say the morning prayers, citing Ps. 5:4, "Lord, in the morning hear my voice...."[5] A good prayer was as effective in propitiating heaven as a sacrifice in the Temple:

> Rava said to R. Ḥiyya b. Abba in the name of R. Yoḥanan, "If one satisfies nature and washes his hands, puts on *tefillen* and says the *Shema'* and the Prayer [Eighteen Benedictions],[6] Scripture accounts it to him as if he had built an altar and offered a sacrifice...."
>
> (b. Ber. 15a)

---

[1] See for example R. 'Ovadyah before Rava, b. Ber. 15b; Rava, b. Suk. 39a, on how to say various prayers.

[2] On saying the *Shema'* nude, Abaye v. Rava, b. Ber. 25b; on the text, b. Ber. 14b, Abaye; on other issues with reference to the Shema, b. Ber. 25a.

[3] b. Ber. 60a.

[4] b. Ber. 32b.

[5] b. Ber. 6b.

[6] Reference to *Prayer* henceforward denotes the Eighteen Benedictions.

The reward of prayer was to come in this world. Rava criticized R. Hamnuna for prolonging his Prayer, and said that he was forsaking study of Torah, which promised eternal life, to occupy himself with merely temporal affairs.[1] Divine response to prayer was regarded as a sign of heavenly love or approval:

> Rava expounded, "What is the meaning of the Scripture, 'I love that the Lord should hear my voice and my supplications (Ps. 116:1)?' The congregation of Israel said, 'Lord of the World, when am I loved before you? When you hear the voicc of my supplications.' 'I was brought low and he saved me (Ps. 116:6).' The congregation of Israel said to the Holy One blessed be he, 'Lord of the Universe, though I am poor in religious deeds [miẓvot] yet I am yours and it is fitting [N'H] that I should be saved.'"
>
> (b. Pes. 118b)

Not only were congregational prayers answered, but also those of individuals. Hence individuals were expected to take account of their own circumstance when praying:

> A man was once traveling through the South Side [of Maḥoza = 'BR YMYN'] when a lion attacked him. He was miraculously saved. He came before Rava. Rava told him, "Whenever you pass that place, say 'Blessed is he who did a miracle for me in this place.'"
>
> (b. Ber. 54a)

Similarly, Rabbah and R. Joseph said that one should say something new in his prayers each day and not merely repeat the required liturgy.[2] Private prayer was best when rabbis guided it:

> Rava heard a certain person praying, "May that girl be destined to be mine!" Rava said to him, "Do not pray thus, for if she is appropriate for you, you will not lose her, and if not, you will have challenged Providence..."
>
> (b. M.Q. 18b)

One had better know what to request of heaven.

Best of all was prayer in a group:

> R. Joseph said, "One should not recite in private the Additional Service on the first day of the New Year during the first three hours of the day, for judgment is then going on, so his deeds may be scrutinized and the prayer rejected." But if so, the same rule should apply to the congregation as a whole. In that case, the merits of the congregation [are collectively greater] so the congregation will not be rejected.
>
> (b. A.Z. 4b)

[1] b. Shab. 10a.
[2] b. Ber. 29b.

Prayer was a risky thing, for it drew the attention of heaven to the praying person and his merits, and hence the community as a whole rather than the individual had best pray together on the day on which men were summoned to judgment. That judgment was for the coming year, and each individual was then assessed.[1] The less the private person was scrutinized the better. If a person prayed improperly, his prayer was regarded as an abomination and could arouse heavenly wrath instead of the desired result.[2]

Of greatest importance was the constant recognition that when praying, a person really faced God. One therefore should not move his feet, and if he does, he returns to the beginning of the prayer.[3] The following reveals how Abaye and Rava envisioned praying:

> "A thousand may fall at thy side, and ten thousand at thy right hand (Ps. 91:7)." Seeing Abaye say 'peace' first to the right, Rava said, 'Do you mean *your* right hand is meant? It is *your* left hand, which is the right of the Holy One...."
>
> (b. Yoma 53b)[4]

In all, when one prays, he must pray fearfully, for which R. Naḥman b. Isaac found Scriptural warrant in Ps. 2:11, "Serve the Lord with fear, and rejoice with trembling."[5]

In the synagogues, old traditions endured, and some of these were not approved by the rabbis.[6] The rabbis however prayed in them, and naturally where great authorities were found, people consulted them. We have a few stories about synagogue prayer under rabbinical supervision, including the following:

> Rafram b. Papa happened to be at the synagogue of 'Abi Gobar [near Maḥoza]. He arose, read in the scroll [of the Torah], saying "Blessed be the Lord", and was silent, [not saying "Who is to be blessed."] The whole congregation cried out, "Blessed be the Lord who is to be blessed." Rava said to him, "Black pot...."
>
> (b. Ber. 50a)

> A certain person went down to lead prayers in the presence of

---

[1] I do not know how faith in astrology was harmonized with faith in annual divine judgment. It is clear that R. Joseph did believe what astrologers said.

[2] b. Ber. 22b.

[3] b. Ber. 29b.

[4] On bowing, see Rava, b. Ber. 28b.

[5] b. Ber. 29b, R. Naḥman b. Isaac discussed the rules about what happens if one moves his feet while saying the Prayer.

[6] Vol. II, pp. 274ff, vol. III, pp. 234-238.

Rabbah. Rabbah heard him say "Truth, truth" twice. Rabbah said, "All truth truly has seized him!"

(b. Ber. 14b)[1]

Abaye cursed anyone who said [an abbreviated form of the Prayer, instead of the full text].

(b. Ber. 29a)

The first two stories indicate that Rava criticized a student for following a custom not accepted in ʾAbi Gobar, and Rabbah criticized a person for changing the liturgy. They do not provide substantial evidence that rabbis could determine the rites of the synagogue, only that they could criticize what was wrongly done, in one instance by a disciple. Abaye's curse must have discouraged some people from saying a prayer of which he did not approve. Other rabbis, however, did accept the abbreviated version, which Samuel had permitted a century earlier, and all Abaye could do was curse those who acted contrary to his own opinion. Whether or not ordinary folk knew Abaye's view we cannot say. The schools, nonetheless, discussed various aspects of public, synagogue worship. Since such worship would have taken place in the schools as well, we cannot readily distinguish between sayings pertinent to the folk-synagogues and those which would have been effective only in the synagogues of the academies.[2]

Characteristic of the academy was stress upon the benediction for various benefits, foods, miracles, and the like. We saw that when a man was saved from a lion, he went to Rava who told him that he must say an appropriate blessing. That the rabbis regarded the art of benedictions as peculiarly their own[3] is seen in the following:

[Tannaitic tradition teaches, It is forbidden for a man to enjoy anything in this world without a benediction ... What is his remedy? He should go to a sage.] What good is that? He has already committed a sin. Rava said, "*Let him go to a sage in the first place, so that the sage may*

[1] See also b. Ber. 33b, Abaye said if one says a prayer in the manner of the *minim*, by inadvertently repeating a word, you call his attention back to what he is doing by hitting him with the hammer of a smith. On repeating words in prayer, see Blau, *op. cit.*, p. 147, *re* b. Meg. 25a.

[2] For example, b. Shab. 24b, Rava on whether the precentor must say a certain prayer; b. Git. 59b, Abaye on the priestly benediction; b. Ber. 14a, Rabbah on how an individual says the Hallel. Note also b. Ber. 33a, R. Joseph explaining the structure of the Prayer, and why certain supplementary blessings are included as they are. I am by no means certain that the academicians did not attend the communal services in towns were schools were located.

[3] See vol. II, pp. 177-180.

> *teach him the blessings, so that he may not commit sacrilege* [by enjoying something in this world without a benediction]." (Italics supplied.)
> (b. Ber. 35a)

It was therefore the sage who knew the proper benedictions, and if a person wanted to learn them, he had to go to the school.

The extensive discussions of blessings for various kinds of food mostly had been completed by this time, and few significant contributions came from the fourth-century schools.[1] Most of the stories about liturgical practices of rabbis concerned how they said benedictions, the Grace after Meals, the Sanctification of the Sabbath Wine, and the *Havdalah* prayer:

> Rabbah b. Mari happened to the house of Rava on a weekday. He saw that he blessed [wine] before the meal and afterward as well....
> (b. Ber. 42b)

> R. Isaac b. R. Joseph happened to come to the house of Abaye on a festival. He saw that he blessed each cup of wine....
> (b. Ber. 42b)

> R. Papa and R. Huna b. R. Joshua and Rava b. Samuel were eating together. R. Papa said, "Let me say grace, because nine pails of water have been thrown on me [so I am ritually pure]...."
> (b. Ber. 22b)

> Rava said the blessing over the light in [a neighboring house] in the *Havdalah* ceremony.
> (b. Ber. 53b)

> R. Huna b. Judah was once at the house of Rava and saw him say the *Havdalah* blessing over spices first...
> (b. Ber. 52b)[2]

> Abaye said, "When I was at Rabbah's house and he recited the Sanctification, he would say to us, 'Eat a little here, lest by the time you reach your lodgings your lamps be upset and you do not recite the Sanctification in the house where you eat....'"
> (b. Pes. 101a)

---

[1] b. Men. 75b, R. Joseph on the blessing for *ḥaviẓah*; b. Ber. 36a, Rava on the blessing over wheat flour; b. Ber. 36b, Rava on the blessing over pepper; b. Ber. 38b, Abaye on the blessing for boiled vegetables, see also b. Ber. 38b, R. Naḥman b. Isaac; b. Ber. 38a, Abaye asked R. Joseph on the blessing over dough baked in a hole in the ground; b. Ber. 37b, Rava on the bread of field workers. On the laws of Grace after Meals, see b. Ber. 48a, Rava, b. Ber. 45b, Abaye. Compare vol. III, pp. 164ff.

[2] See also b. Pes. 103a-b, on *havdalah* at the home of Rava.

Some stories pertained to how various rabbis said their prayers:

> R. Ḥiyya b. R. Huna said, "I observed Abaye and Rava bending to one side [rather than fully prostrating themselves in saying the Prayer] ... Rava kneeled, and was asked why. He said, "Because I saw R. Naḥman and R. Sheshet do so."
>
> (b. Ber. 34b)[1]

> [When Abaye heard the blessing 'Who builds Jerusalem'] he answered in so loud a voice that the workers could hear him and arise...."
>
> (b. Ber. 45b)

It was natural for the students to observe the masters' behavior and to record their actions in matters about which there was some dispute. Grace after Meals, benedictions, the Sanctification of the Sabbath Wine, and similar matters pertained most directly to the schools and the homes of the rabbis. We have no stories whatever about how people who were not academicians or associated with rabbis observed or copied the rabbinical procedures.

VIII. Astrology

The world had been created by the Holy One, blessed be He, and He might alter it at any moment in answer to prayer, but He left its ordinary administration in the hands of his ministers, as the emperor did thus of the empire, and His ministers, though more powerful than the emperor's, were not necessarily better. In general charge of the world were the angels of the stars and planets, whose influence varied according to their characters, and whose power, according to the positions of their stars or planets. Hence, the guide to this cosmic administration was the science of astrology.

While a few rabbis, mostly Palestinian by birth or education, doubted that the Jews were subject to planetary influences, all were quite certain that astrology was a valid science.[2] Most, moreover, believed that its findings pertained to Israel as much as to the gentiles. Some qualified

---

[1] But see above, p. 151, for another reason.

[2] On the rabbis and astrology, see especially S. Lieberman, *Greek in Jewish Palestine* (N.Y., 1942), pp. 97-100. Lieberman stresses that astrology was regarded as an accurate science: "To deny at that time the efficacy of Astrology would mean to deny a well established fact." Lieberman affirms that the rabbis thought astrology a science "but only for the gentiles, not for the pious Jews. The opinion of the Rabbis finally prevailed even on the Gentile Astrologers." Perhaps, but not in this period—and astrology now applied to the most "pious" Jews of all!

that conviction, for they thought that astrological fate could be modified by study of Torah, practice of the commandments, or merits acquired by good deeds. The larger number did not even make that qualification. In this time, not a single master in Babylonia known to us doubted the inexorability of astrological influence.[1]

What is striking, however, is the fourth-century rabbis' failure to leave sayings which indicate their own mastery of astrological sciences. In the stories cited below, we shall see numerous references to Chaldeans and many instances of rabbinical faith in their predictions. Apart from some rather generalized traditions, however, we find no astrological sayings of much consequence, and not a single example in which a rabbi or another Jew prepared a horoscope or otherwise predicted the future upon the basis of the stars. It was a science of the Chaldeans, one which the fourth-century rabbis believed valid, but, in contrast to so many other wonderful capabilities, now did not apparently claim to have mastered.

The Palestinian schools believed that the day and hour of one's birth would affect his fate. In R. Joshua b. Levi's notebook it was recorded that one who was born on the Sabbath would be a seeker, on which R. Naḥman b. Isaac commented,

> "A seeker after good deeds."
>
> (b. Shab. 156a)

R. Ḥanina said concerning R. Joshua's traditions that it was not the constellation of the day, but that of the hour, which was determinative. If born under the constellation of the sun, a man would be distinguished; under Venus, he would be wealthy and unchaste; under Mercury, he would have a retentive memory, because Mercury was the scribe of the sun. He who was born under Mars would shed blood, on which we have the following exchange:

> Rabbah said, "I was born under Mars." Abaye said to him, "You too inflict punishment and kill."
>
> (b. Shab. 156a)

R. Ḥanina flatly stated that planetary influence gives wisdom and wealth, and Israel is subject to it. Some distinguished masters supposedly opposed this view, in particular, R. Yoḥanan, Rav, Samuel, and R. ʿAqiva. In the traditions on alleged opposition to astrology, we find the following:

---

[1] See below, pp. 332-334.

> From R. Naḥman b. Isaac [we learn] Israel is not subjected to the stars. For R. Naḥman b. Isaac's mother was told by Chaldeans, "Your son will be a thief." She did not let him go bareheaded, saying, "Cover your head so the fear of heaven may be upon you, and pray for mercy." He did not know why she said so. One day he was sitting and studying under a palm. His covering fell off his head, and his desire overcame him, so he climbed up, bit off a cluster of dates with his teeth [and thus was a thief.]
>
> (b. Shab. 156b)

Thus R. Naḥman b. Isaac's alleged "rejection" of astrology was based upon the belief that the predictions it made possible might be satisfied in trivial fashions, and thus be insignificant for the individual's life. When, furthermore, one reexamines the stories told to prove that earlier masters had rejected the belief in astrology, we find similarly equivocal evidence. R. Yoḥanan actually did leave a saying that Israel is not subject to the stars, and he cited Jer. 10:2 as evidence. However, the story told in Rav's name was about Abraham's disbelief in the prediction of God that he would have a son. God then replied, "If it is on account of your constellation, go forth from astrology, for Israel is free from astrological influence." God then corrected Abraham's calculation, and, the story concludes, "I will turn Jupiter back and place it in the east" so as to correct your fate.[1] The story about Samuel and 'Ablat proves only that Samuel believed one's merits might overcome his astrological destiny. It was an effort to harmonize astrology with belief in merits, which were achieved in this instance through compassionate action.[2] The story about R. ʿAqiva specifically says that he was worried about a prediction of Chaldeans concerning his daughter; indeed, what they predicted would have come about, had not R. ʿAqiva taken action against it, and had not the girl's own merits protected her. So the pericope about how leading masters did not accept astrology proves only that Yoḥanan was firmly opposed to it. The other materials show quite to the contrary that leading rabbis did believe astrological predictions had to be taken seriously, but in some cases, knew how to overcome the stars, or believed merit would do so. Whoever compiled these stories clearly believed that the ancient rabbis had rejected astrology, and it is clear that one or two of them had left traditions to support his conviction. But most of the materials he tried to include in the passage proved the contrary.

Had a later editor chosen to prepare a pericope to prove that the

---

[1] Vol. II, pp. 84-85.
[2] Vol. I, pp. 162-163.

leading fourth-century masters had faith in astrology or thought that Israel was subjected to planetary influence, he would have included the following:

> R. Papa said, "A Jew who has a case with gentiles should avoid them in 'Av, because his luck [star=MZLYH] is bad, and make himself available in 'Adar when his luck is good."
>
> (b. Ta'anit 29b)

> Rava said, "[Length of] *years, children, and a good living depend not on merit* [*ZKWT'*] *but on one's star* [MZL'] (Italics supplied) for Rabbah and R. Ḥisda were both righteous rabbis. One prayed for rain and it came, and so did the other, [which proves they were both righteous]. R. Ḥisda lived to ninety-two, and Rabbah to forty. R. Ḥisda held sixty marriages, Rabbah, sixty bereavements. [R. Ḥisda was rich, Rabbah ate poorly...]."
>
> R. Se'orim, brother of Rava, was sitting at Rava's deathbed. He saw Rava nodding. Rava said to him, "Do tell him [the angel of death] not to torment me." R. Se'orim said, "Are you not his intimate friend?" Rava replied, "Since my star [MZL'] has been delivered [to him], he takes no heed of me." R. Se'orim said, "Show yourself to me in a dream [after death]." He did so, and was asked, "Did you suffer?" He replied, "No more than the prick of the cupping instrument."
>
> (b. M.Q. 28a)

Abaye offered proof that prophecy continued to be given to the sages, for when a great man makes a statement, the same statement is then reported in the name of another great man. Such a "coincidence" would supposedly indicate that each had received divine revelation. Rava replied,

> "What is so strange? Perhaps both were born under one star."
>
> (b. B.B. 12a)

So the stars, in Rava's explicit view, might even determine a *legal* opinion. One recalls, moreover, that R. Joseph had been told by Chaldeans that he would "reign" for two and a half years, so he declined to accept the headship of the school in fear of abbreviating his life. When he finally did become head, it was for two and a half years.[1]

Not all astronomical observations and comments pertained to astrology. On the Tannaitic teaching, that one who sees "the sun at its turning point, the moon in its power, the planets in their orbits, and the signs of the zodiac in their orderly progress" should say a certain blessing, Abaye explained when these all coincide:

---

[1] b. Ber. 64a, cited above, p. 93.

> "Every twenty eight years, when the [solar] cycle begins again, and the spring equinox falls in Saturn on the evening of Tuesday going into Wednesday."
>
> (b. Ber. 59b)

Abaye similarly possessed traditions on various meteorological phenomena. He said:

> "We have a tradition that a hurricane never comes at night."
>
> (b. Ber. 59a)

The editorial comment was,

> "But behold, we see that it does!"

It is clear that some traditions were tested against actual experience. If so, it stands to reason that the rabbis and ordinary people as well did not doubt that astrological predictions would similarly stand up against the test of experience.

IX. Demons and Angels

Belief in demons was ancient and widespread in Babylonia.[1] What set the rabbis apart from ordinary people was not their conviction that they could see demons, but their claim to be able to master them by Torah or divine assistance elicited on account of merit. Demons were believed the cause of a great many natural inconveniences. Abaye said that demons are more numerous than people, and stand around each person like a ridge around a field. Rava said that the crowding at the *kallah*-assemblies, fatigue in the knees, wearing out of clothing, bruising of the feet—all are caused by demons.[2] Many everyday actions were believed subject to the rule of demons, and hence prohibited by rabbinic tradition:

---

[1] Joshua Trachtenberg, *Jewish Magic and Superstition* (repr. N.Y., 1961), p. 25, "Talmudic Jewry owned a highly elaborated demonology, distinguishing between classes and even individuals.... This lore served a dual need: it conveyed the power of control and at the same time of self-protection. But the rabbis were generally opposed to demon-magic, and though they were not so severe with it as with sympathetic magic (some of the most distinguished Talmudic authorities themselves had recourse to it at times), they frequently expressed their strong disapproval." The stories we shall consider here contain no hint whatever of such allegedly strong disapproval. I know of no stories from this time which make explicit any disapproval, strong or otherwise.

[2] b. Ber. 6a.

> Abaye said, "At first I thought the reason why the last washing [after a meal] may not be performed over the ground was that it made a mess, but now my master [Rabbah] told me that it is because an evil spirit rests on it." (b. Ḥul. 105b)

> Abaye said, "At first I thought one collects crumbs because of tidiness. but now my master [Rabbah] has told me it might lead to poverty. Once the angel [prince] of poverty was following a certain man, but could not prevail over him because the man was careful about crumbs. One day he ate bread on the grass. [The angel] said, "Now he will surely fall into my hand." After eating, he [the man] took a spade, dug up the grass, and threw it [all] into the river. He heard the angel exclaiming, "Alas, he has driven me [lit.: that man] out of his house." (b. Ḥul. 105b)

> Rava thought that some plagues are due to ghosts. R. Papa said some are due to witchcraft. (b. Hor. 10a)

> Abaye said one does not sit under a drain pipe because demons are found there. (b. Ḥul. 105b)

Similarly, one pours off water from the mouth of the jug because demons sip from the top of the jug. As we saw, demons were believed to afflict people especially at the privy, and were driven away by *tefillin*, by the presence of more than one person, or by noise. So Abaye's mother trained a lamb to go with him into the privy, and Rava's wife would rattle a nut in a brass dish. After he became head of the school, she made a window and put her hand on his head to protect him. Apparently rattling a nut was no longer thought sufficiently dignified.[1]

Demons supposedly punished people who drank two, or any multiple of two, cups of wine at the same sitting. R. Joseph was specifically told by the demon Joseph that Ashmedai, king of demons, was in charge of the matter:

> The second cup of wine at a meal was believed by R. Naḥman b. Isaac to be unlucky. (b. Ber. 51b)

> R. Joseph was told by the demon Joseph that Ashmedai, king of demons, is appointed over all "pairs"... R. Papa said that Joseph the demon told him, "we kill for two's, but not for four's. For four's, we harm...." (b. Pes. 110a)[2]

---

[1] b. Ber. 62a.

[2] See b. Pes. 110a, R. Ḥisda and Rabbah b. R. Huna on the seventh cup. Also b. Pes. 110b-111a, wine and beer do not combine for bad luck.

One should therefore be careful not to drink two cups and then go outside. Rabbis, however, knew what to do. They would make some mental or physical effort to avoid "drinking in multiples of two," as in the following stories:

> When he drank a cup of wine, Rava [mentally] counted the beams, so as to avoid drinking "in pairs." When Abaye drank one cup, his [foster-] mother would give him two more.
>
> (b. Pes. 110a)

Rabbis did not have to resort to the magic on which ordinary people depended, for, because of their piety, Torah, and genealogical merits, they were supposed to be able to overcome the influence of demons. Abaye was specifically informed that in heaven, the queen of demons was told to leave him alone:

> ['Igrat daughter of Maḥalat, queen of demons] once met Abaye. She said to him, "Had they not proclaimed concerning you in heaven, 'Take heed of Naḥmani and his Torah', I should have endangered you." He replied, "If I am important in heaven, I order you never to pass through inhabited areas."
>
> (b. Pes. 112b)

We do not know the result. The same discussion continues, "But we see that she *does* pass through [inhabited regions]?" The reply was that demons frequent narrow paths and their horses bolt from there and thus bring them into settled places. What is important is that people believed, or were expected to believe, that because of Abaye's merits, specifically his learning, he and other people were protected from demons, as from other dangers.[1]

A rabbi's prayer was also believed potent against demons:

> ... A certain demon haunted Abaye's schoolhouse, so that when two [disciples] entered even by day they were harmed. [Abaye ordered that R. Aḥa b. Jacob spend the night in the school.] The demon appeared to him in the guise of a seven-headed dragon. Every time [R. Aḥa] fell on his knees, one head fell off. The next day he reproached [the schoolmen], "Had not a miracle occurred, you would have endangered my life."
>
> (b. Qid. 29b)

Abaye had believed that R. Aḥa's merits would be sufficient to exorcize the demon, and the reply, like R. Zera's to Rabbah when the latter

[1] Above, p. 325, below, p. 357.

cut the former's throat and resurrected him, was that in any case one should not rely upon miracles.[1]

Not only merit but also knowledge of astrological laws was believed to operate to protect the rabbis:

> Abaye was walking along with R. Papa on the right and R. Huna b. R. Joshua on his left. Seeing a [certain kind of demon, named] Bitter Destruction [QTB MRYRY, see Deut. 32:24] approaching on the left, he moved R. Papa to the left and R. Huna b. R. Joshua to the right. R. Papa asked, "Why do I differ that you are not afraid on my behalf?" He replied, "For you, the hour [Š'T'] is favorable."
>
> (b. Pes. 111b)

So along with reliance upon Torah, piety, and other merits, the rabbis regarded knowledge of astrological circumstances as consequential in protecting themselves from demons.[2]

Rava explained that if one wanted to see demons, he should take sifted ashes and sprinkle them about his bed. In the morning he will see something like the footprints of a cock. Further, he said,

> "If one wishes to see them, let him take the afterbirth of a black cat, the offspring of a black she cat, the first-born of a first-born, and roast it in fire and grind it up, and fill his eyes with it. Let him pour the rest into an iron tube and seal it with an iron signet, that it should not be stolen from him [by demons]. Let him close his mouth, lest he come to harm." R. Bibi b. Abaye did so and saw them, but came to harm. The rabbis prayed for mercy for him and he recovered.
>
> (b. Ber. 6a)

Obviously if one rubbed ashes into his eyes, he would see something, and his eyes would probably be damaged, at least for a time. One would naturally ascribe what he saw and suffered to the effects of demons.

We have seen, therefore, that the rabbis believed demons were both real and particularly active in the schools. Rabbis knew how to cope with them. They avoided drinking two cups at a time and attracting demons by pouring water or crumbs on the ground. They were able to counteract the demons of the privy by making noise, so frightening them away. Leading rabbis, particularly Abaye and R. Joseph, supposedly had conversations with important demons, who conveyed

---

[1] See b. B.B. 73a-b, Rabbah said he saw Hormin the son of Lilith running on a parapet. However immediately following are stories about Rabbah b.b. Ḥanah's miraculous visions, and it may be that this account belongs to the latter traditions. See Blau, *op. cit.*, p. 12.

[2] On communication with angels, see below, p. 338. For further astrological beliefs, see above, pp. 330ff.

information concerning what orders were given in heaven. Rabbis who were particularly meritorious were able to overcome demons by praying. Others were safe, at least sometimes, on account of their horoscope or their Torah. In the stories considered here we have found neither the slightest trace of disbelief in demonology, nor a single expression of disapproval of such belief *or* of the magic used against them. What is more to the point is that "divine-men" in antiquity were expected to be able to master not only natural phenomena, illness, and death, but also demons.[1] If one supposes that the rabbis were attempting here or elsewhere to purify, ennoble, or elevate the "superstitions" of the ordinary people, and so transform them into "true religion," he simply misses the point of these stories. The point is that *no* "divine-man" could be taken as such who could *not* manipulate or otherwise dominate the world of demons. A rabbi was a rabbi in part because he could do so. It was just as integral to his character to use Torah against demons as it was to learn legal sayings for court-action. The reason the data contain no evidence of rabbinical disapproval of belief in demons is that such disapproval would have been anachronistic and incredible. Just as astrology was an exact science, so were the devices to avert or subjugate demons; these devices required prayer, or incantation, or repeating words of Torah, or astrological good fortune.[2]

The angel of death held seances with some of the rabbis. One recalls that Rabbah was able to keep the angel away because he engaged in study of Torah so fervently that he did not cease even for a moment. In the following story, we see that the angel of death was said to have communicated frequently with R. Bibi b. Abaye, and to have reported that when a man's star "was impaired," he might have power over him:

> R. Bibi b. Abaye was frequently visited by the angel of death. Once the angel told his messenger, "Go, bring me Miriam, the women's hairdresser." He brought Miriam, the children's nurse. He said, "I told you Miriam the hairdresser." "If so," he answered, "I will take her back." He said, "Since you brought her, let her be added [to the

[1] Bieler, *op. cit.*, I, pp. 94ff.

[2] It is deplorable that pious scholars have tried to explain away magical, demonological, astrological, and other supernatural rabbinical exempla in various ways. They are motivated by quite sincere theological convictions. What I regret is their inability to discern where historical scholarship ends, and theological apologetic begins. As I have repeatedly stressed, whatever we find in the Babylonian Talmud is there because the schools and authorities approved of it and wished to preserve it. We assuredly err by imposing our judgment of what is "elevated," or "noble," or "true" religion upon theirs. For a different view of anti-demonic talents, see Josephus's description of Solomon, cited p. 362.

> number of the dead]." "How were you able to get her [before her time]?" The messenger replied, "She was holding a shovel in her hand, heating and raking it over. She took it, and put it on her foot, and burned herself. Her luck [star] was impaired, so I brought her." R. Bibi b. Abaye said to the angel of death, "Do you have the right to act in such a way?" He replied, "Is it not written, 'There is that is swept away without judgment' (Prov. 13:23)." He replied, "But it is written, 'One generation passes away, and another comes' [in due time, not before]? (Qoh. 1:4)" He replied, "I have charge of them until they have completed the generation, and then I hand them over to Dumah [Silence, the angel in charge of the dead]." He asked, "But what do you do with her years [which she should have lived]?" He replied, "If there is a disciple of the rabbis who overlooks his own hurt, I add them to *his* years in her stead."
>
> (b. Hag. 4b-5a)[1]

The following story provided corroborative evidence concerning rabbinic belief in what the angel of death had said:

> Rava said, "One who forgoes his rights is forgiven all his iniquities..." R. Huna b. R. Joshua fell ill. R. Papa went to ask about him, and seeing that he was very ill, said to those present, "Ready provisions for his journey." R. Huna recovered, and R. Papa was ashamed to see him. He asked, "What did you see?" He replied, "It was indeed as you thought [I was really dying] but the Holy One blessed be he said to them [the angels], 'Because he does not insist on his rights, do not be particular about him...'"
>
> (b. R.H. 17a)

Furthermore, rabbis were able to communicate easily with the dead:

> There was a certain Magus ['MGWŠ'] who used to rummage among the graves [to exhume the bodies and expose them to the birds]. When he came to that of R. Tovi b. Mattenah, R. Tovi took hold of his beard. Abaye came and said to [the deceased rabbi], "Pray, leave him." A year later he again came and the same thing happened, but the deceased would not leave the Magus alone until Abaye brought scissors and cut off his beard.
>
> (b. B.B. 58a)[2]

The purpose of telling this story is quite obvious. The Magi desecrate Jewish graves, but that does not mean that they do so with impunity. Dead rabbis can punish them for their actions. Living rabbis can sometimes control dead rabbis and tell them what to do. In any event, rabbis are able to communicate with, and instruct, the dead, and Magi

---

1 See B. Lewin, *Ozar HaGeonim*, IV, part ii, p. 6.

2 See above, Rava appeared to his brother in a dream, b. M.Q. 28a, cited p. 333. See vol. III, pp. 108-109 for other examples.

cannot. This story, like the long account of Bar Sheshakh cited above, is part of the polemical tradition shaped in the schools. That tradition held that pagan magicians were powerful but dangerous; rabbinical magicians were more powerful but benevolent.[1]

Receiving heavenly greetings and other messages was regarded as a sign of heavenly favor, and was not at all uncommon, as we have seen. In the following account, the receipt of heavenly greetings was regarded as recognition of one's ethical or moral merits:

> Abba was a cupper. He daily would receive greetings from the Heavenly Academy. Abaye received greetings every Sabbath eve. Rava annually received them on the eve of the Day of Atonement. Abaye was dejected [lit. "his mind weakened"] because of Abba the cupper. People said to him, "You cannot do what he does ... When he performed operations, he would separate men from women, [and otherwise was fastidious in keeping patients from unchastity.] He had a hidden place where patients deposited their fees ... Those that could afford it put their fees there, and those that could not pay were not put to shame. Whenever a rabbinical disciple consulted him he would accept no fee, but would give him some money..." One day Abaye sent to him two disciples to test him. He received them, gave them food and drink, and in the evening prepared woolen mattresses for them. In the morning they rolled them up and took them to the market [to sell them]. There they met Abba and asked him how much they are worth. He said so-and-so-much. "Perhaps more?" He replied, "That is what I paid for them." They said to him, "They are yours and we took them. By your leave, of what did you suspect us?" He replied, "I thought the rabbis needed money for the redemption of captives and were ashamed to tell me." They said, "Sir, take them back." He answered, "From the moment I missed them I put them out of mind and gave them to charity." Rava was dejected because of Abaye. He was told, "Be content that [through you] the whole city is protected."
> (b. Ta'anit 21b-22a)

The purport of the first story is to show that even an ignorant money-maker may by generosity excell great rabbis in merit and consequent reward. But such a man will respect and think only good of the rabbis (as they indeed deserve). This has several cutting edges, against popular pietists who are critical of the rabbis, against rabbinical students who are unscrupulous, and against the avaricious. For our present purpose the important thing is that it shows a reward dangled before the ava-

---

[1] Bieler (*op. cit.*, I, pp. 24ff) points out that normally the birth of the Θεῖος ἀνήρ was announced in a dream. I know of no rabbinical account of a prediction of the birth of a rabbi by means of a dream or other revelation. Nor are miracle-stories told in connection with the birth of rabbis, compare Bieler, I, 28ff.

ricious was that of daily communion with heaven by means of special messengers or messages. Rava was told that he possesses sufficient merits to protect a whole city. The rabbis certainly believed their presence itself contributed to the protection of the city, and made this an excuse to refuse to pay for the cost of building walls or defending them. So the heavenly message was both believed and put into effect.

x. Dreams and Other Revelations

Conceiving of the world as populated by demons and angels, and presided over by God, with his heavenly court and school, the rabbis thought that the spiritual and heavenly beings communicated with men in various ways, both directly and through signs, wonders, and omens. Direct communication between supernatural beings and men has just been considered. Even the Holy One, blessed be He, might speak to men directly in prophecy—but this prophecy was practically ruled out. One recalls the discussion between Abaye and Rava about whether prophecy had truly ceased. Abaye maintained that prophecy remained in the hands of the sages, but he would probably have given a frigid welcome to any scholar who actually professed himself a prophet. Earlier Pharisaism had denied that prophecy lasted beyond the time of Malachi, Haggai, and Zechariah. Next to prophecy, and terminologically sometimes confused with it, came the utterance of "ominous" sayings, i.e. sayings rarely more than a single sentence, and often only a word or two, which indicated, independently of the speaker's intention, what was to happen. The rabbis shared with non-rabbinic Jews and their pagan neighbors the belief that such sentences might be uttered by anyone. A nice example considered as prophecy and with the high-priest as speaker, occurs in John 11:49, while Augustine's conversion by such an utterance was later to be famous (Confessions VIII, 12, 29). In Augustine's case, the speaker was a child, and the rabbis too shared the common belief that such utterances were particularly likely to come through children and imbeciles, as the following story indicates:

> The daughter of R. Ḥisda was sitting on her father's lap. In front of him were Rava and Rami b. Ḥama. He said to her, "Which of them would you like?" She replied, "Both." Rava said, "And let me be the second."
>
> (b. B.B. 12b).

Quotation by a child of the Scriptural lesson he had just learned might produce a revelation, Rava believed.[1] Omens to be interpreted included any sort of change in the normal routine of daily life, and Rava[2] and Abaye both held that omens were meaningful, should be interpreted and heeded.[3]

After omens, as recognized revelations of the future came dreams. Rava took a rationalistic view of dreaming, saying that if one goes to sleep in good spirits, he will have a good dream.[4] He also held that one dreams only what is suggested by his own thoughts; therefore one does not see in a dream [lit.: they do not show a man]

> a golden palm-tree or an elephant going through the eye of a needle.
> (b. Ber. 55b)

Since such things do not exist, one supposedly will not dream about them. Rava along with all other rabbis of the generation paid attention to the interpretation of dreams, a subject on which the rabbis claimed, and were believed, to speak with authority. Dreams were not only revelations from heaven, but even signs that Israel was not wholly rejected by God. So Rava explained Deut. 31:17, "And I will hide my face in that day,"

> Rava said, "Although I hide my face from them, I shall speak to them in a dream."
> (b. Ḥag. 5b)

Such revelations through dreams were illustrated as follows:

> Two disciples were once sitting before Rava. One reported that in a dream, the following Scripture was read to him, "O how great is your goodness which you have laid up for them that fear you?" (Ps. 31:20), and the other said in his dream he heard the following Scripture, "But let those that ... love your name be joyful in you" (Ps. 5:12). He replied, "You are both completely righteous rabbis, but one is motivated by love and the other by fear."
> (b. Sot. 31a)

To the corpus of the rabbinic traditions about the interpretation of omens and dreams, this generation of authorities added the following sayings:

---

[1] b. Yoma 75b.

[2] b. Yoma 75b. One day his field-hand did not bring him quail, as he ordinarily did.

[3] b. Ker. 6a, Hor. 12a, Abaye said that omens are meaningful, so therefore on the New Year one should eat pumpkin.

[4] b. Shab. 30b.

[In the school of R. Ishmael it was taught that one who experienced a nocturnal emission on the Day of Atonement should be anxious through the coming year, but if he survives the year, he may be sure he will enter the world to come.] R. Naḥman b. Isaac said, "You may know it for all the world is hungry and he is satisfied..."

(b. Yoma 88a)

R. Zera said, "A pumpkin, a palm-heart, wax, and a reed are all good omens in a dream."

(b. Ber. 56b)

[If one sees a camel in a dream, death has been decreed from heaven, but the man has been delivered from it.] R. Naḥman b. Isaac said that this was proved by II Sam. 12:13.

(b. Ber. 56b)

R. Joseph said, "If one sees a goat in a dream, he will have a blessed year. If he sees several goats, he will have several good years. [The proof-text was Prov. 27:27]. If one sees myrtle, he will have good luck with his property; if he has no property, he will inherit some ... If one sees a citron, he is honored in the sight of his Maker [a play on the words *hadar* and *hadur*, with Lev. 23:40 as proof-text]. If one sees a palm branch in a dream, he is single-hearted in devotion to his father in heaven. If he sees a goose, he may hope for wisdom ... and if he dreams of being with one, he will become head of an academy...."

(b. Ber. 57a)

If one dreams that he goes up to the roof, he will attain high position. If he dreams he goes down, he will lose it. Abaye and Rava both say that once he has attained a high position [and dreams he goes down] he will remain there...

(b. Ber. 57a)

The following story[1] indicates that the rabbis, though in this field they claimed to speak authoritatively, believed in the dream-interpretation of others outside of their schools, just as they were prepared to depend upon the predictions of astrologers [= Chaldeans]. It is clear that while it was theoretically the dream which determined matters, and not the intervening interpretation of the dream-interpreter, nonetheless the interpretation here seemed decisive:

Bar Hedya was an interpreter of dreams. To one who paid him he used to give a favorable interpretation and to one who did not pay him he gave an unfavorable interpretation. Abaye and Rava each had a dream. Abaye gave him a *zuz*, and Rava did not give him anything. They said to him, "In our dream we read the verse, 'Thine ox shall be slain before thine eyes' (Deut. 28:31)." To Rava he said, "Your

[1] Trans. Maurice Simon, (London, 1948) pp. 342-347, with minor changes.

business will be a failure, and you will be so grieved that you will have no appetite to eat." To Abaye he said, "Your business will prosper, and you will not be able to eat from sheer joy." They then said to him, "We read in our dream the verse, 'Thou shalt beget sons and daughters but they shall not be thine,' (Deut. 28:41)." To Rava, he interpreted it in its [literal] unfavorable [sense]. To Abaye he said, "You have numerous sons and daughters, and your daughters will be married and go away, and it will seem to you as if they have gone into captivity." [They said to him] "We read the verse, 'Thy sons and thy daughters shall be given unto another people,' (Deut. 28:32)." To Abaye he said, "You have numerous sons and daughters; you will want your daughters to marry your relatives, and your wife will want them to marry her relatives, and she will force you to marry them to her relatives, which will be like giving them to another people." To Rava he said, "Your wife will die, and her sons and daughters will come under the sway of another wife." [They further said]: "We read in our dream the verse, 'Go thy way, eat thy bread with joy,' (Qoh. 9:7)." To Abaye he said, "Your business will prosper, and you will eat and drink, and recite this verse out of the joy of your heart." To Rava he said, "Your business will fail, you will slaughter [cattle] and not eat or drink and you will read Scripture to allay your anxiety." [They said to him]: "We read the verse, 'Thou shalt carry much seed out into the field [and shall gather little in, for the locusts will consume it]' (Deut. 28:38)." To Abaye he interpreted the first half of the verse; to Rava the second half. [They said to him:] "We read the verse, 'Thou shalt have olive trees throughout all thy borders, [but thou shalt not anoint thyself,'] (Deut. 28:40)." To Abaye he interpreted the first half of the verse; to Rava the second half. [They said to him:] "We read the verse: 'And all the peoples of the earth shall see that the name of the Lord is called upon thee' (Deut. 28:10.)" To Abaye he said: "Your name will become famous as head of the college, and you will be generally feared." To Rava he said, "The King's treasury [BDYYN'] will be broken into, and you will be arrested as a thief, and everyone will draw an inference from you." (The next day the King's treasury was broken into and they came and arrested Rava.) They said to him, "We saw a lettuce on the mouth of a jar." To Abaye he said, "Your business will be doubled like a lettuce." To Rava he said, "Your business will be bitter like a lettuce." They said to him, "We saw some meat on the mouth of a jar." To Abaye he said, "Your wine will be sweet, and everyone will come to buy meat and wine from you." To Rava he said, "Your wine will turn sharp, and everyone will come to buy meat to eat with it." They said, "We saw a cask hanging on a palm tree." To Abaye he said, "Your business will spring up like a palm tree." To Rava he said, "Your goods will be sweet like dates." They said to him, "We saw a pomegranate sprouting on the mouth of a jar." To Abaye he said, "Your goods will be high-priced like a pomegranate." To Rava he said, "Your goods will be stale like a [dry] pomegranate." They said to him, "We saw a cask fall into a pit." To Abaye he said, "Your goods will be in demand." ... To Rava he said, "Your goods will spoil and they will be thrown into a pit." They said to him, "We saw a young ass standing by our pillow and braying." To Abaye he said, "You will become a king, and an *Amora* will stand by you." To Rava he said, "The words 'The first-born of an ass' have been erased from your *tefillin*." Rava said to him: "I have looked at them and they are there." He replied to him, "Certainly the *vav* of the word *ḥamor* [ass] has been erased from your *tefillin*."

Rava finally went to him by himself and said to him, "I dreamt that the outer door fell." He said to him, "Your wife will die." He said to him, "I dreamt that my front and back teeth fell out." He said to him, "Your sons and your daughters will die." He said, "I saw two pigeons flying." He replied, "You will divorce two wives." He said to him, "I saw two turnip-tops." He replied, "You will receive two blows with a cudgel." On that day Rava went and sat all day in the school. He found two blind men quarrelling with one another. Rava went to separate them, and they gave him two blows. They wanted to give him another blow but he said, "Enough! I saw in my dream only two."

Rava finally went and gave him a fee. He said to him, "I saw a wall fall down." He replied, "You will acquire wealth without end." He said, "I dreamed that Abaye's villa ['PDN'] fell in and the dust of it covered me." He replied to him, "Abaye will die and [the presidency of] his school will be come to you." He said to him, "I saw my own villa fall in, and everyone came and took a brick." He said to him, "Your teachings will be disseminated in the world." He said to him, "I dreamt that my head was split open and my brains fell out." He replied, "The stuffing will fall out of your pillow." He said to him, "In my dream I read the *Hallel* of Egypt." He replied, "A miracle will happen to you."

Bar Hedya was once travelling with Rava in a boat. He said to himself: "Why should I accompany a man to whom a miracle will happen?" As he was disembarking, he let a book fall. Rava found it, and saw written in it, "All dreams follow the mouth." He exclaimed, "Evil man! It all depended on you and you gave me all this pain! I forgive you everything except [what you said about] the daughter of R. Ḥisda. May it be God's will that this man be delivered up to the government, and that they have no mercy on him." Bar Hedya said to himself, "What am I to do? We have been taught that a curse uttered by a sage, even when undeserved, comes to pass; how much more this of Rava, for justly did he curse." He said, "I will rise up and go into exile." ... He rose and fled to the Romans. He went and sat at the door of the keeper of the King's wardrobe. The keeper of the wardrobe had a dream, and said to him, "I dreamed that a needle pierced my finger." He said to him, "Give me a *zuz*!" He refused to give him one, and he would not say a word to him. He again said to him, "I dreamed that a worm fell between two of my fingers." He said to him, "Give me a *zuz*." He refused to give him one, and he would not say a word to him. "I dreamed that a worm filled the whole of my hand." He said to him, "Worms have been spoiling all the silk garments." This became known in the palace, and they brought the keeper of the wardrobe in order to put him to death. He said to them, "Why execute me? Bring the man who knew and would not tell." So they brought Bar Hedya, and they said to him, "Because of your *zuz*, the king's silken garments have been ruined." They tied two cedars together with a rope, tied one leg to one cedar and the other to the other, and released the rope, so that even his head was split. Each tree rebounded to its place and he was decapitated and his body fell in two. (b. Ber. 56a-b)

The purport of this long account seems at first glancc to be that dream-interpreters are charlatans. They will give you a good interpretation if you pay them and a bad one if you do not. Their interpretations, however, are not doubted. They may not only predict what would happen, but they can also make it happen by their prediction. Nevertheless, even this story ridiculing dream-interpreters indicated that the interpretations of a charlatan were heeded by distinguished masters and came true. Conversely, it took for granted that Hedya recognized miracles would be done for the rabbis. Moreover, Rava's curse proved far more powerful than anything Bar Hedya could do, and brought him to a bad end. It seems, likely, therefore, that the story was meant to warn people against dealing with dream-interpreters who demanded money. If Bar Hedya had not been a Jew, then the people would thus have been told to be careful about having others than qualified Jews, presumably rabbis, interpret their dreams. As in other instances,[1] the rabbis did not doubt that gentile or Jewish non-rabbinical astrologers, magicians, and dream-interpreters knew what they were doing. But they did not want ordinary people to consult with non-rabbinical interpreters of dreams, who used their power only to obtain money. The rabbi, by contrast, could be trusted.

The rabbis not only believed in the interpretation of dreams, but also acted upon that interpretation. Dreams were an accurate vehicle of heavenly revelations. The conflicting Scriptural evaluation of dreams, in Num. 12:6, "In a dream I shall speak concerning him," and Zech. 10:2, "All dreams speak falsely," were harmonized by Rava, who said that when through a dream an angel speaks, it is an accurate revelation, but when a demon does, it is false.[2] Dreams even carried some legal weight, as in the following story:

R. Joseph said, "If one dreamed he has been excommunicated, ten men are necessary for annulling the decree. They must have studied

[1] See for example vol. III, pp. 108-109.

[2] b. Ber. 55b.

law, but if they have only repeated [Tannaitic traditions] they cannot lift the decree..."

(b. Ned. 8a)[1]

Similarly, in the administration of community affairs:

Rava came to Hagronia and ordained a fast, but no rain came. He told the people to fast overnight. The next morning he asked whether anyone had had a dream. R. Eleazar of Hagronia said, "I had a dream, and the following was said to me, 'Good greetings to the good teacher from the good Master who from his goodness gives good to his people.'" Rava exclaimed, "This is a favorable time to pray." He prayed and it rained.

(b. Ta'anit 24b)

Since heaven had been displeased by Rava's actions, its message was conveyed in a dream to R. Safra.[2] Hence a dream might be withheld as a sign of disapproval.

Heavenly communications might come by other means as well. One recalls that the heavenly academy dropped a letter to the earthly one, with reference to Rabbah b. Naḥmani,[3] to tell the rabbis to begin lamenting the death of Rabbah. The letter stated, "He who now holds aloof from lamentation shall be excommunicated." Excommunication was a serious, legal penalty.[4] Nonetheless, R. Joseph held people do not normally go up to heaven and get a legal decision for the earthly academy:

[In expressing his rejection of a view that the law regarded a man as immune from heavenly prosecution if the earthly court did not try him], R. Joseph [sarcastically] said, "Who has gone up [to heaven] and come back [to bring such information]."

(b. Mak. 23b)

XI. Witchcraft, Incantations, and Amulets

Belief in the existence of angels, demons, and spirits of the dead, with whom men could communicate in various ways, provided a "justification" for age-old magical practices, most of them, perhaps, originally impersonal, but many reinterpreted as means of persuading

---

[1] See B. Lewin, *Oẓar HaGeonim*, XI, part i, p. 4.

[2] b. Ḥul. 133a.

[3] b. B.M. 86a, see above, p. 41ff.

[4] Rabbah was unpopular in his town, as we shall see, and some may not have wanted to lament when he was killed.

or compelling supernatural beings to act in the magician's behalf. Such belief in witchcraft seems greatly to have grown in the fourth century.[1] The following account suggests that between the time of Abaye (d. 338) and that of R. Papa (d. 376), fears of witchcraft had so increased that academic discussions were affected:

> [If one gives a loaf to a child, he must tell the mother. What should he do so the mother may know?] Abaye said, "He must rub him with oil and paint him with kohl." But nowadays that we fear witchcraft, what [is to be done]? R. Papa said, "He must rub him with whatever he has given him."
>
> (b. Shab. 10b)

The rabbis certainly shared the convictions of ordinary people that witchcraft was effective. They transmitted traditions about how to prevent or control it, including the following:

> Abaye said that Rabbah told him the reason one should not eat vegetables from the bunch was that one thereby lays himself open to witchcraft.
>
> (b. Ḥul. 105b)

> Abaye said that his mother told him that seven garlands [of a certain vegetable] work against witchcraft.
>
> (b. Shab. 66b)

What is striking is that Abaye's traditions about witchcraft came from two different sources: first, the teaching of his master, Rabbah, second, the tradition of his foster-mother [Rabbah's wife]. No distinction was made between the two, since both women and rabbis were commonly supposed to be authorities on magic. Women were notorious for their practice of it—they had been the first to learn it from the fallen angels. As for the rabbis, their reputation for knowledge, and especially secret and traditional knowledge, led to their being credited with magical knowledge, especially of amulets and healing-incantations, and many of them spoke as authorities on these subjects.

On the other hand, witchcraft or sorcery performed by shady supernatural beings was feared as much as magic performed by ordinary mortals. R. Mari the son of the daughter of Samuel witnessed a miracle performed by angels and warned people against benefitting from it:

> R. Mari son of the daughter of Samuel told, "Once I was standing on the bank of the Papa canal, and saw angels appearing [in the guise of] sailors who brought sand and loaded ships with it, and it turned into

[1] As is clear in the summary table, below, p. 399.

[fine] flour. When the people came to buy it, I warned, 'Do not buy it because it resulted from a miracle.' The next day shiploads of wheat came from Perezina."

(b. Ta'anit 24b)

Traditions about incantations were most commonly repeated in connection with medical remedies.[1] Few remedies were performed without the recitation of some sort of incantation. For example, Abaye reported:

"Mother told me, 'For a daily fever one must take a white (new) *zuz*, go to a salt deposit, take its weight in salt, and tie it up in the nape of the neck with a white twisted cord. But if this is not possible, let one sit at acrossroads. When he sees a large ant carrying something, let him take it and throw it into a brass tube, and close it with lead and seal it with sixty seals. Let him then shake it, lift it up, and say to it, 'Your burden on me and mine on you.'"...

(b. Shab. 66b)[2]

Abaye said, "Mother told me, 'All incantations which are repeated several times must contain the name of the patient's mother. All knots [tied for magical purposes of healing] must be tied on the left ... All incantations are to be repeated the number of times as required in the prescription. Where the number is not prescribed, they should be repeated forty-one times.'"

(b. Shab. 66b)

The source of incantation-magic was not only old-wives tales. Rabbah[3] reported that he had heard an effective incantation to prevent a ship from sinking, as follows:

Rabbah said, "Those who go down to the sea told me, 'The wave that sinks a ship appears with a fringe of white fire at its crest. When hit by clubs on which is engraven, *I am that I am*, *Yah*, *the Lord of Hosts*, *Amen Amen Selah*, it will subside.'"

(b. B.B. 73a)

---

[1] On incantation, Trachtenberg says, "The magic of the Talmud depended largely upon the potency inherent in the form of the incantation, that is, in the word, and upon the magical action, for its most striking effects, and in consequence we find the barbaric word coming to occupy an important place." Trachtenberg, *op. cit.*, p. 88. See also Blau, *op. cit.*, pp. 61-86, on incantations; pp. 86-96 on amulets; pp. 152-156 on the evil eye. On charms, see S. Lieberman, *Greek in Jewish Palestine* (New York, 1942), pp. 100-110.

[2] For other examples of incantations for the purpose of healing, see below, pp. 365-366.

[3] Since the subsequent stories concern Rabbah b. B. Ḥana, this saying may likewise be his, and not Rabbah b. Naḥmani's.

The use of the divine names on these clubs is similar to their use in other magical ways, evidenced both in Palestine and in Babylonia. What is striking is that the *rabbis* preserved stories of how a magical incantation including the divine name was used, and themselves made use of incantations, not only for healing, but also as in the following saying of Abaye:

> Abaye said that it is forbidden to cast a spell over a wasp and a scorpion, though if they are following a man, he may do so.
>
> (b. Ker. 3b)

Whether or not fringes and phylacteries were regarded as charms or amulets—and I am sure they were—the rabbis certainly believed that other charms and amulets could effectively prevent demons or other evil forces from harming a person. Not all amulets were acceptable. The test was a practical one:

> R. Papa said, "It is obvious to me that if three amulets [QMY'] work for three people three times each, both the practitioner [man] and the amulets are approved. If three amulets work for three people once each, the practitioner is approved but not the amulets. If one works for three men, the amulet is approved but not the practitioner. But what if three amulets work for one person? The amulets are not approved, but does the practitioner win approval or not?"...
>
> (b. Shab. 61b)

If the man was approved, R. Papa said, then one would be permitted to go out on the Sabbath wearing an amulet he had prepared.[1] Rava held that no one bothers to make an amulet in the shape of *tefillin*, so he assumed that *tefillin* were not regarded as amulets. But *tefillin* were generally believed to protect against demons, as we have seen.

Like the Magi,[2] some rabbis learned the arts, which were regarded as a form of magic, of juggling:

> Abaye used to juggle before Rabbah with eight eggs or some say four eggs.
>
> (b. Suk. 53a)

Rabbis, however, regarded themselves as greater masters of magic than Magi.[3]

---

[1] b. Shab. 61a.
[2] See Vol. II, pp. 149-151.
[3] Above, p. 339.

XII. The Rabbi's Curse

The rabbis were believed to be able to curse, and so call down evil and even death upon the accursed. The acceptable curse might take the form of words, as when R. Dimi of Nehardea was treated in a manner he thought disrespectful by R. Adda, and complained to R. Joseph. R. Joseph then said the classic imprecation:

> "He who did not delay to avenge the wrong done to the king of Edom will not delay to avenge the wrong done to you..." Shortly afterward, R. Adda b. Abba died. R. Joseph said, "On my account he was punished, because I cursed him." R. Dimi said, "It was on my account, because he made me lose my figs..."
>
> (b. B.B. 22a)

Similarly, one recalls, Rabbah b. R. Huna cursed "whoever cut down" his trees, saying that "his branches should be cut down," and in consequence, during his lifetime the children of Rabbah b. R. Naḥman did not survive.[1]

A rabbi might employ his knowledge of magic to bring down misfortune and even death upon the head of one who displeased him, as in the following case:

> A certain bully was bothering a certain disciple of the rabbis. He came before R. Joseph, who told him, "Go and excommunicate him." The student replied that he was afraid of him. He said, "Then take out a subpoena [PTYḤ'] against him [That is, write out the decree of excommunication]." "I am all the more afraid of him." "Then take it [the decree] and put it in a jar, take it to a cemetery, and blast into it a thousand horn-blasts on forty days." He went and did so. The jar broke, and the bully died.
>
> (b. M.Q. 17a-b)

Another curse was the laying on of the 'evil eye.' One recalls that Abaye cursed the parents of a man of whom he disapproved. He asked where they were, looked in that direction, and the parents died.[2]

If a rabbi was treated dishonorably, heaven itself might automatically avenge the insult. For example, Rava said that Rami b. Ḥama died only because he would not count R. Menashiah b. Taḥalifa for a quorum in reciting the Grace after Meals, despite the fact that R. Menashiah was learned in various Tannaitic traditions. Rami b. Ḥama had thought that he was merely a good memorizer, and did not treat him like a true disciple of the sages. Since R. Menashiah used to hear the rabbis'

---

[1] b. B.M. 108a, above, p. 236.

[2] b. Yev. 106a, cited above pp. 204-205.

discussions and memorize them, he was regarded as of the same status, and hence Rami erred—and died. No explicit curse was issued.[1] One who disobeyed a rabbinical decree might suffer misfortune whether the rabbi cursed him or not. When a certain Pumbeditan was bitten by a snake, it was impossible to prepare the proper antidote. Several apparent accidents prevented it. One antidote was to tear open the embryo of a white ass and sit on it:

> There were thirteen white asses in Pumbedita and they were all torn open and found to be *trefah* [and therefore unusable or ineffective]. On the other side of town was another, but before they could go and get it, a lion ate it. Abaye observed, "Perhaps he was bitten by a snake of the rabbis, for which there is no cure, as it is written, 'And who breaks through a fence, a serpent shall bite him' (Qoh. 10:8) ..."
>
> (b. Shab. 110a)

If people widely believed that dishonoring or disobeying a rabbi would lead to inexorable doom, they would naturally take pains to honor and obey him.

It should be stressed that the rabbis, and other holy men, enjoyed no monopoly over magical arts. Ordinary people might learn the proper incantations and rituals to cast spells, curses, and the like.[2] One such instance is as follows:

> [A woman cursed Rava for making a decision which displeased her.] "May your ship sink," she called out, "Are you trying to fool me?" Rava's clothes were soaked in water [to carry out the curse symbolically, and so prevent its realization] and yet he did not escape the drowning.
>
> (b. B.B. 153a)

It was quite natural for the rabbis to take seriously the curse of an ordinary woman. On the other hand, if magic was real, then the rabbis were surely going to be greater masters of it than anyone else so far as the schools were concerned. Hence their curses would have been regarded as especially potent. While some curses depended upon heavenly assistance, others were not dependent upon angels' or demons' responding to prayer, but rather upon rabbis' knowledge of the proper way to compose and effect the curse. Clearly rabbinic tradition contained uncontingent magical formulae, believed to be useful and in no way reprehensible.

---

1 b. Ber. 47b.

2 See vol. III, p. 108.

XIII. TORAH AS A SOURCE OF SUPERNATURAL AND MAGICAL POWER

If we now review the role of the rabbi in the supernatural world he believed in, we discover a remarkable set of facts. The rabbi was the authority on theology, that is, among other things, on the structure and order of the supernatural world. He knew the secret names of God and the secrets of the divine 'chariot'—the heavens—and of creation. If extraordinarily pious, he might even see the face of the Shekhinah; in any event, the Shekhinah was present in the rabbinical schools. The rabbi was therefore a holy man, overcame the evil impulse which dominated ordinary men, was consequently less liable to suffering, misfortune, and sickness. He knew the proper times and forms of prayer, and could therefore pray effectively. Moreover, the efficacy of his prayers was heightened by his purity, holiness, and merits, which in turn derived from his knowledge of the secrets of Torah, and consequently, his peculiar observances. Therefore not only his prayers in general, but also his prayers for particular purposes, were effective. He could bring rain or cause drought. His blessings brought fertility, and his curses, death. He was apt to be visited by angels and to receive communications from them. He could see demons and talk with them and could also communicate with the dead. He was an authority on the interpretation of omens and of dreams, and on means to avert witchcraft, on incantations for cures, knot-tying (for phylacteries), and the manufacture and use of amulets. He was, in anthropological terms, a medicine man. Could a modern anthropologist spend a few years in ancient Pumbedita, Sura, or Nehardea, to study the social role of the rabbi, his resultant book would certainly be called something like "The Lawyer-Magicians of Babylonia."

Here, however, we must offer an important distinction.[1] The fact that the rabbis performed the functions and claimed the powers characteristic, in primitive societies, of magicians might justify a modern anthropologist in applying to them that term, but it does not prove that they applied the term to themselves or would have approved its application. In fact the rabbis would not have regarded their power

[1] Note also the comment of W. L. Knox, "The boundary between magic and religion on the one hand and medicine on the other is not too easy to fix in the first century A.D. 'He that casteth out devils by Beelzebub' suggests that 'magic' was a term of abuse, implying that you disagreed with your opponent, but could not deny that he produced remarkable results." See his "Pharisaism and Hellenism," in H. Loewe, ed., *Judaism and Christianity, II. The Contact of Pharisaism with Other Cultures* (London, 1937), pp. 61-114. Quotation on p. 106.

as magical or the Torah as a source of magic. The dividing line between true religion and magic was clearly drawn, widely recognized, and by virtue of that recognition, became a social reality. What was approved by society—in this case, the schools—required by custom, and unquestionably seen to be part of the established religion was usually thought to be in no way magical. Abaye said:

> "The sorcerer [who insists upon exact paraphernalia noting different properties of different kinds of magic] works through demons. He who does not, works by [pure] enchantment ... The laws of sorcery are like those of the Sabbath. Certain actions are punished by stoning, some are not punished but forbidden, and others are entirely permitted. If one actually performs [magic], he is stoned. If he merely creates an illusion, he is exempt, but the act is prohibited." What is entirely permitted? Such as [the magic performed by] R. Ḥanina and R. 'Oshai'a', who spent every Sabbath eve studying the Laws of Creation, by means of which they made a third-grown calf and ate it.
>
> (b. Sanh. 67b)

One may only suppose that "magic" was permitted if the rabbis did it. Working through demons and enchantment may be to modern eyes no different from studying the "Laws of Creation" and applying them. But the distinction was important to Abaye.[1]

Jewish society, including the rabbis', was not primitive. It had long since sharply distinguished, by its own standards, between what *it* considered magic, and what *it* considered religion—neither identical with what we should class under those terms—and by *its* standards, the rabbis were not magicians, as I just said. Some of them did practice magic on the side, but this is a different matter. The distinction has been best illustrated by Professor Morton Smith, in an unpublished lecture:

> In antiquity, the practice of magic was a criminal offense and the term 'magician' was a term of abuse. It still is, but the connotation has changed. It now primarily connotes fraud. Then the notion was that of social subversion. The efficacy of magic was almost universally believed and the magician was conceived of as a man who, by acquiring supernatural powers, had become a potential danger to the established authority and to the order that they sought to maintain. Consequently magic was widely practiced but rarely admitted.
>
> For Judaism there was a further limiting factor in the dogma that there was no god save the Lord. This did not lead to a denial of the

[1] Lieberman stresses, "Magic is effective in the case of the ordinary man only, but not in that of the really righteous, whose merit is great ... it is powerless in the face of the virtuous man," *Greek in Jewish Palestine*, (N.Y. 1942), p. 113.

efficacy of pagan magic nor did it prevent Jews from using the same magical practices as pagans. On the contrary, the Jews were famous as magicians, as Josephus says. And new discoveries by Professor M. Margalioth show that as late as the fourth and fifth centuries Jews, steeped in the Old Testament and thoroughly at home in the Synagogue, were composing a magician's handbook which listed pagan deities and prescribed prayers and sacrifices to be offered to them in magical ceremonies. Among the prayers there is an invocation of Helios in transliterated Greek; and the conclusion comes upon reaching the Seventh Heaven with a celebration of Yahweh as the supreme God.

At least the more scrupulous of the Jews distinguished their marvels as performed by the power of the supreme God from those of the pagans whose gods were demons and impure spirits. Rabbi ʿAqiva, complaining of his own ill success in magic, said, "When a man fasts in order that an unclean spirit should rest on him, the unclean spirit does so. It should happen, therefore, that when a man fasts in order that a pure spirit should rest on him, the pure spirit should do so. But what can I do since our iniquities are the cause of our difficulties? For it is said that your iniquities are dividing you from your God." The context leaves no doubt of the magical reference. But ʿAqiva is not, of course, represented in the Talmud as a magician, because that term was a term of abuse. The fact that a man was represented as a supernatural being is in itself a suspicious item, for this was a common claim of magicians and a regular result of magical operation.

Smith's reference, in successive paragraphs, to the handbook discovered by Margalioth [M. Margalioth, *Sefer HaRazim, Hu Sefer Keshafim Mitequfat HaTalmud* (Jerusalem, 1967)], points to the necessity of further distinction, for the two are certainly not in the same class, yet both of them reflect attitudes different from the one common in stories of rabbis whose merits enabled them to pray with good hope that their prayers would be answered. At the pagan end of the scale, we may suppose, was the Jew who simply learned and practiced pagan magic as such, throwing in, perhaps, for good measure a few extra conjurations by the sacred name, Yahweh, or some prayers for him or to the Jewish angels. Of such men we have plentiful evidence in the magical papyri. Next to them come men like the author of *Sefer HaRazim* who took over pagan magic, but made it part of a picture of the cosmos in which Yahweh was the supreme God, to whom all the pagan deities were subordinate. Then there was the position familiar as that of "normative Judaism": the rabbi does not practice "magic" at all, but his "acts of piety and religious observances" so increase his "merits" that he can pray, bless or curse, with the hope that his prayers would be answered and his blessings and curses be made effective by divine or angelic action. Finally there were those who, by study of the Torah, sought to master it so as to be able to use directly, for their own purposes, its creative and miraculous powers; in 'Aqiva's words (which, however, reflect slightly different notions), they "fasted that a pure spirit should rest upon them." Such men could do miracles for and by themselves, not just ask to have them done for them. And this mastery and use of the Torah made Torah a source of magical, not merely supernatural, power. Since these beliefs were preserved within the schools themselves, but were consistently overshadowed, especially in exoteric presentation, by stories and teaching presenting the "normative theory," it is not unlikely that many of the other magical functions of the rabbis, which our texts represent as answers to prayer or acts of divine grace in response to human merit—or do not explain at all—were seen by many contemporaries, and probably by many of the rabbis themselves, as exercises of this supernatural power conferred by study of the Torah. It follows that the rabbis never called themselves magicians. On the contrary, they consistently and explicitly disapproved of "magic," as I have just shown in Abaye's case. But many of the things they did, especially the supernatural character alleged to have been imparted to them by their knowledge of Torah, must be seen in the context of antiquity as appropriate to divine-men or magicians. Unique to the rabbis is the claim that their miracles, supernatural graces, and magical actions derived from the Torah, rather than from some other source of supernatural power. To them this was sufficient justification.

The rabbis were believed to be able to pray more effectively than other people, heads of schools most effectively of all. So we are told that "in the time of R. Joseph," meaning, when he was the head of the school:

> ... there was a famine. The rabbis asked him to offer prayers for mercy. He replied, "If Elisha with whom, when the rabbis departed, there still remained two thousand two hundred disciples, did not offer up prayers for mercy in a time of famine, should I...?"
>
> (b. Ket. 106a)

Further, only when R. Joseph became head of a school was he able to solve a certain legal problem.[1] Rava said that Ahasuerus believed that the rabbis would protect Israel because they were careful to keep

[1] b. B.Q. 66b.

the commandments.[1] One recalls that the Jewish marketman in Be Lapat informed the rabbis when harsh decrees were made against the Jews, "so they would pray and have the decree annuled."[2] There can be no doubt that the basis of the belief that the rabbis enjoyed exceptional powers lay in the anterior conviction that study of Torah and performance of the commandments produced heavenly favor. Rava and Abaye said that sin can be expiated not through sacrifice, but through study of the Torah and good deeds. Rabbah and Abaye were supposedly descended from the house of Eli, but were able to overcome the ancient curse against that house through devotion to Torah and, in Abaye's case, good deeds as well. Hence though descendents of Eli were not supposed to live past the age of twenty, Rabbah was rewarded by a life of forty years, and Abaye, sixty years.[3] It was stated quite explicitly that study of Torah and performance of the commandments were supposed to produce heavenly favor, resulting in protection against evil and also special blessings:

> R. Joseph said that a commandment protects [from suffering] and rescues [from evil inclination] when one is doing it, but afterwards, while it protects, it does not rescue. Rava said that while one is engaged in study of Torah, the act of study protects and rescues, but otherwise, study of Torah protects but does not rescue. As to a commandment, under all circumstances it protects but does not rescue.
>
> (b. Sot. 21a)

The "protection" was from demons and Satan. (R. Aḥa b. Jacob, when swinging the *lulav*, for example, said, "An arrow in the eyes of Satan.")[4]

Obviously study of Torah was supposed to yield exceptional prowess, for when it did not, that was the subject of comment:

> Rava said, "Is there any greatness in propounding problems? In the years of Rav Judah, their whole studies were confined to the laws of *Neziqin*, while we study [much more...], yet Rav Judah [merely] took off his shoes and the rain came, while we cry out but are not heard [lit. "no one pays attention to us"]. But [it is because] the Holy One blessed be he requires the heart...."
>
> (b. Sanh. 106b)

---

[1] b. Meg. 13b. For rabbis as protectors of the community, see vol. III, pp. 102ff., and above, pp. 340-341.

[2] b. Ta'anit 22a, see above, p. 50.

[3] b. R.H. 18a, b. Yev. 5a. See my *Life of R. Yoḥanan ben Zakkai*, p. 64, for an earlier example.

[4] b. Men. 62a.

> R. Papa said to Abaye, "What is the difference between us and the ancients? For them, miracles were done, and for us, no miracles are done. If it is on account of learning, in the years of Rav Judah, they studied only *Neziqin*, and we study all six orders of the Mishnah, and when Rav Judah reached [a certain passage, he was perplexed by it, while we achieve much more in studying that same passage but he could produce rain, ... as above]." Abaye replied to him, "The ancients gave their lives for the sanctification of God's name, but we do not do so..."
>
> (b. Ber. 20a)

> Rabbah once decreed a fast. He prayed, but no rain came. People thereupon remarked to him, "When Rav Judah ordained a fast, rain did fall." He replied, "What can I do? Is it because of studies? We are superior to him, because in the time of Rav Judah ... [as above]. Yet when Rav Judah removed one shoe ... But when we cry out the whole day, no one hears us. Is it because of some deed? If so, let anyone who knows of it tell it. What can the great men of the generation do, however, when their generation does not seem good [warrant miracles]."
>
> (b. Ta'anit 24a-b)

So study of Torah and practice of the commandments would be rewarded by rain as well as protection. Moreover, the disciples of Rava, Abaye, and Rabbah preserved three fundamentally different stories of how the several masters had uttered the same saying on the disparity of learning and miraculous power between their generation and the former one. The saying must therefore be prior to the stories both in time and in importance, and it clearly presupposes some intrinsic relationship between mastery of Torah and the ability to make rain. The masters did not deny it. It was a disappointment to them that they could not do what the ancients, whose achievements in learning were less impressive than theirs, could easily accomplish. The articulated sense of disparity between intellectual achievement and theurgical power leaves no doubt that the former was naturally expected to yield the latter.

The view that the righteous even have the creative power of God is strikingly manifested in the following:

> Rava said, "If a righteous man desires it, he can be a creator of a world for it is written, 'But your iniquities have distinguished...' (Is. 59:2). [That is, but for sin, a man's power would equal that of God, and he could create a world.]
>
> Rabbah created a man [GBR'], and sent him to R. Zera. R. Zera spoke to him, but he did not answer. He said to him, "You are a creature of the magicians [ḤBRY' = Magi]. Return to your dust."
>
> (b. Sanh. 65b)

Learning and piety reshape a man in the likeness of God, and therefore endow him with God's powers of creation. God had made the world through Torah, and masters of Torah could similarly do wonderful acts of creation. Rava said that only sin prevented man from performing miracles, like both Rabbah, who was able to make a man, and R. Zera, who was able to destroy him. The following contains another story of a rabbi's extraordinary power:

> Rabbah and R. Zera feasted together on Purim. They became drunk and Rabbah arose and cut R. Zera's [throat]. The next day he prayed on his behalf and resurrected him. Next year he asked, "Will your honor come and feast with me?" He replied, "A miracle does not always happen."
>
> (b. Meg. 7b)

The rabbi was able to persuade God to resurrect the dead. That does not mean he was "like God." Had Rabbah been able to do it like God, R. Zera would have had no reason to refuse a second invitation, unless he did not want to repeat the experience. The refusal as given indicates that the miracle was not strictly by magic but by prayer and rather uncertain reward for merits. God does miracles without praying to anybody, and the rabbi generally relies upon prayer or merits. That is the difference between this story, which is an ordinary one of prayer and its reward, and the former ones in which the rabbis' own extraordinary powers, probably acquired by prayer, study, or other merits, *now are usable directly and uncontingently*.

Furthermore, if Torah yielded magic, magic could also be used to produce greater Torah. Abaye believed that a certain bird, properly eaten, would help one increase in wisdom. One eats half the right side and half the left, and places the remainder in a brass tube, to be sealed with sixty sealings. This is to be suspended on his arm. One then studies to his heart's content, and finally consumes the other half.[1] That seals in the new learning. If he fails to do so, he will forget what he has learned.

This view of the worldly benefits of studying the Torah, keeping the commandments, and acting virtuously was not the invention of the rabbis. From biblical times, it had been believed that if the Israelites faithfully kept the covenant and did the commandments, they would enjoy rain and other forms of prosperity. Such was the theory of Deuteronomy. The rabbis simply arrogated to themselves and their

---

[1] b. Shab. 90b.

activities promises earlier believed to depend upon the good works of priests, prophets, and other holy men, and upon popular adherence to their teachings.

To summarize: After noting that leading rabbis were said to be able to create men, cows, and rain, one can hardly conclude that the rabbis were not seen as magicians. That people commented upon the disparity between learning and one's capacity to produce rain, furthermore, manifests their sense of an intrinsic relationship between them. Theurgical skills were regarded as an authentication, though not the only one, of the fact that rabbis were holy men, or saints, or righteous. The saying that only sin prevented men from doing the things God could do, followed by the story about how Rabbah created a man, may simply be reversed. If Rabbah could create a man, then he was sinless, a master of great learning and merits. Theurgical ability thus testified to his pure, sinless condition as a master of Torah. That is not to suggest that repeating words of Torah was invariably an incantation, of the same substance as saying an anti-demonic formula. But if, as we have seen, repeating words of Torah could prevent the angel of death from approaching Rabbah and others, or not repeating them in the privy laid one open to demonic mischief so that other anti-demonic measures had to be taken, then repeating words of Torah served on occasion as an incantation. Similarly, great learning in Torah did not lead *only* or invariably to ability to do such wonders as making men, cows, or rain.

The ascription of supernatural power must nonetheless be seen as one frequent attribute of leading masters in the schools.[1] It is the attribute which most closely parallels those of the "divine-man," for, as Bieler stresses,[2] the unity of faith, wisdom, and unusual ability, was everywhere taken for granted. Knowing and "doing" were in no way separable. Bieler states, "Σοφία hat die ganz allgemeine Bedeutung von Wissen und Können." The rabbi's "wisdom" derived from Torah, and so did his supernatural, or magical, skills. To no one in antiquity could such a conception have been alien. The only issue was whose σοφία was really true. Bieler asks, Was the "divine-man" a Magus? Certainly

[1] See the excellent notes of Salo W. Baron, *Social and Religious History*, II, pp. 335-337, ns. 23-27 for a bibliographical survey of Jewish magic in antiquity. My purpose is not to survey that literature, but only to stress that magic, like supernaturalism, was an intrinsic part of the life of the schools, and to call attention to some of the stories which indicate the genres of magic found there. On the sources of Jewish magical science, see Blau, *op. cit.*, pp. 37-49.

[2] *Op. cit.*, I, pp. 73ff.

many "divine-man" of antiquity were so considered, and among them assuredly Jews, who were famed for the excellence of their magic, as in Acts 19:11-20. So far as magicians were disreputable, no faithful community would regard its holy men as magicians. But so far as magic was an expected and normal trait of religious virtuosi, everyone supposed his community's holy men could produce magic. What was "Torah" or perhaps "white magic" to Jews may have been witchcraft or black magic to gentile meighbors, and vice versa. It was, as Bieler says, a subjective distinction at best.[1] Bieler offers a more striking and fruitful distinction, that between "Θεῖος ἀνήρ in den Augen seiner... Zeitgenossen, Θεῖος ἐπιφανής im Glauben seiner Bekenner."[2] It would be foolish to suggest that that distinction applies without modification to the Jewish circumstance. For Jews, the rabbi as living Torah was surely as close as one could possibly come to the Θεῖος ἐπιφανής of Bieler's distinction. It does not, however, seem very remote.[3] We note the striking portrait of the wisdom of Solomon drawn by a first-

[1] Even though the rabbi does not conform to the pattern of the "divine-man" in every detail, the important point in common noted here is striking. Indeed, I wish Bieler had had access to the rich corpus of Talmudic rabbinic hagiography, which would have enhanced his discussion of the "divine-man" as an ideal-type.

[2] *Op. cit.*, I, p. 150.

[3] I note considerable change from Palestine in Tannaitic times. Then miracle-stories were rarely, if ever, told concerning leading Tannaitic authorities, though, to be sure, theurges of various kinds were active within the Jewish community. Morton Smith points out, [*Tannaitic Parallels to the Gospels* (Philadelphia, 1951), p. 81], "For as a matter of fact Tannaitic literature contains almost no stories of miracles performed by Tannaim, and this not because the authorities behind the literature did not believe in miracles, nor yet because they did not like to talk of them, for when they commented on the stories of the Old Testament—which already contain enough miracles for the average man—they added to their accounts many more miracles of the most miraculous sort, but when they came to tell of the doings of the Tannaim they ceased almost altogether to tell miracle stories, and this fact is strikingly obvious from the collection of stories made by Fiebig in his book." Here Smith refers to P. Fiebig, *Jüdische Wundergeschichten des neutestamentlichen Zeitalters* (Tübingen, 1911). Smith then surveys the thirteen passages cited by Fiebig, and shows that most of them do not pertain to Tannaitic authorities, or do not contain what can be called "miracles." Smith's general conclusion (p. 84) is as follows: "As for stories of miracles done by men of that period ... the parallels between the Gospels and Tannaitic Literature are not so important as the difference between them, and that difference is, that stories like these are very frequent in the Gospels, and almost totally lacking in Tannaitic literature." The tables below (pp. 392-399) reenforce Smith's point, for in general, we have only a few miracle-stories from each generation of Babylonian Amoraim. That does not change the fact, which I have stressed here, that the Babylonian Amoraim did suppose there was an intrinsic relationship between Torah and wonderful power (δύναμις = גבורה). Whether that notion characterized Tannaitic masters I cannot say, nor am I certain how it would have been expressed.

century Pharisaic disciple who went on to a career outside of the schools:

> There was no form of nature with which he [Solomon] was not acquainted or which he passed over without examining, but he studied them all philosophically and revealed the most complete knowledge of their several properties. And God granted him knowledge of the art used against demons for the benefit and healing of men. He also composed incantations by which illnesses are relieved, and left behind forms of exorcisms with which those possessed by demons drive them out, never to return. And this kind of cure is of very great power among us to this day....
>
> (Josephus, Jewish Antiquities, VIII, 44-45, trans. H. Thackeray, V, 595).

Healing arts, exorcisms, incantations—these testified to the grace of God, no less than mastery of Torah or other forms of saintliness. Far from disapproving of "magic," the rabbis took pride in their theurgical attainments, which, they said, Torah enabled them to do.[1]

To conclude: Contingent rewards for merit are different from reliably effective magic. We have in the preceding sections noted examples of both kinds of miracles. Rainmaking shows a general expectation that learning produces merit, which produces a claim on the diety for performance of services requested. Rabbah could not raise the dead like God, but only with God's help. We have been careful to examine first the supernatural environment, second some examples of actual uncontingent magical power attributed to rabbis. Miracles therefore must be divided into two kinds, according to the distinction herein inferred, first, those produced by divine grace elicited through right action; second, those produced by rabbinical power attained through Torah. The rabbi's own mastery of Torah produced power he could exert independent of heaven, in the form of witchcraft, amulets, blessings, curses, and the like. Rabbinic tradition often makes the point that these were not powers but merits; even the efficacy of prayer depended on additional moral conditions. In function, however, it is clear that these theoretical distinctions were less conclusive, for the ability to do miracles on one's own, not merely to ask to have them done for him, is evident in some of the stories we have considered.

---

[1] For non-rabbinic, Jewish magicians of the age, see Marcel Simon, *Recherches d'Histoire Judéo-Crétienne* (Paris and The Hague, 1962), pp. 142ff.

XIV. Medicine

Although the rabbis were not physicians, they possessed many kinds of traditions pertaining to hygiene, medicine, and healing. These they acquired from several sources. First, their own schools preserved important medical traditions on account of their relevance to legal issues. Second, they learned whatever they could from folk-medicine. Third, they solicited medical information from other groups in Babylonia, in this period in particular from Tai tribesmen. M. Beer persuasively argues[1] that the rabbis were not professional physicians, never received fees for medical advice, and did not regularly practice medicine. Physicians did exist within the Jewish community but among them were no sages. The physicians of Maḥoza regarded rabbinical medicine as a form of competition with their own practice, especially when the rabbis publicly taught people how to heal themselves, as in the following instance:

> Abaye said, "Mother told me that a salve ['YSPLNYT'] for all pains is seven parts of fat and one of wax." Rava said, "Wax and resin." Rava taught this publicly at Maḥoza. The family of Benjamin the doctor tore up their bandages. He said to them, "I have left you one [unrevealed trade secret] for Samuel said, 'He who washes his face but does not dry it well will have scabs....'"
>
> (b. Shab. 133b)

Rava reported a tradition of Minyomi, which would have been a form of Benjamin:

> Abaye said, "My mother told me that kidneys were made to heal [a pain in] the ear..." Rava said, "Minyomi the physician told me that any kind of fluid is bad for the ear except the juice from kidneys. One should take the kidney of a bald buck, cut it cross-wise, and place it on glowing coals.... [etc.]"
>
> (b. A.Z. 28b)

This same family criticized the rabbis:

> [Who is an *epikoros* ('PYQWRWS)?] R. Joseph said, "Those who ridicule [rabbis, saying], 'Of what use are the rabbis to us? For their own sake they study [Scriptures], for their own sake they repeat [Mishnaic traditions].'" Abaye said, "But this denotes acting impudently against the Torah...." Rava said, "For instance the family of Benjamin the physician, who say, 'Of what use are the rabbis to us? They never permitted us the raven nor forbade the dove.'" When a suspected *trefa* of the

---

[1] Beer, *Ma'amadam*, pp. 114-116.

family of Benjamin was brought before Rava, if he saw reason to permit it, he would remark to them, "'See, I permit you the raven." If there were grounds to prohibit it, he would say, "See, I forbid you the dove..."

(b. Sanh. 99b-100a)

Rava cursed the family of Benjamin as rank disbelievers, saying they were hostile to the rabbis and ridiculed legal decisions.[1] Nonetheless, the physicians subjected themselves to rabbinical rulings on the suitability of food, specifically of slaughtered animals. Rava gave them such rulings, which they presumably obeyed. His sarcastic remark tells us that their criticism stung.

The rabbis' medical traditions focused in part upon matters they were likely to have to know for legal reasons or would have observed as part of a legal inquisition. Rava said, for example, that pregnant and nursing mothers must fast on the 9th of Av.[2] To give such a ruling, he would have had to know whether such a fast would endanger life or not, for if it would, no fasting was allowed. A second issue of forensic medicine concerned whether a youth had passed his minority, which was signified by the appearance of two pubic hairs. Rava had to know how to tell whether a young man was potent or not:

Whenever people came to Rava [to ask about a young man who reached the age of twenty without showing signs of puberty] he would instruct them as follows: "If the youth was thin, he should be fattened. If fat, he should reduce. [For sometimes the signs do not appear on account of emaciation, and sometimes on account of fatness.]"

(b. Yev. 97a)

Similarly, it was necessary for rabbis to know whether to order a circumcision to be delayed past the eighth day, on account of the potential danger to a child's life. As a result, the lessons of midwives were repeated in the schools, even though these did not pertain directly to the narrow and practical legal issue:

Abaye said, "Mother told me an infant whose anus is not visible should be rubbed with oil and stood in the sun, and where it shows transparent, it should be torn crosswise with a barley grain, but not with a metal instrument, which will cause inflammation... If an infant

---

[1] Beer, *Ma'amadam*, pp. 178-180. Beer regards the criticism as a sign of social tension between a non-rabbinical elite and the rabbinical estate. However, it seems plausible that the particular tension was caused in this instance by professional jealousy. Compare Beer's view, p. 116.

[2] b. Pes. 54b. See b. Yoma 78b, Abaye on washing a child on the Day of Atonement.

cannot suck, his lips are cold. Bring a vessel of burning cloths and hold it near his nostrils so as to heat his lips. He will suck... If an infant does not breathe, he should be fanned... If an infant cannot breathe easily, his mother's after-birth should be brought and rubbed over him. He will breathe easily... If an infant is too thin, do the same with the afterbirth from the narrow to the wide end; if too fat, in the opposite direction.... If an infant is too red, so that the blood is not yet absorbed in him, we must wait until his blood is absorbed and then circumcise him. If he is green and anemic, we must wait until he is full-blooded..."

(b. Shab. 134a)[1]

R. Papa said that circumcision should not be performed on a cloudy day.[2] Much of the above data has no direct bearing upon the legal question of whether a circumcision may take place. On the other hand, knowing how to revive a new-born infant would have been important if ordinary people came to rabbis for advice in such a crisis. Because rabbis had to judge paternity cases, it was important for them to know about sexual potency, the healing of perforations in the male membrum, and the like.[3] Other information about sex had no legal bearing. For example, Rava said that if one wants male children, he should cohabit twice in succession.[4] Abaye said that eating a residue of fish hash, as well as vermin in the linen, sleeping on a tanner's hide, pouring hot water over oneself, and treading on egg shells are all debilitating for sexual relations.[5] Other sayings included the following:

Rabbah b. R. Huna said, "If a man who comes home from a journey has sexual intercourse, his children will be weaklings."

(b. Git. 70a)

Abaye said that an aphrodisiac was made by taking three small measures of safflower and grinding and boiling them in wine. One drinks the potion.

(b. Git. 70a)

Cures for various illnesses constituted a mixture of theology, magic, Scriptural exegesis, and practical medicine. Trachtenberg points out that three causes of disease were generally supposed: human, supernatural, or natural. Human agency included the sorcerer; supernatural

---

[1] Trans. H. Freedman (London, 1938), p. 675.

[2] b. Yev. 72a. For other opinions of Abaye and Rava on circumcision, see b. Shab. 135a-b.

[3] See b. Yev. 76a, Rava b. Rabbah asked R. Joseph how to find out whether semen will reopen a closed perforation; Abaye on healing a perforated membrum; b. Yev. 75b, Rava on Deut. 23:2-3.

[4] b. 'Eruv. 100b, b. Nid. 31b.

[5] b. Pes. 112b.

agency, the demon; and natural causes, diet, accident, or old age.[1] The rabbis believed that when a man's star fated him to die, the angel of death had power over him, and no medicine would avail.[2] Rava in the name of Rabin said that the Holy One sustains the sick, which is proved by Ps. 41:4, "The Lord supports him on the couch of languishing."[3] Tannaitic tradition had taught that the Divine Presence was above the pillow of an invalid, so one should not sit on the bed or a seat, but must sit on the ground.[4] Abaye and Rava said one may borrow the medical teachings of other peoples, and did not prohibit them although they were part of the rituals of paganism.[5] Prayer was believed to be an effective medicine. When Rava was ill, after the first day of his sickness he told his attendant to make a public announcement of that fact, so that those who loved him may pray for him.[6] From Jer. 9:20, Rava learned that in time of epidemic, one should close his windows. It was advisable to publicize one's ailments, so that others would pray in one's behalf. The Tannaitic tradition had so taught concerning Lev. 13:45. R. Joseph reported that an incident occurred at Pumbedita in which people prayed for a woman who thus was healed.[7] Abaye said that Mal. 3:20 proved that the motes dancing in the rays of the sun have healing power.[8]

Among many remedies using magic was the following:

> A mad dog rubbed itself against R. Huna b. R. Joshua in the market. He stripped off his garments and ran [quoting Qoh. 7:12].
>
> What is the remedy of a rabid dog bite? Abaye said, "Let him take the skin of a male hyena and write on it, 'I, so-and-so-, the son of such-and-such a woman, write upon the skin of a male hyena, *Kanti* [=*KNTY*] *Kanti*, *qliros* [*QLYRWS*]—some say *Qandy Qandy Qloros—God, God, Lord of Hosts, Amen, Amen, Sela*.' Then let him strip off his clothes and bury them in a grave, leaving them for twelve months. Then he should take them out and burn them in an oven, and scatter the ashes at the cross-roads. During these twelve months he should drink water only out of a copper tube, lest he see the shadow of a demon and be endangered...."
>
> (b. Yoma 84a)

---

1 Trachtenberg, *op. cit.*, pp. 197-199.
2 Above, p. 333.
3 b. Shab. 12b.
4 *Ibid.*, and b. Ned. 40a.
5 b. Ḥul. 77b.
6 b. Ber. 55b, with reference to Prov. 24:17.
7 b. Nid. 66a.
8 b. Ned. 8b.

Other, more naturalistic remedies included these:

> Abaye said, "I tried every remedy [for scurvy] until a Tai recommended, 'Take the pits of olives ... burn them in a fire upon a new rake, and stick them inside of the gums.' I did so and was cured."
> (b. Yoma 84a=b. A.Z. 28a)

> Abaye said, "Mother told me that roasted ears are good for the heart and banish morbid thoughts.... If a man suffers from weakness of the heart, let him take the flesh of the right flank of a male beast and excrements of cattle of the month of Nisan, and if not available, then willow twigs, and let him roast it, eat it, and after that, drink some diluted wine ..."
> (b. 'Eruv. 29b)[1]

> Abaye said, "Mother told me that a child of six whom a scorpion has bitten on his seventh birthday normally does not survive. What is the remedy? The gall of white stork in beer. This should be rubbed into the wound, and then drunk. A child of the age of one year whom a bee has stung on his first birthday does not survive. What is the remedy? The creepers of a palm tree in water should be rubbed in and then drunk."
> (b. Ket. 50a)[2]

> "The cure for *ra'atan* [a disease which causes the eye to tear, the nostrils to run, spittle to flow from the mouth, and flies to swarm about the victim]," Abaye said, "is pila, ladanum, the rind of a nut tree, the shavings of a dressed hide, *melilot*, and the calyx of a red date. These are boiled together and carried into a house of marble, or, if unavailable, a house with walls thick as seven and a half bricks. Three hundred cups are then poured on his head until the cranium is softened, and then the brain is cut open. Four leaves of myrtle must be brought, and each foot [of the insect causing the disease] should be lifted up, and one leaf placed beneath. The insect is then grasped with a pair of tweezers and burned. Otherwise it would return."
> (b. Ket. 77b)

> Abaye said, "Mother told me that for sun-stroke, the remedy is to take a jug of water on the first day. On the second, let blood. On the third, take red meat broiled on the coals and highly diluted wine. For a chronic heat stroke, bring a black hen and tear it lengthwise and crosswise and shave the middle of his head and put the bird on it and leave it there until it sticks. He should then stand in the water up to his neck until he is faint. Then he should swim out and sit down. If that is not possible, he should eat leeks.... For a chill one should eat fat meat broiled on the coals and undiluted wine ..."
> (b. Git. 67b)[3]

---

[1] Trans. W. Slotki (London, 1948), p. 204.

[2] Trans. W. Slotki (London, 1948), p. 287ff.

[3] Trans. M. Simon (London, 1948), pp. 320ff. The following two passages are in M. Simon's translation as well.

"For a toothache," Rabbah b. R. Huna said, "One should take the top of garlic with one stalk only, and grind it with oil, and salt, and put it on his thumb nail on the side where the tooth aches, and put a rim of dough around it, making sure it does not touch his flesh, as it may cause leprosy..."

(b. Git. 69a)

As to a burning in the bones, Abaye said the remedy, told to him by his foster-mother, was this: "All medicines are taken either for three, seven, or twelve days, but he [afflicted with burning in the bones] must go on until cured. All other medicines are taken on an empty stomach. This one is different. After he has eaten and drunk and relieved himself and washed his hands, they must bring a handful of a flour-and-honey mixture, with lentils, a handful of old wine, and mix them together. He must eat it and then cover himself and sleep, and must not be disturbed until he wakes up. When he wakes up, he must remain covered."

(b. Git. 70a)

We have already noted[1] the cures for snakebite and fever.

In addition to cures, the rabbis studied how to prevent diseases. Such "preventive medicine" included warnings about how to avoid arousing demons against oneself.[2] Abaye also was told by Rabbah that the reason one does not drink froth is that it may cause catarrh; but, as we noted, the reason one does not sit under a drainpipe was not because of the waste water, but because demons are found there.[3] Advice on diet included Rava's, that wine and spices have made him wise,[4] and R. Joseph's, that a person should not overeat:

R. Joseph said, "One who eats sixteen eggs, forty nuts, and seven caperberries and drinks a quarter of a *log* of honey on an empty stomach in the summer snaps his heart-strings asunder."

(b. Ḥul. 58b)

Abaye said that a well-boiled broth of beet is good for the heart, eyes, and bowels.[5] Other comments on diet pertained to beer[6] and mustard grain.[7] R. Joseph said that poor eyes were caused by combing one's hair when it is dry, drinking the lees of wine, and putting on

[1] Above, p. 364, b. Shab. 110a.

[2] E.g. b. Ḥul. 105b, one collects crumbs from the floor to avoid the angel of poverty, and above, pp. 334ff.

[3] *Ibid.*

[4] b. Hor. 13b.

[5] b. Ber. 39a.

[6] R. Joseph on Egyptian beer, b. Shab. 110a; on vows against drinking beer, R. Joseph and Rava, b. Pes. 107a.

[7] Abaye would not eat mustard grain, b. Shab. 140a.

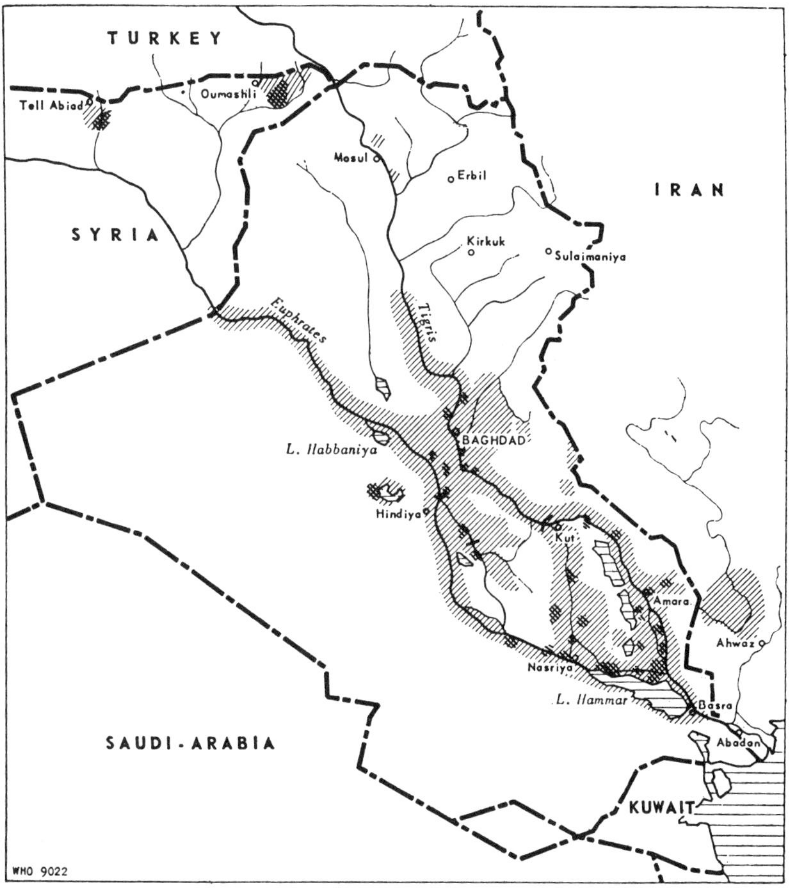

VI: *Distribution of Schistosoma Haematobium in Iraq.*

Source: *Schistosomiasis.* Departments of the Army, Navy and Air Force, Washington, D.C. 20 June 1962, p. 24 figure 7.

shoes when the feet are damp.[1] Rava observed that an abscess is a forerunner of fever[2] and fever, of the angel of death, but it can be a healthy sign as well.[3] As earlier[4] it was believed important to warm oneself after letting blood,[5] as well as to eat a great deal.[6]

A disease endemic in present-day Iraq, *schistosomiasis haematobium*, or Bilharzia disease, is prevalent in irrigation ditches, canals, small streams, and stagnant pools. Infection is acquired through contact with water contaminated with cercariae. Contaminated drinking water infected with feces containing eggs produces the disease as well. The symptoms include nocturnal fever, chills, muscle aches, cough, and the onset is characterized by dysentery and fever, an enlarged liver or spleen, and bloody discharge in the urine and feces. The confused medical traditions cited above include references to many of these symptoms, as in *ra'atan*, but we do not know whether they appeared in the combination likely to yield a diagnosis of schistosomiasis; those of schistosomiasis are easily confused with malaria. The disease is likely to have been one of the causes of some of the symptoms referred to above. Since the larger part of Babylonian Jewry worked the land and made extensive use of irrigation canals, the likelihood of widespread infection cannot be denied.[7]

XV. Scriptural Exegesis

The Written and Oral Torah, and not prayer, incantation, medicine, magic, or astrology, stood in the center of the rabbis' curriculum. Study of Torah made them into rabbis, and so qualified them as saints. Mastery of Torah therefore provided the foundation for supernatural and political power alike. Study of the content and history of Scriptural exegesis in the Babylonian schools, like study of the development of the oral tradition, Mishnah commentary, and law, is tangential to our

---

[1] b. Pes. 111b.
[2] b. A.Z. 28a.
[3] b. Ned. 41a.
[4] Vol. II, pp. 138-139, vol. III, p. 112.
[5] Rabbah, b. Shab. 129a.
[6] R. Naḥman b. Isaac, b. Shab. 129a.
[7] Dr. Elihu D. Richter, M.D., M. P. H., provided the above information, as well as the pamphlet, *Schistosomiasis* (Washington, 1962: Departments of the Navy, Army, and Air Force, TB MEd 167, Nav MEd P-5052-6A, AFP 161-1-7). The best comprehensive account of rabbinic traditions about medicine and hygiene remains Julius Preuss, *Biblisch-talmudische Medizin. Beiträge zur Geschichte der Heilkunde und der Kultur überhaupt* (Berlin, 1923).

present inquiry.[1] Scriptural exegesis is here surveyed as one phenomenon of the life of the schools. We shall merely review the exegetical teachings attributed to various masters in this period.[2] Our purpose now is not to characterize the exegetical tendencies of various individual masters, to investigate their respective legacies, or to search out the sources of exegetical traditions.[3]

Pentateuch: R. Joseph taught (TNY) that the reference to Ashur (Gen. 2:14) meant Seleucia, which, he said, proves that the Bible speaks of things which will come into existence in future times.[4] Rava said that the reward of Abraham for having said, "I am but dust and ashes" (Gen. 18:27) and "I will not take a thread or a shoe latchet" (Gen. 14:23) was that his descendants would receive commandments using ashes and dust, threads, and straps, namely, the ritual of the

---

[1] For earlier data, see vol. I, pp. 157-164, II, pp. 188-240, and III, pp. 179-192. Two questions of particular interest have been discussed, first, the alleged translation of the prophets and Writings by R. Joseph; second, the exegetical innovation of Abaye.

Y. L. Ẓunẓ, *HaDerashot beYisra'el*, ed. Ḥ. Albeck (Jerusalem, 1954), p. 37 and p. 253 n. 21, roundly denies that R. Joseph prepared any such translation. See also Wilhelm Bacher, *Die Agada der Babylonischen Amoräer* (Frankfort a/M, 1913), pp. 101-107, in particular, p. 103 n. 11. The so-called "translation" of R. Joseph is frequently introduced by TNY. Bacher holds that R. Joseph was transmitting Tannaitic traditions. We shall specify those passages. Ẓuri would like to change such a reading to 'MR, "R. Joseph *said*." See also Graetz, *op. cit.*, II, pp. 581-582, and Yavetz, *op. cit.*, VIII, p. 1ff. See also W. Bacher, "Targum," *JE* 12, p. 61.

As to the alleged distinction by Abaye between the PŠT, plain-meaning of Scripture, and MDRŠ, more fanciful exegesis in terms of later values, ideas, or issues, see Bacher, *Agada*, p. 113, but especially Raphael Loewe, "The 'Plain' Meaning of Scripture in Early Jewish Exegesis," *Annual of Jewish Studies*, (London, 1964), pp. 140-185, esp. pp. 160-162. Loewe states (p. 162), "According to Bacher, it was Abaye who first distinguished PŠT from DRŠ as separate exegetical approaches; but the substance of Abaye's distinction cannot be established. It is true that in one of the instances... discussed above, Abaye preferred an explanation which... takes the context into account; but in another, he was apparently content to acknowledge as PŠT an explanation that merely made explicit the entirely arbitrary application of a verse of Proverbs... Yet in Abaye's time there was current the principle, formulated in Pumbeditha, that a text cannot be distorted from the meaning of its *peshat*... This formulation seems to have been employed to counter exorbitant deductions from identity or close analogy of expression...." Loewe also discusses Rava's attention to the plain meaning of Scriptures.

[2] I intend simply to summarize some of the exegetical traditions. It may be useful to specify the part of the *content* of "Torah" revealed by Scriptural commentary and exegesis and that is my sole purpose here.

[3] The best available account of individual rabbis' exegetical legacies remains Bacher, *op. cit.*, for Rabbah b. Naḥmani, pp. 97-101; for R. Joseph, as cited above; for Abaye, pp. 107-113, for Rava, pp. 114-133; for Rava's successors, pp. 133-143.

[4] b. Ket. 10b.

Sotah, the thread of blue in the fringes, and the thong of the *tefillin*.[1] Rabbah exposited Prov. 18:19, "A brother transgressed against a strong city, and their contentions are like bars of a castle," with reference to Gen. 13:11; the brother was Lot, and the contentions were those between Israel and Ammon (Deut. 23:4).[2] Commenting on Ex. 1:13, Rava said that at first the service was in mortar and brick, but afterward in all manner of field work.[3] R. Joseph said that God revealed himself in a bush (Ex. 3:2) because he prefers humility.[4] R. Joseph taught (TNY) concerning Ex. 18:20, "And you will show them the way wherein they must walk and the work which they must do," that the *showing* referred to the source of their livelihood, the *way* referred to deeds of lovingkindness, *they must walk*, to visiting the sick; *wherein*, to burial; *and the work*, to the law; *which they must do*, to the margin of judgment.[5] Rabbah explained the contradiction between Lev. 20:21, "They shall *be* childless" and Lev. 20:20, "They shall *die* childless" by saying that if the sinner has children he will bury them, but if not, he will not have any in the future.[6] On Num. 13:22, "And they went up by the South and he came to Hebron," Rava explained that Caleb went away from the spies, and prayed at the graves of the patriarchs in Hebron that he might be delivered up from the plan of the spies.[7] Rabbah explained how Caleb won the people over with words to the cause of Moses. In the manner of a rhetorician, Caleb first stilled them by pretending to criticize Moses, and then praised Moses.[8] Rava explained the spies' report, that the land consumes its inhabitants (Num. 13:32). God had meant it for the advantage of the spies. Wherever they came, the chief of the city died, so the people were busy with funerals and had no time to bother the spies.[9] Abaye said that the Tammuz of the year of the spies was full, so that the weeping of the people would coincide with the full moon.[10] Rabbah interpreted Deut. 8:26, "Thou shalt cast them away," to mean, "Thou shalt alienate

---

1 b. Ḥul. 88b, Sot. 17b.
2 b. Hor. 10b.
3 b. Sot. 11a.
4 b. Sot. 5a.
5 b. B.Q. 100a.
6 b. Yev. 55a. Other exegeses of Leviticus pertained to legal matters, e.g. b. Yev. 97a, Rava on Lev. 18:10, to prove that a rapist can marry the daughter of the woman he raped; b. Yev. 83b, Lev. 18:22, Rava says, refers to a hermaphrodite, etc.
7 b. Sot. 34b.
8 b. Sot. 35a.
9 *ibid.*
10 b. Pes. 77a. For a translation of R. Joseph for Num. 31:50, see b. Shab. 64a.

them from thee as a stranger."[1] R. Joseph taught (TNY) concerning Deut. 10:2 that both the whole tablets and the fragments were deposited in the ark of the covenant.[2] He taught (TNY) concerning Deut. 11:17 that the "shutting up of heaven" was in respect to clouds and winds.[3] Rava explained Deut. 32:39, "I kill and resurrect, have wounded and heal." He pointed out that if God resurrects, how much the more so does he heal! But the Scripture proves that the Torah so taught the doctrine of divine resurrection of the dead, "What I put to death I revive, just as I have wounded and heal."[4] As a general exegetical principle, R. Joseph said that even those who do not derive lessons from the juxtaposition of texts in all the rest of the Pentateuch do so in interpreting the book of Deuteronomy.[5]

Former Prophets: Abaye said that Delilah knew that Samson was a righteous man, and would not utter the divine name in vain. When he said "I have been a Nazirite to God" (Judges 16:17), she therefore believed that he told the truth.[6] Rava (or, R. Zevid or R. Oshaia) said that I Sam. 17:12, "And the man was an old man in the days of Saul" referred to Jesse.[7] He also said, with reference to I Sam. 16:12, "Arise, anoint him, for this is he," that only he required anointing, but no king not of the Davidic dynasty required anointing.[8] Rava explained I Sam. 19:22, "Where are Samuel and David? One said, Behold they are at Naiot in Ramah," as follows: What was the connection between Naiot and Ramah? It means that they sat at Ramah and were "engaged with the glory of the world". They were discussing, Rava held, the place where the Temple should be built.[9] Rava taught that II Sam. 3:37 originally read, "And all the people came to pierce David" but that it reads"to make him eat bread" [the change of a single letter, KH to **B**] because at first they wanted to destroy him on account of Abner's death, but that he appeased them with words, so they comforted him

[1] b. Shab. 82b.

[2] b. B.B. 14b.

[3] b. Taʿanit 3b.

[4] b. Pes. 68a, b. Sanh. 91b. Note also b. Sanh. 92a, Rava derived the same dogma from Deut. 33:6, "'Let Reuben live and not die,' 'live'--in this world, and 'not die'—in the world to come."

[5] b. Ber. 21b, Yev. 4a. In the same context, R. Abbahu, arguing with a *min*, says that he does not derive lessons from juxtapositions of texts. Hence R. Joseph may be referring to the Babylonian Jewish-Christians, who, he would infer, do derive such lessons from the Book of Deuteronomy.

[6] b. Sot. 9b.

[7] b. Ber. 58a.

[8] b. Hor. 11b.

[9] b. Zev. 54b.

instead.[1] R. Joseph expounded I Chron. 27:23 and II Sam. 16:23. These scriptures show David took counsel with Aḥitofel and consulted the *Urim* and *Tumim* before he went to war.[2] R. Joseph said that the daughter of Pharaoh (I Kings 3:1) had converted to Judaism.[3] Rava said, with reference to I Kings 22:38, that Ahab was frigid, so Jezebel painted the pictures of two harlots on his chariot.[4] R. Joseph translated II Kings 2:12, "And Elisha saw it and cried, My father, my father, the chariots of Israel and the horsemen thereof," as follows: "My master, my master, who was better [protection] for Israel with his prayer than chariots and horsemen."[5]

Latter Prophets: R. Joseph said that Is. 1:9-10, "We should have been like unto Gomorrah... Hear the word of the Lord, you rulers of Sodom," proves that one should never "open his mouth to Satan," that is to say, utter ominous words.[6] Rava interpreted Is. 1:19, "You shall be fed with the sword" to mean, with coarse salt, hard baked barley bread, and onions.[7] Rava said that the Messiah will be able to smell a man and judge him, in explaining Is. 11:3, "He shall not judge after the sight of his eyes... or the hearing of his ears."[8] R. Joseph exposited Is. 12:1, "I will give thanks to you, O Lord, for though you were angry with me, your anger is turned away and you comfort me," as an allusion to two men who set out on a trading expedition. One got a thorn in his foot, could not go along, so he began to curse. Then he heard that his friend's ship had sunk into the sea, and was gratified that he could not join him, so he began to give praise instead.[9] R. Joseph taught (TNY) that Is. 13:3, "I have commanded my sanctified ones" referred to the Persians, who were "sanctified and appointed for Gehenna."[10] He translated Is. 19:18, "One shall be called the city of Ḥeres," as follows: "The city of Beth Shemesh, which is destined to destruction." He pointed out that Job 9:7 uses the word Ḥeres to mean sun.[11] R. Joseph taught (TNY) that "It shall not be stored nor treasured" (Is. 23:18)

[1] b. Sanh. 20a.
[2] b. Ber. 3b-4a.
[3] b. Yev. 76a.
[4] b. Sanh. 39b.
[5] b. M.Q. 26a. For the rabbis as protectors of Israel, see above, pp. 340-341, and vol. III, pp. 118ff.
[6] b. Ket. 8b.
[7] b. Qid. 62b.
[8] b. Sanh. 93b.
[9] b. Nid. 31a.
[10] b. Ber. 8b.
[11] b. Men. 110a.

refers to storehouses or treasurehouses of gold and silver.[1] He translated "Thou shalt fan them, and the wind shall carry them away" (Is. 41:16) as follows: "Thou shall winnow them, and a wind shall disperse them."[2] He taught that the "new thing" referred to in Is. 43:19, was the war of Gog and Magog. The later tribulations will cause the people to forget the earlier ones.[3] R. Naḥman b. R. Ḥisda explained that Cyrus was not really referred to as the Messiah in Is. 45:1. What the verse means is that God said to the Messiah, "I have a complaint against Cyrus on your behalf, for I said 'He shall build my house and gather my exiles' (Is. 45:13) and he merely said that whoever wanted to might go back to Jerusalem."[4] R. Joseph explained to Abaye that despite the virtue of the Jerusalemites of the Second Temple, they were punished because they did not mourn for Jerusalem, citing Is. 66:10, "Rejoice with Jerusalem and be glad for her. All you that love her rejoice for joy with her all you that mourn for her."[5] Rava held that Manasseh tried Isaiah and put him to death, claiming that he was guilty of blasphemy, for Moses had said one could not see God and live (Ex. 33:20) and Isaiah had seen God (Is. 6:1). Isaiah knew that he would not be able to make a convincing defense, so he pronounced the divine name and was magically swallowed up by a cedar. This log was sawn apart. Isaiah died when the saw reached his mouth, as punishment for saying that the Jews had unclean lips.[6] Rava proved from Jer. 5:1 that Jerusalem was destroyed when faithful men ceased to exist in the city.[7] Rava asked Rabbah b. Mari to explain the alleged contradiction between Jer 8:2 and 8:3 as follows: "They shall not be buried... and death shall be chosen rather than life." How could such a death be preferable? Rabbah b. Mari replied that "Death shall be chosen" for the wicked, so they may not live in this world; they thus sin and fall into Gehenna.[8] Rava expounded Jer. 18:23, "But let them be overthrown before you. Deal with them in the time of your anger." He said, "Jeremiah spoke to the Holy One, blessed be he, 'Lord of the world, even when they are ready to do charity, cause them to be frustrated by people unworthy of consideration so they may have no reward for that

[1] b. Pes. 118b.
[2] b. A.Z. 44a.
[3] b. Ber. 13a.
[4] b. Meg. 12a.
[5] b. Git. 57a.
[6] b. Yev. 49b.
[7] b. Ḥag. 14a, Shab. 119b.
[8] b. Yev. 63b.

charity.'"[1] R. Joseph proved that the Davidic kings both judge and are judged, from Jer. 21:12.[2] He paraphrased [translated] Jer. 46:20, "Egypt is a very fair heifer, but the *kerez* [gadfly] out of the north is come...," as follows: "A fair kingdom is Egypt, but murderous nations from the north will come upon it."[3] Rava explained that Jer. 52:6-7 referred to the destructions of the First and Second Temples respectively, so there was no contradiction in the dates of the two verses. Rava saw no conflict between Isaiah's and Ezekiel's visions of God. All that Ezekiel saw, Isaiah also saw. "However," he said, "Ezekiel was like a villager who saw a king, and Isaiah like an urbanite." The one less accustomed than the other to the glory of the throne related more details.[4] R. Joseph taught (TNY) that Ezek. 9:6, "Begin the slaughter with my sanctuary" should be read "My sanctified ones," namely, "those who fulfilled the Torah from first to last."[5] Rava proved from Ezek. 16:14 that Jewish women are not hairy.[6] He showed from Ezek. 18:13 and 18:10 that lenders on interest are like shedders of blood.[7] R. Joseph taught (TNY) that Ex. 12:22, "And none of you shall go out-of-doors until the morning" shows that once the Destroyer has the right to do his work, he does not distinguish between righteous and wicked; and Ezek. 21:8, "I will cut off righteous and wicked," indicates that he begins with the righteous.[8] R. Joseph translated Hos. 4:2, "By swearing, lying, killing, stealing, committing adultery, they spread forth, and blood touches blood" as follows: "They beget children by their neighbors' wives, piling evil upon evil."[9] Rava explained Hos. 7:15, "Though I have trained [yissarti] and strengthened their arms, yet they imagine mischief against me," as follows: "The Holy One, blessed be he, said, 'I thought I would chastise them [YSR] with suffering in this world, so that their arm might be strengthened in the next, yet they..."[10] Rava explained Hos. 13:2 to mean that if one sacrificed his son to the idol, the priest would then praise him, "You have offered a precious gift to it, now come and

---

[1] b. B.Q. 16b.
[2] b. Sanh. 19a.
[3] b. Yoma 32b.
[4] b. Ḥag. 13b.
[5] b. A.Z. 4a.
[6] b. Sanh. 21a.
[7] b. Tem. 6b.
[8] b. B.Q. 60a.
[9] b. Qid. 13a.
[10] b. A.Z. 4a.

kiss it."[1] R. Joseph translated Amos 7:14, "I am no prophet nor a son of a prophet but a herdsman and gatherer of sycamore fruit" as follows: "Behold I am the owner of flocks and possess sycamore trees in the valley."[2] He translated Obadiah 1:6, "How is Esau searched out? How are his hidden places sought out?" as follows, "How was Esau ransacked? How were his hidden treasures exposed?"[3] R. Joseph explained the vision of Habakkuk 3:2, "He stood and measured the earth, he beheld..." "What did he see? He saw the seven commandments accepted by the descendents of Noah, and since some rejected them, he rose up and granted them exemptions."[4] R. Joseph similarly taught (TNY) with reference to Hab. 3:6, "He stands and shakes the earth, he sees and makes the nations tremble," as follows: "He saw the nations did not observe the seven commandments of the sons of Noah, so he released them from those commandments."[5] Rava explained Hab. 3:11, "The sun and moon stood still in their *zevul*, and at the light of your arrows they went" as follows: "The sun and moon ascended from the firmament (*raqiʿa*) to the *zevul* above." He explained that "if God would not punish Koraḥ (Num. 16) they would not go forth. So God shot arrows at them because they were more zealous for the honor of Moses than for his own honor. Therefore they now do not go forth until they are driven to it."[6] R. Joseph translated Zeph. 3:18, "I will gather them that are destroyed because of the appointed season who are of you," as follows: "Destruction comes upon [the enemies of] Israel because they put off until late the times of the appointed seasons in Jerusalem."[7] Rava explained Zeph. 2:14, "Their voice shall sing in the windows, desolation shall be in the thresholds" to mean that "when there is song in a house, destruction lurks on the threshhold."[8] R. Joseph translated Zech. 9:6, "And the bastard shall dwell in Ashdod," as follows: "The house of Israel shall dwell securely in their land, where they were as strangers."[9] He explained Zech. 12:11, "In that day there shall be a great mourning in Jerusalem as the mourning of Hadadrimmon in the valley of Megiddon," saying, "Were it not for the *Targum* of this verse, we should not know what it means: 'On that day there shall be a great

[1] b. Sanh. 63b.
[2] b. Ned. 38a.
[3] b. B.Q. 3b.
[4] b. B.Q. 38a.
[5] b. A.Z. 2b.
[6] b. Sanh. 110a, b. Ned. 39b, Num. R. 18:20.
[7] b. Ber. 28a.
[8] b. Sot. 48a.
[9] b. Qid. 72b.

mourning in Jerusalem like the mourning of Ahab son of Omri who was killed by Hadadrimmon son of Rimmon in Ramoth Gilead and like the mourning of Josiah son of Ammon who was killed by Pharaoh the Lame in the plain of Megiddo."[1]

The Writings: Rava expounded a number of passages in Psalms, like Rav before him, as if they applied to the life of King David. So he explained Ps. 11:1: "What is meant by the verse, 'To the chief Musician, a psalm of David. In the Lord I put my trust. How do you say to my soul, Flee as a bird to the mountain.' Here David was seen as pleading to God, Lord of the Universe, Forgive me that sin [with Bathsheva] so that men may not say, 'Your mountain [the king] has been put to flight by a bird.'" Several other passages in Psalms, particularly Ps. 51:6, 38:18 and 35:15, were seen as referring to the same sin.[2] Rava expounded Ps. 11:7, "For the Lord is righteous. He loves righteousness; the upright shall behold his face" to mean, "Abraham comes and brings redemption to the wicked."[3] He expounded Ps. 25:9, "Good and upright is the Lord. Therefore he instructs sinners in the way," as follows: "Come and see the righteousness of the Holy One... Whoever has the intent of performing a commandment but under duress fails to do so is credited by Scripture as if he had done it, but if he intends to sin, he is not regarded as guilty unless he actually does it."[4] He expounded Ps. 40:6, "Many things have you done, O Lord, my God, even your wonderful works and thoughts toward us," as follows: "Not toward me, but toward us, is this passage written, to teach that Rehoboam sat on David's lap, and David said to him, 'Those two verses [Gen. 18:9 and Ps. 45:14, showing that an Ammonite and a Moabite woman might enter the congregation of Israel] were said concerning you and me [for as descendants of Ammonites and Moabites, we are thereby admitted into the congregation of Israel.]" Concerning Ps. 40:8, "Lo, I am come with the roll of a book which is prescribed for me," Rava explained that David came with a roll but did not know that it was already written about himself [with reference to Gen. 19:15 and Ps. 89:21].[5] Rava interpreted Ps. 62:4, "How long will you imagine mischief against a man? You shall be slain... You are as a bowing wall and a tottering fence." He held that the verse referred to the way of the men of Sodom, who used to cast envious eyes at wealthy men, so

[1] b. Meg. 3a.
[2] b. Sanh. 107a. On Ps. 35:15, see also b. B.M. 59a.
[3] Kallah Rabbati 55a.
[4] Kallah Rabbati 51b.
[5] b. Yev. 77a.

would put them by a wall and push it over on them.[1] R. Joseph taught (TNY) concerning Ps. 104:20, as follows: "'You make darkness and it is night'—refers to this world, which is comparable to night. 'Wherein all the beasts of the forest creep forth'—refers to the wicked of the world, who are like beasts of the forest. 'The sun rises'—for the righteous. 'The wicked are gathered in'—for Gehenna. 'And lay them down in their habitations'—not a single righteous man lacks a habitation appropriate for his honor. 'Man goeth forth to his work'—the righteous go forth to receive their reward. 'And to his labor until the evening'—as one who has worked fully until the very evening."[2] Rava said that the first part of Ps. 112:7 should be explained in terms of the second, or vice versa. "He shall not be afraid of evil tidings, his heart is steadfast, trusting in the Lord." "Either he will not fear evil tidings because his heart is steadfast, or his heart is steadfast and therefore he will not fear evil tidings."[3] The following was in the same mode:

> "It is time to work for the Lord. They have voided your Law." (Ps. 119:126) Rava said the first clause can be taken as explaining the second, or vice versa. Thus, "It is time to work for the Lord because they have made void your law," or "They have made void your law *because* it is time to work for the Lord."
>
> (b. Ber. 63a)

Rava exposited Prov. 18:1, "He that separateth himself seeks his own desire and snarls against all sound wisdom" as a reference to Lot, who separated himself from Abraham.[4] Rava said that Prov. 23:31 proves that only red wine may be used for drink-offerings, including wine for Sanctification.[5] He held that Job lived in the time of the spies (Num. 13), on the basis of an exegesis of 'land of Uz' (Job 1:1) and 'whether there be wood [*'eẓ*] therein' (Num. 13:20), as follows: "Moses said to Israel, 'See if that man is there whose years are as the years of a tree and who shelters his generation like a tree.'"[6] Rava also said that while "In all this, Job did not sin with his lips" (Job 2:10), he did sin with his heart, saying (Job 9:24), "The earth has been given into the hand of the wicked..." Rava expounded Job 10:7, "Although you know that I am not wicked, and there is none that can deliver out of your hand." He said, "Job sought to exculpate the whole world. Job thus said,

[1] b. Sanh. 109a.
[2] b. B.M. 83b.
[3] b. Ber. 60a.
[4] b. Hor. 10b.
[5] b. B.B. 97b.
[6] b. B.B. 15a.

'Lord of the world, you have made the ox with cloven hoofs, and the ass with whole ones; Paradise and Gehenna; righteous and wicked men—and who stands in your way?'" That is to say, God does as he likes, but man has no free will. The companions answered, (Job 15:4), "Yea, you do away with fear and restrain devotion before God"—meaning, "If God created the evil inclination, he also created the Torah as its antidote."[1] Rava held that Job 7:9, "As the cloud that... vanished, so he that goes down to Sheol shall come up no more" proves that Job denied the resurrection of the dead.[2] He taught that Job 12:5 teaches that when Noah rebuked his contemporaries, they made fun of him.[3] He said that Job 37:6 proves that snow is beneficial for the mountains as fivefold rain for the earth.[4]

Of the five Scrolls, the Scroll of Esther elicited the most extensive comments, because the rabbis probably preached in the synagogues at Purim.[5] Rava said, with reference to Esther 1:2, "In those days, when the king sat [on his throne], that "when he sat" means, 'When he began to feel secure.' The king reasoned that sufficient time had passed so that he might now make use of the vessels of the Temple, for the years when redemption had to come, he thought,had gone by with no result.[6] Rava explained "Also Vashti the queen made a feast for the women in the royal house" (Est. 1:9), saying, "It should have said 'the women's house,' but both Ahasuerus and Vashti had no immoral purpose."[7] "The king was very angry" (Est. 1:12) because Vashti accused him of being unable to hold his wine.[8] Rava said that "After these things" (Est. 3:1) referred to God's having created a healing before the blow which was about to fall.[9] Rava's discourse on Esther began with Prov. 29:2, "When the righteous are increased the people rejoice, but when the wicked rule, the people sigh." He said, "'When the righteous are increased' is illustrated by Mordecai and Esther, as it says, 'And the city of Shushan shouted and was glad' (Est. 8:15). 'But when the wicked rules' is illustrated by Haman, as it says, 'But the city of

---

[1] b. B.B. 16a.
[2] b. B.B. 16a.
[3] b. Sanh. 108b.
[4] b. Ta'anit 3b.
[5] See vol. II, pp. 57-64, for an explanation of why the Scroll of Esther attracted disproportionate interest in the Babylonian schools. Sermons would have been preached on all five Scrolls, not only Esther.
[6] b. Meg. 11b. See also Rava an Est. 1:7, b. Meg. 12a.
[7] b. Meg. 12b.
[8] b. Meg. 12b.
[9] b. Meg. 13b.

Shushan was perplexed' (Esther 3:15)."[1] Rava interpreted Est. 9:27, "They confirmed and took upon them" to mean that the Jews reaccepted the Torah in the days of Ahasuerus.[2] R. Joseph held that Est. 9:28 proves that the Scroll of Esther was composed under the inspiration of the Holy Spirit.[3]

Rava said that as a reward for the four tears which Orpah shed upon her mother-in-law, she merited that four mighty wariors should issue from her. The four tears are indicated in Ruth 1:14, "And they lifted up their voice and wept again"; one weeping produced two tears (one from each eye), and the second, two more.[4] We have already noted that Rava interpreted many of the Scriptures in the Song of Songs to refer to study of the Torah,[5] or, in the more common exegetical tradition, to the relationship between God and Israel. His exposition of Song 7:2, "how beautiful are thy steps in sandals, O prince's daughter," was as follows: "How beautiful are the steps of Israel when they go up to celebrate a festival [in Jerusalem]." "O prince's daughter" refers to the daughter of Abraham our father, who is called a prince (Ps. 47:10).[6] The reference was to proselytes, who are regarded as children of Abraham. R. Joseph explained that the book of Ezra, which was narrated by Nehemiah, was not called by Nehemiah's name because he spoke disparagingly of his predecessors, evidence of which is Neh. 5:15.[7]

R. Joseph said that one should not read the book of Ben Sirah, yet he held that one may expound "the good things it contains."[8] Despite his numerous Aramaic paraphrases of Scripture, he said that one should speak either Hebrew or Persian, but not Syriac.[9]

Another kind of exegesis involved the derivation from Scriptures of popular or rabbinical proverbs. Rabbah b. Mari apparently specialized in research on such matters. The following passage recorded some of these traditions:

---

[1] b. Meg. 11a.

[2] b. Shab. 88a. The implication *may* have been that in times of trouble, the Jews should rededicate themselves to the Torah, and would find salvation, as they had in the times of Ahasuerus.

[3] b. Meg. 7a.

[4] b. Sot. 42b.

[5] Above, p. 291f. on Song 7.14, see b. 'Eruv. 21 b; and above, 1 p. 292 on Song 8:10, b. Pes. 87a.

[6] b. Suk. 49b, b. Ḥag. 3a.

[7] b. Sanh. 93b.

[8] b Sanh. 100b.

[9] b. Sot. 49b.

Rava said to Rabbah b. Mari, "Whence can be derived the lesson taught by our rabbis that one who solicits mercy for his fellow while he himself is in need of the same thing [will be answered first]?" He replied, "As it is written: 'And the Lord changed the fortune of Job when he prayed for his friends' (Job. 42:10)."

Rava [again] said to Rabbah b. Mari, "Whence can be derived the proverbial saying that together with the thorn the cabbage is smitten?" He replied, "As it is written, 'Wherefore will you contend with Me, ye all have transgressed against Me, says the Lord' (Jer. 2:29)."

Rava [again] said to Rabbah b. Mari, "Whence can be derived the popular saying that poverty follows the poor?" He replied: "We have learned: 'The rich used to bring the first fruits in baskets of gold and silver, but the poor brought it in wicker baskets made out of the bark of willow, and thus gave the baskets as well as the first-fruits to the priest.'" He said to him: "You derive it from there, but I derive it from this: 'And shall cry unclean, unclean' (Lev. 13:45)."

He [again] said to Rabbah b. Mari, "Whence can be derived the advice given by our rabbis, Have early breakfast in the summer because of the heat, and in the winter because of the cold, and people even say that sixty men may pursue him who has early meals in the mornings and will not overtake him?" He replied, "As it is written, 'They shall not hunger nor thirst, neither shall the heat nor sun smite them' (Is. 49:10)...."

Rava [again] said to Rabbah b. Mari, "Whence can be derived the saying of the rabbis, 'If thy neighbor calls thee an ass put a saddle on thy back?' "He replied: "As it is written: 'And he said: Hagar, Sarai's handmaid, Whence comest thou and whither goest thou? And she said: I flee from the face of my mistress Sarai' (Gen. 16:8)."

Rava [again] said to Rabbah b. Mari, "Whence can be derived the popular saying: 'If there is any matter of reproach in thee be the first to tell it?'" He replied, "As it is written: 'And when the Lord shall have dealt well with my lord then remember thy handmaid' (I Sam. 25:31)."

Rava [again] said to Rabbah b. Mari, "Whence can be derived the popular saying, 'Sixty pains reach the teeth of him who hears the noise made by another man eating while he himself does not eat'?" He replied: "As it is written, 'But me, even me thy servant and Zadok the priest, and Benaiah the son of Jehoiada, and thy servant Solomon, hath he not called' (I Kings 1:26)."

Rava [again] said to Rabbah b. Mari, "Whence can be derived the popular saying, 'Though the wine belongs to the owner, the thanks are given to the butler?'" He replied, "As it is written, 'And thou shalt put of thy honor upon him, that all the congregation of the children of Israel may hearken' (Num. 27:18-20), and it is also written, 'And Joshua the son of Nun was full of the spirit of wisdom, for Moses had laid his hands upon him; and the children of Israel hearkened unto him' (Deut. 24:9)."

Rava [again] said to Rabbah b. Mari, "Whence can be derived the popular saying, 'A dog when hungry is ready to swallow even his [own] excrements'?" He replied, "As it is written, 'The full soul loatheth an honeycomb, but to the hungry soul every bitter thing is sweet' (Prov. 27:7)."

Rava [again] said to Rabbah b. Mari, "Whence can be derived the popular saying: 'Into the well from which you have once drunk water do not throw clods?'" He replied, "As it is written, 'Thou shalt not abhor an Edomite, for he is thy brother, thou shalt not abhor an Egyptian because thou wast a stranger in his land' (Deut. 23:8)."

Rava [again] said to Rabbah b. Mari, "Whence can be derived the popular saying: 'Behind an owner of wealth chips are dragged along'? He replied: "As it is written: 'And Lot also who went with Abram had flocks and herds and tents' (Gen. 13:5)."

(b. B.Q. 92a-93a)[1]

In summary: The various modes and methods of Scriptural exegesis inherited from earlier generations all were represented in the traditions attributed to the fourth-century masters. R. Joseph's many citations of Tannaitic traditions as well as his paraphrastic translations leave no doubt that in a history of Jewish Bible exegesis, he would play a considerable role. Nonetheless, our brief survey has revealed little fundamental innovation. If the distinction between 'plain-meaning' and more fanciful exegesis of Scriptures was widely recognized, we can hardly cite much evidence of that fact in these traditions. The past tendency to read into Scriptures the ideas, concerns, and issues of the current generation continued without significant modification. Indeed, the long citation of Rabbah b. Mari indicates how much interest was now attached to showing the Scriptures to be the ultimate source of all wisdom, just as in earlier times. Various ethical and theological ideas appeared in the context of exegesis. God preferred humility. The right way of living involved deeds of lovingkindness, visiting the sick, burying the dead, keeping the commandments, and showing mercy in judgment. God's ways were forever justified, even when men did not fully comprehend them. Scripture contained many proofs of the coming resurrection of the dead. Pagan monarchs were not to be trusted. Cyrus was not the Messiah. The Persians were destined to Gehenna. Historical events were determined by the moral character of the participants, just as the prophets had said. People must be willing to accept heavenly chastisement in this world, so they may enjoy the

---

[1] Trans. E. W. Kirzner (London, 1948), pp. 533-538. For other popular sayings, see b. Pes. 28a, Abaye, Rava, and R. Joseph; b. Suk. 22b, R. Papa; b. B.M. 107b, Rabbah asked Rava b. Mari about the Scriptural source of a rabbinical proverb.

world to come. The merits of one's ancestors produce blessings for generations to come. Job was a blasphemer, who sinned in his heart and denied the resurrection of the dead. The conventional repertoire of rabbinical exegesis uncovered here could be duplicated in studies of any other generation of rabbinical masters.[1]

XVI. THE KALLAH

In addition to students regularly resident in the vicinity of the schools, many others would come for two months in the year, *'Elul* (August-September) and *'Adar* (February-March) to hear the lectures and discussion. We noted above[2] that Rabbah supposedly attracted as many as twelve thousand students. Being absent from their homes when the census for the head-tax was taken, the students were able to evade their taxes. If that is the case, then we may suppose that among this vast number were some whose interest in not being at home when the tax-collector came exceeded their interest in what they learned at the school.[3] In any event, the *kallah*[4] was one effective means by which the schools retained their influence over students who had completed full-time studies. Large numbers came, as evidenced by Abaye's and Rava's references to great crowding at the sessions.[5]

We noted above[6] stories about younger students' remaining away from home as long as six years at a time. At some point, however, one normally would have to take up a gainful occupation. R. Ishmael and R. Simeon b. Yoḥai had earlier discussed whether one should engage in anything other than study of the Torah, the former holding that one

[1] From the time of Zunz, it has been the assumption of all scholars that the *sitz im leben* of academic exegesis was synagogue preaching. It is difficult to locate in the data considered here, or in vols. II, 188-240, and III, pp. 179-192, examples of actual public sermons. The few clear-cut public speeches referred to in vol. III, pp. 253 and 255, pertained not to Scripture but to the laws of Passover, the Day of Atonement, and the Sabbath; these were introduced by "So-and-so lectured in such-and-such a town...." It seems to me that rabbinic Scriptural exegesis may just as well have been presented in the schools, and mainly for the edification of disciples, as in the synagogues.

[2] b. B.M. 86a, cited above, p. 41.

[3] For imposters at the *kallah*, see R. Naḥman, b. B.Q. 113a.

[4] For the meaning of the term, see the brief but excellent summary of previous suggestions provided by S. K. Mirsky, "Types of Lectures in the Babylonian Academies," in J. L. Blau and others, ed., *Essays on Jewish Life and Thought Presented in Honor of Salo Wittmaye- Baron* (New York, 1959), p. 395, ns. 102-104. See also Tannenblatt. *op. cit.*, pp. 229-230.

[5] See b. Ber. 6a-b.

[6] Above, p. 293.

should combine Torah with a wordly occupation, the latter, that one should study Torah only, and have faith that God will provide. On this discussion Abaye said,

> "Many followed the advice of R. Ishmael and succeeded, and many followed that of R. Simeon b. Yoḥai and did not succeed."
>
> (b. Ber. 35b)

Rava, moreover, advised his students not to come to the school during *Nisan* and *Tishre* (April-May, September-October), after the *ḳallah* ended,

> "So that you do not have to worry about your sustenance for the entire year."
>
> (b. Ber. 35b

These were the months of planting, before the start of summer, in May, and toward its conclusion, in October. Frost may occur any time from November to March. In modern times half the land is left fallow in the summer, and half in the winter. Hence, if the same system was followed then, the farmers would have to plant twice annually, on different parts of their land. The ploughing takes place between January and April, and between August and October. Barley was a winter crop; wheat was also grown generally in the winter. Rice was a summer crop, sown between February and April, and harvested from July to September.[1] While we do not know Rava's specific intentions, they do conform to the pattern of contemporary agriculture and climate. It seems likely that the students, who were mostly either farmers or farm-workers, would have to be home at that time, probably for both harvesting and planting, as conditions required. There was, therefore, a biennial exchange of populations. Former students would come to the schools, and present students would go home. Under the circumstance, the influence of the schools must have radiated throughout the Jewish communities in Babylonia.

Mirsky holds that following the *ḳallah*, others who had not been educated in the schools would come for a month at a time: "The general public flocked to the academy during the months of *Nisan* and *Tishri* to hear lectures on the laws of holidays."[2] I know of no evidence that such gatherings took place in this time. We know that rabbis did

[1] See K. Mason, ed., *Iraq and the Persian Gulf* (London, 1944: Royal Navy Intelligence Division, B.R. 524), pp. 166ff., 447-457. Compare Beer, *Ma'amadam*, pp. 52-53.

[2] *Op. cit.*, p. 401.

lecture about the holiday observance before Passover, but it is not clear whether these lectures took place in the schools or in the synagogues, or whether people really "flocked" to them.[1]

XVII. The Schools and the Streets

The rabbis and their disciples emerged from the masses, distinguished by their carriage, dress, manner of speech, alleged theurgical capacities, and, mainly, learning. Ordinary people thus confronted a kind of man claiming to be something quite different from themselves, namely, the incarnation or realization of the revelation of Sinai, to be honored as much as the Torah of Sinai was honored. Rava so stated explicitly:

> Rava said, "How stupid are those other people who stand up before the Scroll of the Torah but do not stand up before a *great man*...."[2]
>
> (b. Mak. 22b)

Rava explained that the rabbis were able by their interpretation actually to alter the content of the Torah. He pointed out that the Torah prescribed forty lashes, but the rabbis interpreted the passage so as to reduce the figure to thirty-nine. What Rava claimed was not merely that people should respect rabbis, but that they should revere them as masters of oral Torah *just* as they revere the Written Torah itself. Ordinary people certainly honored rabbis in many ways, deferring to them in the synagogue, paying respect to them in the streets, and treating them as holy men in other ways.[3] Rava, however, demanded much more than such natural, ordinary respect. He asked for religious reverence such as was paid to holy objects, even the Torah-scrolls.

The response of ordinary folk is difficult to assess. We noted the critical view of the family of Benjamin the physician, who may have seen rabbis as competition when they gave out medical advice. In regarding as blasphemous infidelity the perfectly normal question of the family of Benjamin, "What good are the rabbis?" the rabbinical advocates transformed mere social criticism into heresy. Not all who opposed the rabbis or disobeyed them, or merely refrained from

---

[1] For two examples, see vol. III, pp. 253, 255. Y. S. Ẓuri, *History of Hebrew Public Law. The Reign of the Exilarchate and the Legislative Academies, Period of Rab Nachman bar Jiẓchak* (320-355) (In Hebrew, Tel Aviv. 1939) discusses data pertaining mostly to the next generation.

[2] On "great man" as a technical term for a rabbi able to reason, see vol. III, p. 83, n. 3.

[3] See the excellent discussion of Beer, *Ma'amadam*, pp. 178-184.

obeying them, were seen as heretics or blasphemers on account of their "disrespect" of rabbis. Some were scoffers to be sure. R. Aḥa b. ʿUlla said those who scoff at the 'words of the sages' will be condemned to boiling excrement.[1] We recall that Rava likewise contrasted the city-dwellers, who rob, swear falsely, and commit adultery, with the students of Torah who live in poverty among disbelievers.[2] That people kept important parts of the law seems beyond doubt. How they responded to the rabbis' political power and religious and cultural leadership may be gauged from the following saying:

> Abaye said, "If a disciple of the rabbis is loved by the townspeople, it is not because of his superiority but because he does not rebuke them for matters of Heaven."
>
> (b. Ket. 105b)

Abaye regarded it as normal for the disciple of the rabbis to be hated, and ascribed the hatred to his rebuke of the ordinary folk for neglect of religious matters.

More concrete evidence of the relationship between local rabbinic authorities and the townspeople derives from the rule of Rava in Maḥoza and of Rabbah at Pumbedita:

> Rava said, "At first I thought all the people of Maḥoza loved me. When I was appointed judge, I thought some would hate me and others would love me. Having seen that the one who loses [in court] today wins tomorrow, I concluded that if I am loved they all love me, and if I am hated they all must hate me."
>
> (b. Ket. 105b)

Rava was referring to the reactions of people who came to him at court. His comments on the Maḥozans in general leave no doubt that *he* hated them:

> "They that strive with the Lord shall be broken to pieces" (I Sam 2:10)... Rava said, "Among them are the best of the people of Maḥoza, and they are called 'sons of Gehenna'."
>
> (b. R.H. 17a)[3]

> "Woe to you, cows of Bashan that...oppress the poor and crush the needy" (Amos 4:1). Rava said, "These are the women of Maḥoza, who eat without working."
>
> (b. Shab. 32b)[4]

---

[1] Above, p. 299, b. ʿEruv. 21a.

[2] Above, p. 292, b. ʿEruv. 21b.

[3] Whatever the variant readings, the "best of Maḥoza [who shall be called] sons of Gehenna" seems a firm one.

[4] Note also Rava's saying, b. Pes. 50b, that the women of Maḥoza are lazy and never work.

> Rava said, "The reason why the people of Maḥoza ... have red spots is that they indulge in sexual intercourse in the daytime ..."
> (b. Ber. 59b)[1]

Maḥoza was a great commercial center, suburb of the capital at Seleucia-Ctesiphon and the center of urban Jewish life. Rava's references to living among infidels and the licentious and immoral people of great cities suggest a preference on the part of the schoolmen for the simpler way of living of the country-folk. The people of Maḥoza were always on the move, Rava said, so it was hard to confirm their signatures.[2] They were delicate, so wine heated them up.[3] They were regarded as sharp "because they drink the waters of the Tigris," Rava said.[4] (The Maḥozan working people felt faint if they were idle.[5]) The women were spoiled, and unlike the farm wives, did not work. Such idleness could hardly win rabbinical approval. But Rava saw the women as the cause of their husband's sharp business practices. In such a setting, it must have been difficult to force or much encourage people to conform to rabbinical standards of life. There was no law against idle women. The rabbis could scarcely prevent people from engaging in sexual relations in the daytime, much as they disapproved because it attracted demons. No wonder, then, that Rava said the best of Maḥozans would end up in hell. It should not be supposed, moreover, that Rava was alone in feeling tension between himself and the city which he served as rabbinical authority. Rabbah at Pumbedita earlier found matters no easier:

> Abaye asked Rabbah, "You whom all the Pumbeditans hate [SNW] —who will mourn for you?" He replied, "You and Rabbah b. R. Ḥanan are enough."
> (b. Shab. 153a)[6]

If the man who informed against Rabbah was a Pumbeditan, Abaye's question cannot have exaggerated matters. Heaven itself supposedly had to force people to mourn for Rabbah. Abaye later on told Rava about the sharp tricks of Pumbeditans, who would cleverly defraud the public if they could.[7] Nor were other places regarded more favorably. Rava said that Harpania was deeper than hell:

---

[1] See above, p. 300.
[2] b. Git. 6a.
[3] b. Shab. 109a.
[4] b. Ber. 59b.
[5] b. B.M. 77a.
[6] Note also Abaye said Rabbah inflicted murderous punishments on the Pumbeditans, above, p. 331.
[7] b. B.B. 46a, see also b. Ḥul. 127a.

> Rava said, "It [Harpania] was deeper than Sheol, for in Scriptures it says, 'I shall ransom them from the power of Sheol, I shall redeem them from death' (Hos. 13:14)—But for the unfitness of these there is no remedy at all. The unfit of Harpania [are forbidden to marry rabbinical Jews] on account of those of Mesene, of Mesene on account of those of Palmyra..."
>
> (b. Yev. 17a)[1]

Harpania was thus seen to be a place of the deepest immorality. The people there had so long ignored rabbinical rules about suitable marriage partners that "good Jews" could not marry them. In earlier times, Rav and Samuel had roundly condemned the Jews of Mesene and other outlying regions.[2] Now, a century or more afterward, Rava repeated that condemnation, which would suggest that matters had improved not at all. Students from such places were not likely to achieve much mastery of Torah. R. Joseph said that coming from Babylon (?) or Borsippa was a bad omen for "Torah."[3] That is to say, one who settles there will quickly forget his learning. Nonetheless, the bitter hatred between sage and *ʿam haʾarez* earlier expressed by the Palestinian schools[4] cannot be said to have characterized the Babylonian academicians. Rabbah b. R. Huna merely said that it was permissible to call an insolent person "wicked,"[5] which is a far cry from the violent language and hostile attitudes of the Palestinians. Nonetheless, the rabbis did try to force people to remain in towns of which they approved:

> Rav Judah in the name of Samuel said, "As it is forbidden to leave the land of Israel for Babylonia, so it is forbidden to leave Babylonia for other countries." Both Rabbah and R. Joseph said, "Even from Pumbedita to Be Kubi." A man once moved from Pumbedita to Be Kubi. R. Joseph excommunicated him. A man once left Pumbedita for Astunia [nearby, Piruz Shapur, according to Obermeyer] and died. Abaye said, "If this young rabbinical disciple wanted it, he could still have been alive."
>
> (b. Ket. 111a)

It therefore seems that rabbinical influence was more effective in some places than in others. Where schools were located, or rabbis adminis-

---

[1] But in the same passage, R. Zera explains "Harpania" as "the mountain [HR] to which all turn [PWNYM]."

[2] Vol. II, pp. 240-249, 268-275.

[3] b. Sanh. 109a. I do not know what town he meant by "Babylon." I do not see how he could have referred to all of Babylonia.

[4] Note that most of the bitter statements against the ordinary folk in b. Pes. 48a-50b derive from Palestinian, *not* Babylonian masters.

[5] b. Taʿanit 7b.

tered the courts and civil affairs, there the rabbis' influence and power were probably substantial. They encouraged ordinary folk to remain in such places and tried to prevent them from going to Jewish communities of which they disapproved.

It is difficult to say whether the rabbis formed a separate economic class or manipulated the people for their own economic benefit. We have already noted that rabbis as a class enjoyed considerable economic benefits. Some of these came in consequence of their public service, for the exilarch's support of the rabbis' market-privilege must be interpreted as a means of compensating them for time spent in study and in court. Others naturally followed upon popular reverence for the rabbis as holy men, whom it would be profitable to include as partners in economic ventures to bring good fortune, to whom it would be wise to marry off one's daughters, whom one ought to entertain and otherwise favor. The complex combination of political and legal power with religious and magical reputation certainly resulted in greater economic advantage than the rabbis would otherwise have enjoyed. I see however no basis whatever to suppose that the rabbis, or any individual rabbi, ever consciously and knowingly fostered belief in rabbinical magic for personal benefit. And yet, the rabbis' economic ideas, examined in connection with slavery, for example, reveal a bias in favor of the proprietary classes against the working classes. While communal funds administered by rabbis were used to ransom people taken captive, they were not available to pay the head-taxes of those who could not do so. Hence impoverished people had to sell themselves into slavery. The rabbis' comments on slaves are typical of people who were not slaves, but owned them. Slaves were lazy, untrustworthy, licentious, and did not deserve the normal dignities afforded to ordinary people. Little if any evidence suggests that in practice rabbis favored improving the lot of slaves; no evidence whatever shows how they attempted to remove the causes of slavery to begin with. Similarly, all the cases of squatters' rights examined earlier revealed the rabbinical judge's ruling in favor of the putative owner and against the squatter. Whether Rava's rulings revealed a consistent policy was not clear. And yet, those rulings remain a fact to be reckoned with. At no point do we find rabbis' decisions in this period on the side of the defendant in a case of land-seizure, and that would suggest, once again, a tendency to favor the proprietary classes, whose property was endangered by the rules of *ḥazaqah*, against the landless classes, for whom the right of squatting constituted the sole realistic hope of gaining a piece of land.

If we had a wider variety of cases and examples, we might conclude that the rabbis as a class did indeed favor mainly the landholding groups within Jewry. In the absence of such evidence, we may only note that most of what we do know points in one direction only. The criticisms of the rich, with their lazy wives and their strange sexual license, do not much change the pattern. It is one thing to fulminate against immorality, but quite another to legislate against the economic interests of those who were supposedly immoral, and this, I think, the rabbis did not do. The rabbis' unabashed use of their position in the courts and schools to favor their own interests, including favoritism of their own estate when trying cases, their asserted claim of tax exemption and their undeniable enjoyment of substantial economic benefits—these, combined with their apparent identification with the interests of the land-holding classes, must help to account for the tension they referred to between themselves and the ordinary people.

XVIII. Summary and Conclusions

The following tables summarize the data concerning various supernatural feats, events, heavenly or demonic visitations, and magical exampla of the first four generations of Babylonian masters. They are intended not only to recapitulate, but also to place into more accurate perspective the magical materials stressed in the preceding pages. It quickly becomes clear that however limited the number of case-reports and other exemplifications of the enforcement of law (above, pp. 256-277), the number of magical accounts is far less still in proportion to the total literature. We actually have relatively few stories about rabbinical magic. I have omitted reference to sayings and stories not associated with a particular rabbi. Even if we were to add the entire corpus of supernatural passages pertaining to Babylonian schools, however, it would not greatly augment the data before us. The first, obvious conclusion is that the editors of the Babylonian Talmud were not concerned to preserve magical sayings and stories. But it is equally clear—and this must be reemphasized—that they did *not* attempt to suppress such data. As I said, the ascription of supernatural powers to various authorities was not only normal and natural but also important. It was taken for granted that rabbis could combat demons and communicate with angels. If the Babylonian Talmudic editors were concerned with systematically providing a hagiographical, instead of legal literature, many more such stories assuredly would have reached us than we now have in hand. It is the nature of the literature, not the attitude or character of the academies, which accounts for the *relative* sparseness of supernatural materials. As in the earlier tables, we must recognize that the specification of an "exemplification of supernatural ability" is somewhat arbitrary. I have not included astrological accounts or stories about how prayers were answered, or would surely be answered, if one did a certain rite, or, more commonly, exhibited a certain moral virtue. The tables are not offered as "proof" of a particular proposition, but rather, as I said, merely as a review of scattered material.

I. *b. Berakhot*

Ca. 220-265	*Ca. 265-310*	*Ca. 310-350*
1. b. Ber. 18b. Samuel talks with deceased father. 2. b. Ber. 58a. Elijah rescued R. Shila.	*[1. b. Ber. 23b. R. Naḥman says *tefillin* keep away demons]. 2. b. Ber. 54b. Rav Judah —guard sick, bridegroom and bride from demons. 3. b. Ber. 58a. Curse of R. Sheshet.	1. b. Ber. 6a. Rava—how to detect demons. 2. b. Ber. 19a. Derogatory remarks about Mar Samuel produced death. 3. b. Ber. 20a. Abaye *re* Rav Judah's ability to make rain. 4. b. Ber. 56a. Abaye's and Rava's dreams, interpreted by Bar Hedya, are realized. 5. b. Ber. 60b. Abaye's privy incantation against demons. 6. b. Ber. 62a. Rava's wife protected him in privy against demons.

* Not counted. General principle.

II. *b. Shabbat*

Ca. 220-265	*Ca. 265-310*	*Ca. 310-350*
*[1. b. Shab. 11a. Rav—fasting is potent against dreams.]	1. b. Shab. 81b-82a. R. Ḥisda and Rabbah b. R. Huna overcome pagan's charms and free boat.	1. b. Shab. 66b. Abaye's mother on correct incantations (2 sayings).

* Not counted. General principle.

II. *b. Shabbat*

Ca. 220-265	*Ca. 265-310*	*Ca. 310-350*
*[2. b. Shab. 32a. Rav and Samuel feared power of Satan over bridge.] 3. b. Shab. 108a. Rav cursed Qarna. 4. b. Shab. 153a. Rav warns he will attend his own funeral. 5. b. Shab. 156b. Samuel predicts miracle.	2. b. Shab. 152b. Rav Judah receives visit from deceased in dream.	2. b. Shab. 66b. Abaye's mother on incantantion over ant to cure fever. *[3. b. Shab. 110a. Abaye said, Snake of the rabbis gives incurable bite.] 4. b. Shab. 134b. Rava fell ill for giving wrong ruling. 5. b. Shab. 156b. R. Naḥman b. Isaac fulfills astrologers' prediction.

*Not counted. General principle.

III. *b. 'Eruvin*

Ca. 220-265	*Ca. 265-310*	*Ca. 310-350*
	1. b. 'Eruv. 43a. Did not Elijah teach in R. Hisda's school at Sura and Rabbah's at Pumbedita on same Sabbath?	

IV. *b. Pesaḥim*

Ca. 220-265	*Ca. 265-310*	*Ca. 310-350*
		1. b. Pes. 110a. Abaye, Rava, and others avoided drinking wine in two-cup sequences, to avoid demons. 2. b. Pes. 110a. R. Joseph talked with demon. 3. b. Pes. 111b. Abaye saw demon. 4. b. Pes. 112b. Abaye saw demon.

V. *b. Yoma, Sukkah, Bezah*

Ca. 220-265	*Ca. 265-310*	*Ca. 310-350*
		1. b. Yoma 22b. R. Naḥman b. Isaac saw vision of Saul in dream. 2. b. Yoma 84a. Abaye gives formula for amulet to cure dog-bite.

VI. *b. Rosh HaShanah, Ta'anit*

Ca. 220-265	*Ca. 265-310*	*Ca. 310-350*
1. b. Ta'anit 20b. R. Adda b. Ahava holds up wall through merit. 2. b. Ta'anit 20b. R. Adda b. Ahava holds up house through his study of Torah. 3. b. Ta'anit 21b. People thought Rav's merit stopped plague.	1. b. Ta'anit 21b. People thought R. Huna's merit stopped fire. 2. b. Ta'anit 24a. R. Naḥman ordained fast, and it finally rained. 3. b. Ta'anit 24b. Rav Judah casts evil eye.	1. b. R.H. 17a. R. Huna b. R. Joshua had vision during illness. 2. b. R.H. 18a [= b. Yev. 105a]. Abaye and Rava averted curse by study of Torah and good deeds. 3. b. Ta'anit 21b. Abaye, Rava regularly received greetings from the heavenly academy. 4. b. Ta'anit 24b. Rabbah *re* Rav Judah rain-making. 5. b. Ta'anit 24b. R. Mari saw angels. 6. b. Ta'anit 24b. Rava makes rain after dream reveals time is propitious.

VII. *b. Megillah, Mo'ed Qatan, Ḥagigah*

Ca. 220-265	*Ca. 265-310*	*Ca. 310-350*
1. b. Meg. 5b. Rav cursed flax. 2. b. Meg. 27b. Rav blessed R. Huna.	1. b. Meg. 29a. R. Sheshet argued with Shekhinah. 2. b. M.Q. 27b. R. Huna cursed woman for excessive mourning, and all her sons died.	1. b. Meg. 7b. Rabbah cut R. Zera's throat and resurrected him. 2. b. M.Q. 17a-b. R. Joseph advises how to put bully to death through magic. 3. b. M.Q. 25b. When Rabbah and R. Joseph died, Euphrates rocks kissed.

VII. *b. Megillah, Mo'ed Qatan, Ḥagigah.*

Ca. 220-265	*Ca. 265-310*	*Ca. 310-350*
		4. b. M.Q. 25b. When Abaye and Rava died, Tigris rocks kissed. 5. b. M.Q. 28a. Rava saw his brother in dream after death. 6. b. M.Q. 28a. Rava communicated with R. Naḥman after latter's death. 7. b. Hag. 4b-5a, R. Bibi b. Abaye visited by angel of death.

VIII. *b. Yevamot*

Ca. 220-265	*Ca. 265-310*	*Ca. 310-350*
		1. b. Yev. 106a. Abaye killed man's parents by evil eye.

IX. *b. Ketuvot*

Ca. 220-265	*Ca. 265-310*	*Ca. 310-350*
1. b. Ket. 67b. Mar 'Uqba's wife immune to fire because of charity.	1. b. Ket. 106a. R. 'Anan received regular visits from Elijah.	1. b. Ket. 61a. Elijah conversed with son of R. Ḥisda. 2. b. Ket. 62b. Roof collapsed on student of Rava.

X. *b. Nedarim, Nazir, Sotah*

Ca. 220-265	*Ca. 265-310*	*Ca. 310-350*
1. b. Ned. 50b. Woman burst for insulting Samuel.		1. b. Sot. 31a. Rava's students dream of Scriptures.

XI. *b. Gittin*

Ca. 220-265	*Ca. 265-310*	*Ca. 310-350*
	1. b. Git. 45a. Birds communicated with R. 'Ilish. 2. b. Git. 45a. Daughters of R. Naḥman were sorceresses.	

XII. *b. Qiddushin*

Ca. 220-265	*Ca. 265-310*	*Ca. 310-350*
		1. b. Qid. 29b. Abaye has R. Aḥa b. Jacob miraculously slay demon.

XIII. *b. Bava' Qamma'*

Ca. 220-265	*Ca. 265-310*	*Ca. 310-350*

XIV. *b. Bava' Meẓi'a'*

Ca. 220-265	*Ca. 265-310*	*Ca. 310-350*
		1. b. B.M. 85a. R. Joseph received message in dream. 2. b. B.M. 86a. Rabbah called up to heaven to settle dispute. 3. b. B.M. 86a. Abaye received letter from heaven. 4. b. B.M. 108a. Rabbah b. R. Huna cursed Rabbah b. R. Naḥman's children, who died.

XV. *b. Bava' Batra'*

Ca. 220-265	*Ca. 265-310*	*Ca. 310-350*
	*[1. b. B.B. 8a. Rav Judah said rabbis do not require protection of walls.] 2. b. B.B. 9b. R. Sheshet cursed colleague, who lost learning and power of speech.	1. b. B.B. 22a. R. Dimi cursed R. Adda b. Abba, who died. 2. b. B.B. 58a. Abaye helped magician free self from corpse. 3. b. B.B. 73a. Rabbah on incantation. 4. b. B.B. 153a. Woman cursed Rava, who suffered on that account.

* Not counted. General rule.

XVI. *b. Sanhedrin*

Ca. 220-265	*Ca. 265-310*	*Ca. 310-350*
1. b. Sanh. 47b. People took dirt from Rav's grave for a medicine.		1. b. Sanh. 65b, 67b. Rava created a man and sent him to R. Zera. [2. b. Sanh. 106b. Rava on Rav Judah's skill at making rain.]

XVII. *b. 'Avodah Zarah*

Ca. 220-265	*Ca. 265-310*	*Ca. 310-350*
		1. b. A.Z. 65a. Bar Shishakh's eye burst for cursing Rava.

XVIII. *b. Horayot, Shevu'ot, Makkot*

Ca. 220-265	*Ca. 265-310*	*Ca. 310-350*

XIX. *b. Zevaḥim, Menaḥot, Ḥullin*

Ca. 220-265	*Ca. 265-310*	*Ca. 310-350*
		1. b. Men. 41a. Angel argued with R. Qattina about fringes. 2. b. Hul. 105b. Abaye said demons sit under drain pipe.

XX. *b. Bekhorot, ʿArakhin, Temurah Keritot, Meʿilah, Tamid*

Ca. 220-265	*Ca. 265-310*	*Ca. 310-350*
		1. b. Ker. 3b. Abaye on casting a spell over wasps or scorpions.

XXI. *b. Niddah*

Ca. 220-265	*Ca. 265-310*	*Ca. 310-350*
1. b. Nid. 37a. Miracle at grave of Rav and Shila.		

XXII. *Summary*

	Ca. 220-265	*Ca. 265-310*	*Ca. 310-350*	*Totals by Category*	
Heavenly Visitations (Dreams, Angels, Elijah)		Rav Judah - 1 R. Sheshet - 1 R. ʿAnan - 1 R. ʿIlish - 1 — 4	Abaye - 3 R. Joseph - 2 R. Naḥman b. Isaac - 2 R. Huna b. R. Joshua - 1 Rava - 5 — 13	17	22.3%

XXII. *Summary* (continued)

	Ca. 220-265	*Ca. 265-310*	*Ca. 310-350*	*Totals by Category*	
Demons -encounters with -magic against	Samuel - 1 Rav - 1 — 2	Rav Judah - 1 Elijah at Sura, etc. - 1 — 2	Rava - 3 Abaye - 5 R. Joseph - 1 R. Mari - 1 — 10	14	18.4%
Rain-making		R. Naḥman - 1 Rav Judah - 1 — 2	[Abaye, Rabbah Rava with reference to Rav Judah]	2	2.6%
Witchcraft, sorcery, magic (except against demons)		R. Ḥisda - 1 Rabbah b. R. Huna - 1 Daughters of R. Naḥman - 1 — 3	Abaye - 3 Rabbah - 2 R. Joseph - 1 Rava - 1 — 7	10	13.1%
Curses and the Evil Eye (Rabbinical)	R. Shila - 1 Rav - 2 Samuel - 1 — 4	R. Sheshet - 1 Rav Judah - 1 R. Huna - 1 — 3	Mar Samuel - 1 Rava - 3 Abaye - 2 Rabbah b. R. Huna - 1 R. Dimi in Babylonia - 1 — 8	15	19.7%
Other Super-natural Stories told about Rabbis	Samuel - 1 Adda b. Ahava - 2 Rav - 4 Mar Uqba - 1 Shila - 1 — 9	R. Huna - 1 — 1	Rabbah - 2 R. Joseph - 1 Abaye - 2 Rava - 3 — 8	18	23.6%
Totals	15	15	46	76	99.7%
Percentages	19.7%	19.7%	60.5%		

We clearly see a fairly random distribution of supernatural stories and sayings of various kinds. Given the content of Tractates *Berakhot*, *Ta'anit*, and the funerary passages of *Mo'ed Qatan*, one can hardly be surprised to find a greater number of magical passages there than elsewhere. While tractates which contained numerous cases of law-enforcement apparently included a disproportionately small number of miracle stories, e.g. *'Eruvin*, *Yevamot*, *Qiddushin*, and *Bava' Qamma'*, it is difficult to regard that fact as significant, since other tractates containing mainly theoretical laws, such as *Horayot*, *Makkot*, *Bekhorot*, *'Arakhin*, and *Temurah*, likewise contain few, if any, such passages. What is more interesting is the obvious increase in the number of supernatural stories and sayings told about, or attributed to, fourth-century rabbis. No single category showed much variation, with the exception of rain-making, so we have an approximately even division. We find by contrast that about three times more stories and sayings pertained to the fourth-century masters than to either preceding group, and twice the two earlier groups put together. In the individual categories, the proportions are equally interesting:

	220-265:310-350	265-310:310-350
Heavenly visitations	—	1:3
Demons	1:5	1:5
Witchcraft	—	1:2
Curses	1:2	1:2
Miscellany	1:1	1:8

Viewed by categories and *in toto*, the corpus of stories quite clearly shows a predominance of fourth-century figures. If, however, we analyze the 310-350 attributions, we find the following:

Rabbah - 4	R. Naḥman b. Isaac - 2	Abaye - 15
R. Joseph - 5	Scattered - 5	Rava - 15

So the preponderance of fourth-century exempla merely shows that more supernatural stories were told about Abaye and Rava, and more magical sayings were attributed to them, than any other Babylonian masters. If we eliminate their exempla, we find that the three periods are represented in approximately equal measure, 15, 15, and 16. We cannot conclude from this evidence that there now was an increase in public or academic credulity, all the more so an increase in actual supernatural events and sayings. However there is so much evidence for a general increase of credulity and particularly an increase of magic in the Roman Empire during the fourth century, that to suppose a similar change in Mesopotamia at that time is not unlikely. Why did Abaye and Rava become the foci of more such stories and sayings? I do not know. Their disciples obviously preserved more fabulous stories than did the disciples of earlier or contemporary masters. Whether or not they did so because Abaye and Rava were more interested in occult matters, and therefore claimed to have done more miracles than others, I cannot say.

To conclude: The rabbis conceived, first, that on earth they studied Torah just as in heaven God, the angels, and Moses "our rabbi" did. The heavenly schoolmen were even aware of Babylonian scholastic discussions, requiring Rabbah's information about an aspect of purity-taboos, acknowledging Abaye's Torah as a prophylactic against demons.

This conception, second, must be interpreted by reference to the belief that the man truly in the divine image was the rabbi, who embodied revelation, both oral and written, and all of whose actions constituted paradigms of not merely correct, but heavenly norms. Rabbis could create and destroy men because they were righteous, free of sin, or otherwise holy, and so enjoyed exceptional grace from heaven.

Third, it follows that Torah was held to be a source of supernatural power. The rabbis enjoyed protection without knowing it; they indeed controlled the power of Torah because of their mastery of its contents. They furthermore used their own mastery of Torah quite independent of heavenly action. They could issue blessings and curses, create men and animals. They were masters of witchcraft, incantations, and amulets. They could communicate with heaven. Their Torah was sufficiently effective to thwart the action of demons. However they disapproved of magic they were expected to do the things magicians do.

A fourth central conception was that all Jews were expected to become rabbis. This belief set rabbinic Judaism apart from Manichaeism, Mazdaism, Oriental Christianity and other contemporary cults, for no one expected that everyone would assume the obligations or attain to the supernatural skills of Manichaean Elect, Mazdean Magi, Christian nuns and monks, or the religious virtuosi and cultic specialists of other groups. The rabbis by contrast wanted to transform the entire Jewish community into an academy where the whole Torah was studied and kept.[1]

These four beliefs enable us to understand the rabbis' view that Israel would be redeemed through Torah. Because Israel had sinned, she was punished by being given over into the hands of earthly empires. When she atones, she will be removed from their power. The means of atonement or reconciliation were study of Torah, practice of commandments, and doing good deeds.[2] These would transform each Jew into a rabbi, hence a saint. When all the Jews had become rabbis, they then would no longer lie within the power of history. The Messiah would come. So redemption depended upon the "rabbinization" of all Israel, that is to say, upon the attainment by all Jewry of a full and complete embodiment of revelation or Torah. The reason was that precisely when Jewry did so, it would achieve a perfect replication of heaven. When Israel on earth became, or attained to, such a replica of heaven, as a righteous, holy, saintly community, it would, like some rabbis even now, be able to exercise the supernatural power of Torah. With access to the consequent theurgical capacities, redemption would naturally follow.

---

[1] See vol. III, pp. 192-194.

[2] See vol. II, pp. 52-64, 180-188, 236-240, and 282-288, and vol. III, pp. 87-94.

CHAPTER FOUR

THE COURTS

I. Introduction

The rabbis carried out crucial community responsibilities as judges and administrators. They were not only holy men, charismatic figures upon whom the people fastened their fantasies about the supernatural world, but also bureaucrats and government officials, the embodiments of routine and order.[1] Pharisaism had long sought to harmonize within itself two antithetical principles, by claiming the inheritance both of the prophets and of the priests. As we have already noted, the rabbi saw himself as the new priest, but also regarded the ancient prophets as *rabbis* qualified by wisdom to speak as they did. Priestly order, prophetic spontaneity—these constituted the polarities of rabbinical life. The rabbis' view of themselves as earthly projections of heavenly values and their conviction that "Torah" above and below came together in their schools preserved the vitality of the rabbinical enterprise. No jot or tittle of the law ever completely lost its referent in supernatural reality, its salvific value. None was utterly disconnected from Sinai at the one side of time or the Messianic order at the other. But the rabbis were not chiefly magicians, miracle-workers, rainmakers, or religious virtuosi of the monastic sort. As I have made quite clear,[2] while stories about rabbinical supernaturalism and magic do occur, they occupy an unimportant part of the whole of the preserved literature of the schools. That they were preserved at all tells us such matters were important to the rabbis, believed by them, regarded as somehow paradigmatic. That the Babylonian Talmud is not chiefly a collection of lives and wonders of the saints (and martyrdoms) but rather a commentary upon a law-code, replete with careful, reasoned, and logical inquiries into legal principles and cases and with stories of legal actions tells us what was truly consequential to the schools, or at least to the fifth and sixth century editors.

[1] My *Life of Rabban Yoḥanan ben Zakkai* (Leiden, 1962) provides a study of the interplay of charisma and routine in the earlier Pharisaic movement, see in particular pp. 16-103.

[2] Vol. IV, pp. 391-401.

The courts constituted the institutions of Jewish government. They concerned themselves not only with torts, damages, and other narrow matters of litigation, but also with issues of personal status based upon exchanges of property. In executing their judgments on such issues, the rabbis' legitimacy rested upon that of the Iranian state. I doubt that they made the effort to incorporate into legal theory that predominating fact, but it was so. Since their judgments normally included the transfer of property from one party to another or the inflicting of other judicial penalities of a similar sort, the courts in no way were irregular, clandestine, or private. The regulation of land-ownership, for example, was a matter of acute concern to the state. If the rabbinical court could determine who owned a piece of property, the only possible basis for effectuating that determination was state support, either given *ad hoc*, or, far more likely, routinely extended to recognized state-functionaries. Litigation over torts and damages, disputed contracts, and other questions about moveable property might have been carried on surreptitiously, but not for long. As a matter of fact, had the losing party had the opportunity to appeal to the Iranian officials scattered throughout the countryside, to the local satrap, or to the high chanceries of Seleucia-Ctesiphon, he certainly would have done so. Yet in three centuries we find not a single instance in which the state routinely intervened in the normal, every-day working of the Jewish courts. The exceptional cases into which the state did make inquiries, sending *parastaks* to ask what was going on, involved either unauthorized capital punishment or tax-evasion. The practical sovereignty exercised by the rabbis as Jewish community judges depended upon Iranian appointment or authorization. As soon as that delegation of power was withdrawn, as probably happened at the time of troubles under Yazdagird II and Peroz, then the Jews simply ceased to live under their own law and were forced to pursue their litigations in Iranian courts.

The reason the Iranian government in a single moment deprived the Jewish courts of their jurisdiction over Jewry, rendering them into merely voluntary courts of arbitration at best, was primarily the disloyalty of the exilarch of that time, not only the disaffection of the rabbis. The rabbis never entered into direct relationship with the Iranian government, except (if the Talmudic tales are true, and I do not think they are) sporadically. The exilarch, long ago established to govern the Jewish *millet* in behalf of the Arsacids, later on able to negotiate a *modus vivendi* with the Sasanians, made use of the rabbis as lawyers and administrators in the government he established. The law schools not only were supported by him but also lay quite within his control. Appointment to the headship of schools primarily rested in his hands, though this was subject to some dispute. The rabbis enjoyed routine and legitimate authority, including power of coercion to effect their decrees, because the exilarch gave it to them as his agents.

We have already devoted considerable attention to the consequent legal and theological tensions between exilarchs and rabbis.[1] To summarize briefly: the exilarch supposed that he both was the descendant of David and would be ancestor of the Messiah. Jewish politics in antiquity invariably turned upon the Davidic and messianic pretensions of various figures who only made such claims long after they enjoyed real, substantial power, obviously to justify or authenticate preexisting authority. It was quite natural to do so. Even the Parthians and Herod found it convenient to assert they were descended, respectively, from the Achaemenids and the Davidic seed! So the exilarch's claim was both normal and necessary, normal in context and necessary for Jewish consumption. It depended upon the assumption that the sole true legitimation of Jewish political power lay in such ancestry. The rabbis entered a different sort of claim of legitimacy, one depending upon Sinaitic revelation of the "Torah" they now taught and enforced in the courts. God himself had determined both the law and the principles for applying the law and developing it. What they said and did God approved of, agreed with, and supported. The rabbis moreover held that when they will have succeeded in reshaping the life of Jewry to conform to the "Torah," then the Messiah would indeed come, brought nearer by a meritorious community wholly worthy to receive him. The basic claims of Jewish politics concerned redemption, reflecting a long-standing obsession with the political dislocation of Jewish life. Whatever the Iranians' intentions, therefore, neither the exilarch nor the rabbis looked to them for ultimate legitimacy, and the rabbis certainly did not think they depended upon Iran for sovereignty. But each party did rely upon Iranian willingness both to cultivate the development of Jewish self-government (or, at the very least, to let the Jews run their own affairs) and to support the actions of that government in normal circumstances.[2]

The rabbis furthermore enjoyed a different sort of power, deriving

[1] Vol. I, 2nd printing rev., pp. 103-121; vol. II, pp. 92-125, Vol. III, pp. 41-94; vol. IV, pp. 73-124.

[2] But of course the Jewish government could not decide cases involving non-Jews, certainly not Iranians, as we noted, vol. IV, p. 236.

from the charismatic qualities alluded to earlier. They were not merely bureaucrats and judges. They presented themselves as holy men, and as such could persuade where they could not actually control, influence when unable to compel. "Spiritual" power mattered precisely because it produced quite worldly results. People fearful of the rabbis' evil eye would not only pay them requisite respect but also obey them in matters supposedly subjects of supernatural concern. Thus while the *courts* could do little to regulate behavior in the homes of Jewish Babylonia, the *rabbis* could do a great deal both by teaching and exemplifying the law, and by cursing, banning, and otherwise discomfiting those who did not keep it. These were extra-legal powers from the perspective of both exilarch and Iranian authority. Little could be done to curb the exercise of influence based upon common fantasies. Indeed, in a measure the rabbis enjoyed an advantage over the exilarch, whom they depicted as chiefly a political figure, "ignorant of Torah" and irrelevant to the supernatural life of Israel. Much of "Torah" and therefore of rabbinical law pertained to just such supernatural matters. Narrowly legal questions such as disposition of contested property or determination of questions of personal status involving property were never settled by the evil eye or curses. Stories about contested property generally end with the court's decision. On the other hand, obedience to religious laws, such as food and sex taboos, or the observance of holy days and the Sabbath apparently was not subjected to court coercion.

That does not mean the rabbis could do nothing as community officials. They could first of all teach, preach, and otherwise impress upon ordinary folk the right way to do things. They could, second, carry out certain official, ritual functions as community authorities, such as establishing the Sabbath-limit and overseeing the ritual acceptability of food sold in the market-place, where in any case they enjoyed supervisory authority for reasons of public order. These actions did not depend upon popular acquiescence but upon administrative authority. Since the rabbi could put a disobedient butcher out of business, he did not have to bother to curse him. On his own he could likewise set up the Sabbath-limit, so he did not have to excommunicate someone who did it improperly. We have no case of public violation of the Sabbath through doing labor everyone agreed would be prohibited, and I doubt that many Jews loyal to the community disobeyed Sabbath laws explicit in Scriptures.

Within the range of the laws as expounded in the rabbinical schools through learned exegesis, however, many violations must have taken place, not through ill-will or apostasy (though these also occurred), but through indifference, ignorance, and more often, the inertial force of habit in following old ways. The rabbinical courts did nothing about such violations. The rabbis did everything they could. The Sabbath simply exemplifies the larger context. I think the people normally kept laws they knew about from Scripture or the traditions of Babylonian Jewry itself. I suppose that by now many of the rabbis' distinctive interpretations of Scripture or peculiar additions to its laws had taken root in the lives of communities intimately subject to their influence, such as Sura, Pumbedita, and similar centers of rabbinical learning. It is probable that the rabbis' influence radiated outward through the disciples who returned to their native towns to live, such as the single student of Mishnah R. Papa found at Tav'akh. (But I wonder what made the old lady think the disciple uniquely "heaven-fearing.") So the range of rabbinical laws likely to have been obeyed by ordinary folk probably broadened in each generation, and the wider the range of rabbinical influence, the more extensive the field of rabbinical power. The process would have been augmented with each success. At first the rabbis found a community loyal to Scriptures and guided by traditional interpretations and applications of scriptural laws. Claiming to know the "whole Torah," both the written part the people knew, and the unwritten part revealed alongside, the rabbis had a fulcrum from which they in time moved the Jewish world.

II. Rabbis and the Exilarch

We earlier considered the data on the exilarchs in the fourth and fifth centuries.[1] Here we return to consider the exilarchic question in the context of the exilarchic-rabbinical *relationship*, for it is the central issue in understanding the basis for rabbinical power in community affairs. As we noted, the holders of the exilarchic office are not frequently specified.[2] Our interest now is specifically in evidences of *how* the exilarchs and the rabbis worked together. We earlier supposed that the exilarchs of the second half of the fourth century drew closer to the rabbinical movement. They were able to do so because former difficulties with the schools had been resolved in favor of the exilarch, who, having successfully asserted complete domination of the rabbinical

[1] See above, pp. 45-69, 95-105, 124-127.

[2] Beer, *PAAJR* 35, 1967, pp. 43-4, esp. p. 43, n. 1.

academies, now sent his heirs and presumably other relatives for a sound training in rabbinical law.

We shall begin by reviewing Geonic and medieval traditions about the exilarchate and then briefly reconsider Talmudic materials on the names designated by the Geonim as exilarchs. These will indicate something about the character of rabbinical-exilarchic relationships. In his second letter, Sherira provides the following:

> The title *Mar* [Master may denote] Babylonian exilarchs ... such as Mar ʿUqba, Mar Yuḥna, Mar Judah, and Mar Zuṭra.
>
> (*Letter of R. Sherira Gaon*, ed. B. M. Lewin, p. 126, lines 13-14)

In addition, as we have already noted, R. Sherira referred to R. Ashi's superiority over the exilarchs of his day. As we saw the exilarchic festival was moved to Mata Meḥasia, where R. Ashi's school was located:

> And Huna bar Nathan who was exilarch in these times, and Maremar and Mar Zuṭra who were after him, all were subjected to R. Ashi and celebrated their festivals in Mata Meḥasia.
>
> (ibid., p. 91, lines 1-5)

R. Sherira thereupon cites the following:

> R. Aḥa b. Rava said, "We too may say that from the days of Rabbi [Judah the Prince] to the times of R. Ashi we do not find Torah and greatness in a single place [= person]." Yet there was Huna bar Nathan? He was subject to R. Ashi.
>
> (b. Giṭ. 59a)

R. Sherira then reports that henceforward for the next hundred years, the festival of the exilarch remained in Mata Meḥasia.[1] The exilarch in the persecutions of ca. 460-480 was Huna Mar b. R. *Ashi*.[2] Immediately thereafter he refers to the death of Huna bar Mar *Zuṭra* the *Nasi* in Ṭevet of 470. Afterward, in 608, R. Huna the exilarch died.[3] So from R. Sherira we directly derive the following names:

Ca. 375-425
- Huna bar Nathan
- Maremar
- Mar Zuṭra

Ca. 465-475
- Huna Mar b. R. Ashi / Huna b. Mar Zuṭra

[1] *Letter*, p. 92, lines 5-15.
[2] *Ibid.*, p. 96 line 16 to p. 97 line 1.
[3] *Ibid.*, p. 98 line 14-15.

Ca. 600
R. Huna

Indirectly, we have in addition:

Mar ʿUqba
Mar Yuḥna
Mar Zuṭra
Mar Judah

These are entirely undated. We may assign Mar ʿUqba to the earlier period and presume that Mar Zuṭra of the second letter is the same person as the contemporary of R. Ashi.

Seder ʿOlam Zuṭa, as we have seen, offers the following names from the time of Abaye and Rava:

Exilarch	*Sages*
Nathan	R. Aḥa and R. Ḥaviva
Mar Kahana his brother	R. Safra
R. Huna	R. Aḥi
Mar Zuṭra	R. Aḥi of Difti
Kahana	Rabina
R. Huna	R. Aḥa b. Nehilai
R. Huna b. R. Kahana	R. Maʾri and R. Kahana

In the year 484, *the world stood without a king.*

There follows the story of the birth of Mar Zuṭra, his rebellion, the final martyrdom of the exilarch, and the exile of Mar Zuṭra son of Mar Zuṭra to Palestine.[1] What does the Talmud report about these men? What was their relationship to the rabbis?

Mar Yuḥna appears in b. Ḥul. 133a. He received a visit from Rava and R. Safra. In b. A.Z. 16b, Abaye was told of customs observed at the home of Mar Yuḥna. In the former passage, Mar Yuḥna prepared for them a calf; in the latter, Mar Judah told Abaye that at Mar Yuḥna's they employ wild asses to turn mills. I share Beer's view that neither passage tells us anything about exilarchs.[2]

Mar Judah appears in b. A.Z. 16b as above, also b. A.Z. 76b, Mar Judah and Baʾṭi b. Ṭuvi were sitting with Shapur the King. Shapur respected the dietary practices of Mar Judah, by making the knife fit for Jewish use. In b. ʿEruv. 24a, Mar Judah visited R. Huna b. Judah's

[1] As above, pp. 45-69.
[2] *op. cit.*, pp. 45-6.

house and commented on the provision for the *'eruv*. In b. 'Eruv. 61b, Mar Judah came to people from Mabrakhta, who were depositing their *'eruvs* in the Be'Agobar synagogue, but was corrected by Rava and called contentious. In b. Qid. 58a, Mar Judah met R. Joseph and R. Samuel b. Rabbah b. b. Ḥana at the door of Rabbah's school. Mar Judah asked certain difficult questions, and Rabbah called him a controversialist. In b. Ḥul. 48a, Mar Judah quoted Abimi. That Mar Judah was informed about parts of the law is beyond question. His appearance before Shapur (II) in the rabbinical account does not by itself prove he was exilarch. The rabbis generally suppressed whatever information they had about exilarchic-royal relationships, but preserved only stories of their own dealings with the emperor. (The reference to Mar Judah's controversies calls to mind that Geniva received the same epithet, but I do not see what difference that makes.) In all, as Beer states,[1] it is impossible to infer from all these references that he was actually an exilarch. As I have shown, however, the systematic exclusion of the exilarchic title from stories about exilarchs of whom rabbis approved makes it very difficult to decide on the basis of Talmudic evidence who was and who was not exilarch. Beer takes as historical the story of the meeting with Shapur II, and "since only heads of schools or exilarchs were granted audiences with the Persian Kings," Mar Judah was probably an exilarch. I do not know the basis of Beer's supposition about whom the emperor received.

Mar Zuṭra has already occurred in many passages already cited. We shall rely on Beer's summary:

> He was prominent and proficient in Halakha, his main discussions in this field being carried on chiefly with R. Ashi and also occasionally with Rabina. His frequent and fruitful contacts with R. Ashi resulted apparently in later generations' forgetting in many instances which of the two was the author of specific Halakhoth.... He would visit R. Ashi's home even though it is evident that R. Ashi was several years his junior. Mar Zuṭra would meet at times with Amemar and Maremar. Similarly we hear of him delivering public discourses on halakhic and aggadic topics and of a court order he issued. All these details imply that Mar Zuṭra was actively engaged in all communal, religious affairs normally the province of the Heads of the Academies.[2]

Beer asks why R. Sherira should have been so certain that Mar Zuṭra was exilarch, for, as we have seen, he explicitly numbers Huna b. Nathan, Maremar, and Mar Zuṭra as holders of that office under R.

---

[1] p. 47.

[2] pp. 50-51.

Ashi. Beer cites the story of b. Ket. 61 a-b, about R. Ashi's miracle at Yazdagird's palace-gate, which was observed by Amemar and Mar Zuṭra, as evidence that Mar Zuṭra actually was exilarch. Beer remarks that R. Sherira probably supposed Mar Zuṭra was both exilarch and a learned master of the law, thus being one of the "rabbis of the exilarchate."

Maremar agreed with Mar Zuṭra on many matters of law. Some of these may pertain specifically to the exilarch:

> Maremar and Mar Zuṭra used to collect ten persons on the Sabbath before a festival [Beer says it was the Sabbath of the exilarch] and say the Prayer...
>
> (b. Ber. 30a)

> Maremar and Mar Zuṭra were carried on the shoulders by means of a sedan chair [following Beer's citation of the Munich manuscript] on the Sabbath before a festival...
>
> (b. Beẓ. 25b)

Both instances, significantly, report what the two men did on the exilarchic festival; both say the two men were nervous because they were about to give a major address before a large crowd. Maremar, like Mar Zuṭra, was also a legal authority who decided laws and officiated as judge. "It follows from here... that he headed an Academy [probably] Sura, since we have evidence of him rendering several legal decisions for the inhabitants of that city."[1] "Maremar was head of some academy, apparently in Sura, about the time of R. Ashi, or a short while prior to R. Ashi's accession to the post of Head of the Academy."[2] He was not only head of a school but also exilarch, proof of which derives from the close association between Mar Zuṭra and Maremar, particularly in their common practices on the festival-Sabbaths of the exilarch and on public fast days. Maremar as exilarch may have headed a court.[3]

Huna b. Nathan is cited thirteen times in the Babylonian Talmud.[4] A summary of the references given earlier is as follows:

b. Ket. 7a-b:	R. Naḥman quoted Huna b. Nathan's citation of a Tanna.
b. Giṭ. 7a:	R. Huna b. Nathan asked R. Ashi about Josh. 15:22.
b. Giṭ. 19b:	R. Ashi said, "R. Huna b. Nathan told me that Amemar ruled that a Persian document signed by Israelite witnesses is sufficient warrant for recovering even from mortgaged property."

---

1 p. 56.
2 p. 61.
3 p. 61.
4 Joseph 'Umanski, *Ḥokhmé HaTalmud* (Jerusalem, 1949), I, p. 65.

b. Giṭ. 59a:	R. Aḥa b. Rava said no one was supreme in both Torah and greatness from Rabbi Judah to R. Ashi. Was there not Huna b. Nathan? He deferred to R. Ashi.
b. Qid. 72b:	Amemar permitted R. Huna b. Nathan to take a wife from Khuzistan. R. Ashi asked his basis for his ruling.
b. B.B. 55a:	Rabbah cited three rules of ʿUqba b. Nehemiah the exilarch, including reference to the poll tax as applying to the person. R. Ashi said Huna b. Nathan told him Amemar found it difficult to accept the view that even barley in the jar may be seized for the poll tax.
b. B.B. 74b:	R. Ashi said R. Huna b. Nathan told him about finding a leg of meat in the desert, roasted it, and found the coals glowing a year later. Amemar told him why.
b. Sanh. 36a:	= b. Giṭ. 59a.
b. Zev. 19a:	R. Ashi reported Huna b. Nathan told him Yazdagird had adjusted his undergarments.
b. Zev. 30a:	R. Huna b. Nathan recited [the passage concerning a Mishnaic dispute about the cult] as did Rava.
b. Bekh. 40a:	R. Naḥman b. Isaac or some say R. Huna b. Nathan [taught concerning a Mishnaic passage].
b. Bekh. 54b:	R. Huna b. Nathan demurred [from Rava's saying about Scriptures dealing with tithing-laws].

The weight of evidence points to two sound conclusions. Huna b. Nathan was certainly exilarch or exceptionally important within the exilarchic regime. He also was a learned rabbi, familiar with the teachings of the earlier generation, particularly with the traditions of Rava. It is true that in some ways Huna b. Nathan respectfully deferred to R. Ashi.[1] The assertion that Huna b. Nathan was Yazdagird's brother-in-law, on account of the marriage of his sister to the emperor, seems to me entirely based upon a gullible and uncritical harmonization of the several sources, Jewish and Iranian.[2] Beer regards it as plausible that R. Sherira understood b. Giṭ. 59a to mean Huna b. Nathan was exilarch, and I agree. He further comments that R. Ashi had moved the celebration of the exilarch's Sabbath to the school in Mata Meḥasia, and "thereby humiliated the Exilarch and the latter's family and glorified and enhanced his own influence as Head of the Academy instead."[3]

[1] Beer's treatment of this subject has little to recommend it. He says that it is self-evident that in matters of law, Huna was subordinate, and this "would need no specific mention. Hence the remark was taken to mean that Huna was restricted in his secular authority... and subject to the control of the Head of the Academy." I do not know what Beer means by "secular authority", but it hardly matters, since his excessively acute assumption as to what would and would not "need specific mention" is groundless.

[2] As above, pp. 8-12.

[3] p. 68.

This seems to me unproven, and in any event is not reflected by any sources known to us.

The Exilarch and the Schools: We further have an important story about a fifth-century succession to the headship of the school of Sura-Mata Meḥasia, as follows:

> Mar b. R. Ashi was standing in the manor [RSTQ'] of Maḥoza when he heard a certain maniac saying, "The Head of the Academy who is to rule in Mata Meḥasia signs his name Ṭavyomi." He said [to himself], "Who among the rabbis signs his name Ṭavyomi? I do. I infer that as for me the hour [S'T'] stands advantageously."
>
> While he was coming, the rabbis voted to appoint R. Aḥa of Difti as the head. When they [the rabbis] heard that he [Mar] was coming, they sent a pair of rabbis to him to consult with him. He detained them. They sent another pair of rabbis to consult him. He detained them as well. So he did until the number reached ten. When there were ten present, he began to expound Tannaitic teachings and Scriptures. [He had waited until then] because one does not open [public discourse] in a group of less than ten. R. Aḥa applied to himself [the saying], "Whoever is ill-treated, he will not quickly be well-treated, and whoever is well-treated, he will not quickly be ill-treated."
>
> (b. B.B. 12a)

This story clearly presumes that the exilarch played no role whatever in the selection of the head of the school at Mata Meḥasia, where Mar b. R. Ashi's father had presided. It quite explicitly states that Mar became aware of his opportunity at the school through an omen uttered by a lunatic and forthwith was able to stop the proceedings. I am not entirely sure what the narrator supposes actually happened. He says that the rabbis had already appointed R. Aḥa. How then did he think Mar b. R. Ashi was really able to reverse matters merely through a legal discourse? We do not know.

Apparently two accounts are joined together. In the first, Mar b. R. Ashi heard bad news. In the second, we learn one should not open a public discourse with less than ten qualified people present. The two stories scarcely relate to each other. R. Aḥa's saying about his bad fortune refers back to the first story, but we do not know what his ill-fortune consisted of. If something of a supernatural character happened, we cannot say what it was. As the passage stands, however, it gives no sign that the exilarch played any part at all. The rabbis were prepared to attribute their rise to power to having dreamed about sexual relations with a goose, but not to having had any connection with the exilarch at all.

The rabbis' relations to the exilarch seem to me consistently better than in earlier centuries. Having carefully reviewed all the data pertaining to later Sasanian times, we can come to no other conclusion. We have, first of all, substantial and credible evidence that the exilarchs were learned in the oral traditions of the schools. Important legal authorities also were exilarchs. The exilarchs of the last half of the fourth-century sent their sons and others in their service to the rabbinical schools.[1] The Geonic stories about the predominance of rabbis over the exilarch seem to me curious, *if* the learned Mar Zuṭra, Huna bar Nathan, and Maremar were exilarchs, for in fact exilarchs also were influential rabbis. While we cannot come to a firm conclusion about Mar Yuhna or Mar Judah, I think it is established as fact that both the Mar Zuṭra known to us in the Babylonian Talmud as R. Ashi's colleague and Maremar were exilarchs or officials in the exilarchate. Of Huna b. Nathan we need entertain no doubt. The exilarchs certainly took leading roles in the life of the schools.

We know how the rabbis represented the situation. R. Ashi had predominated and so had moved the exilarchs to his town for important ceremonial occasions. How would the exilarchs have described matters? Let us suppose, first of all, that they were sincere in their interest in the courts and schools and eager to learn the law. So after a time men like Huna b. Nathan, Mar Zuṭra, or Maremar could indeed have become considerable masters. They would have been eager to make that fact well-known, since it obviously brought credit to them within the rabbinical estate and perhaps beyond. The very frequent representations of R. Ashi with the several exilarchs of his day must be no accident. Indeed the form *Amemar, Mar Zuṭra, and R. Ashi were sitting and such-and-so happened*, or a question was raised—this form doubtless must be assigned to exilarchic tradents. It is strange that three men who were supposedly exilarchs are frequently represented together. I assume there was only one exilarch at a time. I do not know, therefore, why the three alleged exilarchs are thus portrayed. Perhaps Huna was exilarch, the other two his associates in the exilarchate, later on taking the office in turn. But this is only a guess. What the tradents had in mind is a mystery to me. The main consideration, furthermore, is that R. Ashi is contradicted, corrected, or otherwise treated *not* as final authority specifically in these stories. To review:

1. Amemar, Mar Zuṭra, and R. Ashi were once seated. Amemar and

[1] Above, pp. 59-60.

R. Ashi ate vegetables, Mar Zuṭra did not, but could defend his action by reference to R. Isaac's teaching.[1]

2. Amemar, Mar Zuṭra, and R. Ashi were served dates and pomegranates. R. Ashi criticized Mar Zuṭra for throwing the food at him. Mar Zuṭra provided a satisfactory explanation of his action.[2]
3. Amemar, Mar Zuṭra, and R. Ashi blessed wine in different ways, and R. Aḥa asked why.[3]
4. Amemar, Mar Zuṭra, and R. Ashi were once sitting together and reported interpretations of dreams.[4]

What is important is that none of these accounts even *hints* at the alleged subordination of the exilarchs to the rabbis, though, as I said, they may have paid R. Ashi a certain deference. In all of them the exilarch (Amemar? Mar Zuṭra?) figures as equal of R. Ashi in learning.

The move to Mata Meḥasia is represented by R. Sherira as a sign of subordination. Yet how would the exilarchs have viewed things? They could well have regarded their paying special respect to a leading rabbi of their day as perfectly natural and regular, without any implications for the actual power-relationships within the on-going administration of the Jewish government. R. Ashi after all was a considerable personality, enjoying great prestige. The exilarchs likewise were eager to demonstrate their participation in the rabbinical schools and courts and to show themselves worthy of the esteem of other rabbis. How better to do so than through the perfectly characteristic rabbinical practice of paying utmost formal deference to the leading sages? But obviously to the exilarchs it would have been a mere pleasant formality—if R. Sherira's report is accurate to begin with. But given the intense struggle of the Geonic rabbis with the exilarch of their own day, one may discount at least part of R. Sherira's account as pertinent to contemporary, but not historical, times. It would have been important to harp on the subordination of exilarchs in olden times—themselves learned rabbis—to the heads of the very schools in which the Geonim now did their work and carried on their fight with the (unlearned) exilarch of their day.

The appointment to the headship of schools is a far more important issue. As we have observed, no rabbinical account tells us that the exil-

[1] b. Ber. 44b.
[2] b. Ber. 50b.
[3] b. Pes. 103b.
[4] b. Ber. 55b, among other matters.

archs played any role whatever. What the stories do say is that either idiots' mouthings, omens, or random dreams were decisive. We may therefore reject as entirely incredible the rabbis' explanation of matters. We know that the exilarchs ran matters earlier. I see no reason to suppose things had now changed. On the contrary, learned masters of Torah who were also exilarchs obviously could continue as before to appoint the heads of the schools. The rabbis after all actually did elect R. Aḥa to head their academy, but Mar b. R. Ashi, son of the close associate of the exilarch, finally became head of Mata Meḥasia. What happened in-between is not stated. I should imagine that in the meanwhile the exilarch, with close ties to Mata Meḥasia from R. Ashi's day, would certainly not permit the rabbis to make their own appointment, let alone put this choice into effect. I suppose the contrary happened. The exilarch probably had no difficulty in controlling Mata Meḥasia, where he had made his presence felt for nearly a century. But this conclusion can appeal only to probabilities. The editors of the Talmud have preserved no evidence for or against it.

Hostile, Favorable, and Neutral Traditions: Earlier it seemed important to distinguish among rabbinical traditions pertinent to the exilarch, designating stories as on the whole hostile, neutral, and favorable.[1] The viewpoint of the schools obviously serves as the criterion. The results of former studies were hardly satisfactory, for many sayings seemed ambiguous, and few finally revealed a clearcut tendency. Yet it was abundantly evident that where it was possible to shape a tradition into venomous criticism of the exilarch, some circles of tradents gladly did so. Of greater consequence still was the veritable silence about the exilarch, for what we do *not* know far outweighs what we are told about him. The actual workings of the exilarchic institution are never clearly revealed in rabbinical sources. The Geonic traditions considered above[2] are of no consequence in this connection, simply because we do not know how they were shaped or whether they represent opinions actually held in the late fourth and fifth century schools.

Stories about an unnamed exilarch in former times were normally hostile. Now on the whole they seem neutral at worst, but generally favorable. Thus we noted that R. Ḥama instructed the exilarch's servants,[3] as did R. Ashi, Rabina, and R. Aḥa b. R. Ashi.[4] Lectures were

---

[1] See Vol. IV, pp. 102-119.
[2] Above, pp. 45-48, 135-146.
[3] b. M.Q. 12a.
[4] b. Ḥul. 97b, b. B.M. 91b.

given at the gate of the exilarch's palace.[1] The exilarch moreover was presumed to know traditions of R. Ashi and to understand rabbinical discussions of the law. He was further supposed to be tolerant of rabbinical excuses for apparent lapses of paying the respect due to him.[2] The only unambiguously hostile story concerns the murder of R. Zevid.[3] That is, to be sure, no small matter, but compared to what repeatedly was said against the exilarchs of earlier times, it does not amount to much.

Exilarchs mentioned by name included Mar Samuel and Huna b. Nathan. Whether the latter was subordinated to R. Ashi or not is not consequential here. What is important is that all stories told about him reflect the sages' respect. He himself was a learned sage, careful to keep the law, and, of greatest significance, cited as a reliable authority and precedent, both when he quoted his teachers and in his own right. If men such as Maremar and Mar Zuṭra were really exilarchs, as everyone seems to suppose, then the body of traditions relating to the exilarch is not only far more substantial than in the past, but also amazingly affirmative. Mar Yuḥna and Mar Judah were not central figures; yet both generally appear as learned sages, though not important ones. Concerning none of these men do we have a single story we may call hostile.

But none is actually called exilarch either, and that conforms to our earlier observation: Mar ʿUqba was a pious man, but never called exilarch. The exilarch of Mar ʿUqba's day imprisoned Rav and demanded deference from Samuel, but he was never called by his rightful name (assuming it was Mar ʿUqba). In any event, whatever reasons may account for the persistence of this strange phenomenon, the fact remains, as we have already observed, that all the exilarchs, whether named or unnamed, beyond the time of R. Zevid's murder never served as the objects of rabbinical ridicule. No nasty stories were told about them. And some of them appear as the greatest rabbinical leaders of their, or any other, times.

Conclusion: The exilarchate and the rabbis were closely tied to one another by the turn of the fifth century. The fate of one determined that of the other. The rabbis long ago had been dependent upon the exilarch for whatever regular and routine power they exercised. A saying about Huna b. Nathan's subordination to R. Ashi is hardly enough to

[1] b. Beẓ. 23a.
[2] b. Yoma, 78a.
[3] b. A.Z. 38b.

persuade us of the contrary, especially since few, if any, Talmudic stories show how he actually subjected himself to R. Ashi's authority. The saying simply represents matters as the academic rabbis had always maintained they should. The actual situation actually could not have changed much. What changed, as I said, were the relations between the two groups, which seem to me to have vastly improved because of the exilarch's more secure hold over the schools. The authority of the exilarch, however, proved decisive in the end. Further, when the exilarch suffered in the late fifth-century troubles, the schools did also. For the subsequent century and a half of Iranian rule our evidence is insufficient to justify any conclusions at all.

III. Rabbis and the Community

The rabbis' relationship to the community at large was shaped by three factors: first, their reputation as holy men; second, their duties as judges and communal administrators; third, their constant effort to enforce the laws in the streets and homes as much as in the courts. As holy men they were revered. As judges they were obeyed. But in the homes and streets they sometimes must have been found meddlers and nuisances. Of this we may be certain from rabbinical sources. R. Papa for example condemned the inhabitants of Nersh, where he conducted his own academy, for not hearing the word of the Lord:

> R. Papa said, "The ban [be imposed] upon Nersh, its fat, hide, and tail. [All without exception are wicked, including every part of the community.]" *O Land, land, hear the word of the Lord* (Jer. 22:29). R. Papa said, "The inhabitants of Nersh would not hear the word of the Lord."
>
> (b. Ḥul. 127a)

Rabina reported:

> "*'Apikorsim* are common who vex the rabbis."
>
> (b. Ned. 23a)

R. Ashi referred to apostate-Jews who worship in pagan cults, though the reference comes in connection with a theoretical discussion of law.[1] In the same context he also spoke of non-conforming Jews.[2] He clearly supposed that Jews existed who would participate in pagan cults. But such Jews would have been condemned not only by rabbis, but also by ordinary folk. They would not have caused much trouble for the rabbis as an estate, but rather for the community as a whole. We may suppose

1 b. A.Z. 33a.
2 b. Sanh. 61b.

that R. Papa's excommunication of the whole town of Nersh was based upon sound reason. When we realize, moreover, that he and his followers thereupon could no longer maintain social or other ordinary relations with the whole town in which they lived, we understand that R. Papa's action amounted to virtual self-ostracism.

Some places clearly were preferred to others, and we may suppose that the rabbis now as earlier encouraged their followers to remain in towns which were bastions of rabbinical influence:

> R. Mesharsheya said to his sons, "...Better on the dung heap of Mata Meḥasia than in the villas of Pumbedita..."
>
> (b. Hor. 12a)

Formerly, Maḥoza was despised by its rabbinical leadership as a city of sin. Now Pumbedita, long the center of a great academy, was supposedly too luxurious for the rabbinical disciples' residence. Where rabbis were honored and respected, there they preferred to abide. R. Ashi's discussion of whether kings, princes, and others might ignore or forgive disrespect shown to themselves,[1] R. Papa's report that when a certain man made derogatory remarks about Mar Samuel, a log miraculously fell from the roof and cracked his head[2]—sayings and stories such as these tell us how deep was the sages' concern for "honor" shown not merely by disciples but also by townspeople. Hence they chose to live where glory was readily forthcoming.

One source of substantial tension probably lay in the rabbis' using their control of the courts and knowledge of the law to their own advantage. We noted earlier[3] that Mar b. R. Ashi boasted that he was unfit to judge the suit of a rabbinical disciple "for he is as dear to me as myself." Rabbis felt they should not pay for the defense of towns. In rabbinical courts—and these were the only ones in some places—ordinary folk must have felt at a disadvantage, as in the following instance:

> R. Yemar knew some testimony for Mar Zuṭra and came before Amemar. He told them all to sit [which was contrary to normal practice, for witnesses were required to stand. R. Ashi pointed this out to Amemar.] Amemar replied, "This is a positive precept [to stand, based on Deut. 19:17] and that is a positive precept [Deut. 10:20, *Thou shalt fear the Lord thy God*, which, the rabbis said, also includes respect for

---

[1] b. Qid. 32b, Sanh. 19b.

[2] b. Ber. 19a. I suppose this Mar Samuel was an exilarch, and not the third-century master.

[3] Above, p. 172.

> *scholars*], and the positive precept enjoining respect for the Torah [= the sages!] is greater."
>
> (b. Shev. 30b)[1]

The rabbi deserved the honor given to the Torah, and he got it in court. A sage contesting a litigation with an ordinary person would thus enjoy very substantial psychological advantages. We moreover have a case in which R. Papa told both the rabbinical litigant and the outsider to sit down. The court-attendant however advised the outsider to stand up, and R. Papa did not instruct him to take his seat.[2] Rabbah b. R. Huna had earlier said that if a rabbinical disciple knows some testimony but finds it undignified to go to the judge "who is inferior to him," he does not have to go. R. Ashi held that if a man was a rabbinical disciple, he could not be forced to swear an oath in a debt-collection case.[3]

Nor should it be thought that the rabbis' advantages were merely psychological. We have many cases from earlier times similar to the following:

> R. Judah the Indian was a convert and had no heirs. When he was ill, Mar Zuṭra called on him. Seeing that R. Judah was dying, he [Mar Zuṭra] said to his [Judah's] slave, "Take off my shoes and carry them to my house." [The slave would thus be engaged in a service to Mar Zuṭra when Judah died, so he would be acquired as Mar Zuṭra's possession by *ḥazaqah*.]... (b. Qid. 22b)

Rabbinical values did not regard Mar Zuṭra's action as reprehensible. We here have clear evidence of a rabbi's using knowledge of the law of acquisition and possession of property for his own advantage. One recalls Mar Zuṭra's and R. Ashi's explanation of why rabbis do not usually have sons who are rabbis:

> ...because they act high-handedly against the community ... because they call people asses....
>
> (b. Ned. 81a)

In circumstances such as these it is hardly surprising that people would have proved hostile. Whatever the self-imposed limitations of conscience, the rabbis had to be warned against acting high-handedly, calling people asses, using the courts for their own benefit, and otherwise arousing popular hatred against themselves. It cannot be far-

---

[1] Trans. A. E. Silverstone, *Shebuo'th* (London, 1948), p. 170. I have followed his commentary as well.

[2] b. Shev. 30b.

[3] b. Shev. 41a.

fetched to suppose common folk responded in kind. If people so infuriated R. Papa in the town he "controlled" that he excommunicated the whole lot, if Rabina like earlier sages commented on how common were those who vexed the sages, and if, after a century of the Pumbeditan academy's "influence" in the town, it was still better for disciples to live elsewhere,—if such was the case, we need not doubt the true state of affairs. Considerable tension surely characterized day-to-day relations between rabbinical judges and ordinary folk.

IV. Rabbis and the Synagogue

While rabbis did not exercise substantial power over public worship in the synagogue, the generations of the late fourth and fifth century did exert greater control than was enjoyed by their predecessors. That power however was probably limited to the synagogues in the towns in which they lived. I see no way in which they could effectively have ordered synagogues outside of their immediate vicinity to conform to practices approved, or to desist from those disapproved, by the schools. The instrumentalities of government simply did not exist for such widespread social discipline, and even if they did, the exilarch would probably have prevented the sages from upsetting existing arrangements of so intimate and sensitive matter of local, autonomous tradition.

The rabbis certainly determined the disposition of synagogue buildings and property. They did so not as holy men, but because they were judges in community courts. They also composed or instituted certain prayers, and here the basis probably was their prestige as learned and pious men. But at the outset, the prayers must have been said chiefly in the school services. They further legislated about synagogue prayers and behavior in synagogue services, but I see no grounds to think that legislation immediately proved effective. They also lectured in the synagogue on appointed days.[1] We know that R. Ashi, Mar Zuṭra, and Maremar gave such public addresses on the Sabbath before the festival,[2] but

[1] I remain unclear about just when such lectures or sermons were given, who determined the speaker or the subject, and how the schools preserved the contents of such addresses. The *sitz im leben* of rabbinical midrash over the various periods and locations of several authorities remains to be investigated. At present, however, I find it impossible to assume that all, or even most, *aggadic* materials *began* as synagogue lectures.

[2] b. Ber. 30a.

we have no reason to suppose other sages, not heads of schools or exilarchs, did likewise in outlying localities.

Evidences of rabbinical control over synagogue property include the following:

> [A synagogue should not be demolished before another has been built in its place.] Maremar and Mar Zuṭra destroyed and rebuilt a summer synagogue in winter and a winter one in summer.
>
> (b. B.B. 3b)

> [If cracks have appeared in the walls, one may pull down a synagogue even though another has not yet been built.] R. Ashi observed cracks in the synagogue of Mata Meḥasia. He had it pulled down. Then he put his bed there and did not take it out until [even] the gutters [of the new synagogue] had been finished.
>
> (b. B.B. 3b)

> [One may sell a synagogue to buy an ark only in a village, but in a larger town one may not do so since people come from various places to worship there, and the synagogue belongs to a wider public.] R. Ashi said, "Regarding the synagogue in Mata Meḥasia, even though people come from all parts to it, they come at my discretion [or, at my knowledge].[1] Therefore I can sell it if I like."
>
> (b. Meg. 26a)

> Rabina owned the ground of a dismantled synagogue and asked R. Ashi whether he could plant seeds there. He [R. Ashi] replied, "Go and buy it [symbolically] from the seven leaders [lit.: good men] of the village in the presence of the local council [M'MD 'NŠY H'YR], and you may then sow it."
>
> (b. Meg. 26b)

> Rami b. Abba in building a synagogue wanted to tear down the old one so as to use the bricks and beams for the new one. [He was concerned with the rule about not pulling down an old synagogue until building a new one], and he asked R. Papa, who forbade him, and R. Huna, who also forbade him.
>
> (b. Meg. 26b)

These stories make it clear that local rabbis did have to be consulted about the disposition of synagogue property. R. Ashi's control over the synagogue at Mata Meḥasia however proved exceptional. Not many others of his time could claim that people came primarily with his knowledge and consent. Even more striking therefore is R. Ashi's instruction to Rabina to acquire the synagogue from the village authorities at a public ceremony. This can only mean that the village leaders

[1] So Maurice Simon, trans., *Megillah*, p. 156. The text is 'D'T' DYDY.

normally had the right to control the synagogue property, which was part of the public domain. At the same time the rabbis as judges would oversee the exercise of that property right so as to make certain the legal procedures were properly observed.

Control of the synagogue buildings thus implied nothing whatever about supervision of synagogue worship. The one was in the hands of the courts, the other was not. Evidence on what rabbis actually could say about synagogue practice derives from the following:

> R. Papa was once in the synagogue in Abi Gobar [near Maḥoza]. The first person [called to the Torah] read four verses. R. Papa commended him.
>
> (b. Meg. 21b)

> Rabina said, "I visited Maremar at Sura. The reader went down and recited it [the Sanctification of the Wine] in the manner of the Elders of Pumbedita ['s liturgy]. Everyone tried to silence him, but he [Maremar] said, "Let him be. The law follows the elders of Pumbedita." They therefore did not silence him.
>
> (b. Pes. 117b)

> Amemar ordained at Nehardea ... [concerning the lections for the intermediate days of the festival].
>
> (b. Suk. 55a)

We recall also that Amemar wanted to institute the reading of the Ten Commandments but was told not to do so on account of well-established rabbinical rule not to recite them.[1] The practices at Sura and Nehardea would have been readily subjected to rabbinical supervision. Abi Gobar was in a suburb of a major school-town. We know only that R. Papa approved a custom when he visited the place. We do not know what would have happened had he disapproved. Maremar clearly could decide the liturgy of Sura, and Amemar could do the same at Nehardea. The basis for this sort of authority is clear. Local celebrities, ruling the courts and heading the great schools, obviously would be listened to in the synagogues they regularly frequented. It is difficult to think otherwise. But as I have stressed, we can say nothing about what happened elsewhere.

Rabbinical rules about proper synagogue conduct therefore would have proved effective in the synagogues of places like Nehardea and Sura. Prayers said in the schools would surely have followed rabbinical procedures. We need not doubt that a man conforming to the ritual of "being a rabbi" would have observed the following rule:

---

[1] See above, p. 20.

> R. Aḥa b. Rava asked R. Ashi, "If a person wants to call another out of the synagogue [during services], what should he do?" He [R. Ashi] replied, "If he is a rabbinical disciple, let him quote a law. If he is a Tanna, let him repeat a Mishnah. If he is [expert in] Scriptures, let him say a Scriptual verse. If he is none of these, let him say to a child, 'Tell me your verse [which you learned today].' Or else, let him stay a little while and then get up."
>
> (b. Meg. 28b)

The rules for interrupting a person's worship were graded according to one's knowledge, or, more really, status. One who did not learn R. Ashi's instructions obviously would have called a person out not through the graceful or delicate measures R. Ashi proposed, but in a more ordinary fashion. The Palestinian authority R. Ammi had said that *And they that forsake the Lord shall be consumed* (Is. 1 : 28) referred to people who walk out of the synagogue during the lection. R. Papa now asked, "What of going out between one verse and the next?"[1] The rabbis' disciples must have proved more loyal to the sages' ideas on proper conduct at synagogue services than did ordinary folk.

v. The Courts and the Public Welfare

In addition to supervising the observance of some religious laws and taboos and deciding litigation of property and personal status, the courts took responsibility for the poor, the water-supply, the repair of the walls of the towns, and similar matters. The rabbis thus functioned as the agency responsible for many matters of local welfare not connected with the law or with religious rites. They were able to do so partly because of their power through the courts to dispose of the private property of ordinary folk. On that basis they could levy taxes for local needs. R. Papa for example levied a tax on orphans when providing funds to dig a new well in his town.[2] But part of their power to govern local matters depended upon their reputation as learned men. For example, when R. Aḥa and Rabina supervised the teachers of children, it was not because of their power to coerce but rather their prestige as local sages:

> R. Aḥa prohibited by a vow a certain teacher from teaching, because he mistreated the children. Rabina reinstated him because no one else taught so efficiently.
>
> (b. Bekh. 46a = b. Giṭ. 36a)

---

[1] b. Ber. 8a.
[2] b. B.B. 8a.

They also concerned themselves with the ransom of Jews who had been taken captive. R. Ashi took the responsibility so seriously that he ruled money collected for a synagogue might be diverted for the redemption of captives, which was a still greater desideratum.[1] By contrast, the sages did little or nothing to improve the lot of Jews who had sold themselves into slavery in order to pay headtaxes. They regarded slaves as property, never condemned the institution of slavery, and did not use their control of public funds to purchase freedom for enslaved people.[2]

They collected and distributed charity, thus functioning as the social welfare agency within the community. Mar Zuṭra held that even a poor man should give to charity.[3] In general the sages used their influence to encourage folk to contribute:

> Rabina once came to Maḥoza. The women came and threw chains and bracelets to him, and he accepted them [for charity]...
> (b. B.Q. 119a)

They had full control over the division of the proceeds. R. Papa held that one should not give charity to a beggar who goes from door to door.[4] He may have refused a beggar who presented himself at his home:

> As R. Papa was climbing a ladder his foot slipped. He almost fell. He commented, "If that had happened, my enemy [= I] should have been punished like [mere] Sabbath-profaners and idolators [who were punished by heaven-caused accidents]. Ḥiyya b. Rav of Difti said to him, "Perhaps a beggar appealed to you, and you did not assist him."
> (b. B.B. 10a)

If a man is traveling, he should be given a bed and a pillow, and for the Sabbath, food for three meals, R. Papa held.[5] R. Ashi had full power in this matter:

> "I do not even need to stipulate [concerning the use of funds for local poor or outsiders], for whoever comes [to give me funds for charity] relies on my judgment and allows me to give to anyone I want."
> (b. B.B. 9a)

Conditions of life were difficult even in the best days. R. Papa for instance cited a popular saying, "If you hear your neighbor died, you

[1] b. B.B. 3b.
[2] See below, pp. 304-305, Vol. III, pp. 24-29, and IV, pp. 244-247.
[3] b. Giṭ. 7b.
[4] b. B.B. 9a.
[5] b. B.B. 9a.

can believe it. If you hear he became wealthy, do not believe it."[1] In supplying the necessary funds for some unfortunate folk, the rabbis therefore acquired additional influence over the common life. One who was in disfavor or excommunicated could not readily rely upon them. It was best to avoid displeasing important town officials.

The practice of making vows and oaths continued in this time. The rabbis made possible the normalization of life for those who had taken vows they later regretted, for a sage could declare that the original conditions had not contemplated some relevant possibility, and the vow was therefore null and void from the beginning. We have a number of stories about rabbis' annulling vows of rabbis:

> Rabina's wife was under a vow. He appeared before R. Ashi and asked whether the husband can be made agent for his wife's regret...
> (b. Ned. 8b)

> R. Aḥa of Huẓal had a vow in regard to his wife [not to derive benefit from her]. He came before R. Ashi...
> (b. Ker. 13b)

Although sages thus had the authority to annul vows,[2] they discouraged people from taking them in the first place. R. Zevid said that vowing is a sin and cited Deut. 28 : 23 as his proof text.[3] A disciple of R. Papa's school held that one may not annul vows on the Sabbath except when it is necessary for the observance of the Sabbath. He thus limited the possibilities of repairing the damage vows might bring.[4] The basis for the rabbis' power over vows was partly their court jurisdiction, but as holy men they were presumed to know about matters between men and heaven. Still, we do not have much evidence that outsiders scrupulously consulted rabbis to obtain release from vows. Indeed, we do not know whether taking vows was at all characteristic of Jewish society outside of the schools.

vi. Court Procedures

The appointment of judges was in the hands not of the heads of the schools but of the exilarch. It is clear however that the schools did have

---

[1] b. Giṭ. 30b.

[2] For a vow in connection with offerings for the temple, see Rabina and R. Dimi b. R. Huna in b. Men. 81a.

[3] b. Ned. 77b.

[4] b. Shab. 157a.

their own forms of qualification, based upon ordination. R. Aḥa b. Rava asked R. Ashi whether ordination was effected by laying on of hands, and he replied,

> "It is by laying on him with the name. He is called *Rabbi* and given the right to judge cases of fines."
>
> (b. Sanh. 13b)

Mar Zuṭra said that the saying, "If the door to prosperity has been shut to an individual, it will not speedily be opened" refers to ordination.[1] Once one was called *Rabbi* and given the right to judge cases, he had received the approbation of the schools and theoretically possessed the right to take over a court. On the other hand, the schools' "appointment" to a judgeship certainly was not necessary. Judges were appointed who had not even attained their legal qualifications in rabbinical schools. This is clear from R. Simeon b. Laqish's saying that one who appoints an incompetent judge over the community is guilty as though he had planted an *'asherah*, citing Deut. 16 : 18-19, and to this R. Ashi added:

> "And if such an appointment is made where disciples of the sages are to be found, it is as though the *'asherah* were planted beside the holy altar [of the Temple]..."
>
> (b. Sanh. 7b)

R. Ashi also taught concerning the Scripture, *You shall not make with me gods of silver or gold* as follows:

> "This verse refers to judges appointed through the power of silver or gold."
>
> (b. Sanh. 7b)

It therefore stands to reason that the exilarch continued to make appointments without regard to rabbinical approval, placing into positions of power judges who had not studied "Torah" *even* in preference to those who had, and also presumably paying some attention to the judge's material qualifications. It is curious that R. Ashi, to whom Huna b. Nathan had supposedly subordinated himself, made such complaints. Whatever the scholarly attainments of the exilarchs of R. Ashi's time, the exilarchs continued to do pretty much as they pleased with the community's court system, if, as seems likely, these sayings reflect complaints of the rabbis about contemporary conditions.

Whatever favoritism was shown to the disciples of the sages, the courts made a conscientious effort to mete out evenhanded justice to

---

[1] b. B.Q. 80b.

one and all. Rabina quoted a popular saying that if your sister's son is appointed constable [DYYL'], "do not walk before him in the street."[1] That would suggest one could rely on public officials to do their jobs without showing favoritism. R. Papa warned that one should not act as a judge for either a friend or an enemy, for

> "No man can see the guilt of a person he loves or the merits of a person he hates."
>
> (b. Ket. 105b)

In the tradition of earlier sages Amemar showed special care not to accept favors from litigants or even potential litigants:

> Amemar was once engaged in a trial when a bird landed on his head. A man came up and took it off. Amemar asked him, "What brings you here?" The man replied, "I have a suit." Amemar replied, "I am disqualified from judging your case."
>
> (b. Ket. 105b)

In general the court system therefore was probably honest and effective. Justice could not have been much delayed. Judges were on the whole not corrupted. Unless a disciple of the sages was involved in a case, ordinary folk could expect a high standard of justice. I imagine, too, that sayings about favoring disciples should be weighed against others such as R. Papa's above. Hence even sages and their disciples could not invariably have enjoyed a preponderant advantage, even though they clearly enjoyed psychological benefits accruing from their status.

The courts were run according to ancient and well-established procedures. Scriptures provided proof-texts to support contemporary customs. For example, R. Ḥama said that Qoh. 10 : 16f. proves that one judges up to the main meal of the day.[2] Ordinary court decisions were enforced by the threat of excommunication, which generally would have proved sufficient. For example, courts could issue and enforce a subpoena:

> A woman was summoned to appear in Amemar's court in Nehardea. He in the meantime went to Maḥoza, but she did not follow him there. He wrote out a subpoena [under penalty of the ban] against her...
>
> (b. R.H. 31b)[3]

The courts began with a *petiḥa*, which was both a warrant, enforced by anathema, and the opening of the court proceedings:

[1] b. Yoma 18a.

[2] b. Shab. 10a.

[3] Note also b. B.Q. 112b, Rabina said that a summons might be conveyed

> R. Ashi was at R. Kahana's court, and noticed that a certain woman had been summoned on the preceding evening. Since she had failed to appear, a *petiḥa* was already written against her on the following morning [and not for a Monday, Thursday, or Monday, as was usual. He asked the reason...]
>
> (b. B.Q. 113a)

Court oaths were regularly administered:

> A woman was liable to take an oath at the court of R. Bibi b. Abaye. Her opponent suggested to them, "Let her come and take the oath in our town, where she may be ashamed and confess." She countered, "Write out the verdict in my favor so that after I take the oath I may have it." R. Bibi b. Abaye instructed [the court officials] to write it out for her. R. Papa criticized him...
>
> (b. Ket. 85a)

Court oaths, like writs of excommunication, were effective only because all parties believed God would exact penalties for false oaths, and the community would honor writs of excommunication. Both were essentially religious sentiments and lay beyond the exilarch's power of enforcement. But inflicting lashes in addition, as was not infrequent, was quite a different matter.

Amemar held that pleas may be altered before court proceedings begin.[1] Rules of evidence and giving testimony include the saying of Mar Zuṭra that a minor over thirteen and under twenty may give testimony concerning movables but not real estate.[2] R. Zevid disqualified his sharecroppers from acting as witnesses because one stole some barley, another some unripe dates.[3] False witnesses were severely punished when found out.[4] Witnesses were warned, R. Ashi reported in the name of Nathan b. Mar Zuṭra:

> "False witnesses were despised [even] by their own employers, as it is written, *And set two men, base fellows, before him, and let them bear witness against him, saying, 'You did curse God and the King'* (I Kings 21:10)."
>
> (b. Sanh. 29a)

R. Papa ruled in a case that 'Elai and Ṭobia, near relations of a surety to a loan, might testify concerning the loan since they were strangers

through the means of a woman or neighbors, if the party is not in town. If he is, then only the court bailiff may do so, since the man will assume that the summons, if legal, would be served by the bailiff. See b. Sanh. 31b about compelling a defendant to go to the place of the Assembly, in a dispute of litigants on the venue of a trial.

[1] b. B.B. 31a.

[2] b. B.B. 155b.

[3] b. Sanh. 26a.

[4] b. Mak. 7a.

both to the debtor and to the creditor. R. Huna b. R. Joshua pointed out to him that if the debtor proved unavailable, the creditor would have recourse to the surety, and hence the latter's relations should not testify. Testimony was accepted from ordinary people without distinction, R. Papa held.[1] Mar b. R. Ashi permitted a grandson to serve as witness for his grandfather.[2] Another case involving rules of testimony is the following:

> Ṭobia sinned. Zigud alone came and testified against him before R. Papa. R. Papa had Zigud punished. Zigud exclaimed, "Ṭobia sinned, and Zigud is punished!" R. Papa replied, "Yes indeed, for it is written, *One witness shall not rise up against a man* (Deut. 19:5), but you have testified alone against him. You merely [serve to] bring him into ill-repute."
>
> (b. Pes. 113b)[3]

This case bears the marks of an archetypical, conventional story, rather than of an actual event. The names are standard. In case-reports, indeed, the appearance of names is rare. Generally it is "a certain man." Further, the saying that "one sinned and the other is punished" is probably a popular aphorism. R. Papa, as we have noticed, frequently cited such popular aphorisms. In this "case" it may be that he actually replied to the supposed anomaly underlined by folk wisdom, saying that it was quite proper legal procedure to punish a single witness against an otherwise blameless defendant, rather than the accused man. A more likely story is as follows:

> Certain gravediggers buried a corpse on the first day of the festival of Shavuʿot. R. Papa excommunicated them and disqualified them as witnesses [for they had violated the festival law for the sake of their own profit]. R. Huna b. R. Joshua annuled the ban. R. Papa protested, "But they are wicked!" He replied, "They might have thought they were doing a *mizvah*." R. Papa said, "But did I not excommunicate them?" R. Huna replied, "But they may have supposed that the rabbis thereby effected expiation for them."
>
> (b. Sanh. 26b)

Since the rabbis controlled the courts and met no opposition whatever in effectuating their decisions, we have no grounds to doubt that *every* rabbinical rule about giving and evaluating testimony was actually enforced in court.

---

[1] b. Ḥag. 22a, R. Papa says this is in accordance with the view of the Tanna R. Yosi. See also B. M. Lewin, *Ozar HaGeonim*, IV B, p. 45.

[2] b. B.B. 128a.

[3] Trans. H. Freedman, *Pesaḥim* (London, 1948), p. 583.

VII. Court Powers

It is clear that the courts enforced their orders through both social pressure and material fines or physical coercion. Their control over the property of Jewry naturally produced considerable power. First of all, they collected taxes and had it in their discretion to exempt someone, though the community as a whole would have to make up his share of the poll tax. R. Ashi held that an unemployed person had to contribute, but if the tax-collectors themselves exempted him, no further contribution would be exacted, and the man should thank Heaven for its kindness.[1] Since rabbis collected taxes as part of their community administration, they could apparently exercise a small measure of discretion in the matter. Indirect administrative pressures such as this could not have been reliable.

The rabbis enjoyed a far more effective means of enforcing the law by ordering fines or seizure of a person's property in adjudicating conflicting claims. R. Yemar said to R. Ashi that it was a regular practice to do so.[2] The courts certainly levied fines. R. Papa for example ordered the payment of "four-hundred *zuz*," that is, a large sum of money, in damages on account of causing embarassment or shame.[3] We cannot doubt that the courts would efficiently exact such fines. The courts also imposed corporal punishment in the form of lashing.[4] On the penalty of lashing, we have the following exchange:

> [Rava had said that flogging is considered a substitute for the death penalty.] R. Aḥa b. Rava said to R. Ashi, "If so, why do we need medical opinion on the amount of lashes a condemned person can take? Let him be beaten and if he dies, he dies." R. Ashi replied, "Scripture states, *Then your brother should be dishonored before your eyes* (Deut. 25:3), which means that when the lashes are applied, they must be on the back of a living person."
>
> (b. Sanh. 10a)

It seems possible that the courts briefly imprisoned malefactors, though this probably was not the main form of punishment of criminals. R. Papa observed that at the gate of the shop there are many

---

[1] b. B.B. 55a. According to Buddhist records, each family was subjected to a tax of four pieces of silver per man, see S. Beal, trans., *Buddhist Records of the Western World, translated from the Chinese of Hiuen Tsiang* (A.D. 629) (London, 1895), vol. II, pp. 277ff.

[2] b. Ket. 95b.

[3] b. B.Q. 84b.

[4] b. Shev. 41a, Rabina.

friends, at the gate of *ZYYN'* none. The word may refer merely to loss but possibly to prison.[1] No references from this period indicate that criminals ever were sentenced to prison terms. The chief punishments available to the courts therefore do not seem to have included incarceration.[2]

The ban was by far the most common penalty, sometimes in combination with lashing, as in the following:

> Rabina said, "We excommunicate him [for contempt of a court order] until the time comes for his punishment with lashes. [That is, if the man permits thirty days to pass without freeing himself of the ban through appropriate remedial action, he is lashed.] Then we lash him and leave him."
>
> (b. Shev. 41a)

But the ban frequently was imposed by itself. We have noted its use in connection with violation of festival taboos. We have the following cases as well:

> Rabina, once sitting before R. Ashi, observed that a certain person was tying his ass to a palm-tree on the Sabbath. He [Rabina] called out, but he [the man] took no notice. He called out, "Let this man be placed under the ban." He then asked [R. Ashi], "Does such an act as mine [done in your presence] appear as impertinence?" [R. Ashi replied], "*There is no wisdom, understanding, or counsel against the Lord* (Prov. 21:30)—That is, wherever the divine name is being profaned one shows no respect to one's master [but acts on one's own forthwith]."
>
> (b. ʿEruv. 63a)

> Rabina and Rabbah Tosfa'ah were once walking together when they saw a man drawing buckets of water during the intermediate days of the festival. Rabbah said to Rabina, "Shall we place him under a ban?"
>
> (b. M.Q. 4b)

Having discussed the matter, Rabina and Rabbah recognized that the man was not subject to a ban and so refrained from punishing him.[3] Amemar taught that a person excommunicated by three authorities must be released by three authorities.[4] One recalls that the sages found the ban especially effective in maintaining discipline in the schools.[5] This fact underlines the social nature of excommunication. An earlier discussion about why a certain man had not been excommunicated

[1] b. Shab. 32a, and see Jastrow s.v., who gives both meanings.

[2] See below, pp. 318-320, on punishments for thefts and damages, for example.

[3] b. Sanh. 26b, R. Papa excommunicated grave-diggers for burying a corpse on Shavuʿot.

[4] b. M.Q. 16a.

[5] Above, pp. 165-166.

now raised the issue, "Was [he] a great or powerful man that they refrained from banning him?"[1] Clearly both the acquiescence and active support of the community were required to overcome important individuals' resistance to rabbinical decrees, including writs of excommunication. The rabbis could likewise permit people to abuse an evil-doer. R. Ashi said that it was quite proper to abuse a person of poor reputation.[2] The power which the rabbis claimed to suppress rumors may have been a significant, if little used, means of coercion; their power to *start* them was probably more effectual.

Court jurisdiction probably did not extend to capital cases. The Iranian government presumably reserved the right to try such cases. R. Ashi referred to the words opening a murder trial. He said one starts proceedings by saying, "If anyone knows anything in his favor, let him come forward and testify."[3] Mar b. Rabina commented on the rules for accepting testimony in a capital case.[4] It seems to me these were merely matters of legal theory.[5]

VIII. The Sacred Calendar

Observance of the Sabbath and festivals by ordinary folk had earlier remained outside the strict control of the sages. Rabbis could only issue warnings and curses. In general, however, they had little more power than to tell people what to do and promise them heavenly rewards for obedience to "the Torah." The exceptional laws were those about the Sabbath limits. As communal officials, the rabbis could set up the *'eruv* according to the law, and none impeded them. We have similar stories now, such as the following:

> Maremar partitioned off Sura [from the canal] by means of nets...
> (b. 'Eruv. 8a)

We also have sayings on how various rabbis prepared the *'eruv-tavshilin*[6] and on the rules pertaining to fruits carried beyond the Sabbath limit.[7] In this regard the late fourth and fifth century stratum

[1] b. Pes. 53b.
[2] b. Meg. 25b. Note also the saying of R. Ashi on court confirmation or suppression of 'reports' in b. Giṭ. 89b.
[3] b. Sanh. 32b.
[4] b. B.Q. 88a.
[5] See Vol. IV, pp. 186-191.
[6] b. Beẓ. 7a, R. Ashi.
[7] b. 'Eruv. 41b, R. Papa.

is not much different from earlier ones. Where it strikingly differs is in stories about *enforcement* of other aspects of Sabbath-law, for which we have few, if any, earlier equivalents:

> Amemar permitted sprinkling [the floors] in Maḥoza [on the Sabbath]...
>
> (b. Shab. 95a)

> Amemar permitted the drawing of water by means of a wheel at Maḥoza [on the Sabbath]...
>
> (b. ʿEruv. 104a)

> Amemar permitted a gentile to paint an eye [of a Jew] on the Sabbath [for medical purposes] ... Amemar permitted the painting of eyes on the second day of the New Year...
>
> (b. Beẓ. 22a)

In addition, we noted that Rabina discussed with R. Ashi the excommunication of a man who tied his ass to a palm-tree on the Sabbath.[1] These stories suggest that the rabbis were now able to use the ban as a means of enforcing Sabbath-law. I assume that Amemar's decisions were of a practical sort.[2] In the past few such stories were told. If, as seems likely, the ban in Sabbath law-enforcement now proved more effective than earlier, the cause can only be that the public would honor the decree and understand the need to issue it. We therefore may very tentatively suppose that the enforcement of Sabbath-laws proved more feasible than earlier as a result of two and more centuries of rabbinical instruction and exemplification of the law.

Stories of how rabbis themselves observed the Sabbath laws include these:

> R. Papa's household [on the Sabbath] poured wine slowly from one vessel to another...
>
> (b. Shab. 139b)

> Amemar, Mar Zuṭra and R. Ashi were sitting when *barda* [a spice] was brought before them. Amemar and R. Ashi washed their hands in it, but Mar Zuṭra refrained from doing so...
>
> (b. Shab. 50b)

> Mar b. R. Ashi said, "I once stood before my father when his plaster slipped off into his pillow and he replaced it..."
>
> (b. ʿEruv. 102b)

---

[1] b. ʿEruv. 63a.

[2] Compare Vol. IV, pp. 168-9, on the practical significance of *ŠR*ʾ as used by Rava.

> The host of R. Papa ... had some eggs from the Sabbath [which he wished to prepare on the festival]. He came and asked whether he might eat them the next day...
>
> (b. Beẓ. 4a)
>
> A mouse once fell into a spice-box of R. Ashi. He ruled, "Take it out by the tail..."
>
> (b. Beẓ. 36b)

These conventional stories are consistent with those told for several generations. The sages' own actions on the Sabbath set valid precedents, as much as did their teachings. Sayings on Sabbath-observance included discussions on the use of various kind of stoves,[1] spreading mats over bee-hives on the Sabbath,[2] wearing openwork bands on the Sabbath,[3] girding oneself with a *kamara* on the Sabbath,[4] the culpability for throwing objects on the Sabbath[5] and for grinding, kneading, baking,[6] and cooking on the Sabbath,[7] and similar classical legal issues. Rabina held that the Sabbath was sanctified at creation.[8]

Festivals, fasts, and holy days generally exhibited the same pattern. The evidence suggests that the sages had greater success in enforcing the laws than earlier. I conjecture that ordinary folk now both expected them to do so and supported them when they did. The following stories pertain to rabbinical enforcement of laws pertaining to such days:

> Certain gardeners once cut myrtles on the second day of the festival. Rabina allowed people to smell them in the evening immediately [afterward]...
>
> (b. ʿEruv. 40a)
>
> Maremar taught, "The bundles of Sura are valid as a Sukkah-covering..."
>
> (b. Suk. 13b)
>
> Amemar instituted in Nehardea [regarding the lections for the intermediate days of the festival].
>
> (b. Suk. 55a)
>
> The Surans followed the ruling of Maremar [regarding use of the Sukkah species]...
>
> (b. Suk. 46b)

---

[1] b. Shab. 38b, R. Ashi.

[2] b. Shab. 43a-b, R. Ashi was asked by R. ʿUqba of Mesene about doing so in winter when there is no honey.

[3] b. Shab. 57a, R. Huna b. R. Joshua.

[4] b. Shab. 59b, Rabina asked R. Ashi.

[5] b. Shab. 100b, R. Ashi.

[6] b. Shab. 74b, R. Papa and R. Ashi.

[7] b. Shab. 140a, Mar Zuṭra.

[8] b. Beẓ. 17a.

Rabina and Rabbah Tosfa'ah saw a man drawing buckets of water during the festival week. [Rabbah proposed to excommunicate him...]
(b. M.Q. 4b)

R. Ashi allowed the people of Mata Meḥasia to clear obstructions from the canal at Barnish on the festival week, holding that people needed the water for drinking, and it therefore was a public necessity...
(b. M.Q. 4b)

Rabina had lent money ... and asked R. Ashi about going to collect it during the festival week...
(b. M.Q. 10b)

Marion b. Rabina and Mar b. R. Aḥa b. Rava had a yoke of oxen in partnership. After a bereavement of Mar b. R. Aḥa b. Rava, he broke up the team [and did not contribute his animal during the festival week]. R. Ashi ruled...
(b. M.Q. 11b)

R. Papa ordained a fast and no rain fell...
(b. Ta'anit 24b)

R. Papa ordained a fast at Abi-Gobar...
(b. Ta'anit 26a)

The bases for rabbinical actions on festivals were not always the same. Rabina's rule about using the myrtles depended in part on his supervision of the market, for he could prohibit their purchase. But if people could not make use of the myrtles, they would not purchase them to begin with. In larger measure, therefore, his ruling proved effective because people respected his knowledge of religious law. Maremar's teaching does not indicate what people actually did. I suppose that in his town they wanted to build their *Sukkot* in conformity with rabbinical rules. Amemar's ruling about synagogue festival-lections, like those noted above, is of not much greater consequence, for it merely indicates that the synagogues in school-towns would abide by rabbinical rulings.[1] The "Surans" mentioned here may well be the men of the academy, but even if everyone in town followed Maremar's rule—and social pressure probably made it certain most people would—we do not know what happened elsewhere. We earlier noted the willingness of major authorities to excommunicate those who profaned the festival week. R. Ashi's rulings at Mata Meḥasia therefore are of great significance in showing his influence in his own town; like the inquiry of the sons of Rabina and R. Aḥa, Rabina's consultation merely tells us that disciples consulted masters. In all, therefore, we can only imagine that

[1] See above, pp. 262-265.

rabbinical influence tended to increase. The evidence suggests, but does not prove it.

The rabbis also gave public lectures about festival observance. Maremar was asked about the use of glazed vessels on Passover and gave a lecture proving that it was permitted.[1] R. Gevihah lectured at the exilarch's about cooking on the festival.[2] Stories about the rabbis' own festival observances included the following:

> The mother of Mar b. Rabina stored grain for him in a trough [for use on Passover].
>
> (b. Pes. 40a-b)

> Minyamin servant of R. Ashi had his shirt soaked in water and spread it on the *Sukkah*. R. Ashi said to him, "Remove it, lest people think it is permissible to use as *Sukkah*-covering something which is susceptible of uncleanness."
>
> (b. Suk. 10b)

> R. Ashi found R. Kahana placing a *Sukkah*-covering ... [and asked about the law]...
>
> (b. Suk. 19a)

> Mar b. Amemar told R. Ashi, "My father used to pray holding a *lulav*..."
>
> (b. Suk. 41b)

> The wife of R. Ashi sifted flour on the top side of a table [on a festival]...
>
> (b. Beẓ. 29b)

> Rabina said to R. Ashi, "R. Aḥa of Huẓal told me that they pasted up an oven for you on a festival..."
>
> (b. Beẓ. 32b)

> R. Ashi had a wood ... and went to cut it during the festival week...
>
> (b. M.Q. 12b)

> R. Ashi's disciples wore shoes as usual on fast-days ... Maremar and Mar Zuṭra used to shift shoes from one foot to the other...
>
> (b. Ta'anit 12b)[3]

Sayings on festival observance included discussions of chewing ginger on the Day of Atonement,[4] feeding a sick person on that day,[5] cooking

---

[1] b. Pes. 30b.

[2] b. Beẓ. 23a.

[3] R. Ashi's view, like Samuel's, was that there was no public fast in Babylonia except the 9th of Av.

[4] b. Ber. 37b, Rabina to Maremar.

[5] b. Yoma 83a, Mar b. R. Ashi.

on the festivals,[1] watering a field on the intermediate days of the festival,[2] and the like.

I think it significant that R. Ashi assumed people would naturally follow his practice in covering the *Sukkah*. Likewise the possibility of making use of the ban must not be ignored, for the reasons stated earlier. The evidence concerning the Sabbath is more considerable, but the festivals were not much different in character. If the rabbis could now exert greater influence in Sabbath observance than earlier, they probably could do the same with regard to festivals. Keeping festivals and the Sabbath was not subject to court rulings. No one normally was lashed or fined for breaking the festival and Sabbath taboos. The administrative and judicial role of the rabbinate made little difference in enforcing these laws. As holy men, on the other hand, rabbis possessed wide influence over just such matters, and as we have seen, they did not hesitate to use it to enforce the law.

IX. Food Laws

Rabbinical control of the markets naturally included the right to supervise the ritual fitness of food and other products sold there, as we have seen in the ruling about the purchase and use of myrtle after a festival. Food laws produced two kinds of material, first, sayings and stories about the ritual acceptability of various sorts of food and about ways of preparing and storing food. These sayings and stories are rarely, if ever, accompanied by stories of how rabbis instructed others to behave, how ordinary folk had been punished for ignoring rabbinical rulings, or of what Rabbi So-and-so ruled in his court when a "certain woman" prepared something contrary to law. It is important to stress this fact, because the second sort of material is composed of just such stories, most of them in a setting of market-supervision. In fact, the rabbis' control of the markets produced whatever power they had actually to enforce the food laws. That enforcement pertained almost exclusively to the ritual slaughter of animals for Jewish use, the examination of their entrails for marks of disease, the sharpness of the slaughterers' knives, and related matters.

Some of the food laws pertained to hygiene. One should not leave liquids uncovered, for example. R. Papa or R. Huna b. R. Joshua

---

[1] b. Beẓ. 32b, Rabina and R. Ashi.
[2] b. M.Q. 4a, R. Papa and R. Ashi.

would use brine to dilute other liquids that had been left uncovered.[1] R. Ashi and Rabina discussed the rule concerning a mouse's falling into vinegar.[2] Concerning laws on the separation of milk and meat R. Papa taught the dough may not be kneaded with milk.[3] We have numerous stories illustrating how rabbis had behaved in their own homes. Some do not specify the setting at all, as the following:

> An olive's bulk of [forbidden] fat fell into some meat. R. Ashi intended to include in measuring [the meat] absorbed in the pot. The rabbis said to him....
>
> (b. Ḥul. 98a)

> A half of an olive's bulk of fat once fell into a pot of meat. Mar. b. R. Ashi intended to measure it by the standard of thirty-fold, but his father said to him, "Have I not told you not to treat lightly the standard measures [even in prohibitions by] rabbinical ruling..."
>
> (b. Ḥul. 98a)

We simply do not know who, if anyone, consulted R. Ashi and Mar b. R. Ashi in these incidents. It may have been other sages or possibly an ordinary housewife. On the other hand, in the following the practices of the rabbis themselves are preserved for precedent:

> R. Isaac b. R. Mesharsheya once visited R. Ashi. He was served cheese, which he ate, and then meat, which he also ate, but without first washing his hands....
>
> (b. Ḥul. 104b)

> R. Ashi once visited the house of Rami b. Abba his father-in-law, when he saw his brother-in-law putting liver on the spit on top of meat, "How presumptuous is this disciple of the rabbis," he said, "for the rabbis permitted it after the fact but not to begin with..."
>
> (b. Ḥul. 111a-b)

Immediately preceding is the story of Maremar's public exposition that the liver and udder may be cooked on top of the meat only after the fact, but people should not encouraged to do so.[4] We may be certain that the public exposition was heard and obeyed by sages. We cannot say for sure what its impact would have been upon outsiders.

Sayings pertaining to the slaughter of animals do not differ in form from the others. We find a dispute about how to clean a knife used in slaughtering an animal found to be unacceptable,[5] a rule that one should

---

[1] b. Ḥul. 49b.
[2] b. A.Z. 69a.
[3] b. B.M. 91a.
[4] b. Ḥul. 111a.
[5] b. Ḥul. 8b, R. Aḥa and Rabina.

not place the loins on top of the meat for fear that the fat will run and be absorbed by the meat,[1] a test for telling whether the animal's bronchial tubes are intact,[2] a rule on examining an animal which has been injured in a fall[3] or which has been clawed,[4] and many other matters. In this connection we have a story:

> A duck belonging to R. Ashi went among the reeds and came out with its neck smeared with blood. R. Ashi ruled [on the clawing]...
>
> (b. Ḥul. 53b)

The laws concerning ritual slaughter of animals however are accompanied by a number of remarkable cases illustrating points of law. These cases invariably occur in court-settings. They leave no doubt whatever that rabbis effectively decided whether animals had been properly slaughtered and their meat satisfactorily prepared for the Jewish market. R. Ashi would consult the ritual-slaughterers of Mata Meḥasia:

> When a possibly unfit animal was submitted to R. Ashi for inspection, he would call [to consult] all the butchers of Mata Meḥasia in order that "each of them may carry a chip from the beam."
>
> (b. Sanh. 7b = b. Hor. 3b)

This story is told following one about R. Huna, who would gather ten *disciples* to judge cases "so that each may carry..." It is significant that the butchers of R. Ashi's town were believed by him to be sufficiently informed about the law so that their opinion could be solicited and relied upon. Strikingly, the earlier generation produced no such stories.

Further stories illustrating the court enforcement of law or sayings which clearly presuppose practical settings include the following:

> R. Aḥa b. Rava told R. Ashi that R. Kahana required an examination of the slaughter-knife after each animal was slaughtered...
>
> (b. Ḥul. 10b)

> Rabina and R. Aḥa b. Rava were sitting before R. Ashi when a knife was brought to R. Ashi for examination. He asked R. Aḥa to examine it...
>
> (b. Ḥul. 17b)

> In a certain case, a slaughterer did not present his knife for examination by Rava b. Ḥinena. Rava put him under the ban, removed him, and announced publicly that all his meat was unfit. Mar Zuṭra and

[1] b. Ḥul. 8b.
[2] b. Ḥul. 47b, R. Ashi.
[3] b. Ḥul. 5a, Mar Zuṭra.
[4] b. Ḥul. 53b, Amemar.

R. Ashi came by to call on Rava b. Ḥinena. He asked them to look into the case, as there are small children dependent on him. R. Ashi examined the knife, found it satisfactory, and declared him fit again. Mar Zuṭra said, "But are you not concerned about overruling this sage?" R. Ashi replied, "We are only carrying out his instructions."

(b. Ḥul. 18a)

Rabina told R. Ashi, "R. Shaman of Sikara told me Mar Zuṭra once came to our town and ruled that if the knife cut through the arytenoid cartilages ... the slaughtering is valid..."

(b. Ḥul. 18b)

A pair of lungs with an additional lobe was once brought before Maremar. R. Aḥa who was sitting at the gate asked the [butcher] what Maremar had ruled. He replied, "He permitted it." "Then go, take it to him again," said R. Aḥa. Maremar then said, "Go tell him who sits at the gate that the law is not in accordance with Rava..."

(b. Ḥul. 47a)

A pair of lungs with an interjacent lobe was once brought before R. Ashi, who was about to declare it unfit when R. Huna Mar b. Avia said to him...

(b. Ḥul. 47a)

A needle was once found in a portion of the liver. Mar b. R. Joseph was about to declare it unfit, when R. Ashi said to him...

(b. Ḥul. 48b)

A needle was once found in the portal vein of the liver. Huna Mar b. R. Idi declared the animal unfit, and R. Ada b. Manyomi declared it fit. The case came to Rabina who said, "Take away the [rabbinical] cloaks of those who declare it unfit."

(b. Ḥul. 49a)

A date stone was found in the glass-bladder. R. Ashi said, "When we were at the school of R. Kahana, he told us that in such a case..."

(b. Ḥul. 49a)

A goat belonging to Rabina was on the roof and saw through the skylight some peeled barley. It jumped from the roof to the ground. Rabina came to R. Ashi and asked...

(b. Ḥul. 51a)

A ewe belonging to R. Ḥabiba was seen dragging its hind legs. R. Yemar said, "It is suffering from a hip disease." Rabina demurred...

(b. Ḥul. 51a)

R. Ashi said, "When we were at the school of R. Kahana a lung was brought to us. When it was laid down it was firm, but when it was lifted up, it decomposed and fell to pieces. We declared it unfit..."

(b. Ḥul. 53b)

R. Yemar used to examine [the membrane of the brain] with water. R. Aḥa b. Jacob did so with a straw of wheat.

(b. Ḥul. 56a-b)

An animal having two inner rumens was brought before Rabina, who declared it unfit...

(b. Ḥul. 58b)

A tube running from the reticulum to the omasum was once found in an animal. R. Ashi was about to declare it unfit when R. Huna Mar b. Ḥiyya said to him, "But all animals that feed in the open fields have this tube." A tube running from the reticulum to the rumen was once found in an animal. R. Ashi was about to declare it permitted when R. Oshaia said to him...

(b. Ḥul. 58b)

Adda b. Ḥabu had an animal that had been extracted [by caesarean section]. It was attacked by a wolf. He came to R. Ashi who advised him to slaughter it immediately...

(b. Ḥul. 75b)

Mar b. R. Ashi said, "I was once standing before my father when a bird was brought to him which he examined. He found only fifteen tendons..."

(b. Ḥul. 76b)

In the house of the exilarch, sides of meat were once salted with the sciatic nerve inside. Rabina forbade them, but R. Aḥa b. Rava declared them permitted. When the case came to Mar b. R. Ashi, he said...

(b. Ḥul. 97b)[1]

Of the three stories about examining the butchers' slaughter-knives, the third is most striking. We see that Rava b. Ḥinena exercised what amounted to absolute control over the butcher. He could not only excommunicate, but also deprive the butcher of the right to practice his livelihood. He had to take care how he exercised that power, so he consulted other sages. The basis for rabbinical enforcement of food-laws therefore is entirely clear. We moreover have no doubt as to its effectiveness. The ruling of Mar Zuṭra at Sikara and similar decrees certainly were enforced.

Cases in which doubtful matters were brought to rabbis for inspection generally must have been based upon actual events in the courts. Senior authorities, such as Rabina in the case of the needle found in a liver-vein, evidently could overrule the decisions of local officials. Cases such as those reported by R. Ashi from his early years at

[1] All translations in this section are from Eli Cashdan, *Ḥullin* (London, 1948), with minor revisions.

school must have taken place when the master was consulted by a butcher or some other outsider. In deciding the case the master shared the issue with his disciples. We see that sages consulted one another, as was natural.

If, as is clear, the sages enforced all laws dealing with ritual slaughter and sale of animals for Jewish consumption, they could do so because they controlled the markets, but of even greater importance, because they had the power to dispose of the property of Jewry. Animals represented substantial capital; declaring one unsuited for Jewish consumption considerably lowered its value. Even more significant, closing the market to a butcher forthwith deprived him of his livelihood, as we have seen. Under such circumstances the butchers certainly had little choice but to cooperate in every detail with rabbinical instructions. By contrast, not a single rule, custom, or taboo pertaining to food prepared in homes produced an equivalent story or case. I do not think the rabbis enforced or otherwise effectuated any food-laws other than those of ritual slaughter. That is not to suggest people did not keep those laws and taboos. We simply do not know what they did.

x. Sexual Taboos. Circumcision

The biblical laws about refraining from sexual relations during a woman's menstrual period were understood to apply to ordinary folk, not merely priests, and in everyday life, not only in the Temple. Since the common folk believed themselves obligated to keep the laws of the Scriptures revealed at Sinai, they kept the biblical taboo. The rabbis normally and regularly were consulted about doubtful cases. Their reputation as experts in distinguishing the causes and evidences of various kinds of excretions was considerable.[1] Hence the laws, voluntarily kept by most people, did not have to be enforced through either coercive means or the social force of rabbinical influence. The role of the sages depended upon their reputation as sages and holy men, rather than upon their communal position.

Evidence concerning the opinions and practices of the later generations is limited. We have the following:

> R. Kahana stated, "I inquired of the women of the house of R. Papa and of R. Huna b. R. Joshua, 'Do the rabbis coming home from the school-house require you to undergo an examination?' They said no."

[1] Vol. IV, p. 275. See also vol. III, pp. 240-243 and IV, pp. 158-159.

> And why did he not ask the sages themselves? Because they might have imposed additional restrictions on themselves. [The meaning is that the rabbis might have given a lenient ruling applying to everyone, rather than a strict ruling applying to themselves alone. The women would be able to tell the practice of the sages themselves.]
>
> (b. Nid. 12b)

The implication of the later editorial comment is that the rabbis did issue decrees applying to everyone and sterner ones applying to themselves, and we may suppose that they assumed the laws were widely kept. The sages studied the laws of inspecting blood:

> Amemar, Mar Zuṭra, and R. Ashi once sat before a cupper. When the first cupping-horn was taken off Amemar, he saw it and observed, "This is the *red* about which we have studied." When the second was removed he said, "This is a different shade." R. Ashi commented, "One like myself who does not know the differences between bloods must not act as an examiner of blood."
>
> (b. Nid. 20a)

We however have no cases in which rabbis were consulted about blood. Stories cited earlier leave no doubt that sages influenced popular behavior, and we have no reason to suppose their influence later on diminished.

As to other sexual matters, R. Papa taught that it was forbidden to wear trousers in the Iranian manner, for these might cause sexual excitement by contact with the male organ. He held that the breeches referred to in Scriptures (Ex. 28 : 42) were designed to hang loosely, so as to engender no heat in the male sexual organs.

Regarding the rite of circumcision, everyone agreed that the membrum had to be trimmed. The issue was, Who is responsible to do so? R. Kahana held that the surgeon must trim, while R. Papa said that any adult was responsible to do so. R. Ashi agreed with R. Kahana. Similarly, R. Papa said that the surgeon must suck out the wound.[1] We have a case in which rabbis ruled upon the results of circumcision. The cut took the shape of a gutter, and R. Ashi arranged for the corona to be cut into the shape of a reed pen and declared the man fit.[2] I assume the case involved the conversion of an adult male to Judaism.

xi. Holy Objects

When the sages legislated concerning holy objects, such as the scroll of the Torah, the *mezuzah*, *tefillin*, and the like, their intention was both

[1] b. Shab. 133b.
[2] b. Yev. 75b.

to legitimize and to preserve the sanctity of these objects from commonplace defilements. For example, they held that one should not keep a Torah-scroll in a place where people slept. Mar Zuṭra visiting R. Ashi noticed that where Mar b. R. Ashi slept, a scroll of the Torah was kept behind a partition ten handbreaths high. He asked about the legal basis for these arrangements.[1] Similarly with reference to the *mezuzah*:

> R. Papa once visited Mar Samuel and saw a door which had only one doorpost, on the left side, to which a *mezuzah* was attached. [He commented on the legal reason for this situation.]
>
> (b. Men. 34a)

Amemar said that a door in the corner requires a *mezuzah*.[2] We find no legislation, by contrast, dealing with the magical bowls, which were apparently used, like the *mezuzah*, to ward off demons. Since the rabbis probably disapproved of that form of magic, they passed over it in silence. The provision of legislation thus was their mode of indicating approval for particular forms of theurgy.

Tefillin (phylacteries) were characteristically worn by sages and distinguished the sage from outsiders. It was regarded as exceptionally pious to wear *tefillin* all day long. Yet it is possible that ordinary people wore them as well:

> R. Aḥa b. R. Joseph asked R. Ashi, "May one sew [the strap of *tefillin*] together, turning the seam on the inside?" He replied, "Go, see what the people do." (b. Men. 35b)

The meaning may be that ordinary folk also make use of *tefillin*, so we may conform to popular practice. But "people" may denote the men of the school. We can come to no firm conclusion. It is clear that rabbinical practices were preserved as precedents:

> When R. Ashi was once sitting before Mar Zuṭra the strap of his *tefillin* twisted around, and Mar Zuṭra [asked him about it]...
>
> (b. Men. 35b)

> Rabina said, "I was once sitting before R. Ashi when darkness had fallen, and he put on his *tefillin*. I asked him whether his intention was to guard them. He replied, 'Yes.'"
>
> (b. Men. 36b)

> R. Ashi was once sitting before Amemar. Amemar had an injury on his arm and his *tefillin* was exposed [since his cloak had been removed]. R. Ashi said to him, "Does not the master hold 'it shall be a sign to him, but *not* to others'?..."
>
> (b. Men. 37b)

---

[1] b. Ber. 26a.
[2] b. Men. 34a.

Mar Zuṭra reported that R. Papi had said a blessing whenever he put on his *tefillin*. The disciples of R. Ashi said a blessing whenever they touched their *tefillin*.[1]

Similar stories were told concerning fringes (*ẓiẓit*). For instance:

> Rabina was once walking behind Mar b. R. Ashi on a Sabbath preceding the festival, when the corner of [Mar's] garment with its fringe was torn away. Rabina told him nothing about it. When they reached home, he [Rabina] informed him [Mar]. He replied, "Had you said so I would forthwith have thrown it off [for it was not properly provided with fringes.]..."
>
> (b. Men. 37b-38a)

Similarly, Rabina and R. Sama were in R. Ashi's presence, and R. Sama noted that Rabina's fringes were not in accordance with the law. Further:

> R. Aḥa b. Jacob used to take four threads, double them over, insert them through the garment, and then make them into a loop. He held there must be eight threads in the hole of the garment...
>
> (b. Men. 42a)

Knot-tying was a skill characteristic of magicians. The rabbis were certainly expert at it. Yet at no point in their discussion of the laws about fringes do we find reference to their magical value.

The rabbis were not scribes. Professional scribes were employed to copy scrolls of the Torah for synagogue use. R. Ashi reported that he had observed scribes at their work.[2] Scrolls which did not conform to the rabbinical rules would have been rejected in the schools. Scribes employed by courts to prepare documents conformed in every detail to rabbinical law, as we shall see.[3]

XII. Mourning Rites

Well-established mourning rites must have proved among the most difficult practices to modify in accordance with the sages' rules. Yet while earlier, expensive shrouds contrary to rabbinical law had been used,[4] now R. Papa said that it was common practice to employ rough cloth shrouds worth only a *ẓuẓ*.[5] This saying would imply widespread conformity to the rabbis' sumptuary laws. As we have noted, R. Papa

[1] b. Suk. 46a.
[2] b. Men. 29b.
[3] Below, pp. 314-315.
[4] Vol. IV, pp. 156-157.
[5] b. Ket. 8b.

excommunicated men who dug a grave on a festival.[1] The power of excommunication of such men was significant, for perhaps ordinary folk responsive to rabbinical opinion would not then use the diggers' services for their own deceased. On the other hand while butchers made their living at their work, grave-digging required no skill and probably did not constitute a lucrative profession, so not much loss of income could have been incurred.

R. Ashi held that mourning rites commence when the grave is closed with the grave-stone.[2] Another mourning rite now discussed was whether remission by the advent of a festival of the requirement to overturn a couch is effective even though the overturning was first done only very shortly before the festival.[3] Rafram b. Papa cited a teaching that one must not have sexual relations during the seven-day mourning period. He reported that one who did so died.[4] R. Avia expounded that one day of mourning before the New Year and the New Year's day accounted for fourteen of the required thirty days of mourning. Rabina added that by the same reasoning one day of mourning before *Sukkot* plus the festival together accounted for twenty-one days of mourning.[5] R. Papa cited a teaching that a person in mourning should not play with an infant, for the child may amuse him.[6] As to rabbinical practice we have the following stories:

> Amemar's son's son died, and he rent [his clothes]. When his son came, he did so again in the son's presence. He remembered he had done it sitting down, so he stood up and did it a third time, [this time] standing. R. Ashi said, "How do we know that tearing is to be done standing? From *Then Job rose and tore his cloak* (Job 1:20)."
>
> (b. M.Q. 20b)

> R. Ashi visited R. Kahana. A child of R. Kahana died within thirty days of birth. R. Kahana sat and mourned for it. R. Ashi [asked why, since the law was that if the child did not live thirty days, it was not viable and hence is not to be mourned.] He replied, "I know for certain that the months of pregnancy were completed."
>
> (b. Shab. 136a)

We see that the rites of mourning were carefully defined by rabbinical law. It is difficult to assess the extent of compliance by outsiders to rules such as the one about standing up to tear one's cloak or refraining

1 b. Sanh. 26b.
2 b. Sanh. 47b.
3 b. M.Q. 20a, Rabina.
4 b. M.Q. 24a.
5 b. M.Q. 24b.
6 b. M.Q. 26b.

from mourning non-viable children. On the other hand practices done publicly must now have reflected greater conformity to rabbinical views than in earlier times. Furthermore if people believed that acting contrary to rabbinical teaching would be punished by heaven, as allegedly happened, they supposed, to the man who had sexual relations during a bereavement, they would certainly keep the law as the rabbis expounded it. But we really do not know much about popular belief or practice. The use of cheap shrouds suggests, but does not prove, growing conformity to rabbinical law.

XIII. Family Life

The nature of rabbinical authority and influence is most clearly delineated in the various laws and sayings pertinent to family life. Among the many sayings about proper conduct of parents with children and husbands with wives, we find not a single instance in which a sage was able to enforce the law through coercion. On the other hand, contracting marriage and dissolving it were strictly supervised by the sages, who had complete control of the preparation and enforcement of marriage-contracts and writs of divorce. The reason for their effective control was two-fold. First of all, exchanges of property invariably accompanied both marriage and divorce, and rabbis ruled on all disputed property-exchanges. Second, the courts could determine the legal status of children. If a woman married before being properly divorced from her first husband, her children from the second marriage would be regarded by Jewish law as *mamzerim*, that is, of tainted lineage and unable to contract marriage with legitimate Jews. The whole future of families depended upon rabbinical approval of divorce and consequent remarriage. On the other hand the status of the *mamzer* was not conferred upon the product of a marriage improperly contracted between people actually free to marry—let alone of an unmarried couple—so rabbinical influence over marriage-ceremonies generally was limited to the provision of a marriage-contract. Nonetheless in this period that influence probably extended to aspects of marital relations not formerly subjected to rabbinical rulings.

Children were naturally expected to show deference to their parents, who were to be given the respect that disciples paid their masters. Mar b. R. Ashi cited his father, for example, as "My father, my teacher, my rabbi," while his *meturgeman*, or public speaker, cited Mar's father as

"R. Ashi."[1] Mar b. Rabina would not permit his son to lance a pimple on himself, fearing he would thereby incur heaven's wrath upon "the disrespectful child."[2] Nowhere do we find a court's requiring sages to cite their fathers in the manner of Mar. b. R. Ashi, but we may assume that all sages did so, since the schools would have naturally expected compliance to the law. On the other hand, if an outsider's son lanced his father's pimple, the courts probably would not have punished him. Rabina taught that the child of a Jew's daughter and a gentile would be considered a Jew, and this obviously would produce important legal consequences.[3] The child could inherit his family's property and otherwise enjoy the rights of Jewish progeny. These three sayings typify teachings about family life. The first pertained strictly to the inner circle of the sages. The second applied to anyone, but probably was not on that account enforced in the courts. But the third was most definitely a matter of practical, public law.

Still a fourth kind of saying was R. Papa's and R. Ashi's on the importance of marriage to women:

> R. Papa said, "Though her husband be [merely] a *NPẒ'* [=carder? flax-beater?], she calls him to the threshold and sits down [with him.]" R. Ashi said, "If her husband is merely dull [*QWLS'*] she still requires no lentils in her pot."
>
> (b. Yev. 118b = Qid. 75a)

Sages may have approved of marriages but could not impose them. They may have disapproved of such marriages as these, but they could not force the husbands to divorce their wives. These observations therefore theoretically pertained to everyone but actually affected no one.

By contrast Amemar's saying on foundlings would have had important practical consequences:

> Amemar said, "[If a baby was found] in a pit of datestones, he is considerated a foundling; in the swift current of a river, he is not. If found in shallow water, he is a foundling. In the side passages off public thoroughfares, he is not, but in a public thoroughfare, he is."
>
> (b. Qid. 73b)

The result for the child was life-long. If he was a foundling he would have great difficulty finding a mate or living a normal life within the Jewish community. Practical rulings on the legitimacy of children include the following:

---

[1] b. Qid. 31b.
[2] b. Sanh. 84b.
[3] b. Yev. 23a.

Rabina said, "R. Gaza told me, 'R. Yosi b. Abin was at our town when an incident [of a birth from a union between a slave and a free Jewish woman] took place with an unmarried woman, and he declared the child legitimate. When it happened with a married woman, he declared the child illegitimate.'"

R. Aḥa b. Rava said to Rabina, "Amemar was once at our town [when a similar case arose], and he declared the child legitimate in the case of a married as well as of an unmarried woman."

(b. Yev. 45b)

[In a practical case] Rabbah Tosfa'ah decided that a woman [who had given birth after her] husband had gone abroad and remained for a full year [had produced] a legitimate child...

(b. Yev. 80b)

In the last case, the reason was the sages had learned from their traditions that a birth may be delayed beyond the nine month period. Legitimacy-decisions were effective, as I said, mainly because of consequent court power over the child's future marriage and rights of inheritance. R. Papa and R. Huna b. R. Joshua were asked whether women of priestly status could marry men of tainted birth. They said that there was no prohibition.[1] Consequently such marriages would be regarded as legal and the progeny as legitimate. We furthermore know that the rabbis ruled on consanguineous marriages. Amemar supposedly permitted marriage to one's father's father's brother and one's father's father's sister.[2] They also ruled in a practical case on the remarriage of a nursing mother:

R. Papa and R. Huna b. R. Joshua intended to give a practical decision [in accordance with the rule that if a nursing mother gave her child to a wet nurse or weaned him, or if the child died, she may immediately remarry]. An aged woman, however, said to them, "I was in such a position, and R. Naḥman forbade me [to remarry]."

(b. Ket. 60b)

We must distinguish among the many kinds of sayings pertinent to married life and determine which both might produce legal action and actually did so.

Customs observed at marriage ceremonies generally were supposed to conform to rabbinical rituals, but the courts did little to enforce such laws among the common folk. Earlier the weaving of garlands was prohibited, the prohibition being a sign of mourning for the Jerusalem temple. Now we have the following:

---

[1] b. Yev. 8a.

[2] b. Yev. 21b, 40b, Amemar.

> Mar b. R. Ashi was found by Rabina to be weaving a garland for his daughter. He said, "Do you not agree with the interpretation of *Remove the mitre and take off the crown* (Ezek. 21:31) [as a sign of mourning]?" He replied, "The men follow the example of the high priest, but the women do not do so."
>
> (b. Giṭ. 7a)

This hymeneal rite obviously would not be prohibited among the ordinary people. R. Papa reported that in his town, Nersh, the newly-weds would first have sexual relations and then the bride would be placed upon the bridal chair.[1] The rabbis had to take account of common practice; they did nothing to change it.

Some particularly characteristic rabbinical practices were based upon the sages' special interpretation of the law. Thus they held that if a son was married in his father's house, the father would have somehow to signify it was not his intention for the son to acquire ownership of what was in the house:

> Mar Zuṭra married off his son and hung up for himself a sandal. R. Ashi married off his son and hung up for himself a jug of oil.
>
> (b. B.B. 144a)

These rabbinical rites would have been carried out where people knew rabbinical refinements of the law and wished to avoid complications. Elsewhere hanging up a jug of oil may have been a sign of prosperity or fecundity. We cannot however regard hanging up a jug of oil or a sandal as part of the ritual of "being a rabbi" but merely as a sign one was a rabbi, a demonstration of one's knowledge of the law of acquisition of property. There are no cases of a father's neglecting such an observance and the son's acquiring property as a result.

Stories of practical rabbinical influence over aspects of marriage not connected with property exchanges indicate a kind of authority not earlier present. They are not numerous, but that is not important. What is striking is that earlier, stories were rarely told about rabbis' ruling on matters such as these:

> What is to be understood by a rebellious woman [whose divorce is delayed, and who pays from her own marriage-contract for her current expenses]? Amemar said, "One who states, 'I like him but want to bother him.' If she claims that he is repulsive to her, she is not pressured." Mar Zuṭra held that she is pressured [to change her ways.] One such case occurred and Mar Zuṭra pressured the woman [and the couple was reconciled.] R. Ḥanina of Sura was born of the reunion...
>
> (b. Ket. 63b)

[1] b. Yev. 110a.

R. Zevid's daughter-in-law rebelled and took possession of her silk. Amemar, Mar Zuṭra, and R. Ashi were sitting together and R. Gamda was with them, and they ruled, "If a wife rebels she forfeits her worn-out clothing..."

(b. Ket. 63b)

[Rav had taught that one administers lashes on account of a couple's being alone together, but one does not excommunicate the couple.] R. Ashi said, "This applied only to privacy with an unmarried woman but not with a married woman, lest a stigma be cast upon her children."

Mar Zuṭra punished but proclaimed [that the woman had not committed adultery]. R. Naḥman of Paraheṭia said to R. Ashi, "Why do you not punish and proclaim?" He replied, "Some may hear of the one but not of the other [and future children will be thought to be illegitimate.]"

(b. Qid. 8a)

These were exceptional cases. Earlier sages, in particular, did not bring pressure on wives to resume their marital duties. Mar Zuṭra's having done so was regarded as outside of the law, and it was to Providence that R. Ḥanina's birth was attributed. R. Zevid's daughter-in-law's case was a more commonplace situation, producing litigation over property but no effort to reconcile the couple. Similarly Mar Zuṭra's action in going beyond earlier precedents on punishing married women found alone with men who were not their husbands revealed the limits of rabbinical power. R. Ashi feared that the reason for rabbinical rulings would be widely known but misunderstood, which suggests that the rabbis had to take care not to give grounds for false deductions from their actions. This further suggests that people were now attentive to the rabbis' decisions here as in the matters of building *Sukkot* and sexual taboos. Cases more commonplace in earlier times included the following:

R. Zevid permitted [a married couple] to have the first intercourse on the Sabbath [despite the fact that piercing was prohibited as destruction]. Some say that R. Zevid himself had the first intercourse on the Sabbath.

(b. Ket. 7a)

Huna Mar b. Rava of Paraziqa said to R. Ashi, "Shall we also apply a test to the cloth [on which the first intercourse takes place, when the husband claims that he found no blood]?" R. Ashi replied, "Our laundry work is like their washing. [The Palestinians produced finer results and so could rely upon them, while we cannot be certain of ours]. And if you say, let us do laundry work, the smoothing stone will remove [signs of the blood, so the test in any case could not be decisive.]"

(b. Ket. 10a-b)

On this basis, R. Ashi declined to continue the Palestinian practice of seeking to find marks of virginity. Sages could tell people when to conduct the formalities of signing a marriage-contract, but they had no way of preventing newlyweds from engaging in sexual relations when the couple wanted to.

The rabbis thus had some influence over everyday marital life, though we cannot regard it as substantial. They could attempt to reconcile wives to their husbands, but it was easier and therefore more usual to punish wives by fines against their property, in the form of deductions from the marriage-settlements, than to pressure women to change their ways. R. Ashi seemed hesitant about both punishing a woman who spent time alone with another man and testing the sheets for signs of blood. R. Zevid's ruling could hardly have come to court and applied mostly to the faithful few rather than to the larger community. These stories present a striking contrast with the numerous and important rabbinical actions on betrothals, marriage-contracts, and divorces. When the rabbis had no opportunity to work through the courts, their power was severely limited.

XIV. Marriage

Two exchanges of property were effected in connection with marriage, through, first, the token of betrothal, second, the marriage-contract (*ketuvah*) and dowry. Because of the courts' direct control of these matters, related details similarly were under their supervision. Amemar, for example, permitted betrothal on the ninetieth day after divorce or death of the first husband.[1] In the present form of the saying we do not know whether he actually did so in a court case or whether it was his opinion that one *may* do so, but it hardly matters, since in either circumstance he had every possibility of issuing a practical ruling. A more theoretical issue was discussed by R. Ashi and Mar Zuṭra, namely, whether a woman could give the token of betrothal to a man and thereby become engaged.[2] Social conditions would have militated against it. Similarly, R. Papa and R. Ashi raised the question of whether, if a man says, "Your daughter and your cow be mine for a *peruṭah* [penny]," the language means that the daughter comes for a half and the cow for a half, and they similarly wondered about a case in which the language could be used of a daughter and a piece of

[1] b. Yev. 43a.
[2] b. Qid. 7a.

immovable property.[1] Such an issue could not often have arisen in the courts.

Actual reports of court cases on betrothals included the following:

> A man was throwing down dates from a palmtree. A woman came and said to him, "Throw me down a couple." He replied, "If I do, will you become betrothed to me?" She answered, "Oh, do throw them down!" R. Zevid ruled, "Every expression [like] 'Oh indeed do throw them down!' means absolutely nothing."
>
> (b. Qid. 9a)
>
> Two men were drinking wine under mats in Babylonia. One took a cup of wine, gave it to the other, and said, "Let your daughter be betrothed to my son." Rabina ruled, "Even on the view that the father may have consented, we do not hold that the son might." [That is, parents cannot betrothe their children.]
>
> (b. Qid. 45a-b)
>
> A man betrothed a minor with a bunch of vegetables in the market-place. Rabina ruled...
>
> (b. Qid. 45b)
>
> A certain woman was said to have become betrothed to a minor who looked like an adult. R. Mordecai said to R. Ashi...
>
> (b. Giṭ. 89b)
>
> A certain man said [in his will], "Give four hundred *zuz* to so-and-so, and let him marry my daughter." R. Papa ruled, "So-and-so receives the money, but as to the daughter, if he wants to, he may marry her, but if he does not, he need not marry her."
>
> (b. Beẓ. 20a)

The rabbis further concerned themselves with reports or rumors of betrothals. R. Ashi said that a rumor which a court has not confirmed is no rumor, and if rumors are spread after marriage, they are ignored.[2] Deeds of betrothal were supervised by the court. If one was written for a woman without her knowledge, Rava and Rabina held she was nonetheless betrothed. R. Papa denied it.[3] The ancient laws had long since become rooted in everyday life, so that the rabbis' reported decisions concerned exceptional situations. The case of a casual betrothal, for instance, could not have been commonplace. The reports of disputes over more ordinary issues would have produced no legal points of interest, and they therefore were not preserved in our literature. Obviously fathers could not legally betrothe their sons, but it was

[1] b. Qid. 7b.
[2] b. Giṭ. 89b.
[3] b. Qid. 9b.

important to note that the consent of the father did not necessitate taking account of the *possible* consent of the son, a point of theoretical interest.

Disputes over dowries and marriage-contracts had, strictly speaking, little to do with ordinary marriages. A woman could be married on a standard marriage-contract without much additional dowry, and she could routinely collect it upon the death of her husband or on her divorce. In fact, dowries for the bride generally constituted their inheritance from their father's (future) estate and so became a touchy matter. R. Papa's arrangements for his son to marry into the house of Abba of Sura, for instance, involved difficult negotiations and writing a substantial sum into the *ketuvah*.[1] Collections of the marriage-contract had to be done in court when contrary property-claims intervened, such as those of the orphans:

> A daughter-in-law of the house of Bar Eliashiv was claiming her marriage-contract from orphans. When she called them to court and they [shrewdly] said, "It is degrading for us that you come with us in such [poor] clothes," she went home and dressed in all her garments. When they came before Rabina, he ruled ... [concerning assessing the clothes of the widow in connection with the payment of her *ketuvah*.]
> (b. Ket. 54a)

> A man once paid money [in advance] for his father-in-law's dowry [as agent of the father-in-law]. The dowry fell in price. They came to R. Papa [who said to the purchaser], "If you have contracted for the lowest price, you may take at the present prices, but if not, you must pay the original one..."
> (b. B.M. 74b)

> Rabina was writing a large amount for the dowry of his daughter [which was more money than he was actually giving]. They said, "Then let us take possession from you." He replied, "If it is to be by formal possession, then there can be no doubling of the figure, and if there is a doubling of the figure, there can be no formal possession..."
> (b. B.M. 104b)

> A certain man once said, "Give my daughter four hundred *zuz* as her marriage-settlement [*ketuvah*]. R. Aḥa b. R. Avia asked R. Ashi, "Does it mean four hundred *zuz*, hence eight hundred [to be written down], or four hundred *zuz* [as the written sum], and hence [only] two hundred *zuz* is the real dowry?" R. Ashi replied...
> (b. B.M. 104b)

> A certain man sold all his possessions and [then] divorced his wife. R. Joseph b. Rava sent her to R. Papa...
> (b. ʿArakh. 23b)

[1] b. Ket. 54b-53a.

> Rabina was engaged in preparing for the marriage of his son at R. Ḥanina's [or Ḥaviva's]. R. Ḥanina said to him, "Do you intend writing the *ketuvah* four days hence?" He said, "Yes," but when the fourth day came, he waited another four days, and so the matter was delayed for seven days after the day in question...
>
> (b. Nid. 66b)

He did so to accord with the teaching of Rava that one has to allow seven clean [= non-menstrual] days to pass between a proposal of marriage and its fulfillment.

Marriage-contracts thus presented a difficult matter, for while chiefly concerned with property, they involved personal status as well. The collection of marriage-contracts not infrequently required court action, including assessment of what the woman received beside actual cash or land. Use of the dowry in trade obviously would produce litigation over agreements, contracts, and the like. On the other hand, the human tendency to exaggerate the size of gifts such as dowries produced a convention to write twice the actual sum to be paid, and as we noted, this could likewise produce complications. Marriage-contracts thus involved both property and peculiar ritual considerations. One drew up the document in legal forms, but in doing so had to pay close attention to questions of rite and of personal status not related to property at all.

We have seen that the rabbis' control over marriages was based primarily upon their judicial authority over property and personal status. That authority was substantial, yet did not allow sages to enforce obedience to rules of personal behavior, moral principles, and matters of mere custom outside of the narrow jurisdiction of the courts. People could do pretty much as they pleased, except in writing up marriage-contracts and in arranging the formalities of betrothal. Even in such matters, moreover, rabbinical intervention inevitably followed only when gross irregularities were committed. Under normal circumstances people could betrothe and marry without rabbinical supervision. The possibility of rabbinical intervention, however, would have encouraged ordinary folk to conform to the law to begin with, and so would the desire to be "proper" and respectable.

xv. Dissolution of Marriage

Just as ordinary people could marry without rabbinical intervention, so they normally could end their marriages on their own. Marriage terminated with death or divorce. The biblical rule about levirate marriage, moreover, generally was carried out through the ceremony of *ḥaliẓah*, rather than through actual consummation of a new marital connection. Here rabbinical supervision was commonplace. But when a spouse died, sages would intervene only in order to confirm the right to remarriage when death was not readily attested. Similarly, they would involve themselves in a divorce-document (*geṭ*) in the exceptional event of its being improperly written or delivered. The cases recorded thus relate to unusual circumstances. Yet as with marriage and its accompanying legal procedures, the possibility of rabbinical intervention encouraged ordinary folk to avoid necessitating it by scrupulously keeping the law.

The rabbis certainly supervised the ceremony of *ḥaliẓah*. They did not do so because they had to force the people to go through with the ceremony. The biblical laws about the childless widow's either marrying her deceased husband's brother or ceremonially declaring that he refused her, were clearcut, well-known, and widely kept. But the ceremony of *ḥaliẓah* was supposed to take place "at the gate before the elders" (Deut. 25 : 7). The "elders of the city" were not everywhere necessarily sages, but cases of *ḥaliẓah* law would have come to the sages as the most likely "elders" available. Where rabbis were located, there they probably witnessed most, if not all, *ḥaliẓah* ceremonies. Elsewhere, I imagine, people went to the elders of their synagogues. In any event the rabbis' power over *ḥaliẓah* derived only in part from their court authority. The main basis for their influence over the ceremony was their reputation as learned, holy men, equivalent to the "elders" of biblical times. We have the following cases:

> R. Papa and R. Huna b. R. Joshua arranged a *ḥaliẓah* in the presence of five [witnesses] ... in order to give the matter due publicity.
>
> (b. Yev. 101b)

> R. Ashi happened to be at R. Kahana's when R. Kahana said, "You have come [conveniently] to complete a quorum of five..."
>
> (b. Yev. 101b)

> Amemar said, "When a levir submits to *ḥaliẓah* he must press his foot down to the ground..."
>
> (b. Yev. 103a)

> R. Ashi found R. Kahana trying to read out for a woman [without taking a breath] *He will not perform the duty of a husband's brother to me* (Deut. 25:7). R. Ashi asked...
>
> (b. Yev. 106b)

> Mar Zuṭra ruled [the paper for a *ḥaliẓah* certificate] and copied the full text...
>
> (b. Yev. 106b)

> R. Mordecai told R. Ashi, "There was an actual case of this kind [where a *geṭ* was improperly delivered, so a woman was not divorced, and the husband died childless], and she was compelled to give *ḥaliẓah*."
>
> (b. Giṭ. 78b)

Ḥaliẓah was a routine ceremony, which the rabbis could easily require to be performed in an appropriate manner. The practical details of providing sufficient number of witnesses, determining how the ceremony would be performed, preparing the certificate to testify that it had taken place, and the like, all testify to the rabbinical control over the everyday performance of the rite.

Bills of divorce did not have to be drawn up by rabbis or court-scribes, but to be enforceable in court they did have to conform to rabbinical rule. R. Papa held that the witnesses to a *geṭ* must sign in one another's presence.[1] He held that a writ of divorce may be prepared even with spittle, and he showed Papa the cattle-dealer how it was done.[2] R. Kahana, R. Papi, and R. Ashi all acted on the principle that the *geṭ* is valid from the time it is written. R. Papa and R. Huna b. R. Joshua held that it was valid once it was delivered, and they so acted.[3] Mar b. R. Ashi reported that his father held that if the husband died, the agents in charge of delivering the *geṭ* lose their right of agency.[4] An exemplary case is as follows:

> A certain dying man wrote a *geṭ* for his wife. He groaned and sighed. His wife said to him, "Why sigh? If you recover, I am [still] yours." R. Zevid ruled, "These were mere words of consolation [and the writ of divorce is issued unconditionally and—therefore is valid]."
>
> (b. B.M. 66a)

I know of no other reports of actual divorce-cases deriving from this period. The reason cannot be that problems of law did not arise. I do not know why we should have so little evidence of court-actions in matters of divorce. On the other hand there is no basis to suppose the rabbis' power had diminished in the slightest degree.

---

[1] b. Giṭ. 10b.
[2] b. Giṭ. 19a.
[3] b. Giṭ. 18a.
[4] b. Giṭ. 29b.

XVI. Farm and Marketplace

While the rabbinical courts controlled all real estate transactions among Jews,[1] their power also extended to some aspects of land use as well. These were mostly ritual matters, especially taboos originating in Scriptures. To be sure, R. Papa advised that one should raise one's own crops rather than purchase food in the market even if the cost was the same.[2] But in general, we have no rabbinical sayings on the conduct of agricultural life, such as the planting of crops, the way to improve yields, and similar matters. We do have one case of the issuance of a *prosbul*, preventing the cancellation of a debt in the sabbatical year, which suggests that people thought the sabbatical rules applied to debts outside of Palestine:

> R. Ashi would transfer to the debtor the trunk of a date tree and then write a *prosbul* for the creditor. The rabbis of his school used to transfer their debts to one another.
>
> (b. Giṭ. 37a)

Theoretical rulings about inapplicable laws on farming were issued. R. Ashi said that if one trained a vine over a fig-tree, the wine is unfit for libations.[3] Jews could nonetheless drink such wine; libations obviously were offered only in the sacrificial service, which no longer existed.

It is clear that some biblical agricultural taboos observed in Palestine were believed to apply in Babylonia as well. For instance R. Papa and R. Huna b. R. Joshua used to eat new wheat on the night of the sixteenth day of Nisan, holding the view that the prohibition of the new wheat outside of Palestine is rabbinical in origin.[4] The laws against using or sowing mixed species produced a few contemporary sayings. R. Ashi said that neither money-purses nor seed-bags are subject to the prohibition of 'mixing' because it is not the usual practice to warm oneself with these.[5] R. Huna b. R. Joshua said that the coarse felt-mattresses of Nersh are permitted; R. Papa said the law of 'mixing' does not apply to slippers.[6] I know of no sayings on 'mixing' pertinent to actual planting of mixed seeds in gardens.

---

1 See below, pp. 306-311.
2 b. Yev. 63a.
3 b. Bekh. 17a. For a rule on grafting, see also Rabina in b. Ḥul. 60a-b.
4 b. Men. 68b.
5 b. Beẓ. 15a.
6 *Ibid.* See also b. Shab. 27a, R. Papa.

The prohibition of *'orlah*, fruits in the first three years after planting, on the other hand, was certainly observed by sages:

> Rabina once found Mar b. R. Ashi throwing away caparberries [of *'orlah*] and eating the buds. He asked, "What is your view...?"
>
> (b. Ber. 36a)

> Mar b. R. Ashi found Rabina rubbing his daughter with underdeveloped olives of *'orlah*. He said to him, "Granted that the sages ruled [that it was permitted to use these for a remedy] in time of danger, was it so ruled when there is no danger...?"
>
> (b. Pes. 25b)

Mar b. Rabina further held that a gentile may enter an orchard and gather doubtful *'orlah*, but a Jew may not do so.[1] The courts ruled on the use of *'orlah*-fruits:

> A barrel of [stolen] wine was once found in an *'orlah*-vineyard, and Rabina permitted the wine to be used
>
> (b. B.B. 24a)

I think it clear that the *'orlah*-taboo was taken seriously in rabbinical circles. Earlier evidence suggested that ordinary folk kept these laws, having learned them in Scriptures,[2] and the rabbis surely did likewise.

The priestly gifts derived from agricultural produce doubtless were collected by those sages who were also priests. R. Kahana and R. Papa ate priestly gifts on account of their wives, who were daughters of priests. It thus was supposed that the husband of a priest's daughter might receive and consume these gifts.[3] Mar b. Rabina would consume heave-offerings. We may assume people presented heave-offerings.[4]

The most considerable gifts to priests were the first-born of the flocks and herds. These were of value, and priests gladly accepted firstlings if they could get them. But the firstborn had to be perfect, and if it was not, the priest had no claim on it. We have the following stories about rabbinical rulings on first-born animals:

> Rafram of Pumbedita had a firstling without a blemish which he gave to a priest. The latter had it blemished...
>
> (b. Bekh. 36b)

> A case of an animal with an abnormally small eye and an abnormally large one came before R. Ashi, [who ruled it was blemished...]
>
> (b. Bekh. 36b)

1 b. Qid. 39a.
2 See Vol. II, pp. 260-262, III, pp. 296-296, and IV, pp. 143-149.
3 b. Ḥul. 132a. See also b. Ḥul. 131a, R. Papa on gifts for the poor.
4 b. Ber. 39b. See above, p. 169.

> Mar Zuṭra once visited R. Ashi, and was told, "Let the master eat something." They set meat before him and told him, "...it is healthy, for it comes from a firstling." Mar Zuṭra asked, "How did you get this [firstling, since you are not priests]?" They said, "A certain priest sold it to us with its blemish." He replied... (b. Tem. 8b)

I see no reason to doubt that the laws pertaining to firstlings were carried out in rabbinical circles; the sages probably enforced the property-aspects of the law in the courts when possible. The claim to firstlings represented a considerable property-right for the priest; as such it was bound to produce court-action.

Our survey of agricultural laws shows that rabbis had two sorts of power over the farms. First, they could teach about, and try to enforce, some of the taboos. Ordinary folk would have expected sages to do so because of the taboos' biblical origin. Second, when property-rights accrued to priests or others, the rabbis could take court action to support them. But the normal conduct of farm life could not have been much affected by rabbinical influence. Rabbis did not bear any special responsibilities for farming. While they were supposed to oversee fair pricing and fair trading in the markets and therefore regularly visited and patrolled them, they had no such routine obligation nor right to oversee the farms.

Since the rabbis frequented the markets, as was their duty, they therefore learned the practices of trade. R. Papa quoted a popular saying that if it rains in the morning, "lay down your sack, ass-driver, and sleep," because rain will continue to fall, harvests will be abundant, and it will be unnecessary to transport produce from one area to another.[1] R. Papa further advised, concerning business practice, to take nothing for granted, for every bill requires collecting, but one should not be certain of the money until it is in hand; every sale on credit is dubious; even when a bill is paid, it may well be paid in bad money.[2] Sayings such as these show routine familiarity with the insecure conditions of trade. They indicate far wider range of relevant experience than do the agricultural teachings, all of which were bound to narrow issues of law and not one of which reflected much interest in the actual practice of farming.

The rabbis' supervision of the market could be made more effective if ordinary folk believed heaven above, not merely rabbis near at hand, would oversee their practices and punish false-dealing:

---

[1] b. Ta'anit 6b.
[2] b. Pes. 113b.

> Rabina happened to be in Sura on the Euphrates. R. Ḥanina of Sura said to him, "Why did Scripture couple the Exodus from Egypt with the prohibition of reptiles (Lev. 11:44-5)?" Rabina replied, "The Holy One blessed be he said, 'I who distinguished between the first-born and others [in Egypt],—I will also mete out punishment to him who mingles the guts of unclean fish with those of clean fish and sells them to a Jew...'"
> (b. B.M. 61b)

Rabbis could not be everywhere. Although they could severely punish the butcher who did not in all details carry out their instructions, they could hardly know what was put over behind their backs in the market-place, particularly when they would not ordinarily have cause to make inspections. Hence it would be God who would bring down the punishment upon those whose misdeeds were missed by rabbinical inspectors.

Cases of rabbinical practices and of actual market supervision include the following:[1]

> R. Papa and R. Huna b. R. Joshua gave a judgment in an action about coins [in which a debt was to be paid] in accordance with the information supplied by a Ṭai [= Arab] market-commissioner...
> (b. B.Q. 98a)

> Amemar paid for [earthenware which he had ordered] when the potter [had merely] supplied himself with [the necessary] earth [for the clay]...
> (b. B.M. 74a)

> Certain basket-sellers brought baskets to Babylonia. The villagers prevented them [from selling]. They appealed to Rabina. He ruled, "They have come from outside and may sell to outsiders..."
> (b. B.B. 22a)

We have already noted cases of rabbinical supervision of the sale of wine in the Jewish market[2] and Rabina's ruling that stolen wine found in an *'orlah*-vineyard might be drunk, therefore sold for Jewish consumption.[3] The rabbis' control of market-place activities thus produced important ramifications for the enforcement of laws not strictly pertinent to commercial transactions.

Sages further ruled on disputes among partners. For example:

> Two *Kutim* [Samaritans? Jewish-Christians?] entered into a share-partnership [one invested the money, the other traded with it]. One divided the money without his partner's knowledge. R. Papa ruled in

[1] Note also b. 'Eruv 40a, Rabina ruled on purchasing myrtles cut on the second day of the festival, cited above.

[2] Above, pp. 24-25.

[3] b. B.B. 24a, above, p. 301.

> favor of the defendant. The next year they shared wine. The other arose and divided it without his partner's knowledge. R. Papa ruled....
>
> (b. B.M. 69a)[1]

Rulings on business relationships of all kinds either arose directly out of market-place activities or produced important implications for the market. Many of the transactions we are about to consider further reflect rabbinical power over the Jewish economy.

XVII. Workers and Slaves

While Scriptural and rabbinical law legislated about the protection of workers' salaries, we have no cases to show how the rabbis enforced or protected the rights of workers. The only story about rabbis and workers is as follows:

> Judah b. Maremar used to instruct his attendant, "Go and hire workers for me and say to them, 'Your employer is responsible for your wages.'" Maremar and Mar Zuṭra used to engage workers for one another.
>
> (b. B.M. 11a)

They did so in order for each one to be free of the commandment against keeping the worker's wages all night, for the man who engaged the workers was so obligated, but not necessarily the one for whom the work was actually done. It therefore was a subterfuge to permit them to pay the workers at their own convenience.

Slaves were regarded as property. Rabbinical law related to them only as such.[2] No instance of a rabbi's doing anything to alleviate the plight of slaves or to undermine the institution of slavery occurs in sources of this period. The relevant cases are as follows:

> A certain settlement of slaves was sold [by Jews] to pagans. When the second owners died, the slaves appealed to Rabina [to permit them to marry Jewish women]. He said to them, "Go and find the sons of your first owners to write out [proper] deeds of emancipation." The rabbis criticized Rabina, saying, "Did not Amemar rule that if a man declares his slave common property and dies, nothing [whatever] can be done for the slave?..."
>
> (b. Giṭ. 40a)

---

[1] See also Amemar on dissolving partnerships, b. B.B. 13b. I do not know why the *Kutim* came to the rabbinical court. I can find no other examples of non-Jews' resorting to the Jewish judiciary. I find this story difficult.

[2] See above, p. 266.

> A certain slave was owned by two men. One emancipated his half. The other thought, "If the rabbis hear, they will force me to give him up [to allow the man to purchase the other half of himself]." He went and transferred the slave to his son who was a minor. R. Joseph b. Rava submitted the case to R. Papa... (b. Giṭ. 40a)

> Minyamin, slave of R. Ashi, was to be baptized [as initiation to be the slave of a Jew] and was entrusted to Rabina and R. Aḥa son of Rava. "Note that I shall claim him from you," R. Ashi said to them. They put a halter around his neck, loosened it, and tightened it, the former so that nothing might interpose between the water and the flesh, the latter so that he might not forestall them and declare, "I perform the ritual bath in order to procure the status of a free man." While he was raising his head from the water, they put a bucket of clay on it and told him, "Go, carry it home to your master [as a sign that he was legally possessed as R. Ashi's slave]." (b. Yev. 46a)

The rabbis could generally find legal grounds to do what they really wanted to. Consequently their inability to do something for a slave in an anomalous situation tells us that they wanted to do nothing whatsoever. Technicalities of property-law and not considerations of humanitarianism governed their actions. The fact that the rabbis would force a man to allow his slave to purchase the unfree part of himself tells us merely that the rabbis disliked an anomalous situation, not that on principle they made the effort to help the slave to free himself. The behavior of Rabina and R. Aḥa further shows that the sages not only owned slaves but saw nothing wrong in it. They moreover were careful to carry out all the technical requirements of the law so as to keep the man enslaved. (But it also is striking that the slave himself supposedly knew enough of Jewish law to be able to make the required declaration at just the right moment if he got the chance. The rabbis made sure he did not.) No cases testify to the state of affairs outside of rabbinical circles. The appeal to Rabina was based upon the courts' power to approve or disapprove marriages; the rabbis could further determine property-litigations; slaves as property must have come before the courts. So we may assume that the rabbis exercised considerable influence over the fate of slaves. I do not know how effectively they legislated on working conditions or the rights of the free workers, since there is no evidence that they legislated on these subjects at all.

XVIII. Sale and Transfer of Movables

While we may be certain rabbis could rule on all aspects of the transfer of ownership of a property from one man to another, evidence in this period is sparse. We have only one example of court action in a dispute over the sale of movable property

> A man once sold an ass [or, wine] to his neighbor. One *zuz* was unpaid. The seller repeatedly asked for it. R. Ashi considered whether the purchaser had acquired [the item] or not...
>
> (b. B.M. 77b)

The particular rule of law here involved could not have become problem at "just this time," for such problems of unpaid debts must have occurred for many centuries. The real issue concerned the interpretation of a teaching of Rav and other former masters. It was otherwise a routine case.

The disposition of cases involving bailments and disputes over their ownership is illustrated in the following:

> A certain man deposited hops with his neighbor, who himself had a pile of hops. The brewer took the wrong ones ... Yet what loss did the depositor suffer [that it should have been a case in court]? R. Sama b. Rava said, "The beer turned into vinegar." R. Ashi said, "The case involved thorns [inferior hops] and he must pay the value of the thorns [which had benefited the beer]."
>
> (b. B.M. 42b-43a)

R. Papa's own action in acquiring his own far-distant property by symbolic acquisition was also cited.[1] He and R. Huna b. R. Joshua debated on how to set a price by negotiation.[2] The courts further ruled on cases involving the restoration of lost property to a claimant.[3] Other cases involving movables will be considered in connection with gifts, loans, and thefts.

xix. Real Estate and Immovables

The right to decide litigations over the disposition of land and immovable property constituted the court's most important single source of power. Appeal was impossible. The Iranian government firmly stood behind the rabbinical courts' actions. Although on most other subjects the sayings and stories attributed to these last generations have proved sparse and thin, the materials pertinent to real estate transactions of this time are relatively abundant.

Disputes over the conditions of sale of land produced the following cases:

---

[1] b. B.Q. 104b, b. B.M. 46a, b. B.B. 77b, 150b.
[2] b. A.Z. 72a.
[3] b. B.M. 28b, the claimant was R. Papa's father.

> A man once sold an estate to his neighbor without surety. The purchaser was upset, so the seller asked, "Why are you upset? Should it be seized from you [for a debt of mine] I will repay you out of the best of my estate [even] for your improvements and crops." Amemar ruled, "These are merely words of good cheer [and of no legal value.]"
>
> (b. B.M. 65b-66a)

> A man once sold land to his neighbor with security. The purchaser asked, "If it should be seized from me, will you repay me out of your very best land?" He replied, "Not of the very best, but of other *excellent* land I own." The land was seized. The very best land moreover was flooded. R. Papa ruled...
>
> (b. B.M. 66b)

In these cases the issue was the binding value of a sales-talk. In both instances the seller had effusively reassured the purchaser, so the courts later on had to determine the extent of the seller's consequent liability. A guarantee issued at the time of sale produced a parallel case:

> A certain man sold a field, guaranteeing against any accident that might happen to it. The government turned a river through the land. The seller consulted Rabina, who ruled that he had to go and clear it for the buyer, since he had guaranteed against any accident which might happen to the land...
>
> (b. Giṭ. 73a)

Further disputes over the sale of property included the following:

> A certain man said, "I will sell you the land of Ḥiyya's." There were two pieces of land so called. R. Ashi ruled, "He sold him one but not two."
>
> (b. B.B. 61b)

> A certain insane man sold property. Two witnesses testified he was sane when he sold it, and two, that he was insane. R. Ashi ruled...
>
> (b. Ket. 20a)

Retraction of sale was at issue in two further cases:

> A certain man sold a plot of land to R. Papa because he needed the money to buy oxen, but eventually he did not need the money. R. Papa returned the land to him ... [proving that one may retract in this circumstance]. But R. Papa may have acted beyond the measure of the law.
>
> (b. Ket. 97a)

> A certain man sold his property [expressly] intending to emigrate to Palestine, but in the end he did not go. R. Ashi ruled...
>
> (b. Qid. 50a)

In all these cases concerning the sale of real estate, conditions of sale, the right of retraction, and the like, we may readily understand how a case came to trial. Further disputes centered upon conflicting rights to the use of a property, in the often bitter relationship among neighbors, for example:

> Two men were sharing a house. One held the upper room, the other, the lower one. The lower room began to sink, so the owner said to the upstairs neighbor, "Let us rebuild the house." The other declined, saying he was quite comfortable. The lower one asked permission to tear down and rebuild the house, and the upper one countered that he would have no place to live. The former offered to hire a place for the meanwhile. The upper one said it is too much trouble. The lower one said, "I cannot live in my place." The upper one said, "You can get in and out by crawling on your belly." R. Ḥama ruled, "He had a full right to stop him [from rebuilding]..."
>
> (b. B.B. 6b-7a)

> A certain man began to build a wall facing his neighbor's windows. The latter claimed, "You are shutting out my light." The former offered to close up the windows and make new ones above the level of the wall. The latter said, "You will damage my wall." "Then let me take down your wall as far as the place of the windows and then rebuild it with windows in the part above my wall." The latter said, "The lower part will be old and the upper new, and the wall will not be firm" "Then let me take it all down and build it up from the ground with new windows." The latter said, "A single new wall in an old house will not be firm." "Then," the former said, "Let me put up a whole new building." "Meanwhile I will have no place to live." "I shall hire a room for you." "I do not want to be bothered." R. Ḥama said, "He had a perfect right to stop him." (b. B.B. 7a)

Similarly, the obligation not to damage a neighbor's property or impair his rights was at issue in the following cases:

> Papi Yona'ah was a poor man who made some money. He built a country house. Sesame oil makers nearby would make his house shake when they crushed sesame seeds. He appealed to R. Ashi, who ruled...
>
> (b. B.B. 25b)

> When the workers in the house of Bar Marion b. Rabin would beat flax, the dust used to fly and annoy the neighbors, who appealed to Rabina. Rabina ruled... The case was stated before Maremar, who said... (b. B.B. 26a)

A case between rabbis was as follows:

> R. Papa had some date trees near the field of R. Huna b. R. Joshua. He found him [R. Huna] digging up and cutting away the roots, and asked the reason [legal justification]...
>
> (b. B.B. 26a)

It is not necessary to assume this case came to court. The discussion presupposes that it did not. R. Papa adduced adequate legal grounds to prevent R. Huna from doing damage to his trees and went away satisfied that no more damage would be done.

A partnership in property did not require rabbinical approval except in the case of litigation:

> Mar Zuṭra and R. Adda the elder, sons of R. Mari b. Issur, divided their property among themselves. They asked R. Ashi [whether witnesses are required so as to prevent a retraction, or perhaps to give legal force to the transaction.] He replied, "Witnesses were created only against liars."
>
> (b. Qid. 65b)

Thus when a transaction was disputed, just then but not otherwise did it come before rabbinical courts. As we have seen, only when it involved a particularly interesting point of law would the transaction find its way into the court records or into theoretical discussion as contained in the Babylonian Talmud. Hence for each Talmudic story we must suppose there were many thousands of normal, undisputed transactions in every generation, and hundreds of litigations which were settled along conventional lines.

Litigations over the disposition of rented property included the following[1]:

> A certain man once leased a field for sesame [on the basis of sharing the crop]. He sowed wheat instead, but the wheat appreciated to the value of sesame. R. Kahana thought to rule...
>
> (b. B.M. 104b)

> A certain man once leased a field for sesame, sowed wheat, but the wheat subsequently exceeded the sesame in value. Rabina thought to rule...
>
> (b. B.M. 104b)

> A man leased a field to grow fodder for [several] *kors* of barley. When the fodder was grown [in thirty days], he ploughed and resowed barley, which then was blighted. R. Ḥaviva of Sura on the Euphrates sent to Rabina...
>
> (b. B.M. 106b)

> A certain man once leased his mill to another for [an exchange of the services of the second in] grinding [his wheat.] Eventually he became rich and bought another mill and an ass and said, "Until now I have had

[1] See also b. B.M. 109a, a case involving a lease of R. Papa.

> my grinding done at your place, but now, pay me rent [instead]." The other replied, "I shall [continue only] to grind for you." Rabina ruled...
> (b. Ket. 103a)

The sages not only collected taxes but also had to make rulings in court taking into account the existence of strict tax-collections. It was important to pay on time, for one could lose his land for even a modest delinquency. Hence rented property had to be carefully accounted for. Even the land of orphans might be sold in order to facilitate tax-payments without going through the usual procedures:

> Giddal b. Re'ilai rented a field from the owners of a certain property on condition that he would pay the taxes. He paid in advance for three years [of taxes]. The first owners came back and said that while he had paid the tax for the first year and enjoyed the usufruct, now the owner himself will pay and enjoy the usufruct. They appealed to R. Papa...
> (b. Giṭ. 58b)

> R. Ashi said, "R. Kahana and I signed as witnesses to the deed of sale of the mother of the orphan Ze'ira who sold some land in order to pay the poll tax and did so without giving public notice [of thirty days for the sale of the property]..."
> (b. Giṭ. 52b)

Both the wide variety of cases and the content of the specific case-reports leave no doubt about the rabbis' effective control over property transactions of all kinds. Sages' courts decided disputes on the sale of land under various conditions, the use of land to the detriment of neighbors' rights, partnerships in real estate and other properties, rental of real estate, and collection of land-taxes. In sum, not a single aspect of the use of land by Jews for beneficial purposes escaped rabbinical supervision.

I wonder however about the real range of effective rabbinical jurisdiction. Non-Jews did not have to come to rabbinical courts, and we have no evidence, apart from the Kutim, that they often, if ever, did so. Where Jews instituted real estate suits against other Jews, obviously rabbis (or other Jewish officials) decided the case. But the provenance of such suits would have to be territories inhabited almost entirely by Jews. We have considerable reason to suppose that in the larger cities, even in villages round about, Jews lived side by side with gentiles. Who then decided commercial and real estate cases which must have arisen between Jews and gentiles? It was not Jewish judges, for they had no authority. If so, the rabbis' control of the Jewish populations through their *unlimited* power over real estate transactions must indeed have been limited to begin with by the narrow clientele for litigation before their courts. In assessing the *quality* of the courts' power, we must not exaggerate in our own minds what must have been the severely circumscribed range of their jurisdiction, even so far as much of Jewry was concerned.[1]

XX. TESTAMENTS, GIFTS, AND ORPHANS' PROPERTY

Special situations in the transfer of property, both movable and real, were presented by donations through inheritances and other gifts and by ownership of property by minor orphans and other incompetents.

Testaments given in contemplation of death[2] produced the following cases:

> A certain dying man said [to the executors], "A third of my estate to a daughter, a third to the other daughter, and a third to my wife." One of the daughters died. R. Papi intended to rule...
>
> (b. B.B. 132b)

> A certain dying man divided his estate between his wife and son, leaving over a palm-tree. Rabina intended to decide that the wife could have only the one palm-tree. R. Yemar said to him...
>
> (b. B.B. 133a)

> A dying man instructed [his executors] to give a palm tree to his daughter. When he died, it was found he left two halves of a palm tree. R. Ashi wondered, "Do people call two halves of palm tree 'a palm-tree' or not?..."
>
> (b. Ket. 109b)

As earlier, the chief legal issues concerned the special rules applying to testaments made to various heirs, on the one hand, and the peculiarities of the language used in wills, on the other. We have several instances in which the payment of shares in an estate was supervised by the courts:

> R. Minyomi b. R. Reḥumi said, "I was once standing before Amemar, when a woman who claimed [her] tenth of [her deceased father's] estate appeared in his court. He held that if [her brothers] wished to settle with her through a money payment, he would have agreed to the settlement. He heard the brothers say to her, 'If we had the money to settle with you by a cash payment, we would do so,' and he remained silent and said nothing to the contrary."
>
> (b. Ket. 69a)

---

[1] See below, pp. 320 ff.

[2] See Vol. III, pp. 288-290 for an account of the contribution of R. Naḥman b. Jacob to the laws of gifts in contemplation of death.

R. Ashi said, "When we were at the academy of R. Kahana, we authorized the collection [of a daughter's tenth of the estate] from the rent of houses also."

(b. Ket. 69a)

Rabina allowed the daughter of R. Ashi to collect [her tenth] from Mar b. R. Ashi out of his medium-quality land without an oath, but from the son of R. Sama the son of R. Ashi out of his worst land *with* an oath.

(b. Ket. 69a)

Mar Zuṭra of Darishba divided a basket of pepper with his brothers equally. When he came before R. Ashi, R. Ashi told him, "Since you have renounced [your rights in] part [of the estate, namely the pepper], you [are presumed to] have renounced in all of the property."

(b. B.B. 126b)

The means by which secondary claimants (not sons) were to be paid—such as in cash or various sorts of land—would have presented commonplace problems to the courts. Disputes over transfer of property through gifts included these:

A woman owned a palm-tree on ground belonging to R. Bibi b. Abaye. Whenever she went to cut from the tree, he objected. She made it over to him for life [with the understanding that it would revert to her or her heirs afterward]. But he went and gave it to his little son. R. Huna b. R. Joshua ruled...

(b. B.B. 137b)

A certain man gave instructions, "Give to so-and-so a room holding one hundred barrels." The room in question would hold one hundred twenty. Mar Zuṭra ruled, "He gave him [space for] a hundred barrels and no more." R. Ashi said to him...

(b. B.B. 71a)

The mother of R. Zuṭra b. Ṭobia gave her property in writing to R. Zuṭra b. Ṭobia, for she was intending to marry R. Zevid [and wished to dispose of her property beforehand]. She married R. Zevid but was [later] divorced by him. She appeared before R. Bibi b. Abaye [to seek return of her property]. He ruled...

(b. B.B. 151a)

The first case, I suppose, involved an effort to keep property secure from the claim of possession through usufruct; the third, to protect it from the claims of a husband. In the second, the issue was the liberal intent of the donor.

Business affairs of the deceased would naturally pose problems to his heirs. The courts had to assure the rights of legitimate creditors and also to protect the estate from swindlers.[1] The courts certainly carried out their responsibilities, as in the following:

> A man died and left a guarantor. [One had lent money to another, and a third became surety for the debt. The borrower died, rendering the lender liable to take an oath, then the lender died, and the heirs claimed the funds from the surety.] R. Papa thought of ruling...
>
> (b. Shev. 48b)

Examples of court supervision are as follows:

> Rabina had some wine belonging to the orphan Rabina the younger, his sister's son. He also had some wine of his own, which he was about to take up to Sikara. When he came to R. Ashi, he asked, "May I carry [orphan's wine] with my own." R. Ashi told him, "You may, for it is not better than your own [wine]."
>
> (b. Ket. 100b)

> R. Ashi gave a practical decision in reference to an orphan's [mortgage] as though they were adults...
>
> (b. B.M. 67a-b)

> A certain guarantor of orphans' [property] once paid the creditor before the orphans were sued [and sought compensation from the orphans]. R. Papa said, "Repayment [of a verbal loan] to a creditor is a commandment, but orphans are not subject to the performance of the commandments [so the guarantor, *now* their creditor, cannot exact payment.]"
>
> (b. B.B. 174a)

> A certain guarantor to a gentile once paid the gentile before he sued orphans. R. Mordecai said to R. Ashi...
>
> (b. B.B. 174b)

The jurisdiction of the courts extended to these special circumstances quite obviously because of their more general control of property transactions. The rabbis did not set themselves up as protectors of orphans because of any humanitarian sentiments. Their courts simply exercised their powers in these matters as part of their broader responsibilities. But once their right of jurisdiction in these questions was established, their interpretation of the law was clearly intended to work out in practical details the general principles—that orphans are to be protected, but that justice is not to be perverted for the sake of protecting them—which had been laid down in the Bible and perpetuated in earlier rabbinical legislation.

---

[1] See b. B.B. 5b for the practice of R. Papa and R. Huna b. R. Joshua with reference to the collection of debts from orphans' property; and b. B.B. 70b, Mar Zuṭra.

XXI. Legal Documents

Court decisions on property transactions were given effect through legal documents, which were drawn up under close rabbinical supervision by scribes well-trained in the law. The execution of such documents rarely, if ever, depended upon curses, imprecations, or other threats of supernatural intervention. They were regular, routine, and commonplace matters; the courts possessed full powers to do as they liked. The contrast between reports on court documents and those on the preparation of a Torah-scroll is striking. The writing of Torah-scrolls and other theurgical parchments produced no significant examples of popular acquiescence to court decrees, consultations with sages, or other evidences of widespread conformity to rabbinical law. The sages as holy men could urge people to prepare Torah-scrolls and similar documents according to their instructions, but they could do little to invalidate or correct documents they did not approve of. We have on the other hand many examples of effective court action in connection with business and other legal documents.[1]

We know that court decisions were generally accompanied by validating documents. Rava, for example, instructed R. Papa and R. Huna b. R. Joshua on how to deal with his legal documents after his death:

> "When a legal decision of mine comes to you, and you see objections to it, do not tear it up before you have seen me.... After my death do not tear it up but do not infer any law from it either."
>
> (b. B.B. 130b)

Examples of court actions on legal documents include the following, which reveal the required terminology and procedures:

> A certain deed of acknowledgment contained the phrase, "A memorial of the words of so-and-so" [instead of "a memorial of testimony by witnesses"] and was entirely worded like a court document, but did not include the [phrase], "We were in a session of three judges, one of whom absented himself." Rabina thought to rule...
>
> (b. Sanh. 29b-30a)

> A certain document [was brought to court] bearing the signatures of two witnesses, one of whom had died. The brother of the one who was still alive came with another witness to testify to the signature of the deceased. Rabina considered ruling...
>
> (b. B.B. 57a)

[1] Not to mention divorce-documents, marriage-contracts, and other legal instruments.

Rabina considered validating a document drawn up in an [informal] gathering of Aramaeans. Rafram said to him...

(b. Giṭ. 11a)

When R. Papa had to deal with a Persian document drawn up in a pagan registry, he would give it to two pagans to read not in one another's presence and without telling them what it was for. [If they agreed] he would recover even from mortgaged property. R. Ashi said that Huna b. Nathan told him that Amemar ruled that a Persian document signed by Jewish witnesses is sufficient warrant for recovering even from mortgaged property...

(b. Giṭ. 19b)

Amemar once validated a deed on the signature of one witness and the oral evidence of another. R. Ashi said to him...

(b. B.B. 165a)

No court system could operate without official documents to carry out its orders. The Jewish courts were unable to ignore the documents issued by the state, and R. Papa and Amemar showed that they had little choice but to execute Pahlavi documents without too close an investigation of their contents or the circumstances in which they were drawn up. The least plausible reason was sufficient to warrant accepting them. But other documents readily could be dismissed. The language of Jewish documents was carefully examined. The signatures of witnesses were investigated, and rules of validating signatures were studied.

Commercial paper, including bonds of indebtedness, was executed in rabbinical courts. R. Papa held that when one sells a note, he must write in the conveyance, "Acquire it together with its obligations."[1] R. Papi reported that Rabina made a practical decision on the collection of a mortgage.[2] Mar b. Amemar reported his father's actions with reference to the collection of bonds.[3]

xxii. Loans and Usury

Among various kinds of court documents, the ones most frequently subject to litigation were bonds of indebtedness, mortgages, and other testimonies to the existence of loans. The rabbis strongly disapproved of outright usury, which they understood to be any form of "payment for waiting" for one's money. But they accepted various practices

[1] b. Qid. 47b, b. B.B. 76b.
[2] b. B.M. 67a.
[3] b. B.M. 68a.

which made possible the conduct of a reasonably sophisticated business life.[1]

The courts' supervision of the collection of debts is illustrated in the following cases:

> Rabina waited in the case of Mar Aḥa [to issue an *'adrakhta*, an order to trace the debtors property in order to have it seized and handed over to the creditor to settle a delinquent debt] for twelve months, until a caravan was able to go to Khuzistan and back...[2]
>
> (b. B.Q. 112b)

> Rav b. Shava owed money to R. Kahana. "If I do not pay by a certain date, you may exact your debt out of this wine," he stated. R. Papa thought to argue [concerning this come-on...]
>
> (b. B.M. 66b)

> The rabbis commented to R. Ashi that Rabina fulfills all of the rabbinical rules. R. Ashi sent word to him, "Please lend me ten *zuz*, as I have a chance to buy a small parcel of land."
>
> Rabina replied, "Bring witnesses and we will draw up a bond." "Even for me too!" "You, in particular, being busy in your studies, may forget and bring a curse upon me."
>
> (b. B.M. 75b)[3]

> A certain man said to his neighbor, "I believe you as [I would] two [witnesses] whenever you say, 'I have not paid you [what I owe you].'" He went and paid before three [witnesses, and the lender denied having received the money]. R. Papa ruled, "As two he believed him, but not as three..."
>
> (b. Shev. 42a)

> Rabina said, "Mata Meḥasia is a place where one goes out collecting payments due..."
>
> (b. Yoma 86a)

> [Regarding transfer of a debt from one creditor to a new one] R. Ashi said that for the sake of the benefit which the borrower derives from the difference [in time of payment, for he has more time] between the old debt and the new one, he willingly pledges himself to the new creditor [even if the creditor had not been born at the time of the loan]. Huna Mar b. R. Nehemiah said to R. Ashi, "If so, what of people like those of the house of Bar Eliashiv, who force their debtors to pay at once? Do they not acquire possession in such a case as this? And if you say they do, then you apply different standards to different people..."
>
> (b. Giṭ. 14a)

---

[1] See Vol. IV, pp. 225-228.

[2] It normally took a few weeks.

[3] Note also b. B.B. 5b, the actions in debt-collections of R. Papa and R. Huna b. R. Joshua.

It is clear from the first story that the rabbis had considerable power to issue an order to assess, seize, and pay out property of a delinquent debtor. They therefore provided the economy with a stable and secure foundation, making certain people could collect money they had lent or invested. The other stories are of less consequence. The details of paying out debts, drawing up necessary bonds, and so on were illustrated by deeds of the sages rather than by court-reports. I do not suppose on that account that the sages were alone in following their laws. The final story is significant, for it shows that Huna Mar b. R. Nehemiah (who was possibly of the exilarchic house)[1] thought it improper for the rabbis to apply different standards to different people, one of the parties in this case being a powerful merchant-house. If the rabbis did not have to take acount of the relative strength of contestants in their courts, the reason was that they could force any Jew, however powerful, to obey the law.

Cases involving the loan of movable objects include these:

> A man borrowed a bucket from his neighbor and it broke. R. Papa told him, "Bring witnesses that you did not put it to unusual use, and you will be free of liability [to repay]."
>
> (b. B.M. 97a)

> A man borrowed a cat from his neighbor. The mice got together and killed it. R. Ashi considered the problem...
>
> (b. B.M. 97a)

The operative principle in both cases was that an object borrowed and then put to ordinary use did not have to be replaced if it was broken.

Sayings and stories on usury are as follows:

> [Regarding the bonds of the Maḥozans, in which the estimated profit is added to the principal and recorded in a bond, a practice Rava said was not permissible], Mar b. Amemar said to R. Ashi, "My father does so, but when his agents come and declare they have earned no profit, he believes them [and deducts the amount]." He replied, "That is well while he is alive. But what if he dies and the notes are transferred to his heirs [who see the debt recorded and attempt to collect it]?" (This was like *an unwitting order issued by the ruler* [Qoh. 10:5], and Amemar died.)
>
> (b. B.M. 68a)

> R. Ḥama used to hire out a *zuz* for a *peshiṭa* per day [and did not call it a loan, but a fee for hiring out the money]. As a result his money evaporated [as a penalty for usury inflicted by heaven.] He argued, "How does it differ from a spade?" But a spade is returned exactly as

[1] See above, p. 249 and Vol. IV, p. 83. The exilarchic lineage included a Nehemiah followed by a Huna Mar.

it was loaned, and its depreciation is to be assessed. But the self-same coins are not returned and one cannot estimate their depreciation.

(b. B.M. 69b)

Abba Mar b. R. Papa used to take balls of wax from the waxdealers and persuade his father to lend them money. The rabbis protested to R. Papa, "Your son takes usury." He replied, "Such interest we may enjoy, for the Torah forbade only interest coming directly from the borrower to the lender, but here he receives a fee for talking, and this is permitted."

(b. B.M. 69b)

Rabina gave money [for the purchase of wine] to the residents of 'Aqra deShanvata, who supplied him with an additional jug. He asked R. Ashi whether this was permitted [or whether it was usury]?

(b. B.M. 73b)

It is clear that the sages were troubled by the biblical rules against usury and attempted to use their knowledge of the law to overcome the narrow limitations imposed by scriptural law. R. Ḥama's supposed impoverishment was attributed to his taking usury. But R. Papa provided a rationalization for a not dissimilar action. The legal technicality was accepted. We know little of what ordinary businessmen were doing, but we may surmise that if the sages sought a way out of the old prohibitions, ordinary folk, less scrupulous to begin with, found their own solution.

XXIII. Thefts, Torts, and Other Damages

The Jewish courts represented in our sources had no jurisdiction over murder cases. It may be that the exilarch reserved for himself the right to try them.[1] Aspects of other criminal actions, however, were tried in rabbinical courts, particularly those involving injury to persons or damage to property, a fact consistent with our earlier observations about the range of rabbinical court power over property and small claims of various kinds. The following exemplify trials for theft:

Abimi b. Naẓi, father-in-law of Rabina, was owed four *zuz*. The debtor stole a garment and brought it as a pledge and borrowed on it four more *zuz*. He was then caught. The case came to Rabina who ruled, "As to the first four *zuz*, it is a case of a thief's stealing and paying a debt. The plaintiff has to pay nothing at all. In the case of the latter four *zuz* you may demand your money and return the garment..."

(b. B.Q. 115a)

A certain man was forced by pagans to show the wine of Mari b. R.

---

1 See Vol. IV, pp. 186-191.

Pinḥas b. R. Ḥisda. The pagans then said, "Carry the wine and bring it along with us." He did so. When he was brought before R. Ashi, he was exempted [from having to pay a fine or damages]....

(b. B.Q. 117a)

One of R. Zevid's farm-laborers stole a *kav* of barley, and another a cluster of unripe dates. He disqualified them [as witnesses]...

(b. Sanh. 26b)

None of these case-stories specifies how the culprits were caught or what punishment was inflicted upon them for having stolen. The issue consistently was the disposition of the property or the settlement of claims arising from the theft. We do not know from these stories who caught thieves or whether they were punished by imprisonment, fines, or other penalties. It is possible that the rabbis simply did not rule on such questions, and that is the likeliest conclusion. If so, we must suppose that either the exilarch or the Iranians oversaw the protection of persons and property, and I imagine it was the former, for the exilarch was expected to keep the peace in the Jewish community. Since the rabbis probably had little to do with the maintenance of public order through the use of police, they did not record events in connection with the apprehension and punishment of thieves or other felons, except in connection with the results for property-decision. If this surmise is correct, then their role within the Jewish government must have been a modest one.

Negligence cases are as follows:

A company of dealers in perfume divided the baking [of daily bread]. One baked for all each day. One day they said to one of their number, "Go and bake for us." He replied, "Then guard my robe." It was stolen through their negligence. R. Papa held them responsible...

(b. B.M. 81a)

Bar Adda the carrier was leading beasts across the bridge of Nersh when one beast pushed another into the water. R. Papa held Bar Adda responsible...

These were not cases of criminal negligence, so the courts could readily dispose of the minor property issues at hand. As before, we do not know who stole the cloak, how he was caught—if he was—or what happened to him.

Torts done to persons or property were compensated by financial redress. There was no other form of punishment, even when damage was maliciously caused through aggravated assault. All the pertinent cases concern the assessment of compensation, as in the following:

> R. Papa and R. Huna b. R. Joshua in an actual case [of damages done by a human being with his body] ... valued in conjunction with sixty...
>
> (b. B.Q. 59a)

> A certain man kicked another's money box into the river. The owner came and said, "I had so-and-so much money in the box." R. Ashi was sitting and considering the matter.
>
> (b. B.Q. 6a)

> Rafram compelled R. Ashi [to pay damages for destroying the bond of a creditor]...
>
> (b. B.Q. 98b = Ket. 86a)

> A certain man tied his neighbor's animal in the sun and it died. Rabina held him liable. R. Aḥa b. Rav held he was free [of obligation to pay compensation.]
>
> (b. Sanh. 76b)

The sole issue before the rabbinical courts thus was whether and how to assess monetary damages.

xxiv. Summary and Conclusions

The stories and cases we have cursorily considered are summarized in the following tables. While patterns revealed in data of earlier strata do recur, we have observed important variations, and these appear, if slightly, in the statistical summaries. First of all, we have repeatedly noted new *kinds* of cases, formerly rare or entirely absent. These pertain, for example, to enforcement of Sabbath, festival, and other ritual laws. Sprinkling floors on the Sabbath, moving a corpse on that day, allowing the drawing of water, banning Sabbath violators, consulting butchers in matters of law—such stories earlier did not regularly occur. What is equally striking is that while in the earlier materials, Sabbath laws which actually were enforced mainly concerned the Sabbath limits, set up by the rabbis pretty much as they pleased without popular compliance or interference, now the enforcement of Sabbath laws extended to matters of private, not merely public, interest. Thus we have earlier seen many parallels to Maremar's partitioning of Sura by nets, but only a few to the items listed above. Our summary table bears this out. Earlier, *ʿeruv*-laws constituted the majority of the evidence concerning Sabbath and festival observance, fourteen out of nineteen instances in the period from 220 to 310 A.D., for example; most of the other instances concerned enforcement of the laws about publicly working on the intermediate days of the festival. Now only two of the ten instances of the enforcement of Sabbath and festival law pertained to the *ʿeruv*.

Otherwise we see fairly consistent patterns. The proportion of cases pertaining to the enforcement of civil law in all its many forms remains constant after the period of Rav and Samuel, 52.1%, 51,1%, and 49.6%, for the years 265-310, 310-350, and 350-450, respectively. The stories and cases concerning decisions on personal status consistently remain approximately 20% of the whole number of cases. Cases on food and sex taboos, particularly those on the enforcement of the laws of ritual slaughter, which constitute almost the entire evidence pertinent to such matters, produced approximately the same percentages for each period. Since those instances of enforcement of food laws depended upon the sages' control of the markets, they reenforce our earlier conclusion that the sages did not have much power over the dietary habits or private lives of the people. We have little reason to suppose that in this period rabbinical power or influence otherwise increased. The synagogues, as I noted, remained quite outside of their authority. Although the dispositions of cases exemplifying enforcement of other sorts of law were in former times inconsequential, in this period we have none at all.

As to the absolute number of cases, the figure 68 for 220-265 A.D., 163 for 265-310 A.D., 218 for 310-350 A.D., and 131 for 350-450 A.D., must be regarded as partially subjective. I have, as earlier, not counted as an exemplification of law-enforcement a general saying or story which would lead to the conclusion that law was widely carried out. Only specific stories were counted as single units. The variation in the actual numbers of stories probably is a purely literary phenomenon, depending upon the power and effective influence of a head of a school or of a particular school in the formation of the traditions as we now have them. The approximate percentages and proportions perhaps are significant, but the exact numbers of exemplifications must be regarded as very rough estimates at best.

What is more important is the probability that for every case or story we have, thousands of cases must have been tried but not recorded, because they contained only routine and uninteresting points of law. Still more thousands of transactions of civil law and personal status in particular must have been carried out in conformity to rabbinical law, but never have come to the courts. The Babylonian Talmud was no Geniza, in which all sorts of materials were deposited. Alongside trash, the Cairo *geniza* preserved kinds of materials we must have if we are to come to any exact ideas about social, economic, or religious life. On the contrary, the Babylonian Talmud was carefully edited, serving mainly as a commentary on the Mishnah of R. Judah the Prince. Only those cases were actually recorded which revealed important points of law decided by influential sages in those schools the traditions of which were preserved by those responsible for the editing of the Talmud. These are few enough, as we have seen. By consequence we can in no way replicate the precise, exceptionally varied, and rich portrait offered in Goitein's Geniza studies.[1] Even though the issues of this part of our inquiry are much the same, the results, alas, in no way can be compared to Goitein's.

The ability of the courts to enforce the law doubtless produced widespread conformity. Normal commercial life and determinations of, or changes in, personal status followed the lines of rabbinical law without recourse to the courts or even to the schools. On the other hand the utter absence of indications that ritual laws were enforced among the people outside of the marketplace must be regarded as significant. If the courts gave no evidence of being able to carry out the law, the probable reason is that they could not do so. If that was the case, then ordinary folk would have continued along the lines of ancient observance. The rabbinical distinction between laws revealed by Moses at Sinai and laws decreed by the rabbis would have been important for Babylonia. In matters not susceptible to court intervention, the latter must have had little impact upon common people whenever the old traditions of Babylonia were in contradiction or merely silent. Thus R. Joseph remarked that the paragraph in the Grace after Meals concerning God's goodness, ending "...who is good and does good," must not be Scriptural in origin, *for working people omit it.*[2] The converse is that if it were of Scriptural origin, working people presumably would include it. Actually we cannot prove much from a single saying, for whether ordinary folk said the Grace after Meals in a manner similar to the rabbinical formulation, or indeed whether they recited any grace at all, is hardly settled. (I rather doubt that they did.) What is important is R. Joseph's supposition that working people ordinarily would know and carry out biblical ordinances but *not* rabbinical ones. If his supposition was sound, and I see no basis for any other, then the reason must have been the perseverence of patterns of religious life from olden times, long before the arrival in Babylonia of the first

[1] See S. D. Goitein, *A Mediterranean Society* (Berkeley and Los Angeles, 1967).
[2] b. Ber. 46a.

Pharisaic masters and the foundation of rabbinical schools in the second century. Before the coming of rabbinical Judaism, Babylonian Jewry must have developed a rich cultural and religious life based upon reverence for the Scriptures, for the Jerusalem Temple and Yahweh, and upon *ad hoc* interpretations of Scripture and legal decisions of local elders. With their claim that they possessed Mosaic traditions unavailable elsewhere, the rabbis had the basis for reforming Jewish community life. But that theoretical, theological basis by itself could have supported no substantial enterprise. Without the legal authority available through the exilarch from the Iranian government, the rabbis could have changed little if anything. This much is clear from the following summary tables, which indicate, as the earlier ones did, that chiefly those laws which could be enforced through coercive court decisions concerning disposition of property were actually carried out by the rabbis. But by now, after more than three centuries of teaching and exemplifying the laws, the rabbis proved able to enforce some matters which did not depend upon actual court decisions or coercion. This would suggest, as I said, that the rabbis did succeed in widening the range of their influence to include questions other than the enforcement of civil law and the determination of personal status.

It was through the courts that the sages exercised their most direct and effective power over ordinary Jews. Yet, as we have clearly seen, the courts' authority was severely circumscribed. Apart from enforcing civil laws concerning property and making decisions on personal status, many of which also depended upon exchanges of property, the courts could only sporadically coerce obedience to "Torah." Even though "Torah" comprehended a wide range of teachings about the proper conduct of everyday life, the sages through the courts apparently affected only a small part of daily affairs. As we noticed, for example, while the sages' traditions on family life included stress on early marriage and various other extralegal values, the courts could hardly have done much, except episodically, to shape the lives of most families outside of rabbinical circles.

The reason for the rabbis' limited use of their court powers for enforcement of the whole "Torah" is clear. The Iranian government, first of all, did not leave in the hands of the *millet*-communities an unlimited range of power. The rabbinical courts' powers were further circumscribed, second, by the probability that *other* courts exercised jurisdiction over Jews. I conjecture that these competing authorities were likely to have been of three sorts. First, towns mainly inhabited by Jews but not the center of rabbinical schools were probably governed by non-rabbinical authorities, composed of officials such as the "ignorant judges" about whom the rabbis complained. It stands to reason that such judges were also subject to the authority of the exilarch. But they obviously were not educated in rabbinical schools or governed by the discipline of the rabbinical estate. Second, it seems doubtful that the rabbis decided cases involving substantial sums of money, capital punishment, or other weighty matters.[1] Hence either the exilarch or the Iranian government, acting through local satraps, took over the jurisdiction over many sorts of important legal and administrative matters affecting ordinary Jews. The exilarch presided over the only murder trial mentioned in Babylonian rabbinical records. On that basis, we can hardly come to a firm opinion, but it seems likely that the exilarch decided cases involving crimes against persons and thefts. This would account for the concentration of the rabbis' attention on the disposition of stolen goods, with no mention at all of what happened to the thief; references to the "servants" of the exilarch were likely to mean his gendarmes. Third and most important, cases involving Jews and gentiles rarely, if ever, seem to have come before rabbinical courts.[2] Since large numbers of Jews lived in Seleucia-Ctesiphon (Maḥoza) and other places where they were likely to come into contact with gentiles, enter into business-partnerships, and otherwise produce litigation, I can only suppose that the state made provision for disputes among its mixed populations. Hence even though it seems clear that the rabbis made some sorts of decisions, we ought not on that account to exaggerate the extent of their control over the lives of ordinary Jews.

The cases before the rabbinical courts were the exceptional ones in which people deprived others of their property or rights, failed to keep their word, or otherwise lapsed from accepted norms. In normal circumstances the courts played no role whatever, though conversely, the *law* obviously played a great role indeed. But if "*ʾapikorsim* are common who vex the rabbis," and if the men of Nersh "would not hear the word of the Lord," then we may suppose the sages' power also was limited by the difficulties of coercing independent-minded folk to conform at all. People normally kept the law, but they did pretty much as they liked, I imagine, unless they came into direct conflict either with another person's rights or property or with a rabbinical

[1] Vol. IV, pp. 251-253.
[2] Compare Vol. IV, pp. 279-283.

authority actually engaged in the exercise of his duties, as in the market-place, for example. These two factors need, therefore, to be kept in balance. It would have required far more efficient government than existed in late antiquity, combined with a vast and inquisitive police force, to impose "the whole Torah" upon all of Babylonian Jewry. What could readily be imposed was, as I have stressed, a rather small segment of the law. That segment of the law could come to bear mostly when ordinary folk brought one another to court in a litigation. So even judgments of civil law and determinations of personal status by rabbis in the end generally depended upon the compliance of outsiders.

It is therefore remarkable that ordinary folk did not apparently comply with the demands of the holy men-judges about synagogue life, though they probably accepted their decisions about synagogue property. We cannot be certain that common people, if they actually took vows, came before sages to seek absolution. While courts could administer corporal punishment, issue bans of excommunication, and impose fines, only the most "spiritual" of these penalties, the decree of excommunication, applied in matters we should today regard as "religious," such as the violation of holy days, but even here apparently seldom. The Sabbath laws about not working and observing similar taboos were doubtless widely kept because people believed God had commanded them, as Scriptures said. The statutes about the proper arrangement of Sabbath-limits were earlier enforced by rabbis as communal authorities. We now find a few stories in which other rabbinical rules were enforced, and, as I said earlier, not the number but the character of some such stories, which is quite novel, seems to be significant. If Amemar's several rulings represented practical judgments, and I think they do, it would mean that rabbis now enjoyed greater authority than earlier over Sabbath observance by ordinary folk. Definition of permissible work during the festival week-days was earlier well within rabbinical jurisdiction. Control of the markets produced another sort of power, namely the determination of what might be sold, therefore used, in connection with festival observance.

More consequential for our study is R. Ashi's assumption that people would ordinarily copy his observances. Of course we cannot be sure that by "people" he meant merely "rabbinical disciples, masters, and others adhering to our viewpoint." "Men" standing by itself is highly ambiguous. Questions posed by the "men" of such and such a town or instructions to see what "people are doing" both seemed related to rabbinical circles, for in the former case the questions were based upon considerable knowledge of law, and in the latter, upon observance of characteristically rabbinical customs. But R. Ashi supposed people would see how he covered his *Sukkah* and do likewise. Rabbis did not live in isolated neighborhoods, so the people who would see and thereupon copy his practice probably would not have been only rabbinical disciples. I therefore assume that R. Ashi's concern does reflect a tendency of ordinary folk to regard the rabbi as a paradigmatic figure. That would not be surprising in earlier years, for the rabbi was viewed as a holy man. But what now is new is the assumption that *if* people saw how a rabbi carried out in a new way a routine and traditional function—for people had built *Sukkot* for many centuries in some customary fashion—they would change their ways. This is not much evidence, to be sure, but it is a sort of evidence we have not earlier observed.

Enforcement of food laws was quite another matter, and effective power, seen earlier, remained wholly undiminished. If a slaughterer did not present his knife, he could be banned, driven out of business, and deprived of substantial capital. It is doubtful that any Jews outside of rabbinical circles were more completely subjected to rabbinical rules about the conduct of their business affairs than were the butchers. This meant that ordinary folk would not usually purchase other than *kosher* meat in Jewish markets. But it does not mean that in their homes the common people followed rabbinical rulings about preparation of food on ordinary days or Sabbaths, separation of meat from dairy products, and the like.

We have no Talmudic evidence about magical practices of the masses. We do not know what outsiders did with reference to the scroll of the Torah, the *mezuzah*, *tefillin*, and other holy objects. We do know that rabbinical magical objects, amulets, and charms were carefully defined. The rabbis clearly omitted all reference to magical bowls, and presumably to other forms of magic they did not approve of, as well as to practitioners of such magic, not to mention their Jewish and pagan clients. Magical bowls produced by Jews included references to an ancient rabbi who played a minor role in rabbinical traditions available in the Babylonian Talmud. But upon that basis we can hardly come to any firm conclusion except one: the schools out of which the Talmud emerged set their seal of approval upon some forms of theurgy and rejected others. But it is equally obvious that the practices of common folk and perhaps also of schools entirely unknown to us are simply not reflected in the Talmud. Holy buildings, holy objects, holy days, holy or unholy food—to these matters on the whole rabbinical power was peripheral, never very consequential.

Central to the concern and certainly subject to the authority of sages were many kinds and patterns of human relationships, as we have repeatedly observed. We may anachronistically note that while the rabbis had little influence over "religion," they had a great deal of influence over "ethics." But no one then made such a distinction. Behavior in the market-place as much as in the synagogue constituted a matter of "Torah." Indeed the prophets had said "religion" concerned everyday life rather than ritual, and the rabbis rightly saw themselves as heirs of the teachings of the prophets, their best interpreters and true continuators. They therefore devoted themselves to commonplace justice, doing what they could, to be sure, about the sancta and taboos as well. Effecting a reconciliation between husband and wife, preserving the sanctity of marital ties, properly carrying out betrothals, marriages, and, where called for, divorces, protecting the rights of women by providing for their maintenance—these represented human relationships potentially subject to rabbinical control, and therefore, to rabbinical judgments or values. Likewise, the Holy One who knew the difference between the first-born and others in Egypt would also know the difference between honest and dishonest traders. The rabbis would remind marketmen of that fact, forcibly so when they could make effective rulings over what was done in bailments and contracts, exchanges of commerce, trade, movables, transactions over land, settlement of estates, and similar matters. That does not mean their ideas about human rights invariably coincide with those of our own time. It is difficult to share rabbinical views of slavery, for one thing. But in general when it came to property disputes, theirs was a fair standard of justice, and, more important, it was also quick and effective.

The fact that the rabbinical estate could accomplish, not so little, but so much must strike us as astonishing. When the first rabbis came to Babylonia shortly after the Bar Kokhba War, they had no basis for affecting, even interfering in, local affairs. They constituted an outgrowth of a Palestinian party, then several centuries old. I doubt that they earlier had any significant following in Babylonia. Like the Essenes and other Jewish sects, they claimed Moses had founded their group and revealed its peculiar laws and doctrines. But unlike others, they both actively and successfully sought the power to make their claims effective in the everyday life of ordinary Jews. In so doing, they worked to change all Jews into Pharisaic rabbis and to reshape the community according to the model of their sect. At the outset in Babylonia they enjoyed the support of the exilarch, a relatively new authority set in charge of Babylonian Jewry about a half-century earlier. He had sent his son and other relatives to represent him in the Palestinian government, then in the hands of the Pharisaic-rabbinical party. In consequence, the first refugee-rabbis in Babylonia were not an unknown quantity, but perhaps were encouraged to settle permanently in the ancient community. They possessed substantial legal traditions and were men of considerable education. Because of their internal discipline they could be used for the effective administration of a group of far-flung communities. Because of their claim to be holy men, to possess "the whole Torah," and to be the teachers of God's will for Israel, and because of the ability of some rabbis to authenticate these claims through "miracles," they could exercise influence based upon spiritual, not merely physical, coercion. Understanding this, the exilarch probably allied himself with the rabbinate in attempting to overcome the power of local strong-men, antecedent, traditional authorities of the old Babylonian Jewish communities.

It was in the end an uneven contest. The local powers were known and habitually obeyed, to be sure, but the force of inertial obedience in a short time was overcome by the well-organized and well-disciplined sages with the backing of the exilarch and, through him, of the Parthian and (after a time) the Sasanian regimes. The unification of political power within Jewry corresponded to the effort of both Iranian dynasties to organize a single central effective government subject to the control of Ctesiphon. Against the combined force of the imperial government, the central Jewish authority, and the lawyer-magicians who were court judges and administrators backed by both, the pre-existing local authorities could hardly prevail.

The rabbis quickly established their characteristic institution, the school, which over generations transformed ordinary folk not merely into good lawyers and administrators, but rather into rabbis imbued with the convictions, adhering to the singular customs, and educated in the traditions, of the rabbinical estate. The schools certainly proved substantial local influences, quite apart from the court-system, where they were located and, in time, wherever their graduates lived. The schools thus constituted the second major force, besides the courts, for the expansion of rabbinical power. In many ways they were the more important of the two. Through the third and fourth centuries, the schools increased in strength. Local academies related to the great schools known to us in the Babylonian Talmud must have multiplied. The "men" of this town and that, that is, most likely the adherents of rabbinical estate and presumably teachers at lower levels in their own right, constituted local cells of rabbinical disciples. But outside of a few larger centers where the major academies were located, the rabbinical disciples could not have constituted a majority in any one place, as the situation of the single disciple in Tav'akh suggests. In all, the leading authorities and local disciples could by no means have formed a majority of Babylonian Jewry even by the end of Sasanian times. But, as I said, that the handful of masters of ca. 140 A.D. had become by 640 A.D. so powerful a force as to affect all Babylonian Jewry and to dominate a substantial and important part of its everyday affairs remains an extraordinary fact.

If in addition to the Babylonian Talmud we had a considerable body of information about the life of Babylonian Jewry, deriving, for instance, from business documents, exilarchic archives, local chronicles, biographies, martyrologies, poetry, synagogue ruins, liturgies, and records, papyri and ostraca, coins, and other artifacts, Iranian government papers and the like—if we had a Geniza—our view of the history of Babylonian Jewry to be sure would be far broader and certainly deeper, but it could not be much different. The focus of interest would still have to be the relationships between a small group of rabbis and a large mass of people, the creative symbiosis of the organized, active, patient, disciplined few and the inchoate, stubborn, passive, preoccupied many. This is not a new theme in the history of religions or of societies, but I think it is played out in an exceptional, perhaps in a unique, way in the history of Babylonian Judaism and of Babylonian Jewry in Iranian times.

I. *b. Berakhot*

	Ca. 350-380 [*R. Papa, R. Huna b. R. Joshua, etc.*]	*Ca. 380-450* [*R. Ashi and his contemporaries*]
Court Cases Questions from Outside of the Academy Stories and Sayings about Enforcement of, or Obedience to, Law Outside of the Academy		*[1. b. Ber. 12a. Amemar thought of instituting Ten Commandments at Nehardea.]

* Not counted—ambiguous.

II. *b. Shabbat*

	Ca. 350-380 [*R. Papa, R. Huna b. R. Joshua, etc.*]	*Ca. 380-450* [*R. Ashi and his contemporaries*]
Court Cases	1. b. Shab. 94b, R. Naḥman b. Isaac allowed a corpse to be moved in Derokert on Sabbath.	1. b. Shab. 95a, Amemar permitted sprinkling floors in Maḥoza on Sabbath.
Questions from Outside of the Academy		
Stories and Sayings about Enforcement of, or Obedience to, Law Outside of the Academy		

III. *b. ʿEruvin*

	Ca. 350-380 [*R. Papa, R. Huna b. R. Joshua, etc.*]	*Ca. 380-450* [*R. Ashi and his contemporaries*]
Court Cases		
Questions from Outside of the Academy		
Stories and Sayings about Enforcement of, or Obedience to, Law Outside of the Academy		1. b. ʿEruv. 8a, Maremar partitioned Sura by nets. 2. b. ʿEruv. 40a, Rabina permitted people to smell odor of myrtles cut on Second Day of Festival. 3. b. ʿEruv. 61b, Mar Judah told people how to place *ʿeruv*. 4. b. ʿEruv. 63a, Rabina banned Sabbath-violator. 5. b. ʿEruv. 104a, Amemar allowed drawing water on Sabbath in Maḥoza.

IV. *b. Pesaḥim*

	Ca. 350-380 [*R. Papa, R. Huna b. R. Joshua, etc.*]	*Ca. 380-450* [*R. Ashi and his contemporaries*]
Court Cases		
Questions from Outside of the Academy		
Stories and Sayings about Enforcement of, or Obedience to, Law Outside of the Academy		

V. *b. Yoma, Sukkah, Bezah*

	Ca. 350-380 [*R. Papa, R. Huna b. R. Joshua, etc.*]	*Ca. 380-450* [*R. Ashi and his contemporaries*]
Court Cases	1. b. B. 20a, R. Papa ruled on betrothal.	1. b. S. 55a, Amemar instituted in Nehardea *re* lections. 2. b. B. 22a, Amemar permitted eye to be painted by pagan on Sabbath. 3. b. B. 22a, Amemar permitted eye to be painted on Second Day of New Year.
Questions from Outside of the Academy		
Stories and Sayings about Enforcement of, or Obedience, to, Law Outside of the Academy	1. b. B. 4a, R. Papa was asked about egg laid on Sabbath.	

VI. *b. Rosh HaShanah, Ta'anit*

	Ca. 350-380 [*R. Papa, R. Huna b. R. Joshua, etc.*]	*Ca. 380-450* [*R. Ashi and his contemporaries*]
Court Cases		*[1. b. R.H. 31b, Amemar issued court-summons.]
Questions from Outside of the Academy		
Stories and Sayings about Enforcement of, or Obedience to, Law Outside of the Academy		

* Not counted—court procedure.

VII. *b. Megillah, Mo'ed Qaṭan, Ḥagigah*

	Ca. 350-380 [*R. Papa, R. Huna b. R. Joshua, etc.*]	*Ca. 380-450* [*R. Ashi and his contemporaries*]
Court Cases	1. b. Meg. 26b, R. Papa and R. Huna b. R. Joshua *re* property.	1. b. M.Q. 11b, R. Ashi ruled *re* partnership.
Questions from Outside of the Academy		
Stories and Sayings about Enforcement of, or Obedience to, Law Outside of the Academy		1. b. M.Q. 4b, Rabina considered banning man for drawing water during festival week. 2. b. M.Q. 4b, R. Ashi allowed people of Mata Meḥasia to clean canal during festival week.

* Not counted — general rule.

VIII. *b. Yevamot*

	Ca. 350-380 [*R. Papa, R. Huna b. R. Joshua, etc.*]	*Ca. 380-450* [*R. Ashi and his contemporaries*]
Court Cases	1. b. Yev. 91b, R. Papa *re* remarriage. 2. b. Yev. 101b, R. Papa and R. Huna b. R. Joshua *re ḥaliẓah.* 3. b. Yev. 101b, R. Kahana *re ḥaliẓah.* 4. b. Yev. 106b, R. Kahana *re ḥaliẓah.*	1. b. Yev 21b [= 40b], Amemar permitted marriage. 2. b. Yev. 37a, Rafram did not ban a man who betrothed a woman and fled. He did not require a divorce. 3. b. Yev. 43a, Amemar permitted bethrothal on the ninetieth day [after the first husband's death]. 4. b. Yev. 45b, Amemar declared a child legitimate. 5. b. Yev. 75b, R. Ashi supervised circumcision and declared a man fit. 6. b. Yev. 76a, R. Bibi b. Abaye supervised circumcision and declared man fit.
Questions from Outside of the Academy		1. b. Yev. 80b, Rabbah Tosfa'ah *re* legitimacy. *[2. b. Yev. 101b, Mar Zuṭra wrote *ḥaliẓah* certificate.]
Stories and Sayings about Enforcement of, or Obedience to, Law Outside of the Academy		

* Not counted—general rule.

IX. *b. Ketuvot*

	Ca. 350-380 [*R. Papa, R. Huna b. R. Joshua, etc.*]	*Ca. 380-450* [*R. Ashi and his contemporaries*]
Court Cases	1. b. Ket. 7a, R. Zevid permitted first intercourse on the Sabbath. 2. b. Ket. 60b, R. Papa and R. Huna b. R. Joshua *re* remarriage.	1. b. Ket. 20a, R. Ashi *re* sale of land. 2. b. Ket. 54a, Rabina *re* *ketuvah*-settlement. 3. b. Ket. 63b, Mar Zuṭra reconciled quarreling couple. 4. b. Ket. 69a, Amemar *re* settlement of estate. 5. b. Ket. 82a, Mar b. R. Ashi *re* levirate marriage. 6. b. Ket. 86a, R. Ashi ordered collection of damages. 7. b. Ket. 103a, Rabina *re* contract for services. 8. b. Ket. 109b, R. Ashi *re* settlement of estate.
...		
Questions from Outside of the Academy		
Stories and Sayings about Enforcement of, or Obedience to, Law Outside of the Academy		

X. *b. Nedarim, Naẓir, Soṭah*

	Ca. 350-380 [*R. Papa, R. Huna b. R. Joshua, etc.*]	*Ca. 380-450* [*R. Ashi and his contemporaries*]
Court Cases		
Questions from Outside of the Academy		
Stories and Sayings about Enforcement of, or Obedience to, Law Outside of the Academy		

XI. *b. Giṭṭin*

	Ca. 350-380 [*R. Papa, R. Huna b. R. Joshua, etc.*]	*Ca. 380-450* [*R. Ashi and his contemporaries*]
Court Cases	1. b. Giṭ. 40a, R. Papa *re* emancipation of slaves. 2. b. Giṭ. 58a, R. Papa *re* land taxes.	*[1. b. Giṭ. 18a, R. Kahana, R. Papi, and R. Ashi acted on principle that *geṭ* is valid from time of writing.] *[2. b. Giṭ. 19b, R. Papa *re* Persian documents.] 3. b. Giṭ. 40a, Rabina *re* emancipation of slaves. 4. b. Giṭ. 73a, Rabina *re* guarantee of sale of field. 5. b. Giṭ. 78b, R. Ashi *re* *ḥaliẓah*. 6. b. Giṭ. 89b, R. Ashi *re* betrothal.
Questions from Outside of the Academy		
Stories and Sayings about Enforcement of, or Obedience to, Law Outside of the Academy		

* Not counted, general rule.

XII. *b. Qiddushin*

	Ca. 350-380 [*R. Papa, R. Huna b. R. Joshua, etc.*]	*Ca. 380-450* [*R. Ashi and his contemporaries*]
Court Cases	1. b. Qid. 9a, R. Ḥama *re* betrothal. (2) 2. b. Qid, 9a, R. Zevid *re* betrothal.	1. b. Qid. 45a-b, Rabina *re* betrothal. (2) 2. b. Qid. 50a, R. Ashi *re* sale of land. 3. b. Qid. 81a, Mar Zuṭra punished privacy with an unmarried woman. 4. b. Qid. 89b, R. Ashi *re* betrothal.
Questions from Outside of the Academy		
Stories and Sayings about Enforcement of, or Obedience to, Law Outside of the Academy		

XII. *b. Bava' Qamma'*

	Ca. 350-380 [*R. Papa, R. Huna b. R. Joshua, etc.*]	*Ca. 380-450* [*R. Ashi and his contemporaries*]
Court Cases	1. b. B.Q. 59a, R. Papa and R. Huna b. R. Joshua *re* damages.	1. b. B.Q. 62a, R. Ashi *re* damages. 2. b. B.Q. 115a, Rabina *re* theft. 3. b. B.Q. 112b, Rabina *re* collection of debt. 4. b. B.Q. 117a, R. Ashi *re* showing wine to gentile thieves.
Questions from Outside of the Academy		
Stories and Sayings about Enforcement of, or Obedience to, Law Outside of the Academy		

XIV. *b. Bava' Meẓi'a'*

	Ca. 350-380 [*R. Papa, R. Huna b. R. Joshua, etc.*]	*Ca. 380-450* [*R. Ashi and his contemporaries*]
Court Cases	1. b. B.M. 66a, R. Zevid *re* divorce. 2. b. B.M. 66b, R. Papa *re* sale of land. 3. b. B.M. 77b, R. Papa *re* sale of land. 4. b. B.M. 69a, R. Papa *re* partnership. 5. b. B.M. 74b, R. Papa *re* purchase. 6. b. B.M. 81a, R. Papa *re* bailment. 7. b. B.M. 83b, R. Papa *re* negligence. 8. b. B.M. 93b, R. Papa *re* damages. 9. b. B.M. 97a, R. Papa *re* bailment. 10. b. B.M. 104, R. Kahana *re* lease of field. 11. b. B.M. 106b, R. Naḥman b. Isaac *re* lease of vineyard.	1. b. B.M. 65b-66a, Amemar *re* sale of land. 2. b. B.M. 67a, Rabina *re* mortgage. 3. b. B.M. 76a-76b, R. Ashi *re* collection of debt. 4. b. B.M. 73, R. Ashi *re* interest. 5. b. B.M. 77b, R. Ashi *re* sale of ass. 6. b. B.M. 97a, R. Ashi *re* death of cat. 7. b. B.M. 104b, R. Ashi *re* *ketuvah*. 8. b. B.M. 104, Rabina *re* lease of field. 9. b. B.M. 106b, Rabina *re* lease of field.
Questions from Outside of the Academy		
Stories and Sayings about Enforcement of, or Obedience to, Law Outside of the Academy		

XV. *b. Bava' Batra'*

	Ca. 350-380 [*R. Papa, R. Huna b. R. Joshua, etc.*]	*Ca. 380-450* [*R. Ashi and his contemporaries*]
Court Cases	1. b. B.B. 7a, R. Ḥama *re* conflict of neighbors (3). 2. b. B.B. 7b, R. Ḥama *re* bond. 3. b. B.B. 22a, R. Kahana *re* market-supervision. 4. b. B.B. 33b, R. Zevid *re* *ḥazaqah*. 5. b. B.B. 67a, R. Kahana used to collect estate-claims from rent of houses. 6. b. B.B. 132b, R. Papi *re* estate. 7. b. B.B. 151b, R. Huna b. R. Joshua *re* gift. 8. b. B.B. 174a, R. Papa *re* orphans' property.	1. b. B.B. 3b, Maremar and Mar Zuṭra *re* synagogue property. 2. b. B.B. 22a, Rabina *re* market-supervision. 3. b. B.B. 24a, Rabina, *re* use of wine. 4. b. B.B. 25b, R. Ashi *re* inconvenience to home-owner. 5. b. B.B. 26a, Rabina *re* inconvenience to home-owner. 6. b. B.B. 57a, Rabina *re* court document. 7. b. B.B. 61b, R. Ashi *re* sale of land. 8. b. B.B. 11a, Mar Zuṭra *re* gift. 9. b. B.B. 88a, R. Yemar *re* theft. 10. b. B.B. 126b, R. Ashi *re* settlement of estate. 11. b. B.B. 133a, Rabina *re* estate. 12. b. B.B. 143b, Mar b. R. Ashi *re* estate. 13. b. B.B. 165a-b, Amemar validates deed. 14. b. B.B. 174b, R. Ashi *re* orphans' property.
Questions from Outside of the Academy		
Stories and Sayings about Enforcement of, or Obedience to, Law Outside of the Academy		

XVI. *b. Sanhedrin*

	Ca. 350-380 [*R. Papa, R. Huna b. R. Joshua, etc.*]	*Ca. 380-450* [*R. Ashi and his contemporaries*]
Court Cases	1. b. Sanh. 26b, R. Papa banned grave-diggers for burying corpse on first day of festival of Shavu'ot.	*[1. b. Sanh. 7b, R. Ashi judged fitness of meat.] 2. b. B.M. 76b, Rabina *re* damages to animal.
Questions from Outside of the Academy		
Stories and Sayings about Enforcement of, or Obedience to, Law Outside of the Academy		

* General rule, not counted.

XVII. *b. 'Avodah Zarah*

	Ca. 350-380 [*R. Papa, R. Huna b. R. Joshua, etc.*]	*Ca. 380-450* [*R. Ashi and his contemporaries*]
Court Cases	1. b. A.Z. 60a, R. Papa *re* wine. 2. b. A.Z. 72a, R. Kahana *re* sale of land.	1. b. A.Z. 59b, R. Ashi, *re* wine (2). 2. b. A.Z. 60b, R. Ashi *re* wine.
Questions from Outside of the Academy		
Stories and Sayings about Enforcement of, or Obedience to, Law Outside of the Academy		

XVIII. *b. Horayot, Shevu'ot, Makkot*

	Ca. 350-380 [*R. Papa, R. Huna b. R. Joshua, etc.*]	*Ca. 380-450* [*R. Ashi and his contemporaries*]
Court Cases	1. b. Shev. 42a, R. Papa *re* collection of debt. 2. b. Shev. 48b, R. Papa *re* collection of debt from estate. 3. b. Mak. 7a, R. Papa ruled on surety-bond.	[1. b. Hor. 3b = b. Sanh. 7b, R. Ashi ruled on fitness of animals.]
Questions from Outside of the Academy		
Stories and Sayings about Enforcement of, or Obedience to, Law Outside of the Academy		

XIX. *b. Zevaḥim, Menaḥot, Ḥullin*

	Ca. 350-380 [*R. Papa, R. Huna b. R. Joshua, etc.*]	*Ca. 380-450* [*R. Ashi and his contemporaries*]
Court Cases	1. b. Ḥul. 49a, R. Ashi reports on R. Kahana's ruling *re* date-stone in gall-bladder. 2. b. Ḥul. 53b, R. Kahana *re* lung.	1. b. Ḥul. 17b, R. Ashi examined butcher's knife. 2. b. Ḥul. 18a, Rava b. Ḥinena banned butcher for not presenting his knife for examination. 3. b. Ḥul. 18b, Mar Zuṭra ruled on knife. 4. b. Ḥul. 47a, Maremar examined lungs. 5. b. Ḥul. 47a, R. Ashi examined lungs. 6. b. Ḥul. 48b, Mar b. R. Joseph ruled on needle in liver. 7. b. Ḥul. 49a, Rabina ruled on needle in liver. 8. b. Ḥul. 51a, R. Ashi ruled on injured goat. 9. b. Ḥul. 51a, Rabina and R. Yemar *re* injured ewe. *[10. b. Ḥul. 56a, R. Yemar examined membrane.] 11. b. Ḥul. 58b, Rabina *re* rumens. 12. b. Ḥul. 58b, R. Ashi *re* tube from reticulum. 13. b. Ḥul. 75b, R. Ashi *re* animal attacked by wolf. 14. b. Ḥul. 76b, R. Ashi *re* animal's tendons. 15. b. Ḥul. 98a, Mar b. R. Ashi ruled on forbidden fat in pot of meat. 16. b. Ḥul. 105b, Mar b. R. Ashi tried demon for damaging property.
Questions from Outside of the Academy		
Stories and Sayings about Enforcement of, or Obedience to, Law Outside of the Academy		

* Not counted—general rule, not a case.

XX. *b. Bekhorot, ʿArakhin, Temurah, Keritot, Meʿilah, Tamid*

	Ca. 350-380 [*R. Papa, R. Huna b. R. Joshua, etc.*]	*Ca. 380-450* [*R. Ashi and his contemporaries*]
Court Cases	1. b. ʿArakh. 23b, R. Papa *re* divorce.	1. b. Bekh. 36b, R. Ashi *re* firstling.
Questions from Outside of the Academy		
Stories and Sayings about Enforcement of, or Obedience to, Law Outside of the Academy		

XXI. *b. Niddah*

	Ca. 350-380 [*R. Papa, R. Huna b. R. Joshua, etc.*]	*Ca. 380-450* [*R. Ashi and his contemporaries*]
Court Cases		1. b. Nid. 67b, R. Aḥa b. Jacob decreed immersion may be performed on the eighth day in Papunia on account of thieves.
Questions from Outside of the Academy		
Stories and Sayings about Enforcement of, or Obedience to, Law Outside of the Academy		

XXII. *Summary*

	Ca. 350-380	*Ca. 380-450*	*Total*	*Approximate Percentage of Total*
Civil Law (including commercial and real estate, settlement of estates, gifts to charity, maintenance of widows and orphans, collection of debts, marriage contracts, damages and liabilities).	29	36	65	49.6%
Personal Status (including marriage, divorce, *ḥaliẓah*, etc. excommunication for moving from place to place, adultery).	12	16	28	21.3%
Food and Sex Taboos (including slaughter and ritual fitness of wine).	3	21	24	18.3%
Fasts, Holidays, Sabbath.	3	10 (2 *re* Sabbath limits)	13	9.9%
Synagogue Liturgy (including blessings).	—	1	1	0.7%
Punishment for Disrespect to Scholars.	—	—	—	—
Vows and Dedications.[1]	—	—	—	—
Agricultural Rules.[1]	—	—	—	—
Capital Crimes.	—	—	—	—
Total	47	84	131	99.8%

[1] Examples of rabbinical behavior are not counted.

XXIII. *Cumulative Comparisons*

	Ca. 220-265		*Ca. 265-310*		*Ca. 310-350*		*Ca. 350-450*	
	Number	%	*Number*	%	*Number*	%	*Number*	%
Civil Law (including commercial and real estate, settlement of estates, gifts to charity, maintenance of widows and orphans, collection of debts, marriage contracts, damages and liabilities).	23	33.8%	85	52.1%	116	51.1%	65	49.6%
Personal Status (including marriage, divorce, *ḥaliẓah*, excommunication for moving from place to place, adultery).	16	23.5%	24	14.1%	35	15.0%	28	21.3%
Food and Sex Taboos (including slaughter and ritual fitness of wine).	15	22.0%	21	12.9%	31	13.7%	24	18.3%
Fasts, Holidays, and Sabbath.	10	14.7%	19	11.6%	16	7.1%	13	9.9%
Synagogue Litury (including blessings).	3	4%	2	1.2%	6	2.6%	1	0.7%
Punishment for Disrespect to Scholars.	—	—	2	1.2%	4	1.7%	—	—
Vows and Dedications.	—	—	7	4.2%	2	0.8%	—	—
Agricultural Rules	1	1%	3	1.8%	6	2.6%	—	—
Capital Crimes.	—	—	—	—	2	0.8%	—	—
Total by Periods	68	99.0%	163	99.1%	218	95.4%	131	99.8%